Economics and Happiness

Economics and Happiness

Framing the Analysis

Luigino Bruni and Pier Luigi Porta

OXFORD
UNIVERSITY PRESS

*This book has been printed digitally and produced in a standard specification
in order to ensure its continuing availability*

OXFORD
UNIVERSITY PRESS

Great Clarendon Street, Oxford OX2 6DP

Oxford University Press is a department of the University of Oxford.
It furthers the University's objective of excellence in research, scholarship,
and education by publishing worldwide in

Oxford New York

Auckland   Cape Town Dar es Salaam Hong Kong Karachi
Kuala Lumpur Madrid Melbourne Mexico City Nairobi
New Delhi Shanghai Taipei Toronto
With offices in
Argentina Austria Brazil Chile Czech Republic France Greece
Guatemala Hungary Italy Japan South Korea Poland Portugal
Singapore Switzerland Thailand Turkey Ukraine Vietnam

Oxford is a registered trade mark of Oxford University Press
in the UK and in certain other countries

Published in the United States
by Oxford University Press Inc., New York

© Oxford University Press, 2005

ISBN 978-0-19-928628-7

Contents

Contents

List of Figures

List of Tables

List of Contributors

Luigino Bruni, University of Milan-Bicocca

Richard A. Easterlin, University of Southern California

Robert H. Frank, Cornell University

Bruno S. Frey, University of Zurich

Richard Layard, London School of Economics

Matt Matravers, University of York

Martha C. Nussbaum, University of Chicago

Luigi Pasinetti, Università Cattolica S.C., Milan

Charlotte D. Phelps, Temple University, Philadelphia

Pier Luigi Porta, University of Milan-Bicocca

Oded Stark, Universities of Bonn, Klagenfurt, and Vienna; Warsaw University; ESCE Economic and Social Research Center, Cologne and Eisenstadt

Alois Stutzer, University of Zurich

Robert Sugden, University of East Anglia

Bernard M. S. van Praag, University of Amsterdam

Ruut Veenhoven, Erasmus University, Rotterdam

You Qiang Wang, Tsinghua University

Stefano Zamagni, University of Bologna

Introduction

Luigino Bruni and Pier Luigi Porta

> The professed object of Dr. Adam Smith's inquiry is the nature and causes of the wealth of nations. There is another inquiry, however, perhaps still more interesting, which he occasionally mixes with it, I mean an inquiry into the causes which affect the happiness of nations.
>
> Malthus, 1798/1966: 303–4

1. The Return of Happiness in Economics

It is still generally acknowledged that the moral justification of the economist's job is to be found in the persuasion that increases in wealth, income, or goods generally create the preconditions for greater well-being and happiness. In fact, income and wealth are related to many positive goals in life: wealthy people are generally more educated, have better health and longer life spans, and so forth. It should follow that richer people are substantially happier than others.

Another reason for studying economic wealth and welfare is the commonsense conviction that it is very hard to be happy and run a good life in extreme poverty. For this reason political economy, investigating the *means* for a good life, has gained the moral support of society as the "science of wealth", fostering the "hope that poverty and ignorance may gradually be extinguished" and "that all should start in the world with a fair chance of leading a cultured life, free from the pains of poverty and stagnating influences of excessive mechanical toil" (Marshall 1945/1890: 3–4).

Though its goal is far from being accomplished, political economy has inspired economists to study the nature and causes of the wealth of persons and nations and has bred the hope that an ever-increasing number of people could afford to satisfy basic material needs.

Recently, however, something new pertaining to human happiness has begun creeping into economic thought. It is making its way under the umbrella of the "paradoxes of happiness". It is a search to unearth something new about the relationship of happiness to the economic domain. Indeed, as Luigi Pasinetti explains in his contribution to the present volume, the Classical economists, for all their emphasis on wealth, were well aware of the importance of happiness for Political Economy, as is also signaled by Malthus's phrase given as the epigraph to this essay; at the same time Pasinetti observes that the Classical approach was later largely submerged and almost forgotten through the development of economic theory. We have to consider some of the more recent developments of Economics in order to see the signs of a return of happiness in our discipline.

The debate about "the paradoxes of happiness" began explicitly with a paper published by Brickman and Campbell (1971), under the telling title of "Hedonic Relativism and Planning the Good Society". In their study, the two psychologists extended the "adaptation level" theory to individual and collective happiness, reaching the conclusion that bettering the objective conditions of life (income or wealth) has no effect on personal well-being. Such a thesis should have provoked a serious methodological discussion about the meaning of the analysis of the nature and causes of the wealth of nations. Yet it did not; the study remained practically unknown to mainstream economics for years.

Some economists, however, started a very similar research project along parallel lines, taking up and reviving a time-honoured—though increasingly insignificant—strand of economic thinking. We are about to examine that strand in greater detail here. Its hallmark is to give a central place to the wealth–happiness nexus in economic analysis. Initially developed by Italian and Scottish writers in the Classical period in particular,[1] it found fertile ground in Adam Smith's *Theory of Moral Sentiments*. We can trace a line of thinking, linking up, for example, Malthus's *Essay on Population*, Marshall's social economics, Veblen's "conspicuous consumption", Galbraith's criticism of the "affluent society", and, more recently, Duesenberry's (1949) social theories of consumption based on interpersonal comparisons. Utilitarianism too assigned a central place to happiness, although it was precisely in Bentham's theory that happiness came to be reduced to *utility* (or, rather, utility was defined in terms of happiness); and that is one case of reductionism that Stefano Zamagni's chapter draws attention to in the present collection. Robert Sugden's and

Martha Nussbaum's contributions, on the other hand, show that both in Smith and in J. S. Mill theoretical elements are to be found which offer very useful insights into our latter-day debates on the so-called "paradoxes of happiness".

Bernard van Praag, in his doctoral thesis (1968), showed an unusual and heterodox interest in investigating wealth and well-being amidst the almost complete indifference of mainstream economists. But he founded the Leyden School. Van Praag considered utility as cardinally measurable and also accepted interpersonal comparability—as the first Utilitarians had done. In a series of papers, from 1971 onwards, he discovered the empirical phenomenon of "preference drift", that is, the idea that satisfaction adapts to the material level and that therefore the welfare derived from an income increase is appreciated much more *ex ante* than *ex post* (after the increase has taken place), a result curiously similar to, and at the same time independent of, Brickman and Campbell's treadmill effect, and empirically more operational.[2]

More or less in the same period, two other economists, Richard Easterlin (1974) and Tibor Scitovsky (1976), decided to take a direct look at what was going on in Psychology. As a result they focused their economic research directly on *happiness*—while the Leyden school had not *directly* dealt with happiness or life satisfaction—thus introducing the "paradox of happiness" to a wider audience, academic and otherwise. By utilizing empirical research on people's happiness, in 1974, the American economist and demographer Richard Easterlin managed to open up the debate around the *paradox of happiness*. He made use of two types of data. The first database was supplied by the responses to a Gallup-poll type of survey in which a direct question was asked—a question which is still at the heart of most of the present analyses on happiness: "In general, how happy would you say that you are—*very* happy, *fairly* happy or *not very* happy?" (Easterlin 1974: 91). The other set of data Easterlin made use of came from more sophisticated research carried out in 1965 by the humanist psychologist Hadley Cantril (another forerunner of contemporary quantitative studies on happiness), concerning people's fears, hopes, and satisfaction in 14 countries. The subjects interviewed were asked to classify their own satisfaction on a scale from 0 to 10[3]—in today's World Values Survey (WVS) questionnaires, happiness is ranked in "qualitative" terms (from "not very happy" to "very happy"), whereas life satisfaction is measured by a Cantril methodology (a scale from 1 to 10).

Both types of data, then, were based on a subjective self-evaluation of happiness. They both produced, in Easterlin's analyses, the same results.

Within a single country, at a given moment in time, the correlation between income and happiness exists and is robust: "In every single survey, those in the highest status group were happier, on the average, than those in lowest status group" (Easterlin 1974: 100). In cross-sectional differences among countries, on the other hand, the positive association between wealth and happiness, although present, is neither general nor robust and poorer countries do not always appear to be less happy than richer countries. In other words: "if there is a positive association among countries between income and happiness it is not very clear ... The results are ambiguous" (Easterlin 1974: 108).[4] But the most interesting result came from the analysis of time series at the national level: in 30 surveys over 25 years (from 1946 to 1970 in the USA) per capita real income rose by more than 60 percent, but the proportion of people who rated themselves as "very happy", "fairly happy", or "not too happy" remained almost unmodified.[5]

Today the focus of the theoretical debate about the paradox of happiness is contentious. Almost all scholars, from different backgrounds, agree on the latter result, because there is evidence that "over time and across OECD countries rises in aggregate income are not associated with rises in aggregate happiness ... At the aggregate level, there has been no increase in reported happiness over the last 50 years in the US and Japan, nor in Europe since 1973 when the records began" (R. Layard, in this volume).

The main drift of Easterlin's seminal paper came to be developed two years later by Tibor Scitovsky's *Joyless Economy* (1976). Hirsch (1977), Ng (1978), Layard (1980), and Frank (1985) all brought new insights into the new theme of happiness in economics, which grew slowly but steadily (Lane 2000). In 1997 the new theme surfaced in a debate in the *Economic Journal*, thus reaching a wider scientific audience. Today the "paradox of happiness" is gaining greater and greater attention among economists, psychologists, social scientists, and also, through the media, among the general public.

The issue is relevant in economic theory: explaining the happiness paradoxes calls into question some of the basic tenets of contemporary economics.

The income–happiness relationship within a single country at a given moment in time is not controversial today among economists: there is an almost universal agreement that a casual correlation running from income to happiness exists and is robust: "Various studies provide evidence that, on average, persons living in rich countries are happier than those living in poor countries. Various studies provide evidence that, on average, persons living in rich countries are happier than those living in poor countries" (Frey and Stutzer 2001: 10).[6] The income–happiness correlation among countries is, instead, more controversial.[7] Easterlin 1974 found, as we have seen, no clear nor evident correlation between happiness and income between different countries. Today most economists, using data coming from the *World Values Survey* (WVS), agree that a correlation does exist: "Various studies provide evidence that, on average, persons living in rich countries are happier than those living in poor countries" (Frey and Stutzer 2001: 19). However, this second relationship among countries is *not* general. Layard makes an important distinction: "if we compare countries, there is no evidence that richer countries are happier than poorer ones—so long as we confine ourselves to countries with incomes over $15,000 per head . . . At income levels below $15,000 per head things are different, since people are nearer to the absolute breadline. At these income levels richer countries *are* happier than poorer ones. And in countries like India, Mexico, and the Philippines, where we have time series data, happiness has grown as income levels have risen" (Chapter 5, this volume).

Before entering into the main explanations currently being offered for the Easterlin Paradox, thus placing the present volume in the context of the debate, it may be interesting both to know the background to happiness research and to have a glance at what is going on in other social sciences on the issue of happiness.

2. Happiness or What Else?

2.1. *Subjective Happiness and the Good Life*

Mainstream economists have only recently begun to be interested in happiness, trapped as they were by the "iron curtain effect" of the hypothesis of rationality, but social scientists in other fields have been working on the theme for decades. Sociologists were perhaps the first to find "experimental" indicators of the *standard of living* that went beyond GDP per capita. Back in the 1920s William Ogburn[8] launched a social research program on the quality of life which generated the important "movement of social indicators of the quality of life" that a few years later spread from the United States to Europe. In 1954, the United Nations nominated a commission with the task of improving studies on living standards by defining more precisely the items which make up the *standard of living* concept as well as their indicators.

The rise and diffusion of this movement were favoured by the cultural climate of the 1960s, which sought to overcome a purely economic conception of the process of economic growth. There were many economists (e.g. Myrdal, Galbraith, Hirschman) who were also working outside the mainstream of pure economic theory. They were sources of inspiration for sociologists and social scientists, and spawned research projects on the definition of social indicators. The aim was to find operational solutions capable of effectively quantifying the concept of "quality of life" in order to arrive at some sort of "social accountability".

This "quality of life movement" (Offer 2003) emphasizes mainly the "objective" ingredients of a good life, while the later "happiness movement" (discussed above) is characterized by a more "subjective" approach, based on self-reported evaluations (questionnaires). In fact, mostly thanks to Sen, the category of *quality of life* tends to encompass new indicators such as democracy, social capital, health, working conditions, and fundamental capabilities. In the 1980s, a "list of fundamental human needs" was drawn up that was mainly based on Sen's and Nussbaum's theory of capabilities. It developed into the United Nation's *Human Development Indicators*, or HDI.[9]

Sen widens his vision of well-being in scope and definition, and emancipates it from the mere absence or scarcity of material goods. However, his capabilities approach, to which we shall return later, has been criticized for failing to provide convincing solutions to its diagnosis of gaps in traditional theories of well-being.[10] Thus, for the past few years, Martha Nussbaum has been seeking to wed Sen's approach to an Aristotelian and Stoic theory of happiness in order to arrive at an *objectivization* of the "good life".[11] In her search to objectify and operationalize Sen's *capabilities approach*, she concentrates her analysis on constitutional and political applications. Her latest works propose a *normative* approach to well-being. Her theory is based on a list of *ten* fundamental capabilities, called *Central Human Functional Capabilities*, which equip human beings with the capability of *effectively* doing and being well.[12]

So the quality of life approach, or capability approach, considers self-reported happiness as only *one* component of well-being, (a capability or a functioning) which, instead, has to be anchored more objectively.

2.2. Hedonism or Eudaimonia?

In Psychology we find a similar tension between a hedonic-subjective idea of happiness and a eudaimonic-objective one.

In the "hedonistic" approach, happiness is the result of avoiding pain and seeking pleasure. What perspective places emphasis on the acquisition of material goods; in contrast, according to the "eudaimonic" approach, happiness arises as people function and interact within society, an approach that places emphasis on non-material pursuits such as relationality and intrinsic motivation (Deci and Ryan 2001).

More precisely, "hedonism" (Kahneman 1999; Kahneman *et al.* 2003) reflects the view that well-being consists of pleasure or happiness: "Hedonism, as a view of well-being, has thus been expressed in many forms and has varied from a relatively narrow focus on bodily pleasures to a broad focus on appetites and self-interests" (Deci and Ryan 2001: 144). In 1999 Kahneman *et al.* announced the existence of a new field of Psychology. Their title, *Well-Being: The Foundations of Hedonic Psychology*, clearly suggests that, within this paradigm, the terms well-being and hedonism are essentially equivalent.[13]

The second view, both ancient and current, is that well-being consists of more than just hedonic or subjective happiness: "Despite the currency of the hedonic view, many philosophers, religious masters, and visionaries, from both the East and West, have denigrated happiness per se as a principal criterion of well-being" (Deci and Ryan 2001: 145). It lies instead in the actualization of human potential. This view has been called eudaimonism, conveying the belief that "well-being consists of fulfilling or realizing one's *daimon* or true nature". The two traditions—hedonism and eudaimonism—are founded on distinct views of human nature and of what constitutes a good society. Accordingly, they ask different questions concerning how developmental and social processes relate to "well-being, and they implicitly or explicitly prescribe different approaches to the enterprise of living" (ibid. 143). Ryff and Singer (1998, 2000), also drawing from Aristotle, describe well-being not in terms of attaining pleasure, but as "the striving for perfection that represents the realization of one's true potential" (Ryff 1995: 100). Carol Ryff has even proposed to speak of Psychological Well-Being (PWB) as distinct from Subjective Well-Being (SWB): "Whereas the SWB tradition formulates well-being in terms of overall life satisfaction and happiness, the PWB tradition draws heavily on formulation of human development and existential challenges of life" (Keyes *et al.* 2002: 1008).[14]

In the Subjective Well-Being approach, happiness is considered to be a narrower concept than SWB, and different than life satisfaction: life satisfaction and happiness are considered components of SWB. In particular, life satisfaction reflects individuals' perceived distance from their aspirations (Campbell *et al.* 1976). Happiness, instead, results from a balance between positive affect and negative affect (Bradburn 1969).[15]

The philosophical reference point for the hedonic approach is Bentham, while Aristotle is the father of the eudaimonic line. Martha Nussbaum's chapter in this volume contains a synthetic but very clear analysis of both Bentham's pleasure and Aristotle's eudaimonia. Here we would like to stress only two characteristics of eudaimonia, important for the present debate on the paradox of happiness in economics.

One major *fil rouge* of *Nichomachean Ethics* is the *civil* or political nature of *eudaimonia*: "Surely it is strange, too, to make the supremely happy man a solitary; for no one would choose the whole world on condition of being alone, since man is a political creature and one whose nature is to live with others. Therefore even the happy man lives with others; for he has the things that are by nature good. And plainly it is better to spend his days with friends and good men than with strangers or any chance persons. Therefore the happy man needs friends" (*Nic. Ethics*, IX, 9, 1169b).

In its highest expression, friendship is a virtue, and is more important than wealth, according to Aristotle, because it is *a part* of eudaimonia and, therefore, is an end in itself, while wealth is only a means to that end: "For without friends no one would choose to live, though he had all other goods; ... for what is the use of such prosperity without the opportunity of beneficence, which is exercised chiefly and in its most laudable form towards friends? Or how can prosperity be guarded and preserved without friends? The greater it is, the more exposed is it to risk. And in poverty and in other misfortunes men think friends are the only refuge" (*Nic. Ethics*, VIII, 1, 1155a).

To Aristotle, there is an intrinsic value in the commitment to participate in civil or political life, without which human life does not flourish. Though human life must be able to flourish autonomously, in the sense that it cannot be jeopardized by bad fortune, it is also true that some of the essential components of the good life are tied to others and to interpersonal relationships. Participation in civil life, having friends, loving and being loved are essential parts of a happy life. In this sense—this is the second characteristic—eudaimonia is paradoxical: it cannot be reached only through instrumental means. It is the indirect result of virtuous actions, carried out for their intrinsic value, without any ulterior motive. Because it is composed of actions and *relational goods*, the civil life leads to eudaimonia only if it is marked by sincere and gratuitous sentiments. Martha Nussbaum (1986/2001) says that friendship, love, and political commitment are the three principal *relational goods* for Aristotle.

Therefore, they have intrinsic value, are part of eudaimonia, are gratuitous, and cannot be instrumental.

Because they are *made of relationships*, relational goods can be enjoyed only in reciprocity and, for this very reason, they are vulnerable and fragile.

3. Individual Treadmill: Adaptation and Aspiration

Coming back to the link of economics to happiness, those economists working on the "happiness paradox" are following Bentham's methodological line (Kahneman *et al.* 1997). With a few exceptions, happiness is not intended as eudaimonia and is not distinct from individualistic pleasure. As far as sociality is concerned, in the economic explanations, sociality is either (a) not considered as a relevant component of happiness, or (b) intended in terms of positionality. We will refer to (a) as theories based on the "individual treadmill" effects, and to (b) as explanations based on the "social treadmill".

The first economist who attempted to explain the "Easterlin Paradox" via "treadmill effects" was Richard Easterlin himself, in his 1974 paper. His explanation was based on Duesenberry's (1949) "relative consumption" assumption—it has to be noted that this hypothesis is still dominant today among economic explanations.

In his recent contributions Easterlin (2001, 2002) adds to the "relative consumption" hypothesis an explicitly "psychological" explanation based on the concept of *hedonic adaptation* or *set-point* theory. According to set-point theories of SWB there is a level of happiness which remains practically constant during the life cycle because personality and temperament variables seem to play a strong role in determining the level of happiness of individuals; such characteristics are basically innate to individuals. Therefore, life circumstances including health, income, and beauty often account for a very small percentage of variance in SWB: people initially do react to events, but then they return to baseline levels of well-being that are determined by personality factors (Argyle 2001; Lucas *et al.* 2002). Empirical research (Lykken and Tellegen 1996) for instance, concluded that more than 80 percent of the variance in long-term stable levels of SWB could be attributed to inborn temperament. On this basis, researchers have claimed that people have inborn SWB "set-points".[16] The various shocks that hit us in our lifetime affect our happiness only temporarily. We inevitably return to our *set point* after a brief period during which an event has indeed affected our satisfaction levels. As Daniel Kahneman writes: "individuals exposed to life-altering events ultimately return to a level of well-being that is characteristic of their personality, sometimes by generating good or bad outcomes that restore this characteristic level" (1999: 14).

The *hedonic treadmill*, a metaphor coined by Brickman and Campbell (1971), coming from "set-point theory" means that one is running constantly and yet remains in the same place because the treadmill runs at the same pace—or even faster but in the opposite direction.

The set-point theory is also very popular today among economists. On this theory happiness is essentially a congenital matter that mostly depends on subjective elements that are absolute, such as character, genes, or the inherited capacity to live with and overcome life's hardships. In other words, there exists a given level of happiness, around which the various experiences of life fluctuate. This, as an approach, is not far from the thesis of Herrnstein and Murray (1994), who in their *The Bell Curve*, attacked social programs as useless on the grounds that there is an innate level of intelligence that cannot be permanently changed by education.

Although in a quite different methodological tradition, Ruut Veenhoven (this volume)[17] rejects the common stereotype that sees misery, handicaps, and inequality in income distribution as the principal causes of people's unhappiness, reaching the conclusion that there is no "paradox" of happiness in Easterlin's sense. In his *World Database of Happiness*[18] Ghana and Colombia occupy the highest ranks among all nations classified according to their happiness level. France and Italy take a back seat to Guatemala.

In his theory, Kahneman makes a distinction between two types of *treadmill effect*, namely, the *hedonic treadmill* and the *satisfaction treadmill*. Whilst the *hedonic treadmill* depends on *adaptation*, the *satisfaction treadmill* depends on *aspiration* "which marks the boundaries between satisfactory and unsatisfactory results" (1999: 14). A similar distinction between the two treadmill effects is made by Frey and Stutzer: "This process, or mechanism, that reduces the hedonic effects of a constant or repeated stimulus, is called *adaptation*...According to aspiration level theory, individual well-being is determined by the gap between aspiration and achievement" (this volume).

As their incomes increase, people are induced to seek continuous and ever more intense pleasures through consumption in order to maintain the same level of satisfaction. The *satisfaction treadmill* works in such a way that one's *subjective* happiness remains constant even when one's *objective* happiness improves.[19]

To test the aspiration treadmill hypothesis, Easterlin carried out an interesting experiment over a period of 16 years in which he periodically asked the same group of people the following question:

1. We often hear people talk about what they want out of life. Here are a number of different things. [The respondent is handed a card with a list of 24 items.] When you think of the good life—the life you'd like to have, which of the things on this list, if any, are part of that good life as far as you personally are concerned?
2. Now would you go down that list and call off all the things you now have? (Easterlin, this volume).[20]

The first question aims at measuring aspirations, while the second measures means (income). The results showed that with an increase in material means (indicated by the first list), the things that were considered necessary for a happy life change (the second list). Thus, in the first phases of the life cycle, a summer home at the seaside and a second car were not indicated as being important for a good life, while they did enter the list as income increased. The ratio between possessed goods and desired goods remains practically constant over a life span, much as in a treadmill where means and aspiration run, more or less, at the same pace. Layard (this volume) calls this effect the "effect of habit": "if people adopt a higher living standard, they lose the option to return to their former living standard and experience the same utility as before from a given consumption". This mechanism is also very close to one of the most important ideas in modern behavioral economics, the idea that preferences are *reference-dependent* (Tversky and Kahneman 1991).

This idea is not completely new in the tradition of economics.

The first generation of neoclassical economists—up to Pareto—were, as it is well known, very interested in psychological laws, with the aim of basing the new economic science on solid ground, and introspection was considered a scientific source of data for economics: "In the meantime there arose a growing aversion among economists toward 'psychologizing'. The term 'happiness' was abandoned for 'ophelimity' and later on for 'well-being', 'welfare' or for the still less emotionally loaded term 'utility' or 'satisfaction'" (van Praag, this volume). Let us take the example of Francis Ysidro Edgeworth, who, in explaining the law of diminishing sensitivity to stimuli—a very popular law at that time—in his *Mathematical Psychics*, introduced the following consideration: "But not only is the function connecting means and pleasure such that the increase of means does not produce a proportionate increase in pleasure; but this effect is heightened by the function itself so varying (on repetition of the conditions of pleasure) that the same means produce less pleasure" (1881: 62). In other words, the function that specifies the amount of pleasure produced by different quantities of consumption in any given period—the utility function for consumption, as conventionally understood—*shifts according to the individual's consumption experiences in previous periods.* Edgeworth calls this the "Law of Accommodation".[21]

But these marginalist economists did not pursue this line of inquiry. It was left to present-day authors to develop the idea and pioneer a new breakthrough in economic analysis and a fully fledged discussion of possible policy implications.

For example, Frank and Layard have put forward important policy suggestions for offsetting distortions due to self-deception: "inconspicuous consumption should be taxed much less highly than conspicuous consumption". As a consequence, the "design of the tax system to protect inconspicuous consumption from taxation is...extremely important" (Frank, this volume).

Phelps questions the set point model of happiness. With a lifecycle model of personality integrated in a microeconomic model of the family, she explained parenting and work satisfactions in a sample of individuals who were observed at age 5, age 31, and age 41. Like Caspi and Roberts (2001), she thinks that there is continuity and change in personality. She hypothesizes that continuity is a result of attachment processes (Hazan and Shaver 1990; 1994). Her empirical results are consistent with the hypothesis that aspirations for love, achievement, and work competence begin developing from the moment of birth. Learning continues in adulthood. Measures of affect in the voices of the subjects' mothers differentiate outcomes attributable to the subjects' socialization from outcomes attributable to temperament. To improve subjective well-being in the United States, she urges policies to improve the delivery of child care and nurture healthy parent-child interactions.

4. The "Social Treadmill": Relative Consumption and Positional Competition

Explanations based on the relative consumption hypothesis can rightly be considered a development of aspiration theory. The hedonic treadmill based on adaptation is essentially individual and asocial, the satisfaction treadmill is associated with social comparisons, although the satisfaction treadmill can apply even in isolation: it can also occur in Robinson Crusoe's island when he tries to overcome his standards (in cultivation, fishing, etc.). In other words, the hedonic treadmill does not require society to function; the satisfaction treadmill normally occurs in society but neither the hedonic nor the satisfaction treadmill need sociality of necessity. A pure social treadmill is instead the "positional" one.

Not even the relative consumption hypothesis is new in the economics tradition. We have already mentioned that Duesenberry was the first to introduce relative consumption theory explicitly.[22] Duesenberry claimed that a person draws utility, or satisfaction, from his own level of consumption in relation or in comparison to the level of other people's consumption (1949: 32).

In other words, he basically said that we are constantly comparing ourselves to some group of people and that what they buy influences our choices about what we want to buy. It is the old "keeping up with the Joneses" scenario, where the consumption function is constructed upon the hypothesis that our consumption choices are influenced by the difference between our level of income and the level of income of others, instead of the absolute level. Therefore, the utility of a person's level of consumption depends also on the *relative* level and not only on the *absolute* level.

Without going back to Classical authors, where considerations about the social dimensions of consumption were prominent (e.g. in Smith (1759) or Genovesi (1765–7)), more recently Veblen (1899) treated consuming as a social issue, because of the simple fact that the most significant acts of consumption are normally carried out in public, under others' gaze. We could also mention the intuitions of the Classical economists Smith and Genovesi about the social significance of consuming goods, and that the institutional economists in America have always cultivated an interdisciplinary approach to research between economics, psychology, and sociology, with J. K. Galbraith (1959) being one of the most famous. Later, Scitovsky (1976, chap. 6) dealt with the relationship between consumption and status, and Fred Hirsch (1977) coined the term "positional good". The basic element of contemporary positional theory is the concept of *externality*: conspicuous commodities share some characteristics of "demerit goods" (i.e. private goods with negative externalities), with the typical consequence of Pareto inefficiency (for over-consumption):

That many purchases become more attractive to us when others make them means that consumption spending has much in common with a military arms race. A family can choose how much of its own money to spend, but it cannot choose how much others spend. Buying a smaller-than-average vehicle means greater risk of dying in an accident. Spending less on an interview suit means a greater risk of not landing the best job. Yet when all spend more on heavier cars or more finely tailored suits, the results tend to be mutually offsetting, just as when all nations spend more on armaments. Spending less—on bombs or on personal consumption—frees up money for other pressing uses, but only if everyone does it. (Frank, this volume)[23]

Richard Layard moves along the same theoretical lines. He recognizes—following Frank's and Oswald's researches—that "a rise in the average income in the state where you live reduces your happiness by one-third as much as a rise in your own income increases it". And, referring to the labour market, "a rise in wages of comparable workers reduces your job satisfaction as a rise in your own wage increases it" (Layard, this volume). In other words: people, victims of self-deception, consume an excessive amount of conspicuous goods, and, as a consequence, the investment of time for "inconspicuous consumption" is inefficient:

People fail to perceive that because of hedonic adaptation and social comparison aspirations in the pecuniary domain will change commensurately with actual circumstances. As a result, a disproportionate amount of time is devoted to the pursuit of pecuniary goals at the expense of family life and health, and subjective well-being is less than it might be. Clearly, a reallocation of time in favour of family life and health would increase subjective well-being. (Easterlin, this volume)

Thus, relative consumption theory can also be described by using the image of a treadmill: together with our income or consumption something else is running along: the income of others.

Positional explanations of the happiness paradox make use of the economic concept of externality, and, therefore, refer to the non-intentionality of the mechanism that leads people toward unhappiness traps. In particular, in the positional theories the externality A generates affects B's SWB by means of a reduction in the utility of a given level of consumption (or income).

Apart from this kind of positional externality, some authors—Easterlin and Frey and Stutzer in this volume—refer also to a second kind of externality that we can call "relational externality": in this case, the externality problem is related to the interplay of different domains of one's life: A's effort in the materialistic domain affects A's relational domains, which, as we have seen, are the most significant in terms of happiness.

To the question of externality the problem of self-deception is related and, ultimately, of rationality—to these two concepts we devote the next two sections.

These considerations lead us to the implications of the issue of happiness for the concept of economic rationality. In fact, one common denominator of the contributions to this volume is the non-intentionality of the treadmill effects. This brings us to two methodological issues: (a) a reconsideration of the concept of *economic rationality* as we know it in mainstream economics; (b) the recognition that some sort of *deception* is at work in the connection between happiness and the economic domain. In the next two sections we shall analyze these two issues.

5. The Paradox of Happiness as a Challenge to Economic Rationality

In his *Joyless Economy* (1976), Scitovsky perceived something very similar to the treadmill mechanism. He developed an analysis to explain why the increase in consumer goods in the opulent society is not making us any happier. Drawing on psychological and sociological research, he bases his answer on a distinction between comfort and pleasure, that is, a relation between stimulation and the level of "arousal" (i.e. the responsive mental state). Pleasurable arousal is associated with low levels of stimulation, before habit sets in. For this reason, a great source of happiness-pleasure is, for Scitovsky, "creativity" and "novelty", but our consumption of stimulation, variety, and novelty are lower than the optimum level, because "we over-indulge in comfort", because "the economies of scale impose the majority's tastes on the whole society, and when the majority chooses to sacrifice the stimulus of novelty for the sake of comfort, the creation of novelty and the minority's seeking new ways of attaining the good life are both impeded" (1976: 282–3).[24] On the one hand, this makes it very difficult even for the minority of people who are aware of these "consumption traps" to get out of them, while on the other the sad and comfortable majority remains in a state of satiated and bored unhappiness. Consuming things that are comfortable instead of things that are stimulating creates dependence and addiction. Over time, "the cost" of continuously upgrading one's life style also increases and reinforces the vicious circle in a similar pattern to drug addiction. Scitovsky claims that it is not only tobacco, drugs and alcohol that are addictive, but that all consumer goods, in different ways, can be subject to addiction as well.

Scitovsky delivered one of his last talks at a symposium in 1996 in celebration of the twentieth anniversary of the *Joyless Economy*. During that symposium, organized by the *Critical Review*, Scitovsky specified that the consumer addiction pattern is due to the fact that people do not realize, or realize only when it is too late, that improvements in comfort don't make them any happier (1996: 599).[25] In other words, people are affected by some form of *deception* in ordinary economic choice—a topic that we shall develop in the next section.

In the same issue of the *Critical Review*, Sen discussed how the results of Scitovsky's research had shaken the foundations of some of the basic concepts of economic rationality, which can be considered the cornerstone of contemporary economic theory. Sen argued against the theory of economic rationality by saying that the paradoxes of happiness would not arise if people acted rationally. In fact, why obtain excessive levels of comfort if they make us feel worse? Why allocate resources to the production of income if it makes us unhappier? In his discussion, Sen organized Scitovsky's analysis on two levels:

(a) Do people behave in the way that standard economic theory characterizes as rational behavior?

(b) Does the characterization of "rational behavior" in standard economic theory provide an adequate understanding of rationality? (1996: 485)

Most economists would agree today that economic theory should not be interested in the analysis of the *content* of those preferences. Once the subject has expressed his or her preferences, or has made his or her choice, he or she has furnished all that needs to be known in order to understand how he or she will behave:[26] reaching the maximum utility under his or her constraints, where utility represents nothing else than his or her preferences.

If economic rationality were limited to the above description, that is, to a matter of formal consistency in preferences, then Scitovsky's and Sen's criticisms would hardly affect it. Economic theory would see nothing strange in a subject having preferences for things that lead him to boredom, malaise or self-destruction.[27] In the last thirty years Sen has challenged the *formal* conception of economic rationality, claiming—according to us, successfully—that a purely formal concept of economic rationality, without any external (with respect to subject's preferences) reference point, is tautological, or else it describes the behavior of "rational fools": "there is no way of determining whether a choice function is consistent or not *without* referring to something external to choice behavior (such as objectives, values, or norms)" (Sen 2002: 121–2). In this line of research, other scholars believe that economic rationality needs an analysis of the *substantial* nature of desires and beliefs which are involved in the action (Elster 1983: 15). A substantial theory of rationality identifies the individual with a set of objectives and considers a given action rational if it is the most suitable for reaching those objectives (Hargreaves-Heap *et al.* 1994: 3).

If we abandon the hypothesis of formal economic rationality and move to a more substantial approach to rationality, the first question to ask is: what is the content to be maximized? The most common response today is that the individual's well-being is the *maximandum* which would then coincide with the perfect satisfaction of his preferences.[28] This approach to rationality is also known as the *preference-satisfaction approach*: "Orthodox normative economics consequently identifies welfare and preference satisfaction" (Hausman and McPherson 1996: 42). Therefore, the paradoxes of happiness, Scitovsky's in particular, really only hit the *preference-satisfaction approach* because they reveal economic behaviours which do not maximize people's well-being.

Supporters of the preference-satisfaction approach have, however, a possible explanation for the kind of "non-rational" behavior that Scitovsky brought out. In response to Sen's two questions, most economists would make recourse to the abstract nature of economic theory, insisting that a model—to be scientific—must abstract from the many circumstances and factors which influence actual behavior. For example, J. S. Mill and Pareto both said that the *homo oeconomicus* is not the real person because psychological, affective, and other irrational factors intervene in a real man's behavior which make his actions deviate from his rational trajectory. The argument is forced to hypothesize that there must be some areas, such as the market, where the descriptions and forecasts of economic models aren't too far from reality. Otherwise, economics would have to admit the total irrelevance of its attempts to foresee actual human behavior, even in typical domains like buying, selling, and trading, and economic science would lose all its political and material content. All that being said, the defense cannot hold a candle to Scitovsky's argument, because the paradoxes he spotted do not refer to marginal economic areas, but to the *hardcore* of contemporary economic science—ordinary consumer choices.

This response holds even less water when one considers that the application of economic rationality is being extended well beyond its traditional boundaries into such realms as art, politics, religion, and racial discrimination. In the first page of his seminal paper "A Theory of Marriage", Gary Becker wrote: "Indeed, economic theory may well be on its way to providing a unified framework for *all* behavior involving scarce resources, nonmarket as well as market, nonmonetary as well as monetary, small group as well as competitive" (Becker 1973: 814).

6. Happiness and Deception

Not only Scitovsky's *Joyless Economy* but all the theories embracing treadmill effects as explanations of the paradoxes of happiness assume that individual choices are, or can be, affected by a sort of *deception*, that brings us to sub-optimal and inefficient behavior—the contributions of Frank, and above all of Layard, in this volume are strongly based on this assumption. The first author in the tradition of modern political economy who had a theory of happiness based on *deception* was Adam Smith. This emerges in his *Theory of Moral Sentiments* (1759). The argument runs as follows. Emulation of the wealth and greatness of the rich is the engine of both social mobility and economic development. So the "poor man's son" submits "to more fatigue of body and more uneasiness of mind...he labours night and day to acquire talents superior to all his competitors" (1759: 181).

This social engine however, is based upon a process of *deception*—or, better, *self-deception*—namely the idea that the rich man is happier than the poor, or that he possesses "more means for happiness" (ibid. 182). In reality this is not true. Smith brings forward many arguments in support of this thesis (the solitude and dissatisfaction of the old rich man, his anxiety, etc.), recalling also the old proverb: "the eye is larger than the belly"; for physiological reasons (the capacity of the stomach and the limited duration of a healthy life), rich men "consume little more than the poor" (ibid. 184).

At this point the "invisible hand" argument comes into play; given the fallacy that more wealth brings more happiness, given also the impossibility of consuming all the products of his industry, rich men, "in spite of their natural selfishness and rapacity, though they mean only their conveniency, though the sole end which they propose from the labours of all the thousands whom they employ, be the gratification of their own vain and insatiable desires, they divide with the poor the product of all their improvements. They are led by an invisible hand to make nearly the same distribution of the necessaries of life, which would have been made, had the earth been divided into equal portion among all its inhabitants, and thus without intending it, without knowing it, advance the interest of society" (ibid. 184–5).

Smith sees in this mysterious fact the presence of Providence, which "when it divided the earth among a few lordly masters, it neither forgot nor abandoned those who seemed to have been left out of the partition". Nature then has designed the world with endogenous just mechanisms, which *allow the equal distribution not of material means but of happiness*: "In what constitutes the real happiness of human life, they [the poor men] are in no respect inferior to those who would seem so much above them. In ease of body and peace of mind, all the different ranks of life are nearly upon a level, and the beggar, who suns himself by the side of the highway, possesses that security which kings are fighting for" (ibid. 185).[29]

So Smith the philosopher was aware that thinking that wealth, social recognition, and fortune leads to happiness is a *deception* (ibid. 182 ff.). Social dynamics, however, is providentially based on this deception; the individual desires to improve his material conditions, for his happiness, he thinks, is guided by an *invisible hand* towards public happiness, despite the "natural selfishness and rapacity" of the deceived individuals (ibid. 185).

When a few years later he wrote the *Wealth of the Nations* (1776), the title itself defined the object of the new-born political economy. It deals with wealth not with happiness, even if in Smith's choice of the word "wealth" instead of "riches" one can rightly see that the idea that wealth (weal, well-being) is more and different from simply possessing riches.

Given the very rich anthropology and theory of human agency present in the *Theory of Moral Sentiments* and his theory of deception, Smith's political economy (and the whole Classical paradigm) could have become something completely different if, instead of being the "science of wealth", political economy had been defined as the study of how and under what conditions *riches could be transformed into happiness*.

Nevertheless, the philosopher of the deception became an economist studying the wealth of nations. If wealth however does not lead to happiness, if the link wealth–happiness is a deception that the philosopher points out, why would the philosopher study the ways of increasing wealth? Smith's probable answer to this question about happiness (as emerges in particular from the *Theory of Moral Sentiments*) could have been that it is produced by an active life and *modest* wealth, but not by idleness, luxury, and *excessive* wealth. In general, the "wealth of nations" is strictly linked to the happiness of nations, because only a tiny minority are in the idle class. The pursuit of (excessive) wealth is a deception; but it provides the motivational power for the economic system, which provides everyone with subsistence, and people's susceptibility to this deception is one of the mechanisms through which the invisible hand mechanism works. The tradition of economics after Smith (the philosopher) forgot the very complex and slippery relationship between wealth and happiness, as the enthusiasm for the "novelty" of the contemporary paradox of happiness signals.

7. Again, What Kind of Happiness?

In this final section, let us return to the tension between the subjectivist and the objectivist approaches to happiness. In the first two sections we saw that both in Psychology, in Economics, and in general in the social sciences there are two conceptions about happiness: the first being Benthamite-subjective-hedonic-individualistic, and the second Aristotelian-objective-eudaimonic-relational.

Doubtless, the first perspective has gained much support in economics. It is very hard to find in the present debate economists who, when they use the expression "happiness", refer to eudaimonia and to its relational and paradoxical nature. In fact, when today economists use the term "happiness" they are—consciously or not—in line with Bentham, and far from Aristotle.

As far as the authors of this volume are concerned, according to the distinctions we have drawn in this Introduction, van Praag, Layard, Stark, and Veenhoven are closer to the hedonic-subjectivist tradition: happiness is not something different from satisfaction or SWB. All these authors have room for sociality, but normally sociality is intended as "positional competition", and not as an ingredient of happiness. In Frank, Frey and Stutzer, and Easterlin there are, as we have seen, data and emphasis on the importance, in terms of happiness, of relational and family life, a typical eudaimonistic element.

On the other hand, Matravers, Nussbaum, Pasinetti, Sugden, and Zamagni present theories or historical reconstructions where sociality intended as personalized relationality is analyzed as an essential element of a happy life, an approach that is objectively in line with happiness intended as eudaimonia. This approach, which is still marginal in economics, is also close to Amartya Sen's capability approach, a philosophical attitude very close to Aristotle, although Sen denies that his capability approach was inspired originally by Aristotle's readings:

As Aristotle noted at the very beginning of the *Nicomachean Ethics* (resonating well with the conversation between Maitreyee and Yajnavalkya three thousands miles away), "wealth is evidently not the good we are seeking; for it is merely useful and for the sake of something else". If we have reasons to want more wealth, we have to ask: What precisely are these reasons, how do they work, on what are they contingent and what are the things we can "do" with more wealth? In fact, we generally have excellent reasons for wanting more income or wealth. This is not because, typically, they are admirable general-purpose means for having more freedom to lead the kind of lives we have reasons to value. The usefulness of wealth lies in the things that it allows us to do—the substantive freedom it helps us to achieve. But this relation is neither exclusive (since there are significant influences on our lives other than wealth) nor uniform (since the impact of wealth on our lives varies with other influences). It is as important to recognize the crucial role of wealth in determining living conditions and the quality of life as it is to understand the qualified and contingent nature of this relationship. (Sen 2000: 14)

A final remark. The set of papers collected in this volume aims to provide an illustration of the whole field of happiness studies today with a special emphasis on their relationship with economic thought. This volume discusses the state of the art and the main strands and contributions to the "economics of happiness", as a sub-discipline related to political economy. However, the main thrust of the volume is on the *relationship* of happiness studies with economics. The character of the book is therefore interdisciplinary. Moreover, this volume makes a specific contribution to highlighting the comparative role and influence of the subjectivist approach *vis-à-vis* the objectivist approach to human happiness in the current literature in the field.

The ambition of this book is to present the reader with a conceptual framework for a critical understanding of happiness studies and their relationship with economics. While the economic perspective is central, the focus here is on economics *and* happiness rather than the economics *of* happiness.

Notes

The papers collected in the present volume have been contributed by some of the leading scholars on happiness in economics. They were originally prepared for the International Conference "The Paradoxes of Happiness in Economics", held at Milano-Bicocca in 2003.

1. Bruni and Porta (2003), Porta and Scazzieri (2002).
2. In their researches the Leyden school calculated the rate of preference drift β as a numerical value. If $\beta = 1$ the adaptation is complete. In his first article van Praag (1971) found a value of about 0.15 and in most later studies (beginning with van Praag and Kapteyn 1973), values hover around 0.5. Throughout the 1980s the school postulated that, apart from adaptation to *own* income, the income of the social reference group is also an important element. This led to the concept of *"reference drift"* which was estimated at about 0.3. The total effect is about 0.8, which falls short of complete adaptation. Cf. also van Praag (2004).
3. This study (p. 224) also offered important insights into the "hopes" of people in different countries. For example, while Nigeria and the USA attributed the

same value to health in relation to hope, for Nigerians the economic factor was more important (90 vs. 65), and, less obviously, Nigerians gave more weight to the family than did the USA people (76 vs. 47).

4. Cantril's data showed, for instance, that Cuba and Egypt were more satisfied than West Germany (1965: 258). He plotted happiness against the log of income and thus construed a lack of relationship. Veenhoven (1991) criticized Easterlin's thesis about international comparisons. He plotted the same data as Cantril, though using the same scale on both axes, and showed that the relationship follows a convex pattern of diminishing returns. A similar argument has been put forward by Oswald (1997: 1817). A recent paper, Hagerty and Veenhoven (2003), challenges this thesis, claiming that growing gross domestic product (GDP) does go with greater happiness. Easterlin (2004) replied to this paper, defending his original thesis.

5. Nowadays the main source of data comes from the General Social Surveys of the United States (or, in Europe, from the Eurobarometer of the European Commission), which are randomly selected samples of American people. Data are available from 1972 onwards.

6. The same thesis is endorsed by Frank: "When we plot average happiness versus average income for clusters of people in a given country at a given time . . . rich people are in fact a lot happier than poor people. It's actually an astonishingly large difference. There's no one single change you can imagine that would make your life improve on the happiness scale as much as to move from the bottom 5 percent on the income scale to the top 5 percent" (Chapter 2, this volume). And Layard: "Of course within countries the rich are always happier than the poor" (Chapter 5, this volume).

7. Among psychologists the debate is more controversial. Some scholars (e.g. Diener), on the basis of different data from the WVS (World Values Survey), challenge the correlations (also when other variables are under control) between income and happiness in *general* (among countries, within a country and over time).

8. He began with a brief article in the *American Journal of Sociology*, composed almost entirely of 41 graphs, that demonstrated the course of a few social variables chosen as gauges of the quality of life in America during the Great Depression (Ogburn 1935).

9. The HDI turned out to be crucial in development policies. According to Sen (2000), it represents the most important example of putting into operation his *capabilites approach*, which measures individual well-being on the basis of what a person is capable of doing with his goods.

10. For example, Robert Sugden writes, "Given the rich array of functionings that Sen takes to be relevant, given the extent of disagreement among reasonable people about the nature of a good life, and given the unresolved problem of how to value sets, it is natural to ask how far Sen's framework is operational" (Sugden 1993: 1962).

11. In the "Preface to the second edition" of *Fragility* (2001), Martha Nussbaum acknowledges a partial departure from Aristotle and a proximity to Stoic philosophy (for a sense of universal human dignity, a concept absent in Aristotle), Kant (liberty) and Rawls's ("political liberalism").

12. Though Sen shares the idea that the good life is not merely a subjective perception and that it should be measured by how people actually live, the methodological consequences of Nussbaum's response put him off: "I certainly have no great objection to anyone going on that route. My difficulty to accepting that as the only route on which to travel arises partly from the concern that this view of human nature (with a unique list of functionings for a good human life) may be tremendously over-specified, and also from my inclination to argue about the nature and the importance of the type of objectivity involved in this approach. But mostly my intransigence arises, in fact, from the consideration that to use the capability approach as such does not require taking that route, and the deliberate incompleteness of the capabilities approach permits other routes to be taken which also have some plausibility" (Sen 1993: 36).

13. Kahneman's approach to happiness is twofold: in some studies he follows explicitly a hedonistic approach (Kahneman *et al.* 1997, 2003), but in other researches (such as that with Nickerson *et al.* 2003), his conclusion is in line with the Aristotelian approach.

14. Ryff and others presented a multidimensional approach to the measurement of PWB that taps six distinct aspects of human flourishing: autonomy, personal growth, self-acceptance, life purpose, mastery, and positive relatedness. These six constructs define PWB (Ryff and Singer 1998). See also Keyes *et al.* (2002).

15. On SWB see also Diener and Lucas (1999), and Diener (1984).

16. For a review and critical approach to this theory see Lucas *et al.* (2002: 4).

17. It has to be acknowledged that Veenhoven's methodological position is far from the set-point theory. In his 1991 paper, he argued that happiness does not depend on social comparison or culturally variable wants, but rather reflects the gratification of innate human "needs"; and a few years later he rejected the set-point theory (1994).

18. Cf. http://www.eur.nl/fsw/research/happiness/prologue.htm

19. On the basis of the distinction between objective and subjective happiness Kahneman maintains the individual and social importance of improving the *objective* conditions of happiness, even if such improvements are not felt *subjectively*. To drive more comfortable cars or eat better food is an expression of a higher quality of life ("objective happiness", in Kahneman's terms) although, because of the hedonic treadmill, there may be no increase in subjective terms.

20. Similar experiments have also been reported by Layard (this volume).

21. If we take a person's reference point to be some weighted average of his or her previous consumption, Edgeworth's hypothesis "implies that a person's

utility in any given period depends not only on the absolute quantity she consumes of each good in that period, but also on differences between those quantities and the corresponding quantities at the reference point. The psychological concept of 'accommodation' used by Edgeworth is essentially the same as 'adaptation', which present-day psychologists have used to explain reference-dependence" (Bruni and Sugden 2005: 18). A first rank economist at the time, Maffeo Pantaleoni, in his analysis of wants, suggested that there is a tendency for a person's "hedonic scale" at any given time to depend on past consumption (1898: 53)—a very similar concept to Edgeworth's "accommodation". In Pantaleoni, however, there is also an intuition that deserves greater attention in the present debate, namely the idea that the tendency for increases in income to generate new wants is stronger than the tendency for decreases in income to stifle existing wants: "The positive expansion of wants is, as a matter of fact, different from the negative expansion" (p. 53). There would be, thus, an asymmetry in the income/wants-satisfaction relation, something similar to that emphasized by Kahneman in his *objective happiness* (1999).

22. Holländer (2001) refers explicitly to Duesenberry's utility function.

23. Although the paradoxes of happiness are more relevant in high-income societies, they don't have a monopoly on positional or consumer competition. Anthropologists tell us that positional consumerism exists in all types of societies. Even the act of giving is often another way of showing off one's high consumer level in order to reinforce one's status. In the *Theory of the Leisure Class* (1899), Veblen blamed the depersonalization of social relations, typical of modern society, for the increase in conspicuous or positional consumption. While there are many ways to communicate one's social position in villages and small communities, consumerism is the only way to say who we are in today's anonymous society. The tribe's witch-doctor earned respect for his family for generations, the mighty warrior as well, as did the person who taught one's children to read. Now big cars and homes tell the neighbors, whom we don't know, just who we are. Goods have become almost the only means to communicate status.

24. A comment made by Hirschman to Scitovsky stressed that relational activity (civil and political commitment, doing interesting things with friends, in particular "commensality") can be *at the same time* both stimulating and comforting: "My principal argument against Scitovsky was his utter neglect of the *public* dimension. He did not conceive of politics, participation in public life, pursuit of the public interest (or of the 'public happiness', in the language of the eighteenth century) as alternative sources of stimulation" (Hirschman 1996: 536).

25. In the same talk, Scitovsky (p. 600) was keen to highlight a point which he felt he had neglected in his book. Besides the rich who are bored and unhappy because of their excess in comfort, he stressed that there are many people who

are unhappy because of the too few comforts which indigence affords. Unfortunately, this is an often forgotten aspect in the analysis of the paradoxes of happiness, which, instead, needs to be addressed.

26. Founding this vision on economic action, Pareto clearly said that an individual can disappear once he has left his map of preferences (1906, chap. III, § 57).

27. The idea that economic rationality should not say anything concerning the content of preferences has a long history. At the end of the nineteenth century, Pareto introduced the term *ophelimity* as distinct from utility and set the foundations for economics in non-substantial bases. Economists following the "theory of revealed preferences" are moving totally along this Paretian path (cf. Bruni 2002).

28. Individual well-being does not imply egotism. The well-being of an individual can also imply the well-being of others, or the pleasure of caring for others. This characteristic of rationality is also called "philosophical egoism" as distinct from "psychological egoism" (cf. Hollis 1998).

29. We find a similar thesis (Providence = invisible hand) in G. B. Vico, the Neapolitan philosopher and Genovesi's master (Vico 1725: 59).

References

Argyle, M. (2001), *The Psychology of Happiness*, New York: Taylor & Francis.

Aristotle (1980) *Nicomachean Ethics*, Oxford: Oxford University Press.

Becker, G. (1973), "A Theory of Marriage: Part I", *The Journal of Political Economy*, 81: 813–46.

Bradburn, N. M. (1969), *The Structure of the Psychological Well-Being*, Chicago: Aldine.

Brickman, P., and Campbell, D. T. (1971), "Hedonic Relativism and Planning the Good Society", in M. H. Apley (ed.), *Adaptation-Level Theory: A Symposium*, New York: Academic Press, 287–302.

Bruni, L. (2002), *Vilfredo Pareto and the Birth of Modern Microeconomics*, Cheltenham: Edward Elgar.

—— and Porta, P. L. (2003), "*Pubblica felicità* and *Economia civile* in the Italian Enlightenment", *History of Political Economy*, suppl. no. 35: 361–85.

—— and Sugden, R. (2005), "The Road not Taken: How Psychology was removed from Economics, and how it might be brought back", forthcoming in *The Economic Journal*.

Campbell, A., Converse, P. E., and Rodgers, W. L. (1976), *The Quality of American Life: Perceptions, Evolutions, and Satisfactions*, New York: Russell Sage Foundation,

Cantril, H. (1965), *The Pattern of Human Concerns*, New Brunswick, NJ: Rutgers University Press.

Deci, R. M., and Ryan, E. L. (2001), "On Happiness and Human Potentials: A Review of Research on Hedonic and Eudaimonic Well-Being", *Annual Review of Psychology*, 52: 141–66.

Diener, E. (1984), "Subjective Well-Being", *Psychological Bulletin* 95: 542–75.

—— and Lucas, R. E. (1999), "Personality and Subjective Well-Being", in Kahneman *et al.* (1999), 213–29.

—— and Seligman, Martin, E. P. (2003), "Beyond Money: Toward an Economy of Well-Being", *Psychological Science in the Public Interest*, 51: 1–31.

Duesenberry, J. (1949), *Income, Saving and the Theory of Consumer Behavior*, Cambridge, Mass.: Harvard University Press.

Easterlin, R. (1974), "Does Economic Growth Improve Human Lot? Some Empirical Evidence", in P. A. Davis and M. W. Reder (eds.), *Nation and Households in Economic Growth: Essays in Honor of Moses Abromowitz*, New York and London: Academic Press.

—— (2001), "Income and Happiness: Towards a Unified Theory", *The Economic Journal*, 111: 465–84.

Easterlin, R. (ed.) (2002), *Happiness in Economics*, The International Library of Critical Writings in Economics, Cheltenham: Edward Elgar.

—— (2004), "Feeding the Illusion of Growth and Happiness: A Reply to Hagerty and Veenhoven", mimeo.

Edgeworth, F. Y. (1881), *Mathematical Psychics*, London; reprinted New York: Kelly, 1967.

Elster, J. (1983), *Sour Grapes*, Cambridge: Cambridge University Press.

Frank, R. (1985), *Choosing the Right Pond*, New York: Oxford University Press.

Frey, B. (1997), *Not Just for the Money*, Cheltenham and Brookfield, Vt.: Edward Elgar.

—— and Stutzer, A. (2001), "Happiness, Economy and Institutions", *The Economic Journal*, 111: 918–38.

Galbraith, J. K. (1959), *The Affluent Society*, Boston: Houghton Mifflin Company.

Genovesi, A. (1765–7), *Lezioni di commercio o sia di economia civile*, 2 vols., Naples: Stamperia Simoniana.

Hagerty, M. R. and Veenhoven, R. (2003), "Wealth and Happiness Revisited—Growing National Income *Does* Go with Greater Happiness", *Social Indicators Research*, 64: 1–27.

Hargreaves-Heap, S., Hollis, Martin, Lyons, Bruce, Sugden, Robert, and Weale, Albert (1994), *Rational Choice: A Critical Guide*, Oxford: Blackwell.

Hausman, D. M., and McPherson, M. S. (1996), *Economic Analysis and Moral Philosophy*, Cambridge: Cambridge University Press.

Herrnstein, R. J., and Murray, C. (1994), *The Bell Curve: Intelligence and Class Structure in American Life*, New York: Free Press.

Hirsch, F. (1977), *Social Limits to Growth*, London: Routledge.

Hirschman, A. O. (1996), "Melding the Public and Private Spheres: Taking Commensality Seriously", *Critical Review*, 104: 533–50.

Holländer, H. (2001), "On the Validity of Utility Statements: Standard Theory versus Duesenberry's", *Journal of Economic Behaviour and Organization*, 45: 227–49.

Hollis, M. (1998), *Trust within Reason*, Cambridge: Cambridge University Press.

Lane, R. (2000), *The Loss of Happiness in Market Economies*, New Haven and London: Yale University Press.

Layard, R. (1980), "Human Satisfactions and Public Policy", *The Economic Journal*, 90: 737–50.

Lucas, R. E., Clark, A. E., Georgellis, Y., and Diener, E. (2002), *Unemployment Alters the Set-Point for Life Satisfaction*, Working Paper 2002/17, Paris: Delta.

Lykken, D., and Tellegen, A. (1996), "Happiness is a Stochastic Phenomenon", *Psychological Science*, 7: 186–9.

Kahneman, D. (1999), "Objective Happiness", in Kahneman *et al.* (1999).

——Diener, E., and Schwartz, N. (eds.) (1999), *Well-Being: The Foundations of Hedonic Psychology*, New York: Russell Sage Foundation.

——Krueger, A. B., Schkade, D. A., Schwarz, N. and Stone, A. A. (2003), "A Survey Method for Characterizing Daily Life Experience: The Day Reconstruction Method (DRM)", mimeo, Princeton.

Kahneman, D., Wakker, P.P., and Sarin, R. (1997), "Back to Bentham? Explorations of Experienced Utility", *Quarterly Journal of Economics*, 112: 375–405.

Keyes, C. L. M., Shmotkin, D., and Ryff, C. D. (2002), "Optimizing Well-Being: The Empirical Encounter of Two Traditions", *Journal of Personality and Social Psychology*, 826: 1007–22.

Malthus, T. R. (1798/1966), *An Essay on the Principle of Population*, reprinted, London: Macmillan, 1966.

Marshall, A. (1945/1890), *Principles of Economics*, London: Macmillan.

Ng, Yk (1978), "Economic Growth and Social Welfare: The Need for a Complete Study of Happiness", *Kyklos*, 314: 575–87.

Nickerson, C., Schwarz, N., Diener, E., and Kahneman, D. (2003), "Zeroing the Dark Side of the American Dream: A Closer Look at the Negative Consequences of the Goal for Financial Success", *Psychological Science*, 14: 531–6.

Nussbaum, M. (1986/2001), *The Fragility of Goodness: Luck and Ethics in Greek Tragedy and Philosophy*, Cambridge: Cambridge University Press.

Offer, A. (2003), "Economic Welfare Measurements and Human Well-Being", in Paul A. David and Mark Thomas (eds.), *The Economic Future in Historical Perspective*, Oxford: Oxford University Press.

Ogburn, W. F. (1935), "Indexes of Social Trends and their Fluctuations", *American Journal of Sociology*, 40: 822–8.

Oswald, A. J. (1997), "Happiness and Economic Performance", *The Economic Journal*, 107 (November): 1815–31.

Pantaleoni, M. (1998), *Pure Economics*, London: Macmillan.

Pareto, V. (1906), *Manuale di economia politica, con una introduzione alla scienza sociale*, Milan: Società editrice libraria.

Porta, P. L., and Scazzieri, R. (2002), "Pietro Verri's Political Economy", *History of Political Economy*, 34: 83–110.

Ryff, C. D. (1995), "Psychological Well-Being in Adult Life", *Current Directory of Psychological Science* 4: 99–104.

—— and Singer, B. (1998), "The Contours of Positive Human Health", *Psychological Inquiry* 9: 1–28.

—— —— (2000), "Interpersonal Flourishing: A Positive Health Agenda for the New Millennium", *Personal and Social Psychological Review* 4: 30–44.

Scitovsky, T. (1976), *The Joyless Economy: An Inquiry into Human Satisfaction and Consumer Dissatisfaction*, Oxford: Oxford University Press.

—— (1996), "My Own Criticism of the *Joyless economy*", *Critical Review*, 10: 595–605.

Sen, A. K. (1993), *Capability and Well-Being*, in M. Nussbaum and A. Sen (eds.), *The Quality of Life*, Oxford: Clarendon Press, 1993.

—— (1996), "Rationality, Joy and Freedom", *Critical Review*, 10: 481–94.

Sen, A. K. (2000), *Development as Freedom*, New York: A. Alfred Knopp.

—— (2002), *Rationality and Freedom*, Cambridge, Mass: Belknap Press of Harward University.

Smith, A. (1984/1759), *The Theory of Moral Sentiments*, ed. D. D. Raphael and A. L. Macfie, Indianapolis: Liberty Fund.

—— (1904/1776), *An Inquiry into the Nature and Causes of the Wealth of Nations*, 2 vols., London: Methuen.

Sugden, R. (1993), "Welfare, Resources and Capabilities: A Review of Inequality Reexamined by Amartya Sen", *Journal of Economic Literature*, 31: 1947–62.

Tversky, A., and Kahneman, D. (1991), "Loss Aversion in Riskless Choice: A Reference Dependent Model", *Quarterly Journal of Economics*, 1064: 1039–61.

van Praag, B. M. S. (1968), *Individual Welfare Functions and Consumer Behavior: A Theory of Rational Irrationality*, Ph.D. thesis, Amsterdam: North Holland Publishing Company.

—— (1971), "The Welfare Function of Income in Belgium: An Empirical Investigation", *European Economic Review*, 2: 337–69.

—— (2004), *Happiness Quantified—A Satisfaction Calculus Approach*, Oxford: Oxford University Press.

—— and Kapteyn, A. (1973), "Further Evidence on the Individual Welfare Function of Income: An Empirical Investigation in the Netherlands", *European Economic Review*, 4: 33–62.

Veblen, T. (1899), *The Theory of the Leisure Class*, New York: Prometheus Books.

Veenhoven, R. (1991), "Is Happiness Relative?", *Social Indicators Research*, 24: 1–34.

—— (1994), "Is Happiness a Trait? Tests of the Theory that a Better Society Does Not Make People any Happier", *Social Indicators Research*, 32: 101–60.

Vico, G. B. (1725), *The New Science*, English translation by Thomas Goddard Bergin and Max Harold Fisch, Ithaca, NY: Cornell University Press, 1948.

1

Building a Better Theory of Well-Being

Richard A. Easterlin

1. Introduction

I take the terms "well-being", "utility", "happiness", "life satisfaction", and "welfare" to be interchangeable and measured by the answer to a question such as that asked in the United States General Social Survey (GSS): "Taken all together, how would you say things are these days— would you say that you are very happy, pretty happy, or not too happy?"[1] A substantial methodological literature has developed on the reliability, validity, and comparability of the answers to such questions (Frey and Stutzer 2002a 2002b; Veenhoven 1993). For the present purpose, I take the responses to be meaningful and reasonably comparable among groups of individuals, and focus on the determinants of happiness, so measured.

The title of this chapter, "Building a Better Theory of Well-Being", raises the question, "Better than what?" My answer is, better than the prevailing theories of well-being in psychology and economics. This is not to suggest that there is unanimity in either field; the theories discussed below are what one might view as the central tendency of each discipline. I try to take advantage here of work in both fields plus social survey data to suggest the shape of a theory more consistent with what people have to say about their feelings of well-being.

In psychology, the tendency is towards "setpoint theory".[2] Each individual is thought to have a setpoint of happiness given by genetics and personality. Life events such as marriage, loss of a job, and serious injury may deflect a person above or below this setpoint, but in time hedonic adaptation will return an individual to the initial setpoint. One setpoint theory writer states flatly that objective life circumstances have a negligible role to play in a theory of happiness (Kammann, 1983: 18).

If the goal of public policy is to improve subjective well-being (SWB), this theory leads to a nihilistic view of economic and social policy. Setpoint theory implies that any measures taken to improve economic or social conditions can have only a transient effect on well-being, since each individual will in time revert to his or her given setpoint of happiness. This implication of the theory has been explicitly recognized by psychologists in the recent encyclopedic volume on hedonic well-being edited by Kahneman *et al.* (1999). Ed Diener and Richard E. Lucas state, for example: "The influence of genetics and personality suggests a limit on the degree to which policy can increase SWB...Changes in the environment, although important for short-term well-being, lose salience over time through processes of adaptation, and have small effects on long-term SWB" (Diener and Lucas 1999: 227). Moreover, if setpoint theory is correct, not only is public policy likely to be ineffective but there is little an individual can do to improve his or her well-being, except, perhaps, consult a psychologist.

In contrast, in economics, life circumstances and particularly, income and employment, are believed to have lasting effects on well-being. The prevailing theory might be termed "more is better". As a general matter economists prefer not to theorize about subjective states of mind and to deal only with observed behavior. Their argument, termed "revealed preference", is that if an individual is observed to buy a combination of goods, say, x_2, y_2, when an alternative combination, x_1, y_1 is affordable with a person's given income and prevailing prices, then (based on certain axioms) the individual is deemed to prefer x_2, y_2 to x_1, y_1 and hence, to be better off. A major implication of this theory is that one can improve well-being by increasing one's own income, and that public policy measures aimed at increasing the income of society as a whole lead to greater well-being. Economists recognize that well-being depends on a variety of circumstances besides material conditions, but typically they assume that if income increases substantially, then overall well-being will move in the same direction. As A. C. Pigou put it many years ago, "there is a clear perception that changes in economic welfare [the level of real income] indicate changes in social welfare in the same direction, if not in the same degree" (Pigou 1932: 3).

In what follows, I argue that neither the prevailing psychological nor economic theories are consistent with accumulating survey evidence on well-being, and based on this analysis, I try to sketch the outlines of a better theory. My empirical work takes, for the most part, a life-cycle approach, applying the demographer's technique of cohort analysis to survey data, usually the GSS. Generalizations about life-cycle experience are obtained by following each of several cohorts over the 28-year span between 1972 and 2000 covered by the GSS. Because some cohorts are at the beginning of the adult life cycle in 1972, while others are in their middle or later years, it is possible to infer patterns over the full adult life span by bringing together the different segments of life-cycle experience represented by younger and older cohorts. The total sample size of the annual surveys is typically about 1,500, except after 1994 when they are almost twice as great. In what follows I sometimes use three- or five-year averages in order to minimize the problem of small sample size that arises when one subdivides the total sample by characteristics such as age, gender, and health, marital, or work status. The three-option happiness question is scaled from $3 =$ very happy to $1 =$ not too happy to compute mean happiness for various population groups.

2. Is there a Setpoint of Happiness?

Let me start with the psychological theory. The critical issue is not whether *any* adaptation to life events occurs, but whether adaptation is *complete*, that is, whether individuals return to their initial level of happiness.[3] There are, in fact, psychological studies that make clear that with respect to some experiences, such as noise and cosmetic surgery, hedonic adaptation by people is typically less than complete, that is, these experiences have a lasting effect on well-being (Frederick and Loewenstein 1999).

The survey evidence presented here suggests, in addition, that individuals do not fully adapt to changes in either health or marital circumstances. A deterioration in health has a permanently negative effect on happiness, and the more severe the deterioration in health, the greater the adverse impact. With regard to marital status, the formation of unions has a positive and lasting effect on happiness; the dissolution of unions, a permanently negative effect. Needless to say, I am speaking of averages; there is considerable dispersion about the mean.

2.1. Health and Happiness

The seminal article repeatedly cited in the psychology literature as demonstrating adaptation to adverse changes in health is a study by

Brickman *et al.* (1978). This article reports that serious accident victims (paraplegics and quadriplegics), when compared with a group of controls, "did not appear nearly as unhappy as might have been expected" (p. 921). The sample size in this analysis is very small (29 accident victims versus 22 controls). The problem of small sample size is aggravated by the dubious comparability of the controls, who are chosen from a phone book because they "lived in approximately the same areas of the city as . . . lottery winners [a third and quite different group in the analysis]" (p. 919). In any event, the study does *not* find that accident victims are as happy as controls. On the contrary, accident victims, compared with controls, "rated themselves significantly *less* happy" (p. 924, emphasis added). Setpoint (or "adaptation level") theory is saved in this study only by introducing a quite different comparison, one between accident victims and what "might have been expected". What "might have been expected" is never explained or quantified; the reader's intuition presumably fills in the blank.

There have been a number of studies since, some supporting the notion of complete adaptation, others contradicting it. Most of these suffer from similar problems of sample size or other shortcomings. To my knowledge the most comprehensive and careful investigation is one that examines the life satisfaction (on a five-point scale) of a *national* sample of persons reporting disabling conditions (n = 675) and compares them with a *national* sample of nondisabled persons (n = 1064) (Mehnert *et al.* 1990).

What does this study find? First, the life satisfaction of those with disabilities is, on average, significantly less than those who report no disabilities (Table 1.1). Second, within the disabled group, happiness is less for those with greater difficulties. Life satisfaction is lower, the more severe the disabling condition (see Table 1.2, item 1). Life satisfaction is less for those who have more than one disabling condition (item 2). Those with mental, physical, or "other serious health" disabilities are less satisfied with their lives than those with sensory disabilities (item 3). The more limited one is in daily activities, the less satisfied he or she is (item 4). Finally, if one's disability is more likely to be noticed by persons who know the respondent fairly well, life satisfaction is less (item 5).

A question is sometimes raised as to which way the causal arrow runs—from health to life satisfaction or life satisfaction to health? If health is conceived unidimensionally, a plausible a priori argument can be made that life satisfaction affects health, as well as vice versa. But when health is characterized by a variety of physically disabling conditions, as in Table 1.2, it seems highly unlikely that it is differences in life satisfaction that are causing the observed variations in health problems. The more

Table 1.1. Percent Distribution by Life Satisfaction of Persons by Self-Reported Disability Status, 1986

Disability status	(1) (2) Life Satisfaction		(3)	(4)	(5)	(6) n
	Satisfied		Neither	Dissatisfied		
	Very	Somewhat		Somewhat	Very	
Nondisabled	50	40	4	5	1	1064
Disabled	37	31	5	18	9	675

Source: Mehnert et al. (1990: 13). The question is, "How satisfied are you with life in general—very satisfied, somewhat satisfied, neither satisfied nor dissatisfied, somewhat dissatisfied, or very dissatisfied?" Respondents who were not sure or refused (2 percent or less) are classified as "neither".

Table 1.2. Percent Distribution by Life Satisfaction of Persons with Self-Reported Disability, by Characteristic of Disabling Condition, 1986

	(1) Life satisfaction	(2)	(3)	(4) n
	Very or somewhat satisfied	Neither	Somewhat or very dissatisfied	
All persons with disability	68	5	27	675
1. *Severity*				
Slight	86	2	12	108
Moderate	80	6	14	216
Somewhat severe	61	5	34	196
Very severe	49	6	45	155
2. *Multiple conditions*				
No	74	2	24	493
Yes	57	5	38	182
3. *Type of disability*				
Sensory	86	1	13	88
Mental[a]	72	5	23	61
Physical	68	3	29	303
Other serious health	65	5	30	196
4. *Limitation of activities*				
None	91	0	9	61
Limited in amount, kind of work[b]	75	6	19	317
Cannot work, keep house, etc.	56	6	38	297
5. *Feels close others[c] perceive respondent as disabled*				
No	78	[d]	22[d]	371
Yes	58	[d]	42[d]	304

Notes:
[a] Mental retardation, developmental, mental illness.
[b] Includes "other activities limited".
[c] Persons who know respondent fairly well.
[d] "Neither" included with "somewhat or very dissatisfied".

Source: Mehnert (1990: 10, 12).

plausible inference is that greater health problems result systematically in less happiness.

Thus, the results of Tables 1.1 and 1.2 imply that, on average, an adverse change in health reduces life satisfaction, and the more adverse the change in health, the greater the reduction in life satisfaction. The results do not mean that no adaptation to disability occurs. It is reasonable to suppose that the initial impact on happiness, say, of an accident or serious disease, is greater than its long-term impact. Adjustment to a disabling condition may be facilitated by health devices such as hearing aids or wheelchairs, and by a support network of friends and relatives. Moreover, the impact varies depending on the individual affected, and the extent of adaptation may depend, among other things, on personality character-istics. But the evidence does suggest that there is a lasting negative effect on happiness of an adverse change in health.

This study is based on nationally representative samples, and the sys-tematic results relating life satisfaction to the magnitude of health diffi-culties are impressive. It is true, however, that it is a point-of-time investigation, and does not follow persons over the life cycle. Let me turn, therefore, to some life-cycle evidence based on sampling the same persons in a given birth cohort at successive points in time as the cohort progresses through the adult life cycle.

There is no question that among adults real health problems increase over the life cycle. But what do people *say* about their health? If adaptation were complete to adverse changes in health, then the life course trend in self-reported health should be flat.[4] Is this the case?

In fact, self-reported health declines throughout the life course. Since 1972, the GSS has asked the following question: "Would you say your own health, in general, is excellent, good, fair, or poor?" (National Opinion Research Center 1999: 172). If one follows successively older ten-year birth cohorts for 28-year segments of the life span, one finds for each cohort a clear (and statistically significant) downtrend in mean self-reported health (Figure 1.1). (The mean health rating is obtained by scaling the responses from excellent = 4 down to poor = 1.) The trends for women and men separately are similar to that for both sexes combined as shown here. In the two oldest cohorts, the apparent leveling off of self-reported health beyond age 60 is due to the truncation of the sample caused by mortality; those reporting poorer health do, in fact, die more rapidly. The conclusion suggested by the data on self-reported health is the same as that for the preceding data on disability. There is not complete hedonic adaptation to adverse changes in health.[5]

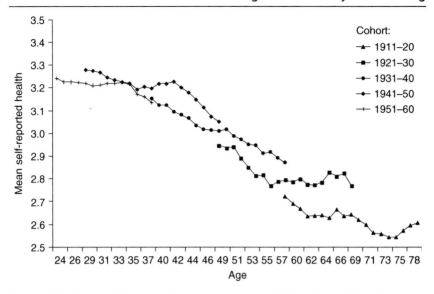

Figure 1.1. Mean self-reported health, cohorts of 1911–20 to 1951–60, by age (five-year average centered of each age)

Table 1.3. Mean Happiness by Self-Reported Health Status, Birth Cohorts of 1911–20 to 1951–60, 1972–2000

(1) Birth cohort	(2) Stage of life cycle	(3) Mean happiness	(4)	(5)	(6)
		Excellent health	Good health	Fair health	Poor Health
1951–60	Ages 23 to 45	2.36	2.12	1.85	1.63
1941–50	Ages 27 to 55	2.37	2.17	1.92	1.74
1931–40	Ages 37 to 65	2.43	2.23	1.98	1.74
1921–30	Ages 47 to 75	2.48	2.24	2.06	1.83
1911–20	Ages 57 to 85	2.52	2.27	2.12	1.96

Source: Unless otherwise indicated, the source for all tables and figures is the United States General Social Survey, 1972–2000 (cf. National Opinion Research Center 1999).

Throughout the life cycle, those who report they are healthier also say they are happier. For both younger and older cohorts happiness is greater, on average, the better the state of self-reported health (Table 1.3). This finding is consistent with the results above on life satisfaction and disabling conditions (Tables 1.1 and 1.2), and with numerous studies that find significant negative associations between happiness and self-reported health with controls for a variety of socio-economic circumstances (Argyle

1999; Blanchflower and Oswald 2004; Frey and Stutzer 2002*a*, 2002*b*; Michalos *et al.* 2000). The latter studies, which control for income, make clear that the impact of deteriorating health on happiness is due to non-pecuniary effects as well as any loss of income that may come with poor health. The conclusion to which all of these results consistently lead is that adverse health changes have a lasting and negative effect on subjective well-being, and that there is less than complete adaptation to deteriorating health.

2.2. *Marital Status and Happiness*

Curiously, despite claims by setpoint theory proponents that life circumstances have virtually no lasting effect on well-being, little evidence on marital formation or dissolution has been advanced to support this view. Indeed, one enthusiastic supporter of the setpoint model makes a specific exception for marriage, without explaining how one reconciles this with setpoint theory (Myers 1992, cf. chaps. 3 and 9). The effect of widowhood is perhaps most studied, and the results on this suggest that adverse effects of bereavement on life satisfaction persist, on average, for at least a decade (Frederick and Loewenstein 1999: 312).

A recently published evaluation of the setpoint model, using German longitudinal data to study the effects on well-being of changes in marital status, concludes, contrary to the setpoint model, that "all happiness is not due to temperament" (Lucas *et al.* 2003: 538). The empirical analysis, which focuses on marriage and widowhood, finds, however, a curious asymmetry: there is complete adaptation to marriage, but not (quite) to widowhood. Apparently, whatever is lost in happiness due to the dissolution of a union by widowhood is not gained by the formation of a union via marriage. There is no analysis of divorce or remarriage. Although the study is presented as a critique of the setpoint model, it is at best a weak one, for it states in its conclusions: "On average people adapt quickly and completely to marriage, and they adapt more slowly to widowhood (though even in this case, adaptation is close to complete after 8 years)" (ibid.).

Study of the life-cycle experience of cohorts suggests a much stronger departure from the setpoint model. Marriage (and remarriage) have a positive and lasting effect on happiness, and marital dissolution, whether divorce or widowhood, a permanently negative effect. At ages 18–19 when most women and virtually all men have not yet married, their mean

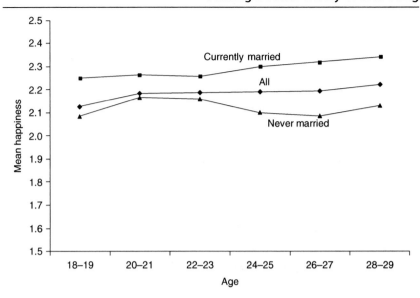

Figure 1.2. Mean happiness of females by marital status, cohort of 1953–72 from ages 18–19 to 28–29

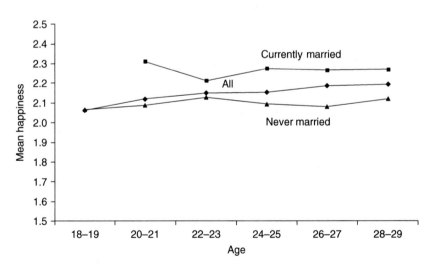

Figure 1.3. Mean happiness of males by marital status, cohort of 1953–72 from ages 18–19 to 28–29

happiness is around 2.1 (Figures 1.2 and 1.3). Over the next ten years, as up to 50 percent or more of a cohort becomes married, those who are married report happiness levels of around 2.2 to 2.3, while those who have never married remain at about 2.1 (ibid.).

These results cannot be due to selection effects. Persons who marry in the first decade of the adult life cycle could not have been happier than others, on average, before they got married. If this were true, then as these persons married and left the never-married group, the average happiness of the remaining never-married would have fallen. In fact, the happiness of those never-married remains constant as more and more persons marry (Figures 1.2 and 1.3). As a result, the mean happiness of the cohort as a whole increases as the proportion married increases. One would not observe these happiness patterns for the married and never-married, and for the cohort as a whole, if those with personalities that predisposed them toward greater happiness were typically the ones getting married.[6]

Beyond age 30 the proportion of a cohort currently married tends to level off and then decline as the effect of marital dissolution due to divorce, separation, and widowhood outweighs that due to the formation of unions through marriage and re-marriage. Throughout the adult life cycle, however, there is a marked and persistent gap between the average happiness of those in a cohort who are currently married and those who are not, for both women and men (Figures 1.4 and 1.5).

Within the group of married persons, there is little difference in happiness between those who are still in their first marriage and those who are remarried (Table 1.4). When married respondents are asked specifically about their marital, rather than overall, happiness, it is again true that those who are remarried are, on average, as satisfied with their marriage as those still in their first marriage (Table 1.5). The noticeably higher average values of marital compared with overall happiness (around 2.5–2.6 versus 2.3) is because a very large proportion (about two-thirds) of respondents choose the "very happy" response when asked specifically about marital happiness, and almost all of the rest choose "pretty happy".[7]

For those still in their first marriage the average length of marriage ranges from 10 years or less in the youngest cohort, that of 1951–60, to over 35 years in the oldest, that of 1921–30. (Duration of marriage for remarried persons is not available in the GSS data.) The mean level of both overall happiness and marital happiness for these two cohorts is virtually

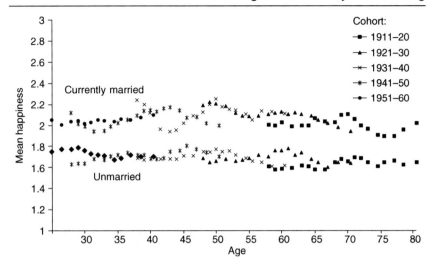

Figure 1.4. Mean happiness of currently married and unmarried females in specified cohort, by age (five-year average centered at each age)

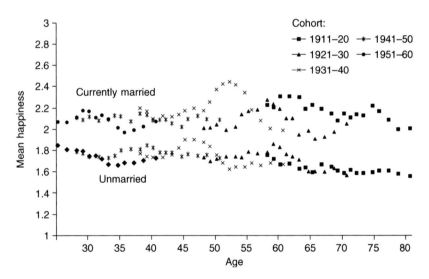

Figure 1.5. Mean happiness of currently married and unmarried males in specified cohort, by age (five-year average centered at each age)

the same despite their much different marriage durations (Tables 1.4 and 1.5). Furthermore, the overall happiness of married persons in each of these two cohorts is significantly above that of their counterparts who are not currently married, and significantly above overall happiness at the

Table 1.4. Mean Happiness of Currently Married Women by Number of Times Married, Birth Cohorts of 1921–30 to 1951–60, 1972–2000

(1) Birth Cohort	(2) Stage of life cycle	(3) Mean happiness	
		First marriage	Second or later
1951–60	Ages 23 to 45	2.31	2.27
1941–50	Ages 27 to 55	2.35	2.32
1931–40	Ages 37 to 65	2.36	2.32
1921–30	Ages 47 to 75	2.36	2.28

Table 1.5. Mean Marital Happiness[a] of Currently Married Women by Number of Times Married, Birth Cohorts of 1921–30 to 1951–60, 1972–2000

(1) Birth Cohort	(2) Mean marital happiness	(3)
	First marriage	Second or later
1951–60	2.58	2.54
1941–50	2.57	2.58
1931–40	2.58	2.51
1921–30	2.60	2.50

Notes:
[a] The question asked, with assigned numerical value in brackets, is: "Taking things altogether, how would you describe your marriage? Would you say that your marriage is very happy [= 3], pretty happy [= 2], or not too happy [= 1]?"

start of the adult life cycle when very few people are married (Figures 1.2 and 1.3). If complete hedonic adaptation to marriage were occurring, it is hard to understand why married persons are persistently happier than others, and why the happiness of those still in their first marriage remains high at increasing durations of marriage.

Just as the formation of marriage affects happiness positively, the dissolution of marriage has a negative effect. Although the mean happiness of those not currently married (i.e. persons who are never-married, widowed, and divorced or separated) is significantly below that of their married counterparts, those who have experienced marital dissolution are significantly less happy than those who never married. Never-married persons at later stages of the life cycle report happiness levels around the 2.1 value of the large proportion of never-married persons at the start of the life cycle, but those widowed, divorced, or separated have mean

Table 1.6. Mean Happiness of Women Not Currently Married by Marital Status, Birth Cohorts of 1921–30 to 1951–60, 1972–2000

(1) Birth cohort	(2) Stage of life cycle	(3) (4) Mean happiness		(5)
		Widowed	Divorced or separated	Never married
1951–60	Ages 23 to 45	1.98	1.96	2.07
1941–50	Ages 27 to 55	1.95	2.01	2.05
1931–40	Ages 37 to 65	2.00	1.97	2.11
1921–30	Ages 47 to 75	1.97	2.00	2.15

happiness levels of around 2.0 or less (Table 1.6). One might speculate that personality effects had sorted out those who end up divorced or separated, but there is no significant happiness difference between them and persons who are widowed. The widowed are unlikely to have been selected on the basis of personality, and the fact that their mean happiness and that of the divorced or separated group is virtually the same suggests that one is observing here the effect of marital dissolution on happiness, not personality.

These life-cycle results on the association between marital status and happiness are consistent with cross-sectional regression analyses of survey data in which controls are introduced for a variety of socio-economic circumstances (Argyle 1999; Blanchflower and Oswald 2004; Frey and Stutzer 2002a, 2000b), and with other studies that focus on specific marital circumstances such as divorce and widowhood (Johnson and Wu 2002; Wortman et al. 1993). They are also consistent with a new panel study of divorce that tracks respondents over a five-year period (Waite et al. 2002). The results do not mean that no adaptation occurs after unions are formed or dissolved. But they certainly suggest that adaptation is less than complete, and that the formation of unions has a lasting positive effect on happiness, while dissolution has a permanently negative effect.[8] If the setpoint model of happiness is correct, it is hard to see how one can reconcile it with the survey evidence on either marriage or health.[9]

3. Is More Better?

To turn to economic theory, a basic problem with the revealed preference approach is that the judgment on a person's well-being is made, not by the individual concerned, but by an outsider who is observing the person's consumption choices (Holländer 2001). If one takes the view that the only one who can make authoritative observations on a person's feelings of well-being is the person concerned, then one is led to look at self-reports on well-being.

Does the evidence support the view that income and well-being go together? The answer depends on whether one looks at cross-sectional or time series data. Support for the hypothesis of a positive association comes from point-of-time regressions, which invariably find a significant positive association between income and happiness, with or without controls for other factors (Argyle 1999; Blanchflower and Oswald 2004; Frey and Stutzer 2002a, 2000b; Graham and Pettinato 2002). Over the life cycle, however, as income increases and then levels off, happiness remains unchanged, contradicting the inference that income and well-being go together (Figure 1.6).

If one uses education as a proxy for income, then the life cycle data too reveal the positive cross-sectional association between well-being and income. Over the life span those with more education are consistently happier than those with less (Figure 1.7). What is even more noteworthy, however, is the life cycle *change* in happiness for the more and less educated. If happiness were moving in accordance with the income trajectories of these two educational groups, then the happiness of both groups would increase, with that of the better educated increasing more, and the happiness differential by educational status widening. In fact, happiness remains flat at both educational levels, and the differential unchanged (Figure 1.7). Although those fortunate enough to start out on the higher income trajectory remain happier throughout the life cycle than those on the lower income trajectory, there is no evidence for either group that happiness increases with income.

These life cycle patterns clearly contradict the expectation based on economic theory that well-being increases with income. But don't they support the setpoint model that has heretofore been called into question? The answer is that they do; indeed, these findings have often been cited by psychologists in support of complete hedonic adaptation. But while there may be (fairly) complete hedonic adaptation with regard to income, this does not mean that there is complete adaptation with regard to all sources of happiness. As has been seen, the evidence on health and family conditions suggests that adaptation in these areas is less than complete, and that changes in these circumstances have a lasting effect on well-being.

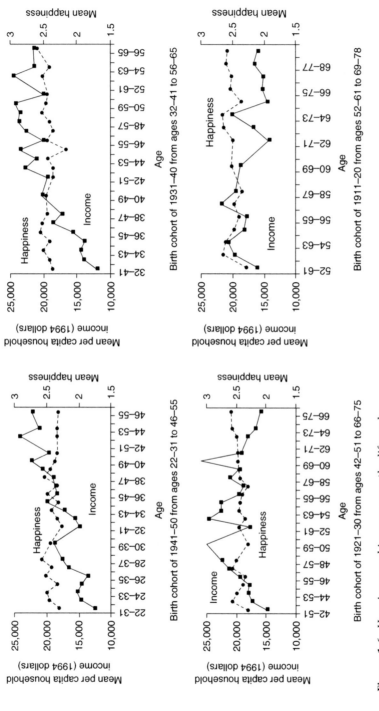

Figure 1.6. Happiness and income over the life cycle

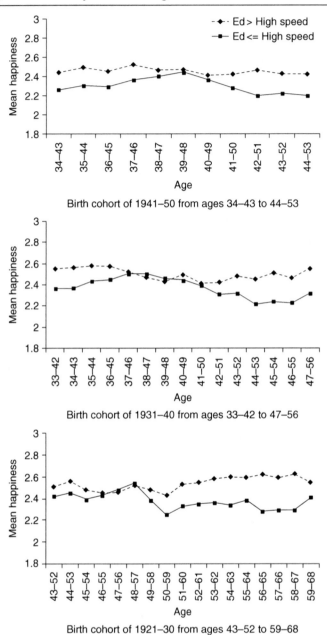

Figure 1.7. Life cycle happiness by level of education

4. Aspirations and Adaptation

But why should the extent of adaptation differ with regard to the circumstances, or, as psychologists say, "domain", under study? The answer, I suggest, is that people's *aspirations* in each domain respond differently to changes in their circumstances. Complete adaptation implies that aspirations change to the same extent as one's actual circumstances. This seems to be what happens when income changes. As a result, one gets no nearer to or farther away from the attainment of one's material aspirations, and well-being is unchanged. Less than complete adaptation means that aspirations change less than the actual change in one's circumstances. If things change for the better, there is greater goal-fulfillment and well-being increases; if, for the worse, there is a greater shortfall from one's goals, and well-being declines. This seems to be what happens with regard to marriage and health.

Is there any evidence that the response of aspirations to actual circumstances varies by domain? The answer is "yes" with regard to the economic and family domains, for which relevant data are available. In what follows, I draw chiefly on nationally representative surveys carried out in 1978 and 1994 that include questions on the "good life". In these surveys the questioning procedure is as follows (see Appendix 1.1 for the full survey question):

1. We often hear people talk about what they want out of life. Here are a number of different things. [The respondent is handed a card with a list of 24 items.] When you think of the good life—the life you'd like to have, which of the things on this list, if any, are part of that good life as far as you personally are concerned?
2. Now would you go down that list and call off all the things you now have?

The great value of these two questions is that they yield information rarely available—on both aspirations and the attainment of aspirations. The answers to question 1 tell us about desires for certain goods and also for marriage and a family; those to question 2 tell us where the respondents stand in relation to these desires—to what extent they are fulfilled. These responses thus make it possible to follow a cohort's aspirations and attainments over the 16 years between 1978 and 1994, and see to what extent aspirations change as a cohort's actual circumstances change.

Let me start with the responses for ten big-ticket consumer goods that are included on the "good life" list. These goods range from a home, car,

Table 1.7. Ownership of and Desires for Ten Big-Ticket Consumer Goods over Three 16-Year Segments of the Adult Life Cycle[a]

| | (1) (2) Stage of life cycle segment | | (3) Change over life cycle segment |
	Start	End	
A. Early life cycle			
1. Mean number of goods owned	1.7	3.1	+1.4
2. Mean number of goods desired	4.4	5.6	+1.2
B. Mid life cycle			
1. Mean number of goods owned	2.5	3.2	+0.7
2. Mean number of goods desired	4.3	5.4	+1.1
C. Late life cycle			
1. Mean number of goods owned	3.0	3.2	+0.2
2. Mean number of goods desired	4.4	5.0	+0.6
D. Average for all three segments			
1. Change in mean number of goods owned	—	—	+0.8
2. Change in mean number of goods desired	—	—	+1.0

Notes:
  [a] Early life cycle is from ages 18–29 in 1978 to 30–44 in 1994. Mid-life cycle is from ages 30–44 in 1978 to 45–59 in 1994. Late life cycle is from ages 45–59 in 1978 to 60 and over in 1994.
Source: Roper-Starch Organization (1979, 1995).

and television set to travel abroad, a swimming pool, and a vacation home. Over each stage of the life cycle—early, mid-life, and older years—persons typically acquire more of these big-ticket items (Table 1.7, rows A-1, B-1, C-1). But their aspirations for these goods—what they view as part of the good life—also rises (rows A-2, B-2, C-2). Moreover, the increase in the number of goods desired is, on average, roughly equal in magnitude to that in the average number owned (panel D, column 3).

What is happening is that as people acquire those goods for which aspirations were fairly high to start with (a home, a car, a TV) their aspirations increase for goods which were initially much less likely to be viewed as part of the good life. Thus, in each segment of the life cycle, travel abroad, a swimming pool, and a vacation home are increasingly named as part of the good life, reaching values of nearly 40 percent or more of respondents (Table 1.8, cols. 1 and 2). The proportion that ever actually has any of these items, however, is typically less than 10 percent (col. 3). There is clearly a suggestion in these data that new material aspirations arise as previous goals are reached, and, to judge from the mean number of goods desired, to about the same extent.

This inference of complete adaptation in the economic domain is further supported if we divide the cohort by level of education, and consider

Table 1.8. Desires for Specified Big-Ticket Consumer Goods and Attainment of Desires over Three 16-Year Segments of the Adult Life Cycle[a]

	(1) Desires over life cycle: percent who want good at		(3) Attainment: percent who have good at end
	Start	End	
A. *Early life cycle*			
1. Travel abroad	39	46	7
2. Swimming pool	28	41	5
3. Vacation home	26	47	3
B. *Mid-life cycle*			
1. Travel abroad	33	45	12
2. Swimming pool	22	38	6
3. Vacation home	28	45	6
C. *Late life cycle*			
1. Travel abroad	33	37	8
2. Swimming pool	14	23	2
3. Vacation home	26	33	3

Note:
[a] For life cycle stages see Table 1.7.
Source: Roper-Starch Organization (1979, 1995).

the two segments of the life cycle in which income is increasing. In each segment the increase in the number of goods owned is greater for those with more education, as one would expect based on their differential income growth (Table 1.9, panel A). The increase in number of goods desired is also greater for those with more education (panel B). Moreover, for each educational group, the increase in desires is of the same order of magnitude as the increase in the number of goods owned (col. 3, compare row A-1 with B-1, and row A-2 with B-2). Thus, material aspirations are increasing commensurately with material possessions, and the greater the increase in possessions, the greater the increase in desires. It is this differential change in aspirations corresponding to the differential change in income that explains the constancy of happiness over the life cycle for each educational group (Easterlin 2001*a*).[10]

The responses cited so far are for specific goods. Is there evidence suggesting that income aspirations in general rise in proportion to income? The answer is "yes". Consider the answers from a different survey that asks people how much income is needed by a family of four to get along. Over a 36-year period "get along" income increases, on average, to the same degree as actual income. This result was obtained by sociologist Lee Rainwater (1994) who concluded that the elasticity of "get along" to actual income is one.[11]

Table 1.9. Change in Ownership of and Desires for Ten Big-Ticket Consumer Goods in Specified Life Cycle Stage, by Level of Education[a]

	(1) Early life cycle	(2) Mid- life cycle	(3) Mean of Cols. 1 and 2
A. *Change in mean number of goods owned*			
1. Education greater than 12 years	1.6	1.0	1.3
2. Education 12 years or less	1.1	0.4	0.8
B. *Change in mean number of goods desired*			
1. Education greater than 12 years	1.4	1.3	1.4
2. Education 12 years or less	1.0	0.9	1.0

Notes:
[a] For life cycle stages see Table 1.7.
Source: Roper-Starch Organization (1979, 1995).

Responses to another item on the good life list—whether people consider a lot of money as part of the good life—also suggest that income aspirations increase in proportion to income, or at least, roughly so. In the 16-year span covered by the good life data, cohort real per capita income increased by 27 percent in the early years of the adult life cycle and 22 percent in the middle years. One might expect that because of this growth of income, the proportion of a cohort that says it has "a lot of money" would increase somewhat. There is, in fact, an increase, but it amounts to only a few percentage points (Table 1.10). The striking feature of the responses is that throughout the life cycle hardly anyone—never more than seven persons in 100—thinks he or she has a lot of money.

Let me turn from the economic to the family domain. The desire for a happy marriage is a common one; at every point in the life cycle, three-quarters or more of respondents say that a happy marriage is part of the good life (Table 1.11, rows A-1, B-1, C-1). The proportion that actually has a happy marriage increases in the early life cycle, and declines thereafter as divorce, separation, and widowhood take their toll (rows A-2, B-2, C-2). There is a shortfall of actual circumstances relative to aspirations for a happy marriage among a fifth or more of the population throughout the life cycle.

If adaptation were complete, then one would expect that married persons who are not in a happy marriage would abandon their desires for such a marriage. Similarly, if divorced, separated, or widowed persons revised their marriage aspirations to accord with their changed marital status, they too should give up their aspirations for a happy marriage.

In fact, aspirations for a happy marriage persist among more than half of those respondents who do not, in fact, have a happy marriage

Table 1.10. Percent of Cohort that has "a Lot of Money" at Beginning and End of Three 16-Year Segments of the Adult Life Cycle[a]

	(1) Stage of life cycle segment	(2)
	Start	End
1. Early life cycle	2	4
2. Mid-life cycle	1	7
3. Late life cycle	4	3

Note:
[a] For life cycle stages see Table 1.7.
Source: Roper-Starch Organization (1979, 1995).

Table 1.11. Desires for a Happy Marriage and Attainment of Desires over Three 16-Year Segments of the Adult Life Cycle[a]

	(1) Stage of life cycle segment	(2)
	Start	End
A. *Early life cycle*		
1. Percent wanting a happy marriage	83	79
2. Percent who have a happy marriage	44	51
B. *Mid-life cycle*		
1. Percent wanting a happy marriage	84	76
2. Percent who have a happy marriage	62	51
C. *Late life cycle*		
1. Percent wanting a happy marriage	85	75
2. Percent who have a happy marriage	66	46

Note:
[a] For life cycle stages see Table 1.7.
Source: Roper-Starch Organization (1979, 1995).

(Table 1.12, col. 1). Even among persons for whom the prospect of remarriage is quite low—divorced, separated, or widowed persons ages 45 and over—marriage aspirations continue to be above 50 percent (col. 3). Among persons who have been *single* their entire lives and are ages 45 and over, more than four in ten cite a happy marriage as part of the good life as far as they personally are concerned (ibid.). It is true that among all of these groups aspirations for a happy marriage are below the average for the whole population. But if those who have been single for more than 30 years had adjusted their marital aspirations to accord with their actual status, one would hardly expect more than four out of ten to cite a happy marriage as part of the good life as far as they *personally* are concerned.

Table 1.12. Percent of Persons Wanting a Happy Marriage Among Those Who Do Not Have One, by Marital Status and Age, 1994

Marital status	(1)	(2)	(3)
	Percent wanting happy marriage		
	All ages	Ages 18–44	Ages 45 and over
Married, not in happy marriage	56	58	55
Divorced or separated	63	73	55
Widowed	62	a	62
Never-married	65	68	43

Note:
[a] Sample size less than 20.
Source: Roper-Starch Organization (1979, 1995).

Similarly, if aspirations eventually adjusted to actual circumstances, one would hardly expect that more than half of widows and divorcees 45 years and older would still say that they view a happy marriage as part of the good life. Thus, in contrast to the economic domain, hedonic adaptation seems to be occurring only to a limited extent with regard to marriage circumstances. The substantial persistence of aspirations for a happy marriage among those widowed, divorced, separated, and never-married explains, I believe, why these groups are less happy, on average, than married persons, among whom aspirations for a happy marriage are more nearly fulfilled.

What about aspirations for children? Economists like to draw an analogy between the demand for children and the demand for consumer durables. We have seen that as more big-ticket consumer goods are acquired, desires for such goods tend to grow to about the same extent. Is this true of children—as people have more children, do their family size desires increase commensurately? The answer is no. At all stages of the life cycle the number of children desired is virtually constant, whether measured by the percentage of adults who want children or the average number of children wanted (Table 1.13, row 1 in panels A, B, C). Although actual family size changes, especially in the early life cycle (row 2), family size aspirations change hardly at all.

Is it possible that aspirations for the "quality", if not quantity, of children increase over the life cycle? Perhaps, but there is not much sign of increasing aspirations for a highly expensive dimension of child quality, a college education for one's children. The proportion who consider such an education to be part of the good life rises mildly in the early life cycle, from 56 to 65 percent; thereafter, it changes very little (Table 1.14, cols. 1, 2).

Table 1.13. Desires for Children and Attainment of Desires over Three 16-Year Segments of the Adult Life Cycle[a]

	(1) Stage of life cycle segment		(3) Change over life cycle segment
	Start	End	
A. *Early life cycle*			
1. Desires: (a) Percent who want one or more children	71	69	—
(b) Mean number wanted	2.3	2.4	0.1
2. Attainment: Mean number have	1.0	2.0	1.0
B. *Mid-life cycle*			
1. Desires: (a) Percent who want one or more children	72	66	—
(b) Mean number wanted	2.6	2.7	0.1
2. Attainment: Mean number have	2.0	2.2	0.2
C. *Late life cycle*			
1. Desires: (a) Percent who want one or more children	71	65	—
(b) Mean number wanted	3.0	2.8	−0.2
2. Attainment: Mean number have	2.6	2.4	−0.2

Note:
[a] For life cycle stages, see Table 1.7. Mean number of children "wanted" and "have" is for persons who want children.
Source: Roper-Starch Organization (1979, 1995).

Table 1.14. Desires for "a College Education for My Children" and Attainment of Desires over Three 16-Year Segments of the Adult Life Cycle[a]

	(1) Desires over life cycle: percent who want good at		(3) Attainment: percent who have good at end
	Start	End	
A. *Early life cycle*			
Percent wanting children's college education	56	65	7
B. *Mid-life cycle*			
Percent wanting children's college education	65	65	24
C. *Late life cycle*			
Percent wanting children's college education	56	59	30

Note:
[a] For life cycle stages, see Table 1.7.
Source: Roper-Starch Organization (1979, 1995).

While income growth over the life cycle is accompanied by persistent growth in aspirations for big ticket consumer goods, income growth is seemingly not associated with growth in desires for either the number or quality of children.

I have no data on health aspirations. If such data were available, however, I suspect that "good health" would be checked off as part of the good life, irrespective of age.[12] Since self-reported health declines with age, this would imply that adaptation to actual health circumstances is less than complete over the life cycle. I think there is evidence too of less than complete adaptation in regard to other life circumstances such as friendship, loss of a job, and retirement (Clark and Oswald 1994; Easterlin 2003; Gallie and Russell 1998; Myers 1999; Oswald 1997; Winkelman and Winkelman 1998).

5. Building a Better Theory of Well-Being

We can now begin to see the outlines of a better theory of happiness. Let us start with the economist's notion that the typical individual has a utility or happiness function such that well-being depends on a variety of pecuniary and nonpecuniary conditions, or domains. To judge from unconstrained self-reports, the domain that is typically of most importance is material living level; this is followed by family concerns and health, and then, work and personal character concerns such as emotional stability and self-discipline (Figure 1.8). The importance of living level and family concerns does not change with life-cycle stage, but health concerns become higher at an older age, and job concerns, lower (ibid.; Crimmins and Easterlin 2000).

The typical person is taken to have certain goals or aspirations in each domain (such as a home of one's own, a car, a happy marriage, two children, good health, etc.) and a current state of attainment in each domain (a rented apartment, a spouse and child, and so on). The overall happiness of the individual depends on the shortfall between aspirations and attainments in each domain, and the relative importance of each domain in the individual's utility function.

Economic analysis typically assumes that well-being depends only on attainments in each domain, but there are two strands of theory—habit formation and interdependent preferences—that recognize the effect on well-being of aspirations. Habit formation stresses that the utility one derives from a given set of goods is affected by comparisons with one's past

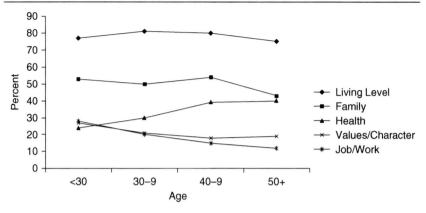

Figure 1.8. Percent of population naming specified item as important for their happiness, by age, around 1960 (average for 12 countries)

Notes: The countries are Brazil, Cuba, Dominican Republic, Egypt, India, Israel, Nigeria, Panama, Philippines, United States, West Germany and Yugoslavia. The rank order of items is virtually identical in all countries.

Source: Cantril (1965, appendix E).

experience. Interdependent preferences point out that the utility created by one's having a given amount of a good depends partly on the amount of that good that others have. The counterpart in psychology of the economists' concept of habit formation is hedonic adaptation, and of interdependent preferences, social comparison. I use the psychologists' terms in what follows, because these are more common in the happiness literature.

The central point of the present theory of happiness is that neither hedonic adaptation nor social comparison operate equally across all domains or constituents of domains. Hedonic adaptation, as we have seen, is less complete with regard to family circumstances and health than in the material goods domain. I suggest that social comparison is also less in family life and health than in the material goods domain, because these domains are less accessible to public scrutiny than material possessions. (Recall that in Table 1.2 life satisfaction is less if one's disability is more likely to be noticed by persons who know the respondent fairly well.)

Moreover, hedonic adaptation and social comparison do not operate equally with regard to all constituents of a given domain. With regard to the goods domain, Scitovsky (1976) has argued that cultural goods, such as music, literature, and art, are less subject to hedonic adaptation than "comfort" goods, like homes and cars. Similarly, the distinction drawn between positional and nonpositional goods by Frank (1985), Hirsch (1976),

53

Ng (1978), and others is an example of a classification of goods based on whether or not their utility is affected by social comparison.

Each individual has only a given amount of time to allocate among different domains and their constituents. Clearly, the happiness of an individual can be increased by allocating his or her time to those domains and constituents of domains in which hedonic adaptation and social comparison are less important. Based on the evidence above, this implies that happiness would be increased by greater attention to family life and health rather than economic gain, and, within the economic sphere, to nonpositional and cultural goods. With regard to macroeconomic policy, reducing unemployment and inflation increases happiness, but the pursuit of rapid economic growth as a policy objective is questionable.

Do individuals currently achieve the optimal allocation of time among domains? My answer is "no"; people are likely to allocate a disproportionate amount of time to the pursuit of pecuniary rather than nonpecuniary objectives, as well as to "comfort" and positional goods, and to shortchange goals that will have a more lasting effect on well-being (cf. also Frank 1997). This misallocation occurs because in making decisions about how to use their time, individuals take their aspirations as fixed at their present levels, and fail to recognize that aspirations may change because of hedonic adaptation and social comparison. In particular, people make decisions assuming that more income, comfort, and positional goods will make them happier, failing to recognize that hedonic adaptation and social comparison will come into play, raise their aspirations to about the same extent as their actual economic gains, and leave them feeling no happier than before. As a result, most individuals spend a disproportionate amount of time working, and sacrifice family life and health, domains in which aspirations remain fairly constant as actual circumstances change, and where the attainment of one's goals has a more lasting impact on happiness.

What about the interdependence between pecuniary and nonpecuniary pursuits—doesn't more money, for example, make the attainment of family and health goals easier? The answer is "no", because the causal effects on nonpecuniary goals of pecuniary success are negative as well as positive. More income may contribute to a more comfortable family life, and may facilitate health through exercise machines and recreational expenditures. But time spent in the pursuit of income takes away from the time available for family, exercise, and recreation. Moreover, the net balance of effects tends to be negative. This is because of the inability of people to foresee the differential change in aspirations by domain. This failure to anticipate the change in aspirations assures that the allocation of time to the pecuniary domain will be excessive and that the more rewarding domains of family and health will consequently receive insufficient attention. In family life, the result is a substitution of goods for time spent with one's spouse and children.[13]

One may ask if social learning occurs—don't people eventually realize how their material aspirations escalate with economic achievement, and become aware of the self-defeating nature of the pursuit of pecuniary goals? Perhaps, but the evidence on material aspirations that I have given fails to show evidence of such social learning. Moreover, the change in material aspirations itself works against social learning. When asked how happy they were five years ago, people, on average, systematically underestimate their well-being at that time, because they evaluate their past situation in terms, not of the lower material aspirations they actually had at that time, but on the basis of the new higher level of aspirations they have now acquired (Easterlin 2001a, 2002). As a result, they tend to think they are better off than they were in the past, rather than realizing that there has been no net improvement.

6. Summary

My interest here is in developing a theory to explain people's feelings of well-being as reported in social surveys. To judge from responses to open-ended questions, both pecuniary and nonpecuniary circumstances (domains) affect well-being. The most important factor is pecuniary, one's material living level. Next, and about equal in importance, are two non-pecuniary factors, family life and health. After this come job circumstances (work utility) and considerations having to do with personal character. Each individual has certain goals (or aspirations) in each domain. One's overall well-being depends on the extent to which the various goals are fulfilled, and the relative importance of the domains in one's utility function.

Mainstream economic theory sets aside goals or aspirations. It focuses chiefly on pecuniary conditions and assumes that an increase in the material goods at one's disposal increases well-being. The implicit assumption is that the utility associated with a given set of consumption goods is unaffected by one's past experience or what others have, that is, that habit formation and interdependent preferences play no part in determining feelings of well-being—the utility attributed to a given consumption set.

A better theory of well-being—one more consistent with the evidence—sets aside this assumption. It recognizes that one's feelings about any given set of circumstances depend partly on one's history, and partly on comparison with the situation of others. The evidence suggests that these influences are especially important with regard to material living level. The satisfaction anticipated *ex ante* from a given increase in consumption turns out *ex post* to be less than expected, as one adapts to the new level of living, and as the living levels of others improve correspondingly. Improvements in material circumstances are found to yield little change in well-being over the life cycle, because material aspirations change commensurately with actual circumstances.

In the nonpecuniary domain of family life, however, the evidence indicates that aspirations do not change to the same extent as actual circumstances. The attainment of family life goals does not lead to further escalation of these goals, and, as a result, subjective well-being is permanently increased. Failure to attain such goals has a lasting negative effect on feelings of well-being. With regard to health, too, it seems likely that aspirations do not simply mirror the change in one's actual condition, that is, that one merely downgrades one's notion of good health as actual health declines. Because the conception of and desires for good health remain fairly constant, the increasing shortfall of actual relative to desired health over the life course reduces feelings of well-being. Attempts to reduce this shortfall by more exercise and changes in life style would moderate the decline in well-being.

People fail to perceive that because of hedonic adaptation and social comparison aspirations in the pecuniary domain will change commensurately with actual circumstances. As a result, a disproportionate amount of time is devoted to the pursuit of pecuniary goals at the expense of family life and health, and subjective well-being is less than it might be. Clearly, a reallocation of time in favor of family life and health would increase subjective well-being.

Because mainstream economic theory views individual preferences as given and sacrosanct, economic policy proposals are typically confined to manipulation of the socio-economic context. Viewed in terms of the present analysis, some of these policies, such as measures to improve health or maintain full employment, are consistent with greater well-being. Beyond this, however, the assumption that preferences are beyond the realm of policy is called into doubt, once the role in shaping preferences of hedonic adaptation and social comparison is recognized. It is hard to see how individuals who are unaware of some of the forces shaping their behavior can be expected to make choices in the allocation of their time that will successfully maximize their subjective well-being. It is time to recognize that serious policy attention needs to be directed to education as a vehicle for shaping more informed preferences (cf. Scitovsky 1976; Layard 1980).

In closing, let me touch on a few research needs, already apparent from the many gaps in this chapter, in order to build a better theory of well-being, beyond those in economics and sociology. In psychology, as has been seen, the recent literature has emphasized the role of genetic and personality factors in determining well-being, a view that carried to the extreme, as in the setpoint model, leaves little or no room for individual and collective action to improve well-being. Social survey evidence of the type I have cited contradicts the setpoint model. But this is not to say that genetic and personality factors do not influence well-being. They clearly do, and one promising line of research is to explore the interplay between personality and life events in shaping well-being (cf. McCrae and Costa 1990, chap. 9).

There is need too for incorporating internal biological mechanisms in a better theory of well-being. The importance to well-being of family life in this analysis may be seen as a proxy for a broader network of social support that extends to friends, community and religious organizations, and the like. There is ample biological evidence that social support promotes physical health, while social isolation is detrimental (Berkman and Glass 2000). Similarly, an inverse association between symptoms of stress and position in the social hierarchy has been established in both humans and animals (Seeman and Crimmins 2001). One suspects that a fair share of the research on the association between social conditions, biological mechanisms, and physical health could be usefully applied to develop a more comprehensive theory of subjective well-being that includes underlying biological mechanisms.

There is, finally, the question of why the adjustment of aspirations to actual circumstances differs by domain, a question that suggests the need for research in evolutionary psychology. It is possible that the differences among domains may be due to evolutionary influences (cf. Frederick and Loewenstein 1999: 314). The persistence of aspirations for a happy marriage among those who are in broken unions may reflect the importance to group survival of mating and reproduction. Correspondingly, the disproportionate importance of adaptation in the economic domain may be because those whose material aspirations were never satisfied were more likely to survive, and, as a result, we have inherited their genes (Buss 1996; Kasser 2002). If so, we are paying the price today in happiness foregone of our forebears' survival success.

Appendix 1.1. **Good Life Questions from Roper Surveys 79-1, 95-1**

77. We often hear people talk about what they want out of life. Here are a number of different things. (HAND RESPONDENT CARD) When you think of the good life—the life you'd like to have, which of the things on this list, if any, are part of that good life as far as you personally are concerned?

78. Now would you go down that list and call off all the things you now have? Just call off the letter of the items. (RECORD BELOW)

	77. PART OF THE GOOD LIFE	78. NOW HAVE
a. A home you own		
b. A yard and lawn		
c. A car		
d. A second car		
e. A vacation home		
f. A swimming pool		
g. A happy marriage		
h. No children		
i. One child		
j. Two children		
k. Three children		
l. Four or more children		
m. A job that pays much more than average		
n. A job that is interesting		
o. A job that contributes to the welfare of society		
p. A college education for myself		
q. A college education for my children		
r. Travel abroad		
s. A color TV set		
t. A second color TV set		
u. A five day work week		
v. A four day work week		
w. Really nice clothes		
x. A lot of money		

Notes

Prepared for presentation at the conference "Paradoxes of Happiness in Economics", University of Milano-Bicocca, 21–23 March 2003. This paper builds substantially on prior work by other scholars, especially, in economics, Robert H. Frank, Andrew J. Oswald, Tibor Scitovsky, and Bernard M. S. van Praag; and in psychology, Paul T. Costa, Robert R. McCrae, David G. Myers, and, for their path-breaking volume on well-being, Daniel Kahneman, Ed Diener, and Norbert Schwarz. Finally, my thanks to James A. Davis, Tom W. Smith, and Ruut Veenhoven for their invaluable data collections, without which this work would not have been possible. I am grateful too for the excellent assistance of Donna Hokoda Ebata, Pouyan Mashayekh-Ahangarani and Paul Rivera. Financial assistance was provided by the University of Southern California.

1. The same question may be asked with more response options, for example, by presenting the respondent with an integer ladder from 0 to 10 and asking where on the ladder the respondent currently stands.
2. See Costa *et al.* (1987); Cummins *et al.* (2003); Lykken and Tellegen (1996); Myers (1992). For a differing view by a psychologist, see Argyle (1999). A good critical summary of the setpoint model is given in Lucas *et al.* (2003).
3. The time dimension of adaptation seems to be overlooked in the psychological literature. Does complete adaptation mean return to the setpoint within a day, month, year, decade, or more? I suggest that adaptation that requires around a decade or more to return to the initial level is not complete adaptation, because a departure from the setpoint for as long as a decade amounts to perhaps one-sixth of the adult life span, a considerable spell of exhilaration or depression.
4. It would also be flat if persons implicitly evaluate their health only by comparison with others of their age. For example, as actual health declined with age, if an older person simply compared herself with others of her age, then, on average, there should be no deterioration in self-reported health.
5. Can we believe self-reports on health? I think so. Patterns in self-reports of health other than life cycle change are also consistent with objective data on health. At a given age, younger cohorts are healthier than older (compare, for example, the three cohorts in Figure 1.1 for which observations around age 50 are available). Also, in each cohort males report better health than females. (Men have higher mortality rates than women because their health problems are more lethal, but women have a considerably higher prevalence than males of less lethal health problems, such as arthritis.) Indeed, self-reports of health are not only meaningful, but they apparently contain information on a respondent's state of health over and above that given by objective data. If, in predicting mortality, self-reported health is included along with objective measures of health (whether one has heart disease, diabetes, etc.), self-reported health is statistically significant (Idler and Benyamini 1997; Smith *et al.* 2001).
6. These conclusions come from following a 20-year birth cohort, that of 1953–72, from ages 18–19 through 28–29. The large size of the birth cohort and two-year age spans yield big enough samples of married persons to permit meaningful inferences of their average happiness (except for married males ages 18–19, who are omitted here because the sample size is very small). When the sample is subdivided into two ten-year cohorts, the same pattern is found for each ten-year cohort separately as for the combined cohort, but the variability is greater.
7. Blanchflower and Oswald (2004) find that those remarried are significantly less happy than those in their first marriage. This difference from the present results

may come from the fact that they do not control for cohort. Younger cohorts are, in general, less happy than older, though not to a great extent. Since a larger number of remarried persons are in younger cohorts, failure to control for the cohort effect may lead to the conclusion that those remarried are less happy than those still in their first marriage.

8. I cannot explain the different results for marriage of the longitudinal analysis by Lucas *et al.* (2003) discussed in the text, but let me note two possibilities. First, no allowance is made for the possibility that in Germany a fair proportion of couples were cohabiting for some period of time prior to marriage, so one is not really observing the effect on happiness of the formation of unions. Second, although presented as a longitudinal analysis, the study is not actually following the same individuals over time—the number of persons observed at marriage (t) and the years immediately before and after ($t-1$, $t+1$) is considerably greater than those observed two or more years prior to and after marriage ($t-2$, $t+2$, $t-3$, $t+3$, etc.).

9. Survey evidence on happiness by race and gender is also difficult to reconcile with the setpoint model. Blacks are consistently less happy than whites; is this because of different setpoints resulting from genetic and personality differences? Also, beyond age 60, the life-cycle excess of female over male happiness is reversed; it is hard to explain this without reference to differences by gender in life events (Easterlin 2001*b*, 2003).

10. The point-of-time happiness differential is also explained by aspirations (Easterlin 2001*a*). At the start of the adult life cycle, material aspirations differ very little between the two education groups; hence the better-educated come closer to fulfilling their aspirations, and are happier. Subsequently, aspirations rise more for the better-educated, but at any point in time the dispersion in aspirations continues to be less than that in income, and the happiness differential by education persists.

11. A much earlier analysis of "get-along" income based on responses for only a 14-year period, 1957 to 1971, found an income elasticity of 0.6 (Kilpatrick 1973). Pioneering theoretical and empirical work relating variations in income norms to actual income has been done by the Leyden School, founded by Bernard van Praag (van Praag 1968; van Praag and Frijters 1999). Additional support for Rainwater's conclusion comes from a study by members of this school (van de Stadt 1985; Kapteyn 2002). Using panel data and a model taking account of both habit formation and interdependent preferences, this study finds an elasticity of the income norm on actual income equal to one.

12. I added "good health" to the end of the good life list and ran the survey in an undergraduate class and faculty seminar ($n = 50$). Good health is checked as part of the good life by every single respondent.

13. The change in childrearing attitudes is indicative of this substitution (Crimmins *et al.* 1991: 125–6).

References

Argyle, M. (1999), "Causes and Correlates of Happiness", in Kahneman *et al.* (1999), 353–73.

Berkman, Lisa F., and Glass, Thomas (2000), "Social Integration, Social Networks, Social Support, and Health", in Lisa F. Berkman and Ichiro Kawachi (eds.), *Social Epidemiology*, Oxford: Oxford University Press, 137–73.

Blanchflower, D. G., and Oswald, A. J. (2004), "Wellbeing over Time in Britain and the USA", *Journal of Public Economics*, 88/7–8: 1359–86.

Brickman, Philip, Coates, Dan, and Janoff-Bulman, Ronnie (1978), "Lottery Winners and Accident Victims: Is Happiness Relative?" *Journal of Personality and Social Psychology*, 36/8: 917–27.

Buss, D. M. (1996), "The Evolutionary Psychology of Human Strategies", in E. T. Higgins and A. W. Kruglanski (eds.), *Social Psychology: Handbook of Basic Principles*. New York: Guilford Press, 3–38.

Cantril, H. (1965), *The Pattern of Human Concerns*, New Brunswick, NJ: Rutgers University Press.

Clark, A. E., and Oswald, A. J. (1994), "Unhappiness and Unemployment", *Economic Journal*, 104: 648–59.

Costa, Paul T. Jr., Zonderman, Alan B., McCrae, Robert R., Cornoni-Huntley, Joan, Locke, Ben Z., and Barbano, Helen E. (1987), "Longitudinal Analyses of Psychological Well-Being in a National Sample: Stability of Mean Levels", *Journal of Gerontology*, 42/1: 50–5.

Crimmins, Eileen M., and Easterlin, Richard A. (2000), "What Goals Motivate Individual Behavior?" in K. Warner Schaie and John Hendricks (eds.), *The Evolution of the Aging Self*, New York: Springer Publishing Company, 159–68.

——— Easterlin, Richard A., and Saito, Yasuhiko (1991), "Preference Changes among American Youth: Family, Work, and Goods Aspirations, 1976–86", *Population and Development Review*, 17/1 (March): 115–33.

Cummins, Robert A., Eckersley, Richard, Pallant, Julie, van Vugt, Jackie, and Misajon, Rose Anne (2003), "Developing a National Index of Subjective Well-being: The Australian Unity Wellbeing Index", *Social Indicators Research*, 64: 159–90.

Diener, Ed, and Lucas, Richard E. (1999), "Personality and Subjective Well-Being", in Kahneman *et al.* (1999), 213–29.

Easterlin, Richard A. (2001a), "Income and Happiness: Towards a Unified Theory", *The Economic Journal*, 111/473 (July): 465–84.

——— (2001b), "Life Cycle Welfare: Trends and Differences", *Journal of Happiness Studies*, 2: 1–12.

——— (2002), "Is Reported Happiness Five Years Ago Comparable to Present Happiness? A Cautionary Note", *Journal of Happiness Studies*, 3: 193–8.

——— (2003), "Happiness of Women and Men in Later Life: Nature, Determinants, and Prospects", in M. Joseph Sirgy, Don Rahtz, and A. Coskin Samli (eds.),

Advances in Quality-of-Life Theory and Research, Dordrecht, The Netherlands: Kluwer Academic Publishers, 13–26.

Frank, Robert H. (1985), "The Demand for Unobservable and Other Nonpositional Goods", *American Economic Review*, 75 (March): 279–301.

Frank, Robert H. (1997), "The Frame of Reference as a Public Good", *The Economic Journal*, 107 (November): 1832–47.

Frederick, Shane, and Loewenstein, George (1999), "Hedonic Adaptation", in Kahneman *et al.* (1999), 302–29.

Frey, Bruno S., and Stutzer, Alois (2002a), *Happiness and Economics: How the Economy and Institutions Affect Well-Being*, Princeton: Princeton University Press.

————(2002b), "What Can Economists Learn from Happiness Research?" *Journal of Economic Literature*, 40 (2 June): 402–35.

Gallie, D., and Russell, H. (1998), "Unemployment and Life Satisfaction: A Cross-Cultural Comparison", *Archives Européennes de Sociologie*, 39/2: 248–80.

Graham, Carol, and Pettinato, Stefano (2002), *Happiness and Hardship: Opportunity and Insecurity in New Market Economies*, Washington: Brookings Institution Press.

Hirsch, F. (1976), *Social Limits to Growth*, Cambridge, Mass.: Harvard University Press.

Holländer, Heinz (2001), "On the Validity of Utility Statements: Standard Theory versus Duesenberry's", *Journal of Economic Behavior and Organization*, 45 (3 July): 227–49.

Idler, Ellen L., and Banyamini, Yael (1997), "Self-Rated Health and Mortality: A Review of Twenty-Seven Community Studies", *Journal of Health and Social Behavior*, 38/1 (March): 21–37.

Johnson, D. R., and Wu, J. (2002), "An Empirical Test of Crisis, Social Selection, and Role Explanations of the Relationship between Marital Disruption and Psychological Distress", *Journal of Marriage and the Family*, 64 (February): 211–24.

Kahneman, Daniel, Diener, Ed, and Schwarz, Norbert (eds.) (1999), *Well-Being: The Foundations of Hedonic Psychology*, New York: Russell Sage Foundation.

Kammann, R. (1983), "Objective Circumstances, Life Satisfactions, and Sense of Well-Being: Circumstances across Time and Place", *New Zealand Journal of Psychology*, 12: 14–22.

Kapteyn, Arie (2002), "Relative Utility and Income Growth: An Example", in Richard A. Easterlin (ed), *Happiness in Economics*, Northampton, Mass.: Edward Elgar, 143–5.

Kasser, Tim (2002), *The High Price of Materialism*, Cambridge, Mass.: MIT Press.

Kilpatrick, Robert W. (1973), "The Income Elasticity of the Poverty Line", *Review of Economics and Statistics*, 55/3 (August), 327–32.

Layard, R. (1980), "Human Satisfactions and Public Policy", *Economic Journal*, 90 (December): 737–50.

Lucas, Richard E., Clark, Andrew E., Georgellis, Yannis, and Diener, Ed (2003), "Reexamining Adaptation and the Set Point Model of Happiness: Reactions to

Changes in Marital Status", *Journal of Personality and Social Psychology*, 84/3: 527–39.

Lykken, David, and Tellegen, Auke (1996), "Happiness is a Stochastic Phenomenon", *Psychological Science*, 7/3 (May): 180–9.

McCrae, Robert R., and Costa, Jr., Paul T. (1990), *Personality in Adulthood*, New York: Guilford Press.

Mehnert, Thomas, Kraus, Herbert H., Nadler, Rosemary, and Boyd, Mary (1990), "Correlates of Life Satisfaction in Those with Disabling Conditions", *Rehabilitation Psychology*, 35/1: 3–17.

Michalos, A. C., Zumbo, B. D., and Hubley, A. (2000), "Health and the Quality of Life", *Social Indicators Research*, 51: 245–86.

Myers, David G. (1992), *The Pursuit of Happiness*, New York: Avon.

—— (1999), "Close Relationships and Quality of Life", in Kahneman *et al.* (1999).

National Opinion Research Center (1999), *General Social Surveys, 1972–1998: Cumulative Codebook*, Chicago: National Opinion Research Center.

Ng, Yew-Kwang (1978), "Economic Growth and Social Welfare: The Need for a Complete Study of Happiness", *Kyklos*, 31/4: 575–87.

Oswald, Andrew J. (1997), "Happiness and Economic Performance", *Economic Journal*, 107/445 (November): 1815–31.

Pigou, A. C. (1932), *The Economics of Welfare*, London: Macmillan.

Rainwater, Lee (1994), "Family Equivalence as a Social Construction", in D. Ekert-Jaffe (ed.), *Standards of Living and Families: Observation and Analysis*, Montrouge, France: John Libbey Eurotext, 25–39.

Roper-Starch Organization (1979), *Roper Reports 79–1*, Storrs, Conn.: University of Connecticut, The Roper Center.

—— (1995), *Roper Reports 95–1*, Storrs: Conn.: University of Connecticut, The Roper Center.

Scitovsky, Tibor (1976), *The Joyless Economy*, Oxford: Oxford University Press.

Seeman, Teresa E., and Crimmins, Eileen (2001), "Social Environment Effects on Health and Aging: Integrating Epidemiologic and Demographic Approaches and Perspectives", in Maxine Weinstein, Albert I. Hermalin, and Michael A. Stoto (eds.), *Population Health and Aging: Strengthening the Dialogue between Epidemiology and Demography*, Annals of the New York Academy of Sciences, Vol. 954, New York: The New York Academy of Sciences, 88–117.

Smith, V. Kerry, Taylor, Jr., Donald H., and Sloan, Frank A. (2001), "Longevity Expectations and Death: Can People Predict their Own Demise?" *American Economic Review* 91/4 (September), 1126–34.

van de Stadt, Huib, Kapteyn, Arie, and van de Geer, Sara (1985), "The Relativity of Utility: Evidence from Panel Data", *Review of Economics and Statistics*, 67/2 (May): 179–87.

van Praag, Bernard (1968), *Welfare Functions and Consumer Behavior: A Theory of Rational Irrationality*, Amsterdam: North Holland.

van Praag, Bernard, M. S., and Frijters, Paul (1999), "The Measurement of Welfare and Well-Being: The Leyden Approach", in Kahneman *et al.* (1999), 413–33.

Veenhoven, Ruut (1993), *Happiness in Nations, Subjective Appreciation of Life in 56 Nations 1946–1992*, Rotterdam, the Netherlands: Erasmus University.

Waite, Linda J., Browning, Don, Doherty, William J., Gallagher, Maggie, Luo, Ye, and Stanley, Scott M. (2002), *Does Divorce Make People Happy? Findings from a Study of Unhappy Marriages*, New York: Institute for American Values.

Winkelman, L., and Winkelman, R. (1998), "Why are the Unemployed So Unhappy? Evidence from Panel Data", *Economica*, 65: 1–15.

Wortman, C. B., Silver, R. C., and Kessler, R. C. (1993), "The Meaning of Loss and Adjustment to Bereavement", in M. S. Stroebe, W. Stroebe, and R. O. Hansson (eds.), *Handbook of Bereavement: Theory, Research, and Intervention*, New York: Cambridge University Press, 349–66.

2

Does Absolute Income Matter?

Robert H. Frank

One of the principal findings of the literature on human well-being is that within a country at a given point in time, measured well-being is strongly positively associated with relative income. A second important finding is that, beyond a fairly low income threshold, measured well-being changes little as the incomes of population members rise in tandem over time. In this chapter I briefly survey the relevant literature and attempt to explain why, despite the latter finding, we should be reluctant to conclude that absolute income has no bearing on human well-being.

Measuring Subjective Well-Being

The main method that psychologists have used to measure human well-being has been to conduct surveys in which they ask people whether they are: (a) very happy; (b) fairly happy; or (c) not happy.[1] Most respondents are willing to answer the question and not all of them respond "very happy", even in the United States, where one might think it advantageous to portray oneself as being very happy. Many people describe themselves as fairly happy, and others confess to being not happy. A given person's responses tend to be consistent from one survey to the next.

The happiness surveys also pose other questions. For example, they ask people to indicate, on a scale from 0 to 5, the extent to which they agree with statements like these:

"When good things happen to me, it strongly affects me."
"When I get something I want, I feel excited and energized."
"When I'm doing well at something, I love to keep at it."[2]

Many people respond to such statements with a 5 on the five-point scale, indicating strong agreement. Yet others don't seem to be able even to recall an episode that provoked feelings like the ones described. With remarkable consistency, the people who agree strongly with these statements are the ones who rate themselves as very happy in response to survey questions. Those who say they're not happy tend to disagree strongly with these statements.

Other psychologists attempt to measure emotional well-being by tracking the amplitude and frequency of electrical waves in different regions of the brain. Subjects with a preponderance of electrical activity in the left prefrontal region are much more likely to agree with the statements described above, and also much more likely to characterize themselves as happy in response to survey questions. But subjects with a preponderance of electrical activity in the right prefrontal region are far more likely to respond negatively in the earlier measures.[3]

People who say they're happy or who are revealed as happy by the various measures are also more likely to be rated as happy by their friends. And all the happiness measures are strongly correlated with observable behaviors that we associate with well-being.[4] If you're happy, for example, you're more likely to initiate social contacts with your friends. You're more likely to respond positively when others ask you for help. You're less likely to suffer from psychosomatic illnesses—digestive disorders, other stress disorders, headaches, vascular stress. You're less likely to be absent from work, or to get involved in disputes at work. And you're less likely to attempt suicide—the ultimate behavioral measure of unhappiness. These happiness measures are consistent, valid, and reliable.[5] In sum, it appears that human happiness is a real phenomenon that we can measure.

That fact permits us to investigate the factors that influence happiness. Much of the interpersonal variation in happiness is hereditary. If you're a child of happy parents, you're much more likely to be happy than if your parents were unhappy.

But although inborn factors are important, environmental factors also account for some of the variation in human happiness. People who have many close friends, for example, tend to be significantly happier than others, and also to live longer.

Income and Happiness

How does happiness vary with income? As noted earlier, studies show that when incomes rise for everybody, measures of well-being don't change

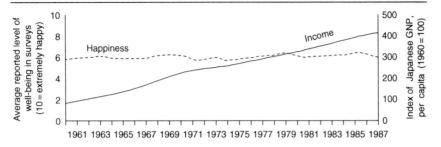

Figure 2.1. Average happiness versus average income over time in Japan
Source: Veenhoven (1993).

much. Consider the example of Japan, which was a very poor country in 1960. Since then, its per-capita income has risen several-fold, and is now among the highest in the industrialized world. (See Figure 2.1.) Yet the average happiness level reported by the Japanese is no higher now than in 1960. They have many more washing machines, cars, cameras and other things than they used to, but they haven't registered significant gains on the happiness scale.

The pattern shown in Figure 2.1 consistently shows up in other countries as well, and that's a puzzle for economists. If getting more income doesn't make people happier, why do they go to such lengths to get more income? Why, for example, do legal associates work 100 hours a week hoping to become partners in law firms? Why do tobacco company CEOs endure the public humiliation of testifying before Congress that there's no evidence that smoking causes serious illnesses?

It turns out that if you measure the income–happiness relationship in another way, you get just what the economists suspected all along. Consider Figure 2.2, which shows this relationship for the United States during a brief period during the 1980s. When we plot average happiness versus average income for clusters of people in a given country at a given time, as in the diagram, rich people are in fact a lot happier than poor people. It's actually an astonishingly large difference. There's no one single change you can imagine that would make your life improve on the happiness scale as much as to move from the bottom 5 percent on the income scale to the top 5 percent.

The patterns portrayed in Figure 2.1 and Figure 2.2 are not only consistent with the view that relative income is a far better predictor of happiness than absolute income, but they also seem to suggest that absolute income may not matter at all. Some social scientists who have pondered the significance of this finding have concluded that, at least for people in

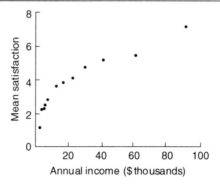

Figure 2.2. Income versus satisfaction in the US, 1981–4

Source: Diener *et al.*, (1993: 195–223).

the world's richest countries, no useful purpose is served by further accumulations of wealth.[6]

On its face, this should be a surprising conclusion, since there are so many seemingly useful things that having additional wealth would enable us to do. Would we really not be any happier if, say, the environment were a little cleaner, or if we could take a little more time off, or even just eliminate a few of the hassles of everyday life? In principle at least, people in wealthier countries have these additional options, and it should surprise us that this seems to have no measurable effect on their overall well-being.

There is indeed independent evidence that having more wealth *would* be a good thing, provided it were spent in certain ways. The key insight supported by this evidence is that even though we appear to adapt quickly to across-the-board increases in our stocks of most material goods, there are specific categories in which our capacity to adapt is more limited. It is in these categories that additional spending appears to have the greatest capacity to produce significant improvements in well-being.

Adaptation

The human ability to adapt to changed circumstances is one of the most remarkable features of our species. It spans the range of biological functioning, all the way down to molecular changes at the cellular level. Thus autonomic changes in pupil dilation, photochemical changes in the retina, and neural changes in the visual cortex of the brain allow us to see, more or less normally, in environments whose actual physical luminosity varies by a factor of more than one million.[7]

Our power to adapt is no less impressive at the level of the entire organism. Asked to choose, most people state confidently that they would rather be killed in an automobile accident than to survive a quadriplegic. And so we are not surprised to learn that severely disabled people experience a period of devastating depression and disorientation in the wake of their accidents. What we do not expect, however, are the speed and extent to which many of these victims accommodate to their new circumstances. Within a year's time, many quadriplegics report roughly the same mix of moods and emotions as able-bodied people do.[8] There is also evidence that the blind, the retarded, and the malformed are far better adapted to the limitations imposed by their conditions than most of us might imagine.[9]

We adapt swiftly not just to losses but also to gains. Ads for the New York State Lottery show participants fantasizing about how their lives would change if they won. ("I'd buy the company and fire my boss.") People who actually win the lottery typically report the anticipated rush of euphoria in the weeks after their good fortune. Follow-up studies done after several years, however, indicate that these people are often no happier—and indeed, are in some ways less happy—than before.[10]

In short, our extraordinary powers of adaptation appear to help explain why absolute living standards simply may not matter much once we escape the physical deprivations of abject poverty. This interpretation is consistent with the impressions of people who have lived or traveled extensively abroad, who report that the struggle to get ahead seems to play out with much the same psychological effects in rich societies as in those with more modest levels of wealth.[11]

These observations provide grist for the mills of social critics who are offended by the apparent wastefulness of the recent luxury-consumption boom in the United States. What many of these critics typically overlook, however, is that the power to adapt is a two-edged sword. It may indeed explain why having bigger houses and faster cars doesn't make us any happier; but if we can also adapt fully to the seemingly unpleasant things we often have to go through to get more money, then what's the problem? Perhaps social critics are simply barking up the wrong tree.

I believe, however, that to conclude that absolute living standards do not matter is a serious misreading of the evidence. What the data seem to say is that as national income grows, people do not spend their extra money in ways that yield significant and lasting increases in measured satisfaction. But this still leaves two possible ways that absolute income might matter. One is that people might have been able to spend their money in other ways that would have made them happier, yet for various reasons did not, or could not, do so. I will describe presently some evidence that strongly supports this possibility.

A second possibility is that although measures of subjective well-being may do a reasonably good job of tracking our experiences as we are consciously aware of them, that may not be all that matters to us. For example, imagine two parallel universes, one just like the one we live in now and another in which everyone's income is twice what it is now. Suppose that in both cases you would be the median earner, with an annual income of $100,000 in one case and $200,000 in the other. Suppose further that you will feel equally happy in the two universes (an assumption that is consistent with the evidence discussed thus far). And suppose, finally, that you know that people in the richer universe would spend more to protect the environment from toxic waste, and that this would result in healthier and longer, even if not happier, lives for all. Can there be any question that it would be better to live in the second universe?

My point is that although the emerging science of subjective well-being has much to tell us about the factors that contribute to human satisfaction, not even its most ardent practitioners would insist that it offers the final word. Indeed, it is easy to envision ways in which across-the-board increases in incomes might facilitate changes for the better that would be unlikely to have much impact on subjective well-being as currently measured. Of course, we must not simply *assume* that across-the-board increases in incomes will automatically lead to such changes. But neither should we be blind to this possibility. Whether growth in national income is, or could be, a generally good thing is a question that will have to be settled by the evidence.

And there is in fact a rich body of evidence that bears on this question. One clear message of this evidence is that, beyond some point, across-the-board increases in spending on *many types* of material goods do not produce any lasting increment in subjective well-being. Sticking with the parallel-universes metaphor, let us imagine people from two societies that are identical in every respect save one: In Society A, everyone lives in a house with 4,000 square feet of floor space, whereas in Society B each house has only 3,000 square feet. If the two societies were completely isolated from one another, there is no evidence to suggest that psychologists and neuroscientists would be able to discern any significant difference in their respective average levels of subjective well-being. Rather, we would expect each society to have developed its own local norm for what constitutes adequate housing, and that people in each society would therefore be equally satisfied with their houses and other aspects of their lives.

Moreover, we have no reason to suppose that there would be other important respects in which it might be preferable to be a member of Society A rather than Society B. Thus the larger houses in Society A would not contribute to longer lives, more freedom from illness, or indeed any other significant advantage over the members of Society B. Once house size achieves a given threshold, the human capacity to adapt to further across-the-board changes in house size would appear to be virtually complete.

Of course, it takes real resources to build 4,000-square-foot houses instead of 3,000-square-foot houses. Put another way, a society that built a 4,000-square-foot house for everyone could have built 3,000-square-foot houses instead, freeing up considerable resources that could have been used to produce something else. Hence this central question: Are there alternative ways of spending these resources that could have produced lasting gains in human welfare?

An affirmative answer would be logically impossible if our capacity to adapt to every other possible change were as great as our capacity to adapt to larger houses. As it turns out, however, our capacity to adapt varies considerably across domains. There are some stimuli, such as environmental noise, to which we may adapt relatively quickly at a conscious level, yet to which our bodies continue to respond in measurable ways even after many years of exposure. Indeed, there are even stimuli to which we not only do not adapt over time, but actually become sensitized. Various biochemical allergens are examples, but we also see instances on a more macro scale. Thus, after several months' exposure, the office boor who initially took two weeks to annoy you can accomplish the same feat in only seconds.

The observation that we adapt more fully to some stimuli than to others opens the door to the possibility that moving resources from one category to another might yield lasting changes in human well-being. I turn now to a summary of evidence that bears on this possibility.

Spending Categories that Matter

A convenient way to examine this evidence is to consider a sequence of thought experiments in which you must choose between two hypothetical societies. The two societies have equal wealth levels but different spending patterns. In each case, let us again suppose that residents of Society A live in 4,000-square-foot houses while those in Society B live in 3,000-square-foot houses. I use these figures because each is significantly larger than the current average house size in the US (and by an even larger margin larger than the average dwelling in Europe), which means that most of you will be able to contemplate a move from A to B without having to imagine moving to a smaller house than the one in which you now live. If your current house is larger than 3,000 square feet, simply replace 3,000 with the size of your current house and suppose that the house in Society A is 1,000 square feet larger than that. (For example, if you currently live in a 6,000-square-foot house, let the houses in Society B be 6,000 square feet and those in A be 7,000.)

In each case, the residents of Society B use the resources saved by building smaller houses to bring about some other specific change in their living conditions. And in each case we shall ask what the evidence says about how that change would affect the quality of their lives.

> Which would you choose: Society A, whose residents have 4,000-square-foot houses and a one-hour automobile commute to work through heavy traffic; or Society B, whose residents have 3,000-square-foot houses and a 15-minute commute by rapid transit?

The only difference between these societies is that they have allocated their resources differently between housing and transportation. The residents of Society B have used the same resources they could have employed to build larger housing to instead transform the nature of their commute to work. Let us also suppose that the cost savings from building smaller houses are sufficient to fund not only the construction of high-speed public transit, but also to make the added flexibility of the automobile available on an as-needed basis. Thus, as a resident of Society B, you need not give up your car. You can even drive it to work on those days when you need extra flexibility, or you can come and go when needed by taxi. The *only* thing you and others must sacrifice to achieve the shorter, less stressful daily commute to work of Society B is additional floor space in your houses.

A rational person faced with this choice will want to consider the available evidence on the benefits and costs of each alternative. As concerns the psychological cost of living in smaller houses, the evidence provides no reason to believe that if you and all others live in 3,000-square-foot houses, your subjective well-being will be any lower than if you and all others live in 4,000-square-foot houses. Of course, if you moved from Society B to Society A, you might be pleased, even excited, at first to experience the additional living space. But we can predict that in time you would adapt, and simply consider the larger house the norm.

Someone who moved from Society B to Society A would also initially experience stress from the extended commute through heavy traffic. Over time, his consciousness of this stress might diminish. But there is an important distinction: Unlike his adaptation to the larger house, which will be essentially complete, his adaptation to his new commuting pattern will be only partial. Available evidence clearly shows that, even after long periods of adjustment, most people experience the task of navigating through heavy commuter traffic as stressful.[12]

In this respect, the effect of exposure to heavy traffic is similar to the effect of exposure to noise and other irritants. Thus, even though a large increase in background noise at a constant, steady level is experienced as less intrusive as time passes, prolonged exposure nonetheless produces lasting elevations in blood pressure.[13] If the noise is not only loud but intermittent, people remain conscious of their heightened irritability even after extended periods of adaptation, and their symptoms of central nervous system distress become more pronounced.[14] This pattern was seen, for example, in a study of people living next to a newly opened noisy highway. Whereas 21 percent of residents interviewed four months after the highway opened said they were not annoyed by the noise, that figure dropped to 16 percent when the same residents were interviewed a year later.[15]

Among the various types of noise exposure, worst of all is exposure to sounds that are not only loud and intermittent, but also unpredictably so. Subjects exposed to loud, aperiodic noise in the laboratory experience not only physiological symptoms of stress, but also behavioral symptoms. These subjects become less persistent in their attempts to cope with frustrating tasks, and suffer measurable impairments in performing tasks requiring care and attention.[16]

It is plausible to suppose that unpredictable noise is particularly stressful because it confronts the subject with a loss of control. David Glass and his collaborators confirmed this hypothesis in an ingenious experiment that exposed two groups of subjects to a recording of loud, unpredictable noises. Whereas subjects in one group had no control over the recording, subjects in the other group could stop the tape at any time by flipping a switch. These subjects were told, however, that the experimenters would prefer that they not stop the tape, and most subjects honored this preference. Following exposure to the noise, subjects with access to the control switch made almost 60 percent fewer errors than other subjects on a proofreading task and made more than four times as many attempts to solve a difficult puzzle.[17]

Commuting through heavy traffic is in many ways more like exposure to loud, unpredictable noise than to constant background noise. Delays are difficult to predict, much less control, and one never quite gets used to being cut off by others who think their time is more valuable than anyone else's. A large scientific literature documents a multitude of stress symptoms that result from protracted driving through heavy traffic.

One strand in this literature focuses on the experience of urban bus drivers, whose exposure to the stresses of heavy traffic is higher than that of most commuters, but who have also had greater opportunity to adapt to those stresses. Compared to workers in other occupations, a disproportionate share of the absenteeism experienced by urban bus drivers stems from stress-related illnesses such as gastrointestinal problems, headaches, and anxiety.[18] Many studies have found sharply elevated rates of hypertension among bus drivers relative to a variety of control groups, including, in one instance, bus drivers themselves during their pre-employment physicals.[19] Additional studies have found elevations of stress hormones such as adrenaline, noradrenaline, and cortisol in urban bus drivers.[20] And one study found elevations of adrenaline and noradrenaline to be strongly positively correlated with the density of the traffic with which urban bus drivers had to contend.[21] More than half of all urban bus drivers retire prematurely with some form of medical disability.[22]

A one-hour daily commute through heavy traffic is presumably less stressful than operating a bus all day in an urban area. Yet this difference is one of degree rather than of kind. Studies have shown that the demands of commuting through heavy traffic often result in emotional and behavioral deficits upon arrival at home or at work.[23] Compared to drivers who commute through low-density traffic, those who commute through heavy traffic are more likely to report feelings of annoyance.[24] And higher levels of commuting distance, time, speed, and months of commuting are significantly positively correlated with increased systolic and diastolic blood pressure.[25]

The prolonged experience of commuting stress is also known to suppress immune function and shorten longevity.[26] Even spells in traffic as brief as 15 minutes have been linked to significant elevations of blood glucose and cholesterol, and to declines in blood coagulation time—all factors that are positively associated with cardiovascular disease.

Commuting by automobile is also positively linked with the incidence of various cancers, especially cancer of the lung, possibly because of heavier exposure to exhaust fumes.[27] Among people who commute to work, the incidence of these and other illnesses rises with the length of commute,[28] and is significantly lower among those who commute by bus or rail,[29] and lower still among non-commuters.[30] Finally, the risk of death and injury from accidents varies positively with the length of commute and is higher for those who commute by car than for those who commute by public transport.

In sum, there appear to be persistent and significant costs associated with a long commute through heavy traffic. We can be confident that neurophysiologists would find higher levels of cortisol, norepinephrine, adrenaline, noradrenaline, and other stress hormones in the residents of Society A. No one has done the experiment to discover whether people from Society A would report lower levels of life satisfaction than people from Society B. But since we know that drivers often report being consciously aware of the frustration and stress they experience during commuting, it is a plausible conjecture that subjective well-being, as conventionally measured, would be lower in Society A. Even if the negative effects of commuting stress never broke through into conscious awareness, however, we would still have powerful reasons for wishing to escape them.

On the strength of the available evidence, then, it appears that a rational person would have powerful reasons to choose Society B, and no reasons to avoid it. And yet, despite this evidence, the United States is moving steadily in the direction of Society A. Even as our houses continue to grow in size, the average length of our commute to work continues to grow longer. Between 1982 and 2000, for example, the time penalty for peak-period travelers increased from 16 hours per year to 62 hours; the period of time when travelers might experience congestion increased from 4.5 hours to 7 hours; and the volume of roadways where travel is congested has grown from 34 percent to 58 percent.[31] The Federal Highway Administration predicts that the extra time spent driving because of delays will rise from 2.7 billion vehicle hours in 1985 to 11.9 billion in 2005.[32]

Several of the next thought experiments ask you to choose between societies that offer different combinations of material goods and free time to pursue other activities. Each case assumes a specific use of the free time and asks that you imagine it to be one that appeals to you. (If not, feel free to substitute some other activity that does.)

Which would you choose: Society A, whose residents live in 4,000-square-foot houses and have no time to exercise each day; or Society B, whose residents live in 3,000-square-foot houses and have 45 minutes available to exercise each day?

Again we have two societies that have different bundles from the same menu of opportunities. Residents of Society B could have built larger houses, but instead they spent less time at work each day and devoted the time thus saved to exercise. As before, we assume that there are no other relevant differences between the two societies. And imagine yourself to be someone who views exercise as neither more nor less intrinsically pleasurable than work.

Let us again take as given that no reduction in well-being will result from the mere fact that everyone lives in a smaller house in Society B. The only question, then, is whether the additional time available for exercise will result in a significant increase in well-being. And on this question, the evidence could hardly be more clear.

Thus numerous studies have documented a variety of positive physiological and psychological effects of regular aerobic exercise.[33] Exercisers report more frequent and intense positive feelings and tend to have better functioning immune systems.[34] Exercisers also have higher life expectancy and are less likely to suffer from heart disease, stroke, diabetes, hypertension, and a variety of other ailments.[35]

Evidence for the causal nature of these relationships is seen in the fact that subjects randomly assigned to exercise programs experience improved physical and psychological well-being.[36] For example, people diagnosed with moderate depression who were randomly assigned to an aerobic exercise program experienced recovery rates comparable to others being treated by psychotherapy, and both groups fared substantially better than controls.[37]

Some critics have expressed concern that the psychological benefits found in many studies may really be the result not of exercise itself but of the fact that subjects experience a break in their normal routines. Some support for this possibility emerged in a study in which one group of 32 volunteers was assigned to an aerobic exercise program and another group of 32 to a hobby class.[38] Both groups experienced measurable improvements in mood. But the breaks in routine that both groups enjoyed cannot be the entire explanation, since the mood improvements were significantly larger for the exercise group. Thus the exercise group experienced improvements in each of six mood indicators, all but two of which were large and statistically significant. Although the hobby-class group improved on five of the six indicators, their improvements were smaller and only two were statistically significant.

Even programs of relatively light exercise, such as walking, yield significant physiological and psychological benefits. One experiment, for example, showed that premenopausal women randomly assigned to a supervised walking group experienced significant reductions in heart rate and blood pressure, and significant improvements in self-esteem relative to non-walkers.[39]

Despite the compelling evidence for the beneficial psychological and physical effects of regular exercise, and despite the evidence that no discernible increase in life satisfaction results when all have larger houses, it is difficult to insist that all rational persons would necessarily choose Society B over Society A. Indeed, many people are so averse to physical exercise that they would be willing to give up material goods in order to *escape* having to do it.

Many of these people might change their minds if they stuck with an exercise program for just a little while. For although people often report that exercise is an unpleasant experience at first, especially if they try to do too much too soon, most adapt to it quickly and come to think of it as pleasurable. In the end, however, even this knowledge may not tip the balance in favor of Society B for some people. If you are in this group, just think of Society B as providing a little more time for some other daily activity, or mix of activities, that you might like to pursue.

In any event, lack of time is the reason most frequently cited by people who say they wish they could get more exercise. Thus Jon Robison, co-director of the Michigan Center for Preventive Medicine in Lansing, says that most exercise regimens are doomed from the start because people try to cram an hour of exercise into a daily schedule that is too busy to begin with, and end up quitting because they can't find the time.[40] Extra time is readily available, however, if we spend less time working to acquire goods. The evidence strongly suggests that our lives would be healthier, longer, and more satisfying if we all made that choice. Yet, the average American is in fact exercising less than in the past and spending more time at work.

Which would you choose: Society A, whose residents have 4,000-square-foot houses and one evening each month to get together with friends; or Society B, whose residents have 3,000-square-foot houses and get together with friends four evenings a month?

The question is again whether one use of time produces a larger impact on subjective well-being than another. Because the residents of Society A work longer hours, they can build larger houses but have less time to socialize with friends. Here again, the evidence suggests that whereas the payoff when all have larger houses is small and fleeting, the pleasures that result from deeper social relationships are both profound and enduring. People with rich networks of active social relationships are much more likely to call themselves happy, and are much more likely to be described as happy by friends.[41] In the findings of one survey by the National Opinion Research Center, for example, persons who could name five or more friends with whom they discussed matters of personal importance were 60 percent more likely to feel "very happy" than others who listed no personal confidants.[42] Another survey of 800 college graduates found that subjects whose values emphasized high income and occupational prestige were twice as likely as others to describe themselves as "fairly unhappy" or "very unhappy".[43]

It might seem natural to wonder about the direction of causation in the link between social integration and subjective well-being. Does having close relationships make people happy, or is it just that happier people are more likely to enjoy close relationships? Without discounting the second possibility, I note that there is at least some evidence that social integration is an important causal factor. Thus one study found that soldiers assigned to small, stable, cohesive units scored significantly higher on several important measures of subjective well-being than did others assigned to large units with high turnover.[44]

Even more striking is the link between networks of close personal relationships and physical health. People who lack such networks tend to be less physically healthy, and confront a higher risk of dying at every age. For example, in a study of leukemia patients about to undergo bone marrow transplants, the two-year survival rate was 54 percent for those who experienced strong emotional support from family and friends, but only 20 percent for those who experienced little social support.[45]

A more broad-based study investigated whether the presence or absence of various kinds of social relationships—marriage, contact with friends, membership in churches and other organizations—predicted subsequent rates of death for a sample of 2,229 men and 2,496 women living in Alameda County, California. For both men and women across all age groups, people who were low or lacking in such relationships at the beginning of the study in 1965 were from 30 to 300 percent more likely to have died during the subsequent nine years.[46]

Here, too, one might wonder about the causal link between mortality and social integration. Could the higher mortality of the less socially integrated subjects have been in part a reflection of the fact that pre-existing poor health caused them to be less socially integrated at the time of the initial interview? The results of a later study seem to rule out this interpretation. Based on a sample of 1,322 men and 1,432 women in Tecumseh, Michigan, investigators found essentially the same relationship between mortality and social integration even after controlling for the results of a physical examination conducted at the beginning of the study.[47]

In sum, the evidence is clear that closer social ties promote both physical health and subjective well-being. But close social ties cannot be achieved by waving a magic wand. Relationships take time, and as economists correctly insist, time is money. Is this money well spent? The answer is almost surely yes, if the alternative is to use that money to build larger houses for all. Here again, it appears that a rational person has compelling reasons for choosing Society B, in which everyone has a smaller house but more time to spend with friends. Yet, as a nation, Americans have been moving in precisely the opposite direction.

> Which would you choose: Society A, whose residents have 4,000-square-foot houses and one week of vacation each year; or Society B, whose residents have 3,000-square-foot houses, and four weeks of vacation?

If we all lived in smaller houses, or drove less expensive cars, we could all take more weeks of vacation each year. The physical and psychological benefits of periodic breaks in routine have long been established.[48] Thus studies of people on vacation find that they are less tired, irritable, and worried than at other times.[49] Vacationers also experience reduced incidence of stress-related disorders such as indigestion, constipation, headaches, and insomnia.[50]

Vacations offer the opportunity to see new places, visit distant relatives and friends, take up a new sport, read books, lie on a beach, hike in the wilderness, or whatever the spirit moves you to do. Provided they are of sufficient duration, vacations have also been found to have restorative effects that persist long after people return to work. Citing evidence of these effects, German legislation encourages vacation leave to be taken "as a single, uninterrupted period unless pressing requirements of the establishment or of the employee make it necessary to split leave into parts".[51] The German legislation goes on to say that if the statutory minimum of 24 vacation days is split into parts, "one of the parts ... shall comprise at least twelve consecutive working days".[52]

Despite the manifold advantages of longer vacations, few entry level-jobs in the US offer more than ten days of paid vacation a year, and many offer less. There appears little doubt that a package with a lower annual salary and a longer vacation allotment would increase subjective well-being by more than enough to offset an across-the-board move to slightly smaller houses. And yet Americans must work longer now than in the recent past to earn each day of paid vacation.

> Which would you choose: Society A, whose residents have 4,000-square-foot houses and a relatively low level of autonomy in the workplace; or Society B, whose residents have 3,000-square-foot houses and a relatively high level of autonomy?

Because most of us spend the majority, or at least a large proportion, of our waking hours on the job, our satisfaction with our lives as a whole depends importantly on how satisfied we are with our jobs. A consistent finding in the industrial psychology literature is that job satisfaction increases with the degree to which workers enjoy autonomy and choice with respect to which tasks they do and the manner in which they perform them.[53] In laboratory experiments, for example, subjects allowed to choose their own activities spent significantly longer times on task than did those to whom activities were assigned arbitrarily.[54]

Autonomy is of course not the only factor that influences job satisfaction. For example, workers tend to find greater satisfaction in jobs that provide greater opportunities to make use of their skills.[55] And numerous studies have found that job satisfaction increases with the variety of tasks workers are called on to perform.[56] The list is endless. Thus, if pay were the same, people would choose safe jobs over risky jobs; quiet jobs over noisy jobs; jobs with convenient parking over jobs without; jobs with security over jobs without; and so on.

Giving workers more autonomy sometimes results in greater productivity, sometimes not. Where it does, it will of course be in the interests of profit-seeking employers to grant additional autonomy. But beyond some point, greater autonomy usually comes at the expense of profits. And once this point is reached, workers can enjoy increased autonomy only by accepting lower salaries. The same holds true for other valued job characteristics. To the extent that workers become more productive the more they specialize, pay cuts will be necessary if workers are to enjoy more variety and the opportunity to utilize more fully the various skills they possess. Likewise, additional safety equipment, employment security, parking spaces, office privacy, and other amenities inevitably mean lower paychecks.

For the purposes of this thought experiment, we assume that the only consequence of gaining these desirable working conditions is an across-the-board reduction from 4,000 to 3,000 square feet of housing space, a move that entails essentially no sacrifice in subjective well-being. Yet there is a lasting gain in well-being when everyone gains additional autonomy on the job—or when all gain additional variety or safety. Here again, the available evidence strongly favors the choice of Society B. Yet the combination of alternatives in Society B is just what we seem to be moving away from.

Inconspicuous Consumption

The choice in each of the thought experiments considered thus far has been between conspicuous consumption (in the form of larger houses) and what, for want of a better term, I shall call "inconspicuous consumption"—freedom from traffic congestion, time with family and friends, vacation time, and a variety of favorable job characteristics. In each case the evidence suggests that subjective well-being will be higher in the society with a greater balance of inconspicuous consumption.

The list of inconspicuous consumption items could be extended considerably. Thus we could ask whether all living in slightly smaller houses would be a reasonable price to pay for higher air quality, for more urban parkland, for cleaner drinking water, for a reduction in violent crime; or for medical research that would reduce premature death. And in each case the answer would be the same as in the cases we have considered thus far.

Although many forms of inconspicuous consumption—the use of rapid transit systems to alleviate traffic congestion, for example—entail expenditures in the public domain, many others do not. Spending additional time with family and friends, for example, is a form of private inconspicuous consumption.

Many private goods, such as automobiles, embody elements of both conspicuous and inconspicuous consumption. And if we fix the total amount spent on such goods, we confront a tradeoff between these two kinds of consumption. If we all buy faster or more luxuriously appointed cars (conspicuous consumption), the evidence suggests that we will experience little lasting improvement in subjective well-being. But the outcome will be different if we all buy safer, more reliable cars (inconspicuous consumption). In the case of safety, the distribution of the increase in well-being will be highly uneven: a small proportion of us will escape the pain and suffering that follows a serious injury or the loss of a loved one. In the case of reliability, a large majority of us can escape the stress of repeated mechanical breakdowns.

My point in the thought experiments is not that inconspicuous consumption is always preferable to conspicuous consumption. Indeed, in each of the individual thought experiments, we might envision a minority of rational individuals who might choose Society A over Society B. Some people may simply dislike autonomy on the job, or dislike exercise, or dislike spending time with family and friends.

But if we accept at face value the evidence that there is little sacrifice in subjective well-being when all move to slightly smaller houses, the real question is whether a rational person could find *some* more productive use for the resources thus saved. Given the absolute sizes of the houses involved in the thought experiments, the answer to this question would seem to be "yes".

And this suggests that the answer to the question posed in my title ("Does absolute income matter?") is that it depends. Considerable evidence suggests that if we all work longer hours to buy bigger houses and more expensive cars, we do not end up any happier than before. As for whether increases in absolute income *could* buy happiness, however, the evidence paints a very different picture. The less we spend on conspicuous consumption goods, the better we can afford to alleviate congestion; the more time we can devote to family and friends, to exercise, sleep, travel, and other restorative activities; and the better we can afford to maintain a clean and safe environment. On the best available evidence, reallocating our time and money in these ways would result in healthier, longer, and more satisfying lives.

So Why Hasn't Subjective Well-Being Been Rising?

It might seem natural to suppose that when per-capita income rises sharply, as it has in most countries since at least the end of World War II, most people would spend more on both conspicuous and inconspicuous consumption. In many instances, this is in fact what seems to have happened. Thus the cars we buy today are not only faster and more luxuriously equipped, but also safer and more reliable. If both forms of consumption have been rising, however, and if inconspicuous consumption boosts subjective well-being, then why has subjective well-being not increased during the last several decades? (Recall that Japan's average subjective well-being remained essentially unchanged during a period of more than fivefold growth in per-capita income.)

A plausible answer is that whereas some forms of inconspicuous consumption have been rising, others have been declining, often sharply, during the period in question. Thus, as discussed earlier, there have been increases in the annual number of hours spent at work in the US during the last two decades. Traffic has grown considerably more congested; savings rates have fallen precipitously; personal bankruptcy filings are at an all-time high; and there is at least a widespread perception that employment security has fallen sharply. Declines in these and other forms of inconspicuous consumption may well have offset the effects of increases in others.

The much more troubling question is *why* we have not used our resources more wisely. If in fact we could all live healthier, longer, and more satisfying lives by simply changing our spending patterns, why haven't we done that? As even the most ardent free-market economists have long recognized, the invisible hand cannot be expected to deliver the greatest good for all in cases in which each individual's well-being depends on the actions taken by others.

This qualification was once thought to justify collective action in only a limited number of arenas—most importantly, the regulation of environmental pollution. We now recognize, however, that the interdependencies among us are considerably more pervasive. For present purposes, chief among them are the ways in which the spending decisions of some individuals affect the frames of reference within which others make important choices.

Many important rewards in life—access to the best schools, to the most desirable mates, and even, in times of famine, to the food needed for survival—depend critically on how the choices we make compare to the choices made by others. In most cases, the person who stays at the office two hours longer each day to be able to afford a house in a better school district has no conscious intention to make it more difficult for others to achieve the same goal. Yet that is an inescapable consequence of his action. The best response available to others may be to work longer hours as well, thereby to preserve their current positions. Yet the ineluctable mathematical logic of musical chairs assures that only 10 percent of all children can occupy top-decile school seats, no matter how many hours their parents work.

That many purchases become more attractive to us when others make them means that consumption spending has much in common with a military arms race. A family can choose how much of its own money to spend, but it cannot choose how much others spend. Buying a smaller-than-average vehicle means a greater risk of dying in an accident. Spending less on an interview suit means a greater risk of not landing the best job. Yet when all spend more on heavier cars or more finely tailored suits, the results tend to be mutually offsetting, just as when all nations spend more on armaments. Spending less—on bombs or on personal consumption—frees up money for other pressing uses, but only if everyone does it.

What, exactly, is the incentive problem that leads nations to spend too much on armaments? It is not sufficient merely that each nation's payoff from spending on arms depends on how its spending compares with that of rival nations. Suppose, for example, that each nation's payoff from spending on nonmilitary goods also depended, and to the same extent as for military goods, on the amounts spent on nonmilitary goods by other nations. The tendency of military spending to siphon off resources from other spending categories would then be offset by an equal tendency in the opposite direction. That is, if each nation had a fixed amount of national income to allocate between military and nonmilitary goods, and if the payoffs in each category were equally context-sensitive, then we would expect no imbalance across the categories.

For an imbalance to occur in favor of armaments, the reward from armaments spending must be *more* context-sensitive than the reward from nonmilitary spending. And since this is precisely the case, the generally assumed imbalance occurs. After all, to be second-best in a military arms race often means a loss of political autonomy; clearly a much higher cost than the discomfort of having toasters with fewer slots.

In brief, we expect an imbalance in the choice between two activities if the individual rewards from one are more context-sensitive than the individual rewards from the other. The evidence described earlier suggests that the satisfaction provided by many conspicuous forms of consumption is more context-dependent than the satisfaction provided by many less conspicuous forms of consumption. If so, this would help explain why the absolute income and consumption increases of recent decades have failed to translate into corresponding increases in measured well-being.

Notes

H. J. Louis Professor of Economics, Johnson Graduate School of Management, Cornell University. This chapter draws heavily on chapters 5 and 6 of my 1999 book, *Luxury Fever*.

1. See Easterlin (1974).
2. Goleman (1996, C3).
3. Davidson (1992).
4. For surveys of this evidence see Frank (1985, chap. 2); and Clark and Oswald (1996).
5. Diener and Lucas (1998).
6. See e.g. Townsend (1979).
7. Loewenstein and Frederick (1999).
8. Bulman and Wortman (1977).
9. Cameron (1972); Cameron *et al.* (1976).
10. Brickman *et al.* (1978).
11. Myers (1993: 36).
12. For a survey, see Koslowsky *et al.* (1995).
13. Glass *et al.* (1977).
14. ibid.
15. Weinstein (1982).
16. Glass *et al.* (1977).
17. ibid., figures 5 and 6.
18. Long and Perry (1985).
19. Ragland *et al.* (1987); Pikus and Tarranikova (1975); and Evans *et al.* (1987).
20. ibid.
21. Evans and Carrere (1991).
22. Evans (1994).
23. Glass and Singer (1972); Sherrod (1974).
24. Stokols *et al.* (1978).
25. ibid., table 3.
26. DeLongis *et al.* (1988); and Stokols *et al.* (1978).
27. Koslowsky *et al.* (1995, chap. 4).
28. Koslowsky *et al.* (1995).
29. Taylor and Pocock (1972); Koslowsky and Krausz (1993).
30. European Foundation for the Improvement of Living and Working Conditions (1984).
31. Schrank and Lomax (2002).
32. Clark (1994: 387).
33. For a survey, see Plante and Rodin (1990).
34. Fontane (1996).
35. Blair (1989).
36. Palmer (1995).
37. Greist *et al.* (1979).
38. Lichtman and Poser (1983).
39. Palmer (1995).
40. Sharp (1996: 4M).
41. Argyle (1999).

42. Burt (1986).
43. Perkins (1991).
44. Manning and Fullerton (1988).
45. Colon *et al.* (1991).
46. Berkman and Syme (1979).
47. House *et al.* (1982).
48. Argyle (1996).
49. Rubenstein (1980).
50. ibid.
51. Weiss (1991: 141).
52. ibid.
53. For a survey, see Warr (1999); see also Agho *et al.* (1993); Fried (1991); Kelloway and Barling (1991); Spector and O'Connell (1994); Spector *et al.* (1988); Wall *et al.* (1996); and Xie and Johns (1995).
54. Deci (1971).
55. Campion and McClelland (1993); and Warr (1990).
56. Agho *et al.* (1993); Fried (1991); Kelloway and Barling (1991); Warr (1990); and Xie and Johns (1995).

References

Agho, Augustine O., Mueller, Charles W., and Price, James L. (1993), "Determinants of Employee Job Satisfaction", *Human Relations* (August): 1011–19.

Argyle, Michael (1996), *The Social Psychology of Leisure*, New York: Penguin.

——(1999), "Causes and Correlates of Happiness", in Kahneman *et al.* (1999).

Berkman, L. and Syme, S. (1979), "Social Networks, Host Resistance, and Mortality: A Nine-Year Follow-up Study of Alameda County Residents", *American Journal of Epidemiology*, 109: 186–204.

Blair, S. N. (1989), "Physical Fitness and All-Cause Mortality: A Prospective Study of Healthy Men and Women", *Journal of the American Medical Association*, 262: 2396–401.

Brickman, P., Coates, D., and Janoff-Bulman, R. (1978), "Lottery Winners and Accident Victims: Is Happiness Relative?" *Journal of Personality and Social Psychology*, 36 (August): 917–27.

Bulman, R. J., and Wortman, C. B. (1977), "Attributes of Blame and 'Coping' in the 'Real World': Severe Accident Victims React to their Lot", *Journal of Personality and Social Psychology*, 35 (May): 351–63.

Burt, R. S. (1986), *Strangers, Friends, and Happiness*, GSS Technical Report No. 72, Chicago: National Opinion Research Center, University of Chicago.

Cameron, P. (1972), "Stereotypes about Generational Fun and Happiness vs. Self-Appraised Fun and Happiness", *The Gerontologist*, 12 (Summer): 120–3.

——Titus, D., Kostin, J., and Kostin, M. (1976), *The Quality of American Life*, New York: Russell Sage, 1976.

Campion, M., and McClelland, C. (1993), "Follow-up and Extension of the Interdisciplinary Costs and Benefits of Enlarged Jobs", *Journal of Applied Psychology*, 78: 339–51.

Clark, Andrew, and Oswald, Andrew (1996), "Satisfaction and Comparison Income", *Journal of Public Economics*, 61, 359–81.

Clark, Charles S. (1994), "Traffic Congestion", *The CQ Researcher* (6 May): 387–404.

Colon, E., Callies, A., Popkin, M., and McGlave, P. (1991), "Depressed Mood and Other Variables Related to Bone Marrow Transplantation Survival in Acute Leukemia", *Psychosomatics*, 32: 420–5.

Davidson, Richard J. (1992), "Anterior Cerebral Asymmetry and the Nature of Emotion", *Brain and Cognition*, 6: 245–68.

Deci, Edward L. (1971), "Effects of Externally Mediated Rewards on Intrinsic Motivation", *Journal of Personality and Social Psychology*, 18: 105–15.

DeLongis, Anita, Folkman, Susan, and Lazarus, Richard S. (1988), "The Impact of Daily Stress on Health and Mood: Psychological and Social Resources as Mediators", *Journal of Personality and Social Psychology*, 54: 486–95.

Diener, Ed, and Lucas, Richard E. (1999), "Personality and Subjective Well-Being", in Kahneman *et al.* (1999).

——Sandvik, Ed, Seidlitz, Larry, and Diener, Marissa (1993), "The Relationship between Income and Subjective Well-Being: Relative or Absolute?" *Social Indicators Research*, 28: 195–223.

Easterlin, Richard (1974), "Does Economic Growth Improve the Human Lot?" in Paul David and Melvin Reder (eds.), *Nations and Households in Economic Growth: Essays in Honor of Moses Abramovitz*, New York: Academic Press.

——(1995), "Will Raising the Incomes of All Increase the Happiness of All", *Journal of Economic Behavior and Organization*, 27: 35–47.

European Foundation for the Improvement of Living and Working Conditions, (1984), "The Journey from Home to the Workplace: The Impact on the Safety and Health of the Community/Workers", Dublin: European Foundation for the Improvement of Living and Working Conditions.

Evans, Gary W. (1994), "Working on the Hot Seat: Urban Bus Drivers", *Accident Analysis and Prevention*, 26: 181–93.

——and Carrere, S. (1991), "Traffic Congestion, Perceived Control, and Psychophysiological Stress among Urban Bus Drivers", *Journal of Applied Psychology*, 76: 658–63.

——Palsane, M., and Carrere, S. (1987), "Type A Behavior and Occupational Stress: A Cross-Cultural Study of Blue-Collar Workers", *Journal of Personality and Social Psychology*, 52: 1002–7.

Fontane, Patrick E. (1996), "Exercise, Fitness, and Feeling Well", *American Behavioral Scientist*, 39 (January): 288–305.

Frank, Robert H. (1985), *Choosing the Right Pond*, New York: Oxford University Press.

——(1999), *Luxury Fever*, New York: The Free Press.

Fried, Y. (1991), "Meta-analytic Comparison of the Job Diagnostic Survey and Job Characteristics Inventory as Correlates of Work Satisfaction and Performance", *Journal of Applied Psychology*, 76: 690–7.

Glass, D. C., and Singer, J. (1972), *Urban Stressors: Experiments on Noise and Social Stressors*, New York: Academic Press.

——— and Pennegaker, James (1977), "Behavioral and Physiological Effects of Uncontrollable Environmental Events", in Daniel Stokols (ed.), *Perspectives on Environment and Behavior*, New York: Plenum, 1977.

Goleman, Daniel (1996), "Forget Money; Nothing Can Buy Happiness, Some Researchers Say", *New York Times* (16 July): C1, C3.

Greist, J. H., Klein, M., Eischens, R., Faris, J., Gurman, J., Gurman, A., and Morgan, W. (1979), "Running as a Treatment for Depression", *Comparative Psychology*, 20: 41–54.

House, James S., Robbins, C., and Metzner, H. M. (1982), "The Association of Social Relationships and Activities with Mortality: Prospective Evidence from the Tecumsah Community Health Study", *American Journal of Epidemiology*, 116: 123–40.

Kahneman, Daniel (1999), "Assessments of Individual Well-Being: A Bottom-Up Approach", in Kahneman *et al.* (1999).

——Diener, Ed, and Schwartz, Norbert (eds.) (1998), *Well-Being: The Foundations of Hedonic Psychology*, New York: Russell Sage.

Kelloway, E., and Barling, J. (1991), "Job Characteristics, Role Stress, and Mental Health", *Journal of Occupational Psychology*, 1: 291–304.

Koslowsky, Meni, Kluger, Avraham N., and Reich, Mordechai (1995), *Commuting Stress*, New York: Plenum.

——and Krausz, Moshe (1993), "On the Relationship between Commuting, Stress Symptoms, and Attitudinal Measures", *Journal of Applied Behavioral Sciences* (December): 485–92.

Lichtman, Sharla, and Poser, Ernest G. (1983), "The Effects of Exercise an Mood and Cognitive Functioning", *Journal of Psychosomatic Research*, 27: 43–52.

Loewenstein, George, and Frederick, Shane (1999), "Hedonic Adaptation: From the Bright Side to the Dark Side", in Kahneman *et al.* (1999).

Long, L., and Perry, J. (1985), "Economic and Occupational Causes of Transit Operator Absenteeism: A Review of Reserch", *Transport Reviews*, 5: 247–67.

Manning, F. J., and Fullerton, T. D., (1988), "Health and Well-Being in Highly Cohesive Units of the US Army", *Journal of Applied Social Psychology*, 18: 503–19.

Myers, David G. (1993), *The Pursuit of Happiness: Who is Happy and Why?* New York: Avon.

——(1999), "Close Relationships and Quality of Life", in Kahneman *et al.* (1999).

Palmer, Linda K. (1995), "Effects of a Walking Program on Attributional Style, Depression, and Self-Esteem in Women", *Perceptual and Motor Skills*, 81: 891–8.

Perkins, H. W. (1991), "Religious Commitment, Yuppie Values, and Well-Being in Post-Collegiate Life", *Review of Religious Research*, 32: 244–51.

Pikus, W., and Tarranikova, W. (1975), "The Frequency of Hypertensive Diseases in Public Transportation", *Terapevischeskii Archives*, 47: 135–7.

Plante, Thomas G., and Rodin, Judith (1990), "Physical Fitness and Enhanced Psychological Health", *Current Psychology: Research and Reviews*, 9 (Spring): 3–24.

Ragland, D., Winkleby, M., Schwalbe, J., Holman, B., Morse, L., Syme, L., and Fisher, J. (1987), "Prevalence of Hypertension in Bus Drivers", *International Journal of Epidemiology*, 16: 208–14.

Rubenstein, Carin (1980), "Vacations", *Psychology Today* (May): 62–76.

Schrank, David, and Lomax, Tim (2002), *The 2002 Urban Mobility Report*, Texas Transportation Institute (June): http://mobility.tamu.edu/.

Sharp, David (1996), "Stress!" *The Buffalo News* (14 July): p. 4M.

Sherrod, D. R. (1974), "Crowding, Perceived Control, and Behavioral Aftereffects", *Journal of Applied Social Psychology*, 4: 171–86.

Spector, P., Dwyer, D., and Jex, S. (1988), "Relation of Job Stressors to Affective, Health, and Performance Outcomes: A Comparison of Multiple Data Sources", *Journal of Applied Psychology*, 73: 11–19.

——and O'Connell, B. (1994), "The Contribution of Personality Traits, Negative Affectivity, Locus of Control and Type A to the Subsequent Reports of Job Stressors and Job Strains", *Journal of Occupational and Organizational Psychology*, 67: 1–11.

Stokols, Daniel, Novaco, Raymond W., Stokols, Jeannette, and Campbell, Joan (1978), "Traffic Congestion, Type A Behavior, and Stress", *Journal of Applied Psychology*, 63: 467–80.

Taylor, P. and Pocock, C. (1972), "Commuter Travel and Sickness: Absence of London Office Workers", *British Journal of Preventive and Social Medicine*, 26: 165–72.

Townsend, Peter (1979), "The Development of Research on Poverty", in *Social Security Research: The Definition and Measurement of Poverty*, Department of Health and Social Research, London: HMSO.

Veenhoven, Ruut (1993), *Happiness in Nations: Subjective Appreciation of Life in 56 Nations*, Rotterdam: Erasmus University.

Wall, T., Jackson, P., Mullarkey, S., and Parker, S. (1996), "The Demands-Control Model of Job Strain: A More Specific Test", *Journal of Occupational and Organizational Psychology*, 69: 153–66.

Warr, Peter (1990), "Decision Latitude, Job Demands, and Employee Well-Being", *Work and Stress*, 4: 285–94.

——(1999), "Well-Being and the Workplace", in Kahneman *et al.* (1999).

Weinstein, N. D. (1982), "Community Noise Problems: Evidence against Adaptation", *Journal of Environmental Psychology*, 2: 82–97.

Weiss, Manfred (1991), "Legislation in the Federal Republic of Germany", in R. Blanpain (ed.), *International Encyclopedia for Labor Law and Industrial Relations*, Boston: Kluwer.

Xie, J., and Johns, G. (1995), "Job Scope and Stress: Can Job Scope Be Too High?" *Academy of Management Journal*, 38: 1288–309.

3

Correspondence of Sentiments: An Explanation of the Pleasure of Social Interaction

Robert Sugden

Everyone knows that, for us human beings, interaction with others is an important source of happiness. Of course, not all interactions are enjoyable; some—bullying and harassment for example—can cause deep distress. Still, it is surely a matter of common experience that, when social interaction takes place in an atmosphere of friendliness and goodwill, it is predominantly pleasurable. The aim of this essay is to examine the mechanisms by which the right kinds of social interaction create pleasure and the wrong kinds create pain.

I will argue that, if we are trying to understand the affective qualities of social interaction, the theoretical strategies of modern economics are not merely unhelpful, but actually encourage us to ask the wrong questions. I will propose an alternative way of thinking about how social interaction impacts on happiness. This proposal derives from Adam Smith's theory of moral sentiments. The idea of using ideas that are almost 250 years old as the starting point for psychological theorizing may seem eccentric, but I hope to persuade the reader that Smith's hypotheses are broadly consistent with current psychological and neurological knowledge. I will end by suggesting that some of the processes that traditionally have supplied opportunities for social interaction are breaking down. These developments make it particularly important for economists and social theorists to understand the relationship between social interaction and happiness.

1. Some Evidence

Most empirical research on happiness relies on people's reports of their overall affective states, averaging across all the episodes of their current lives. For example, a typical self-rating question asks people to respond on a five-point scale to the question: "Taking the good with the bad, how happy and contented are you on the average now, compared with other people?"[1] Recently, however, Daniel Kahneman (2000) has argued for an alternative *moment-based* approach, in which respondents report their affective states separately for each short episode (e.g. "having lunch" or "travelling to work") in an actual day. If the aim is to investigate people's actual hedonic experiences, this approach has many advantages.

The moment-based approach reduces the effects of biases resulting from the limitations of memory and from cognitive dissonance. (To report that you are unhappy with your life as a whole, or even with your marriage as a whole, your job as a whole, or your holiday as a whole, feels like a confession of failure. It is much easier to say that the hour you spent having dinner with your partner was dull, that the hour you spent dealing with the angry customer was stressful, that the hour you spent looking round the museum was boring.) In the context of this essay, it is particularly significant that the moment-based approach reduces the problem of determining directions of causation. Suppose we find (as in fact we do) that there is a positive correlation between being happy with one's life as a whole and having close relationships with other people. Is that evidence that close personal relationships are a source of happiness, or that happy people are more likely to be successful in maintaining close personal relationships? The second interpretation seems entirely credible, given what is known about the heritability of subjective well-being and about the tendency for depression to induce social withdrawal (Lykken and Tellegen 1996). In contrast, the moment-based approach allows us to compare the hedonic qualities of different episodes in the same person's life. If we find a systematic tendency for episodes of social interaction to be perceived as more pleasurable than episodes in which the respondent is on her own, that is evidence that the causation runs from social interaction to happiness.

Kahneman *et al.* (2003) report the results of a moment-based study in which a random sample of 909 employed women from two cities in Texas reconstructed a day in their lives. Each respondent was asked to think about the previous day, to decompose it into episodes and then, for each episode, to say who if anyone she was interacting with and to describe how she felt during it by giving a rating on a 0 to 6 scale for each of a list of feelings. Three of these feelings have positive affective quality ("happy", "warm/friendly", "enjoying myself") and six have negative ("frustrated/annoyed", "depressed/blue", "harassed/pushed around", "angry/hostile", "worried/anxious", "criticized/put down").

The results show a very clear association between positive affect and interaction with others. Averaging across all episodes, positive affect (defined as the average rating for the three positive feelings) was highest in episodes in which respondents were interacting with friends (a score of 4.36), followed by interaction with relatives (4.17), with the respondent's partner (4.11), with her children (4.04), with clients or customers (3.79), with co-workers (3.76), and with her boss (3.52). Episodes in which the respondent was alone generated less positive affect than any form of interaction (3.41). Ratings on the negative affect scales were generally much lower (i.e. respondents did not report much unhappiness). Negative affect (the average rating for the six negative feelings) was also associated with interaction. It was highest for interaction with the boss (1.09), followed by interaction with clients or customers (0.95), with co-workers (0.92), with relatives (0.80), with the partner (0.79), and with children (0.75). Episodes in which the respondent was alone (0.69) generated less negative affect than any form of interaction except interaction with friends (0.67). The implication, then, is that interaction with others generates stronger positive feelings *and* stronger negative feelings than being alone; but positive feelings predominate. This evidence supports the intuition that, for most people, most of the time, interpersonal interaction is a source of pleasure.

It is less clear whether this pleasure is dependent on what would normally be understood as "close" or "deep" relationships, as contrasted with more casual relationships based on friendliness and goodwill. For the women in the study, even interactions with customers were more pleasurable than being alone. Friends, rather than partners or children, were the people with whom interaction was most pleasurable. One possibility is that, for the respondents, relationships with friends were closer than relationships with partners and children. However, an alternative interpretation is that the deepest relationships do not necessarily generate the most pleasurable feelings.[2] You might think of your relationship with your children as fundamental to the meaning of your life, and still find chatting with a casual friend of your own age more pleasurable than trying to keep your young child amused or trying to have a conversation with your teenage son or daughter. The theory I will present in this essay is at least consistent with this second interpretation.

2. How Economics Models Sociality

Can economic theory help us to understand the mechanisms by which interpersonal interaction contributes to happiness? If the official methodological position of economics is taken at face value, it seems that the answer should be an unequivocal "No". What is required is a theory of the social causes of affective states, but such states are not part of the conceptual framework within which economic theory is constructed.

Affective states were expelled from economic theory in a theoretical revolution that took place at the beginning of the twentieth century, led by Vilfredo Pareto (1909). Before that revolution, neoclassical economists grounded their theories on general assumptions about the nature of pleasure and pain. Those assumptions were broadly compatible with what were then recent findings in psychophysics, and were explicitly justified by reference to those findings. The affective states that were most relevant, given the subject matter of economics at that time, were those associated with consumption. Thus, economists were particularly interested in psychological hypotheses about diminishing sensitivity to sensory stimuli and about hedonic adaptation—hypotheses that were thought to explain the main properties of demand functions. However, at least one early neoclassical economist, Francis Edgeworth (1881/1967), suggested the hypothesis that people derive happiness from the happiness of others, and considered its implications for behavior in bargaining problems. Pareto's revolutionary proposal was to eliminate psychological assumptions from economics, and instead to ground economic theory on assumptions about rational choice.[3]

Pareto's position has become the official methodology of economics. As a result, the concept of "utility" has undergone a change of meaning. In nineteenth-century economics, the utility of a commodity was its capacity to induce feelings of pleasure for its consumers. As a kind of shorthand, the feelings themselves also came to be called "utility". After Pareto's approach was adopted, *preference* rather than hedonic experience became the fundamental concept in the theory of choice.[4] "Utility" then came to be used as the name for a function which represents a preference ordering by assigning a number to every possible object of choice. In this usage, to say that one bundle of goods has more utility than another for a given consumer is just another way of saying that the consumer prefers the first to the second. In the terminology adopted by Kahneman and his associates, the nineteenth-century concept is *experienced utility*, while the modern concept is *decision utility* (Kahneman and Varey 1991; Kahneman *et al.* 1997). On a strict interpretation, these two kinds of utility are conceptually independent of one another. That is, there is no necessary connection between the pre-consumption preferences that are registered as decision utility and the post-consumption affective states that are registered as experienced utility. Any connection between the two is a matter of empirical contingency. The empirical question that is at issue here—the question of how far *ex ante* preferences correspond with accurate predictions of *ex post* hedonic experiences—was removed from the domain of economics by Pareto's move.

However, the nineteenth-century meaning of "utility" has never been completely expunged from the language of economics. In practice, economists often find themselves speaking about pleasure and pain. In many circumstances, it is natural to suppose that people's preferences over goods are also preferences over the hedonic experiences that those goods will in fact generate. (If you know that I consistently prefer tea to coffee as a breakfast drink, it's natural for you to infer that I have found the experience of drinking tea more pleasurable.) Conversely, if, as a theorist, you are trying to decide what assumptions about preferences to make in a particular model, or are trying to justify the assumptions you have made, it is tempting to appeal to common experience of pleasure and pain. (Suppose you are building a model in which the consumption of certain goods convey social status. If you are an economist, it is an obvious move to assume that people have a preference for status. Then, if you are called on to defend the credibility of this assumption, it is natural to suggest that it is a matter of common experience that people derive pleasure from status.) Thus, it is often difficult to avoid thinking of utility as representing *both* preference *and* hedonic experience.

This ambivalence in the concept of utility has had unfortunate consequences for economists' understanding of sociality. The problem is this. According to its official methodology, economics is concerned with people's social orientations only in so far as these are revealed in their choices. Thus, in their models, economists have focused on those elements of sociality that can be represented as decision utility. But then, in the interpretation of these models, there has been conceptual slippage from decision utility to experienced utility. There has been an implicit assumption that the affective experience of social interaction is described by the utility functions that are used to explain individual behavior in social settings.

To be more specific, economic models of socially oriented behavior typically assume some form of *altruism*. That is, an altruistic individual is assumed to have a utility function with the property that his utility depends not only on his own consumption of goods, but also (and positively) on other people's consumption or on other people's utility. If the aim is to explain non-selfish behavior while retaining as much as possible of conventional economic theory, assuming altruism is at least a natural first step. In fact, models which try to explain non-selfish behavior in terms of altruism lead to some wildly false implications about voluntary contributions to public goods and charitable activities.[5] In response to these problems, new theories have been proposed in which altruism takes more sophisticated forms. For example, Ernst Fehr and Klaus Schmidt (1999) propose that individuals have preferences for equality in the distribution of resources. In Fehr and Schmidt's model, each individual derives negative utility both from "advantageous inequality" (others being worse off than oneself) and from "disadvantageous inequality" (others being better off than oneself). Matthew Rabin (1993) proposes that altruism (and its opposite, malevolence) is reciprocal. Thus, individuals derive positive utility *both* from conferring benefits on people who are altruistic toward them *and* from conferring disbenefits on people who are malevolent toward them.

A common feature of all these altruism-based theories is that socially oriented attitudes are represented in terms of preferences with respect to other people's consumption, wealth or utility. In such a theory, to have a positive orientation toward another person is to be willing to incur personal costs in order to confer benefits on her. In this essay, I am not concerned with the question of how successful these theories are at explaining behavior in the domains in which they are intended to be applied.[6] However successful they may be in this sense, it would be a mistake to suppose that their assumptions about decision utility give an adequate description of the affective experiences of social interaction. That is, we should not automatically assume that the positive affective qualities of social interaction occur as a result of each person's deriving happiness from the happiness of others.

As an example of the consequences that can follow from this (as I see it) mistaken assumption, I exhibit a well-known paper by Douglas Bernheim and Oded Stark (1988). The paper purports to explain the (supposed) observation that "nice guys finish last": in the game of social life in which people sort themselves into marriages or couples, it is a dis-advantage to be "nice". The crucial assumption is that to be nice is to be altruistic. Bernheim and Stark use a concept of "felicity" which seems to correspond with happiness or experienced utility. Each individual is assumed to derive felicity from his or her own consumption of economic goods. An altruistic person also derives felicity from his or her partner's felicity. It follows easily from these assumptions that people who derive relatively little happiness (or "felicity") from consumption and who are themselves altruistic will prefer to have partners who are not altruistic toward them. Thus, the authors claim, nice guys may be rejected as potential partners because they are too altruistic. They say: "The explanation is quite simple. An altruistic type A [i.e. man] would be depressed by his partner's low level of felicity. Since the type B [i.e. woman] cares about her partner, she would in turn be disturbed by the fact that she has made him unhappy". In other words: if you are unhappy, other people's sympathy with your unhappiness is an additional cause of unhappiness for you.

I suggest that this hypothesis is contrary to the facts of experience. When we are unhappy, we *want* sympathy; other people's sympathy makes us feel less unhappy, not more. We want partners who will sym-pathize with our pleasures *and our pains*. There is surely something deeply wrong with Bernheim and Stark's model of sympathy as altruism. This is a cue for me to introduce Smith's theory of sympathy.

3. Smith's Theory of Mutual Sympathy[7]

Among economists, Smith's *Theory of Moral Sentiments* is best known for the claim made in its opening sentence: "How selfish soever man may be supposed, there are evidently some principles in his nature, which interest him in the fortune of others, and render their happiness necessary to him, though he derives nothing from it except the pleasure of seeing it" (1759/1976: 9). It might seem that Smith is proposing a hypothesis similar to Bernheim and Stark's: that each person derives happiness from the happiness of others. Indeed, this hypothesis is one component of Smith's theory; but there is much more to the theory than this.

Smith proposes a very general psychological tendency for what he calls *fellow-feeling* and what would now be called *emotional contagion*. Fellow-feeling occurs when one person B has a lively consciousness of some affective state experienced by another person A, and when B's consciousness has similar affective qualities to A's state, as perceived by B. Smith gives the example of what he takes to be a normal human response to seeing someone being beaten:

When we see a stroke aimed and just ready to fall upon the leg or arm of another person, we naturally shrink and draw back our own leg or our own arm; and when it does fall, we feel it in some measure, and are hurt by it as well as the sufferer. (pp. 9–10)

Smith's hypothesis is that there is a general tendency for fellow-feeling among human beings with respect to all affective states, whether pleasurable or painful. However, the strength of fellow-feeling is greater, the more closely related the individuals are, and the more vividly the circumstances of the person directly affected are represented to the observer. In most cases, the fellow-feeling of the observer is much weaker than the feeling that is experienced by the person directly affected. Smith also proposes that some kinds of affective states are more effective in inducing fellow-feeling than others. In particular, emotional pains are more conducive to fellow-feeling than physical pains.

Subsequent research in biology, psychology, and neuroscience has confirmed many of Smith's insights about fellow-feeling.[8] There is strong evidence of processes of emotional contagion working below the level of conscious control, and present not only in humans but also in many other social mammals. Emotional contagion seems to be particularly robust in relation to the emotions of fear and distress. Its effect is generally stronger, the greater the familiarity of the "object" (the individual with the directly induced affective state) to the "subject" (the individual in whom a corresponding affective state is induced by emotional contagion), the greater the similarity between object and subject, the more experience the subject has of the state experienced by the object, and the greater the salience of the cues which direct the subject's attention to the object.

Given what we now know (but Smith did not) about the way our brains are organized, the prevalence of emotional contagion should not be surprising. In a system made up of a dense network of inter-connections, we should expect that perceptions that have significant common features will be processed in overlapping ways, and thus have some tendency to activate similar affective states. For example, it is now known that in both monkey and human subjects, seeing the hand of another monkey or human grasping an object with apparent purposefulness does not merely activate in the subject's brain a *visual* representation of that act, as seen from outside. It also activates a *motor* representation of the performance of the act, *as performed by the subject.* In other words, the subject's consciousness of another individual's act of grasping has much of the neural content of *actually grasping.* There is some evidence that affective states are subject to similar mirroring. For example, when sad stories are read to human subjects, neural structures that are known to be involved in emotional processing are activated.

So far, Smith's theory of sympathy may seem to have much the same structure as modern economic theories of altruism, the main difference being that Smith focuses on affective experience rather than preference. Now for the crucial difference. Smith proposes an additional psychological mechanism, which he calls "the pleasure of mutual sympathy". This is the hypothesis that human beings derive pleasure from all forms of fellow-feeling.

Smith introduces this hypothesis by considering the implications of a model in which fellow-feeling is the only mechanism, and feelings are simply "reflected" from person to person. Consider a case in which one person A is in pain. Another person B experiences fellow-feeling for A's pain. By the nature of fellow-feeling, this is painful for B. But then what if A becomes conscious of B's fellow-feeling for her? The same analysis would seem to imply that this consciousness is *painful* for A, since A is conscious of a painful affective state in B. Recall that this is exactly the implication of Bernheim and Stark's theory that offends against common experience. Smith takes the side of common experience:

The sympathy, which my friends express with my joy, might, indeed, give me pleasure by enlivening that joy: but that which they express with my grief could give me none, if it served only to enliven that grief. Sympathy, however, enlivens joy and alleviates grief. It enlivens joy by presenting another source of satisfaction; and it alleviates grief by insinuating into the heart almost the only agreeable sensation which it is at that time capable of receiving. (p. 14)

Smith's hypothesis is that A's consciousness of B's fellow-feeling for her pain is *pleasurable.* The desire for correspondence is particularly strong in relation to emotional states that are perceived as painful. Smith suggests that this is particularly true of resentment:

...we are not half so anxious that our friends should adopt our friendships, as that they should enter into our resentments. We can forgive them though they seem to be little affected by the favours which we may have received, but lose all patience if they seem indifferent about the injuries which may have been done to us...(p. 14)

Notice that, for Smith, the pleasurable consciousness of fellow-feeling is "another source of satisfaction": it is the product of a mechanism that is additional to fellow-feeling. The source of the satisfaction is the *correspondence of sentiments* between the two people: "this correspondence of the sentiments of others with our own appears to be a cause of pleasure, and the want of it a cause of pain, which cannot be accounted for [by a theory of reflected feelings]" (p. 14). Smith seems to be proposing the following general mechanism. Whenever one person A is conscious of a correspondence between his own affective response to some state of affairs and the response of another person B, that consciousness in itself has a positive affective quality for A. Conversely, if A is conscious of dissonance between his response and B's, that consciousness has a negative affective quality for A. Smith thinks that the pleasure derived from the correspondence of sentiments (and the pain induced by dissonance) is sufficiently strong that we are *pleased* when we are able to feel sympathy for the painful feelings of others, and feel *hurt* when we are unable to do so—a hurt that is often expressed as contempt for the other person (pp. 15–16).[9]

The pleasures of mutual fellow-feeling can be enjoyed in any joint activity between people whose sentiments are suitably aligned. Smith gives an example of one person reading aloud to another, which will strike a chord with many parents:

When we have read a book or poem so often that we can no longer find any amusement in reading it by ourselves, we can still take pleasure in reading it to a companion. To him it has all the graces of novelty; we enter into the surprise and admiration which it naturally excites in him, but which it is no longer capable of exciting in us; we consider all the ideas which it presents rather in the light in which they appear to him, than in that in which they appear to ourselves, and we are amused by sympathy with his amusement which thus enlivens our own. On the contrary, we should be vexed if he did not seem to be entertained with it, and we could no longer take any pleasure in reading it to him. (p. 14)

For Smith, fellow-feeling is closely linked to approval and disapproval. His first formulation of this link is the claim that we approve of other people's sentiments just to the extent that we "go along with" them:

When the original passions of the person principally concerned are in perfect concord with the sympathetic emotions of the spectator, they necessarily appear to this last just and proper, and suitable to their objects...To approve of the passions of another, therefore, as suitable to their objects, is the same thing as to observe that we entirely sympathize with them. (p. 16)

He goes on to qualify this formulation by allowing that we can approve or disapprove of another person's sentiments by recognizing that we are *capable of* going along with them, even if, because of the particular circumstances of the case, we do not actually do so; this is "conditional sympathy" (pp. 17–18). Still, the fundamental idea is that approval expresses a correspondence of affective states between the approver and the approved, while disapproval expresses dissonance. This is the core hypothesis of Smith's theory of moral sentiments. This theory represents the formation of morality as a social process in which the sentiments of different individuals are brought into alignment. The force which brings about this alignment is the human desire for the correspondence of sentiments.

For my present purposes, this analysis of approval is significant because it suggests that the pleasure induced by correspondences of affective states has a normative aspect. When we find that our sentiments are shared by others, we perceive that correspondence as conferring approval on—as validating—our own sentiments. Smith's example of resentment illustrates this mechanism. Suppose A resents some action of B's. A's perception that C shares this resentment makes it easier for A to feel justified in his hostility toward B. Through this mechanism, correspondences of sentiment can support feelings of self-worth. An important component of self-worth is the perception that one's life is made up of worthwhile projects—of things that are worth doing. If Smith's theory is correct, social interaction between people who are pursuing similar projects is likely to enhance each person's sense that her own projects are worthwhile.

The correspondence-of-sentiments mechanism postulated by Smith does not seem to be central to modern psychological theories of sympathy and empathy. Nevertheless, I think the modern literature reveals evidence that there is such a mechanism.

In particular, there is strong evidence, not only for human adults but also for human infants and for some non-human social mammals (including apes, monkeys, and rats), that individuals not only are distressed by the distress of another individual of the same species, but also will sometimes perform acts which, at some cost to themselves, help the other by relieving its distress. Some theorists interpret this as evidence of "genuine" empathy (the actor is seeing the world from the perspective of the person in distress); others interpret it as an aversive response to emotional contagion (the actor is trying to "switch off" the painful feelings induced by contagion); still others deny the validity of this distinction. For my purposes, what is most interesting is that acts of comforting are treated as paradigm cases of "helping". For example, one of the main forms of evidence of helping behavior in human infants concerns cases in which the infant subject comforts an object (a child, an adult, a pet, or a toy that is treated as a living thing) which is in apparent distress. Such comforting often involves simple gestures (hugging, stroking hurt places) which express sympathy. Another characteristic form is for the subject to offer one of her own possessions to the object. Often this possession is one which the subject uses to comfort herself (a favourite doll, a comfort blanket) and which, to her, has the character of a sympathetic living thing (Zahn-Waxler *et al.* 1992).

Comforting behavior is not restricted to human beings. In chimpanzee societies, comforting is one of the most universal forms of interaction, taking forms that are remarkably similar to comforting among humans. For example, if one chimpanzee has been injured in a fight, other chimpanzees hug, pat, and groom it. Another parallel between the two species is that when a chimpanzee is distressed it *demands* comforting from others—by pouting, whimpering, or if all else fails, throwing a temper tantrum (de Waal 1996: 53–62). Similar behavior patterns are well known in young children; any self-aware adult will recognize that the urge to solicit comforting in distress does not disappear with age, even if we learn to suppress its most blatant expressions.

This evidence suggests that for human beings, and for at least some other social mammals, there is a deep-rooted desire to receive comfort when distressed, and an equally deep-rooted motivation to engage in comforting behavior in response to other individuals' distress. This in turn suggests that both sides of the comforting activity have positive affective qualities.

But what *is* comforting behavior? In many of its characteristic forms, the benefit to the object seems to be entirely affective: there is no "objective" help. If there is a problem in explaining why individuals comfort others who are in distress, there is just as much a problem in explaining why those who are in distress want to be comforted. Comforting behavior, I suggest, typically has two affective components. Most obviously, it is a means by which the subject expresses an affective state of her own which in some way reflects the distress of the object: that is, it is a vehicle for the expression of fellow-feeling. But at the same time, this expression *calms* the object's more direct and intense emotions. The connection between these two components is not straightforward: for example, when the object experiences fear, the calming effect of comforting behavior comes through the subject's expression of reassurance rather than of her own fear. But even when (as in the case of fear and reassurance) the affective state expressed by the subject is not an exact replica of that experienced by the object, fellow-feeling still seems to be implicated in calming: it is an essential part of the comforting that the subject is expressing fellow-feeling for the object's distress. Thus, I suggest, the core ingredient of comforting behavior is a correspondence of affective states between subject and object. The fact that humans and chimpanzees spontaneously engage in and solicit such behavior is strongly suggestive of a fundamental desire for the correspondence of sentiments.[10]

4. Correspondence of Sentiments as an Element of Happiness

Smith's correspondence-of-sentiments mechanism may help to explain the affective qualities of social interaction. If Smith's hypothesis is right, social interaction tends to generate happiness when it provides an environment in which participants become aware of shared affective states, or (in the longer term) when it provides a medium for the cultivation of such states.

Notice that this is a hypothesis about causal relationships *between affective states*. It tells us how, given certain configurations of affective states within a group of people, further affective states are induced. As such, it lies well outside the domain of economics, as that has usually been understood. Even Pareto's neoclassical predecessors were interested in pleasure and pain as determinants of consumption, and so focused on causal relationships linking affective states to behavior. In contrast, Smith's theory is not directly concerned with behavior at all. It is for this reason, I think, that so many modern economists have overlooked the role played by the correspondence-of-sentiments mechanism in the *Theory of Moral Sentiments*. For the same reason, this mechanism cannot easily be represented in the theoretical framework of modern economics. But if we want to investigate the determinants of human happiness, we need to take account of interactions between affective states.

As a first indication of the value of Smith's approach, consider what is wrong with Bernheim and Stark's altruism-based theory of how people sort themselves into couples. According to that theory, the essential ingredients to make a happy couple are two separately happy individuals who take pleasure in each other's happiness. Each person's happiness is then augmented by sympathetic thoughts about the happiness of the other. Conversely, two separately unhappy but mutually sympathetic individuals constitute an unhappy couple in which each person's unhappiness is augmented by sympathetic thoughts about the unhappiness of the other. If one person is happy and the other is unhappy, their being a mutually sympathetic couple is a mechanism by which the unhappy partner is able to siphon off some of the happiness of the other. There is no sense that *facing life together*, sharing the pains as well as the pleasures, is part of the happiness of being a couple.

As a starting point for an alternative model of happiness in couples, think of the story which is familiar to game theorists as the Battle of the Sexes game. Alice and Bill have a free evening. They can go to the cinema together; or they can go to the football match together; or one can go to one and one to the other. Alice prefers films to football, Bill prefers football to films, but each prefers being with the other at the less preferred entertainment to being alone at the more preferred one. The story serves its purpose because this kind of choice problem is common in everyday life, and because the assumptions that it makes about preferences accord with common experience. But if Alice and Bill's feelings for one another were like those of Bernheim and Stark's couples, would the problem arise? If all they felt for one another was altruism, the optimal solution would be for Alice to go to the film and Bill to the football. Alice would get happiness from watching the film; she would get more happiness from knowing that Bill was getting happiness from the football; she would get yet more happiness from knowing that Bill was getting happiness from knowing that she was getting happiness from the film; and so on. And similarly for Bill. How could either of them be made happier overall by one of them not going to his or her preferred entertainment? The common-sense answer is that Alice and Bill get happiness *from going together* to wherever they go, and that this source of happiness is somehow connected with their positive feelings for one another. But this idea cannot be expressed in a model in which each person's positive feeling for the other takes the form of altruism.

I suggest that Smith's account of reading aloud provides the model we need. The point of this example is that the two people derive pleasure from their consciousness of shared emotional responses (admiration, surprise, amusement) to a common stimulus (the words of the book). The closer the correspondence between the sentiments of the people involved, and the more vivid their mutual consciousness of this correspondence, the greater the tendency for pleasure to be induced. If I read *Treasure Island* to my young son, I can *share* his feelings of thrill and suspense: we are feeling them *together*. If someone else reads it to him while I read something completely different, I can merely be pleased that he is enjoying the book. Similarly, if Alice and Bill are at the football match together, and if their team's striker moves into a goal-scoring position, they can share one another's excitement. If Alice is at the cinema and Bill is at the match, each can be pleased in a general way about the other's enjoyment, but the vividness and specificity of shared feelings is lost.

If Smith is right, it is not essential that the sentiments that Alice and Bill share are pleasurable in themselves. What matters is that they are *shared*. Suppose that they go to the match together. It is pouring down with rain and they get soaked walking to the ground; the match is dull; their team lose. Although the affective qualities of their first-order feelings (being cold, being wet, being bored, being disappointed) are negative, the correspondence of these feelings between the two people is pleasurable for each of them—or, at least, it makes the feelings less painful than they would have been if experienced alone.

So Smith's theory of the correspondence of sentiments suggests a recipe for happiness in interpersonal relations that is very different from Bernheim and Stark's. What is primarily required for a happy couple is that the partners have similar repertoires of affective responses to the stimuli that they are likely to confront together. Meeting this requirement is partly a matter of initial similarities of tastes and disposition. But, in choosing what to do in their life together, given their tastes and dispositions, two partners can make it more or less likely that the stimuli they confront will induce correspondences of sentiment. To some degree, too, corresponding tastes, dispositions, and emotional cues can be cultivated; and they can evolve out of common activities, common objectives, and common experiences.

Of course, it also matters what general feelings people have for one another. The closer the emotional relationship between two people, the stronger the fellow-feeling that each has for the affective states of the other, and so the more pleasure they can derive from correspondences of sentiment. This is particularly important for cases in which correspondences of sentiment depend on sympathy rather than (as in the case of the book or the football match) on parallel experiences. For example, suppose Alice suffers distress from some cause (say, an illness) that does not directly impact on Bill. Then it is only through sympathetic fellow-feeling that Bill can come to experience a reflection of Alice's distress; and it is only if Bill *does* experience this that there is a correspondence of sentiment.

However, it is a recurring theme in Smith's argument that the human capacity for sympathetic fellow-feeling, even between intimate friends and close relatives, is limited.[11] He stresses the potential for dissonance between the intense feelings of a person who is directly affected by a painful stimulus and the weak feelings of a sympathetic onlooker. For example, he suggests that "our sorrow at a funeral generally amounts to no more than an affected gravity" (p. 47). Or:

[W]hen we condole with our friends in their afflictions, how little do we feel, in comparison of what they feel? We sit down by them, we look at them, and while they relate to us the circumstances of their misfortune, we listen to them with gravity and attention. But while their narration is every moment interrupted by those natural bursts of passion which often seem almost to choak them in the midst of it; how far are the languid emotions of our hearts from keeping time to the transports of theirs? We may be sensible, at the same time, that their passion is natural, and no greater than what we ourselves might feel upon the like occasion. We may even inwardly reproach ourselves with our own want of sensibility, and perhaps, on that account, work ourselves up into an artificial sympathy, which, however, when it is raised, is always the slightest and most transitory imaginable; and generally, as soon as we have left the room, vanishes, and is gone for ever. (p. 47)

This form of affective dissonance is crucial for Smith's moral theory. For Smith, a disposition to comport oneself in ways that are conducive to correspondences of sentiment is one of the principal human virtues. Our natural endowment of this virtue is limited, but (Smith thinks) we should strive to cultivate it. In part, this virtue consists in a propensity, as an onlooker, to sympathize with other people's pleasures and pains. But— and Smith gives particular emphasis to this—it also consists in a propensity, as the person directly affected by a stimulus, to "bring down our passion to that pitch, which the particular company we are in may be expected to go along with" (p. 23). It is because Smith thinks human sympathy is weak, while dissonances of sentiment are painful, that "self-command"—that is, emotional self-control—is such an important virtue in his account of the moral sentiments.

Some evidence that Smith is giving us a realistic account of human psychology (rather than, as a harsh critic might allege, displaying the limitations of his own sensibility) can be found in modern studies of hedonic adaptation.[12] One general finding of these studies is that, when an individual suffers a major setback in life—such as divorce, the death of a spouse, or the loss of a limb—hedonic adaptation is facilitated by social contact *with others who have had similar experiences.* Conversely, people who have suffered such setbacks commonly perceive the attentions of friends and relatives who have not had similar experiences as unhelpful and intolerant. For example, those friends and relatives are perceived as underestimating how long grief lasts, and as expecting the widowed and divorced to be thinking about remarriage before they have had time to come to terms with their sense of loss. It seems that correspondence of sentiment is difficult to achieve through sympathy alone, even among people who are emotionally close. It is more easily achieved between people who, although perhaps less intimately related, have similar first-order experiences. In other words, what matters is not so much person-to-person sympathy, one person giving the sympathy and the other receiving it, as consciousness of common emotional responses to common stimuli.[13]

A similar phenomenon is reported in many memoirs of World War I. Men who lived through the trench warfare of the western front report horrific experiences that have been seared into their memories; but they also report intensely positive feelings of comradeship with their fellow-soldiers. A common theme in these memoirs is the difficulty that soldiers found, when on leave, in resuming relationships with lovers, friends, and relatives who had not shared their experiences—despite genuine attempts at sympathy on both sides. It seems that, in trying to cope with the trauma of the war, soldiers drew on the positive affective qualities of correspondences of predominantly painful sentiments.

These examples highlight the distinction between *caring about* another person and *finding pleasure in their company*. To care about someone is to want that person to have a happy and successful life, and to be willing to incur personal costs to help bring this about. This is the attitude to others that is represented in theories of altruism. In contrast, Smith's correspondence-of-sentiments mechanism is primarily concerned with people's finding pleasure in one another's company. If, as Smith's analysis seems to imply, correspondences of sentiment are most reliably generated by parallel first-order experiences, we should not expect that the interactions we find most pleasurable are always with the people we most care about. For example, it seems clear that feelings of caring and altruism are particularly strong on the part of parents toward their children. This hypothesis has theoretical and empirical support from evolutionary biology, from anthropology, and from the evidence of interpersonal transfers of resources in modern societies. It is confirmed in the literature of all cultures, and in everyday experience. Yet, because of the differences of age and lifetime experience in the parent–child relationship, the degree of correspondence of affective responses to common experiences may be less than in friend–friend relationships.

This may help to explain why the mothers in Kahneman *et al.*'s study perceived their interactions with their children as less pleasurable than their interactions with their friends.

In reaching such conclusions, it is important to recognize the limitations of the moment-based approach to the measurement of happiness. That approach is designed to investigate the affective qualities of individual episodes of a person's life. In contrast, many important elements of human happiness depend on our perceiving our lives as made up of continuing projects. We derive subjective well-being from an overall sense that our lives are going well for us, that we are achieving things that we perceive as worth achieving. Such a sense of well-being gives our lives an affective tone which cannot easily be decomposed into individual episodes of hedonic experience. Thus, the satisfaction that a person derives from doing well in her career may not be separable into pleasurable episodes at work; the satisfaction that she derives from guiding her children toward adulthood may not be separable into pleasurable episodes of child care.

I do not want to play down the importance for happiness of deep personal relationships and long-term emotional commitments. Rather, my aim is to identify and to understand one component of episodic happiness: the pleasurable feelings generated by correspondences of sentiment. My suggestion is that this particular component of happiness is less dependent on continuing projects and commitments than one might think. Indeed, for reasons I explained in Section 3, the direction of causation may sometimes go the other way. Episodic correspondences of sentiment may underpin our more long-term sources of happiness by helping us to maintain the sense that our projects and commitments are worthwhile. For example, think of the importance of social contacts in maintaining the well-being and self-esteem of parents of young children. However much one may have looked forward to the event, having a child has life-changing implications that are not altogether dissimilar to the effects of divorce or widowhood or the loss of a limb. It is surely a matter of common experience that, just as the widowed look to the widowed for emotional support, so parents of young children look to (current or past) parents of young children. Interactions among parents help to sustain a shared sense that the sacrifices of parenthood are worthwhile. It seems that even our most fundamental emotional commitments can be supported by correspondences of sentiment that are generated in recurrent episodes of social interaction.

5. Taking Social Interaction for Granted

I have argued that everyday episodes of social interaction are an important source of human happiness. This conclusion is significant when set against the evidence that long-term social and economic trends are systematically eroding many of the situations in which such episodes have traditionally occurred.[14]

Historically, many forms of social interaction have been by-products of economic activities that have had other professed objectives. Social interaction occurs among workers, as a by-product of team-based productive activities. It occurs among consumers when groups of individuals come together to consume indivisible goods (e.g. when the members of a household watch a television program together). It occurs between producers and consumers when services are delivered on a person-to-person basis (e.g. between nurse and patient, or between shopkeeper and customer). It occurs in voluntary associations when individuals combine to produce public goods (e.g. in the branch meetings of trade unions or among volunteers working on environmental projects). In addition, interaction in voluntary associations has often provided participants with incidental benefits that go beyond the intrinsic pleasures of sociality. For example, participation in civic society has been a means of gaining information about the trustworthiness of potential trading partners and of building networks for cooperation and the exchange of favours (think of Adam Smith's famous remark about how often social interactions among people of the same trade end in contrivances to raise prices).

However, many current trends seem to work against activities which supply social interaction as a by-product. Collective consumption activities are being replaced by individualized ones. (Think of the effect of increasing car ownership on the amount of social interaction associated with travel, or of the effect of increasing ownership of personal audio equipment on the amount of social interaction associated with consumption of music.) Developments in service delivery are displacing person-to-person contacts. (Think of the decline of local grocery shops and their replacement by large supermarkets, or the transition from high-street banking to telephone and Internet banking, or—a recent development in the British National Health Service—the supply of medical advice through telephone call centres.) Charities, pressure groups, and political parties are increasingly shifting their organizational structure from networks of local activists to centralized professional staffs raising funds through mailshots. The value of civic associations as channels for local information transmission and the exchange of favors has been undermined by the increasing scale of firms and by increasing integration of markets. (Think of how assessments of creditworthiness are now made by accessing large databases rather than through the judgments of local bank managers, or of how the growth of national distribution networks has reduced the discretion of local retail managers to make contracts with people they know personally.)

The preceding paragraph may read like a random list of exhibits, but the underlying tendencies are systematic. They are the results of increasing disposable income, increasing market integration, and developments in information technology—perhaps supplemented by an increasing taste for privacy. What we are seeing is the progressive unbundling of what formerly were joint products. It would be complacent to think that we can continue to rely on the fortunate coincidence of joint products for the supply of opportunities for social interaction.

In thinking about these trends, it may be interesting to consider two analogues in current public debate.[15] The first is the changing relationship between the farming industry and environmental conservation. In Britain until quite recently, the main policy of environmental conservation has been the restriction of industrial and housing development in rural areas; even the British national parks are essentially areas of privately owned land that are subject to particularly strict land-use controls. The implicit assumption behind this policy has been that landscape and wildlife conservation are by-products of the farming industry, and hence that conservation can be secured by maintaining agricultural land use.[16] It is only in the last few years that public policy has begun to take serious account of the conflicts between intensive agriculture and conservation. Now policies are being introduced which pay farmers directly for their participation in specific conservation programmes. In parallel, there has been growth in nature reserves managed by environmental charities. These developments are part of a general trend toward the unbundling of agricultural production and conservation, and toward seeing conservation as a matter of deliberate planning rather than merely of letting nature take its course.

The second analogy is the rising trend in obesity, which has recently begun to register in public consciousness. Among the causes of this trend is the decreasing role of physical exercise in work, travel, and recreation as a result of increasing income, improvements in technology, and perhaps also changes in tastes. To put this another way, physical fitness was formerly a by-product of activities which were carried out with other ends in mind. Increasingly, these joint products are being unbundled. Maintaining one's fitness is becoming something that can be achieved only by deliberate intention. While some people become overweight and put their health at risk, others have come to see exercise as a good to be bought on the market, and are willing to pay for it—as can be seen in the growth of private fitness centres.

These examples show the potential instability of social practices which supply valuable goods as by-products. They also show how what formerly were thought of as by-products—or were enjoyed without being consciously thought about at all—can come to be seen as distinct goods for which a price has to be paid. This mental transition may not be easy to make, because it requires us to take an instrumental attitude toward what we have been used to treating as a natural feature of the world or of our lives. Thus, some farmers find it demeaning to be paid to conserve the landscape rather than to grow crops or raise animals. Some old-fashioned people (of whom I am one) feel self-conscious about the deliberate pursuit of fitness, and try to camouflage their exercise regimes within other activities. Still, perceptions can and do change.

I suggest that the positive affective quality of social interaction is a traditional by-product which may be reaching the stage at which this transition has to be made. As the cases of environmental conservation and physical fitness illustrate, the first stage in such a transition is the recognition that something we previously have taken for granted is a definite good, that it has a specific value for us, and that its supply is not guaranteed, but is governed by particular mechanisms which need to be understood. Adam Smith's analysis of the correspondence of sentiments provides a possible starting point for understanding why certain forms of social interactions are valuable and how this value is generated.

Notes

In developing the ideas presented in this essay, I have benefited from discussions with Luigino Bruni, Jean Decety, Benedetto Gui, Shaun Hargreaves Heap, Daniel Kahneman, Stephanie Preston, Giacomo Rizzolatti, and Jung-Sic Yang.

1. This question was used in a study of the degree of correlation between the self-reported happiness of twins (Lykken and Tellegen 1996).
2. A third possibility is that this is a statistical artefact. It might be that the activities which respondents liked most were disproportionately carried out in the presence of friends, while duller activities tended to be carried out in the presence of partners and children. The activities which rated highest were (in this

order) "intimate relations", "socializing", and "relaxing", well ahead of "shopping", "preparing food", "taking care of my children", and "housework".

3. Bruni and Sugden (2004) review the arguments that were advanced for and against Pareto's proposal to remove affective states from economics, and compare these with some current controversies about the status of behavioural economics.

4. In the "revealed preference" variant of choice theory, the primitive concept is choice, and preference is interpreted as a relation that is revealed in choices. On my understanding of modern economics, the revealed-preference interpretation of choice theory is generally seen as viable but non-standard.

5. These problems in the simple theory of altruism (and in the formally equivalent standard theory of voluntary contributions to public goods) are explained in Sugden (1982, 1985).

6. My own view is that many forms of socially oriented behavior are better explained by theories in which each individual is motivated to do his part in mutually beneficial collective actions, conditional on the expectation that sufficient others will do their parts too. See Sugden (1984, 1993). That economists are so inclined to interpret non-selfish behaviour as altruism rather than cooperation reflects the dominance of the utilitarian tradition in the discipline.

7. This section draws on my discussions of Smith's theory in Sugden (2002, 2004).

8. The following discussion draws on Preston and de Waal's (2002) comprehensive survey of research on empathy. The discussion of mirror systems draws on Rizzolatti *et al.* (2001) and Chaminade and Decety (2003).

9. This is not quite the same thing as saying that the acts by which we express sympathy are, on balance, pleasurable. What is pleasurable is *finding oneself feeling sympathy* for the other. Many well-motivated acts of sympathy take place against a background of dissonance of affective states. For example, visiting his terminally ill friend A, B may be painfully conscious of the dissonance between the intensity of A's distress and the weakness of his own emotional response. B's act may be an appropriate expression of friendship and yet, because of this dissonance, painful.

10. De Waal (1996) interprets chimpanzee behavior as revealing a correspondence-of-sentiments mechanism, and offers some suggestions about the biological functions of this mechanism. As de Waal recognizes, some of the ideas he is proposing are present in Smith's *Theory of Moral Sentiments*.

11. Smith allows that "parental tenderness" is an exception to this general rule. He suggests that nature has made parental sympathy uniquely strong because "the continuance and propagation of the species" depend on it (p. 142).

12. The evidence summarized in this paragraph is reviewed by Frederick and Loewenstein (1999).

13. While Smith would have understood the psychological mechanisms involved in this kind of mutual emotional support, he would not have approved of it as

a strategy for coping with distress. He stresses the importance of interaction with people in general—with strangers and casual acquaintances rather than with intimate friends—as a method of regaining "composure" and "tranquility" after emotional shocks (pp. 23, 146–7). Smith's emphasis on self-command and equability of temper expresses an eighteenth-century sensibility.

14. Putnam (2000) marshals a large body of evidence pointing to a long-run decline in social interaction in the United States, beginning in the 1960s. For a critical review of Putnam's argument, see Durlauf (2002). While I agree with many of Durlauf's criticisms of the looseness of Putnam's analysis, I also agree with his conclusions that Putnam *has* discovered a genuine downward trend in participation in voluntary organizations, and that "something 'feels' correct" about Putnam's main thesis. Gui and Sugden (2004) discuss some of the implications of this thesis for economics.

15. I have deliberately chosen one example of a by-product which is clearly public (environmental conservation) and one which, on the face of it, is private (physical fitness). Gui (2000) offers reasons for thinking that "relational goods" (a class which includes the affective components of interpersonal interactions) are public. Hargreaves Heap (2002) suggests that "conversational resources" are public goods. A book, film, television program, or sporting event is a conversational resource in a population if individuals' separate exposure to this common stimulus facilitates social interaction between them. Translating into the theoretical framework I am using, conversational resources are shared cues for corresponding affective responses. The issue of how far social interaction is a public good is orthogonal to the topic of this essay.

16. The landscape of the British countryside is predominantly a human creation; the original vegetation of ancient woodland was almost completely lost centuries ago. Thus, the idea that agriculture and conservation can coexist has been more credible in Britain than in countries such as Australia, the United States, and Canada, where the most highly prized landscape and wildlife are found in wilderness areas.

References

Bernheim, R. Douglas, and Stark, Oded (1988), "Altruism within the Family Reconsidered: Do Nice Guys Finish Last?", *American Economic Review*, 78: 1034–45.

Bruni, Luigino, and Sugden, Robert (2004), "The Road Not Taken: Two Debates about the Role of Psychology in Economics", Unpublished paper, University of East Anglia.

Chaminade, T., and Decety, Jean (2003), "Neural Correlates of Feeling Sympathy", *Neuropsychologia*, 41: 127–38.

de Waal, Frans (1996), *Good Natured: The Origins of Right and Wrong in Humans and Other Animals*, Cambridge, Mass.: Harvard University Press.

Durlauf, Steven N. (2002), "Bowling Alone: A Review Essay", *Journal of Economic Behavior and Organization*, 47: 259–73.

Edgeworth, Francis (1881/1967), *Mathematical Psychics*, New York: Kelley.

Fehr, Ernst, and Schmidt, Klaus (1999), "A Theory of Fairness, Competition and Cooperation", *Quarterly Journal of Economics*, 114: 817–68.

Frederick, Shane, and Loewenstein, George (1999), "Hedonic Adaptation", in Daniel Kahneman, Edward Diener, and Norbert Schwarz (eds.), *Well-Being: The Foundations of Hedonic Psychology*, New York: Russell Sage Foundation.

Gui, Benedetto (2000), "Beyond Transactions: On the Interpersonal Dimension of Economic Reality", *Annals of Public and Cooperative Economics*, 71: 139–69.

——and Sugden, Robert (2005), "Why Interpersonal Relations Matter for Economics", Forthcoming in Gui and Sugden (eds.), *Economics and Social Interaction*, Cambridge: Cambridge University Press.

Hargreaves Heap, Shaun (2002), " 'Everybody is Talking About It': Intersubjectivity and the Television Industry", in Edward Fullbrook (ed.), *Intersubjectivity in Economics*, London: Routledge.

Kahneman, Daniel (2000), "Experienced Utility and Objective Happiness: A Moment-Based Approach", in Amos Tversky and Daniel Kahneman (eds.), *Choices, Values, and Frames*, Cambridge: Cambridge University Press.

——Kreuger, Alan, Schkade, David, Schwarz, Norbert, and Stone, Arthur (2003), "A Survey Method for Characterizing Daily Life Experience: The Day Reconstruction Method (DRM)", Unpublished Paper.

——and Varey, Carol (1991), "Notes on the Psychology of Utility", in Jon Elster and John Roemer (eds.), *Interpersonal Comparisons of Well-Being*, Cambridge: Cambridge University Press, 127–63.

——Wakker, Peter, and Sarin, Rakesh (1997), "Back to Bentham? Explorations of experienced utility", *Quarterly Journal of Economics*, 112: 375–405.

Lykken, David, and Tellegen, Auke (1996), "Happiness is a Stochastic Phenomenon", *Psychological Science*, 7: 246–53.

Pareto, Vilfredo (1909), *Manual d'economie politique*, Geneva: Librairie Droz. English translation published as *Manual of Political Economy*, New York: Kelley, 1971.

Preston, Stephanie D., and de Waal, Frans B.M. (2002), "Empathy: Its Ultimate and Proximate Bases", *Behavioral and Brain Sciences*, 25: 1–71.

Putnam, Robert (2000), *Bowling Alone: The Collapse and Revival of American Community*, New York: Simon & Schuster.

Rabin, Matthew (1993), "Incorporating Fairness into Game Theory and Economics", *American Economic Review*, 83: 1281–302.

Rizzolatti, Giacomo, Fogassi, Leonardo, and Gallese, Vittorio (2001), "Neurophysiological Mechanisms underlying Action Understanding and Imitation", *Nature Reviews: Neuroscience*, 2: 661–70.

Smith, Adam (1759/1976), *The Theory of Moral Sentiments*, Oxford: Oxford University Press.

Sugden, Robert (1982), "On the Economics of Philanthropy", *Economic Journal*, 92: 341–50.

—— (1984), "Reciprocity: The Supply of Public Goods through Voluntary Contributions", *Economic Journal*, 94: 772–87.

—— (1985), "Consistent Conjectures and the Voluntary Provision of Public Goods: Why the Conventional Theory does Not Work", *Journal of Public Economics*, 27: 117–24.

—— (1993), "Thinking as a Team: Towards an Explanation of Non-selfish Behavior", *Social Philosophy and Policy*, 10: 69–89.

—— (2002), "Beyond Sympathy and Empathy: Adam Smith's Concept of Fellow-Feeling", *Economics and Philosophy*, 18: 63–87.

—— (2004), "Fellow Feeling", Forthcoming in Robert Sugden and Benedetto Gui (eds.), *Economics and Social Interaction*, Cambridge: Cambridge University Press.

Zahn-Waxler, C., Radke-Yarrow, M., Wagner, E., and Chapman, M. (1992), "Development of Concern for Others", *Developmental Psychology*, 28: 126–36.

4

Testing Theories of Happiness

Bruno S. Frey and Alois Stutzer

1. Introduction

Happiness research in economics takes reported subjective well-being as a proxy measure for utility. This allows for the testing of "old hypotheses" in a new way. Present research deals, for example, with the relationship between happiness and income, unemployment, inflation, inequality, and democratic institutions. This research has put forward many interesting findings. However, future research on subjective well-being has to be further developed in order to provide additional valuable insights. We envisage two main directions for fruitful research.

First, happiness research offers new ways of testing the basic assumptions of the economic approach and of approaching a new understanding of utility in economics. Based on data on reported subjective well-being, it is possible to address fundamental questions like, for example, "Do people consciously maximize their utility?" or "Can people successfully predict their future utility/preferences?" These questions are closely related to the research program of scientists in behavioral economics.

Second, happiness research provides a new way of discriminating between models that predict the same patterns in behavior but predict differences in experienced utility. This complementary evidence thus helps us to reject particular models and their policy recommendations. Models may come from areas as different as the micro-foundations of macroeconomics (e.g. on voluntary versus involuntary unemployment) and addiction (rational addiction versus limited self-control).

We present our own application to both directions of research. In an initial study, we analyze the role of income aspirations in the notion of relative utility. We present new evidence for the effect of income aspirations on people's satisfaction with life in longitudinal data for Germany. A second application uses data on subjective well-being to test Becker's model of household production and the division of labor in marriage compared to sociological theories of marriage.

The remainder of the chapter is structured as follows: in the next section, we briefly describe the current state of happiness research in economics. In Section 3, we outline two directions for future research. Both directions are illustrated with examples and extended applications in Section 4. Section 5 offers some concluding remarks.

2. The Current State of Happiness Research in Economics

Research on happiness has been one of the most stimulating new developments in economics in recent years. It attracts economists of all ages and some findings have already attracted the attention of a broader audience in government administrations, as well as among the public. Happiness research provides the tools and measures to test "old hypotheses" in a new way. The result is a substantial amount of new and insightful complementary evidence. We do not want to summarize these findings here (for overviews see Easterlin 2002; Frey and Stutzer 2002*a*, 2002*b*; Oswald 1997). However, we sketch them briefly as a contrast with what we expect to be successful research in the future.

In a nutshell, current research is guided by the question: how does x affect happiness? X can be any factor supposed to affect human happiness, examples being income, inflation, or unemployment. We plot trends, measure simple correlations, and estimate microeconometric happiness functions. Sometimes our work is more data and measurement driven than theory based. Some of our findings come from explorative analyses and *ex post* rationalizations of their results.[1]

We want to devalue neither research efforts in this direction nor the empirical findings that—in our view—are quite remarkable. However, we think that research on happiness can make an even bigger impact on modern economics.

3. Future Research on Subjective Well-Being

Empirical research on happiness in economics has a short history. The marginal benefits of the study of subjective well-being are still very high in almost every area where questions have so far been addressed.

117

Further analyses of survey data on subjective well-being will be worth-while, for example, (i) to study the relationship between discrimination of women in the labor market and their life satisfaction (e.g. Clark 1997), (ii) to understand the interdependencies in well-being at the family level (Winkelmann 2002), (iii) to test how various indicators of the quality of life, like crime, environmental quality, or commuting are related to individual well-being (e.g. Michalos and Zumbo 2000), or (iv) to analyze whether social capital has positive external effects on people's well-being (e.g. Helliwell 2003). Special efforts will be made to establish causality.

Promising future research can also be expected on how happiness affects individual behavior (for a theoretical investigation, see e.g. Hermalin and Isen 1999). People's level of subjective well-being may influence many important economic decisions, like consumption activities, work behavior, risk taking in investment or even political engagement and voting behavior.

The future will, of course, bring improvements in the methods that are applied to research on happiness and economics (see e.g. the interesting contribution by van Praag in this volume). However, this progress sometimes tends to stifle innovation and the relevance of research questions.

There is much room, on the other hand, for improvements in the quality and understanding of happiness measures. In this area, scientists around Daniel Kahneman are currently coming up with valuable new insights (see e.g. Kahneman *et al.* 2004). One question is whether people's instantaneous level of happiness can be captured by self-reported measures of well-being or whether there is a difference between people's hedonic experiences and their explicit reflective appraisals of experiences in reported subjective well-being (e.g. Schooler *et al.* 2003). People are sometimes fully engaged in challenging activities and thereby experience great pleasure (or flow in the sense of Csikszentmihalyi 1997). By the very nature of this situation, people will never assess and report their well-being when in such a state and thus set boundaries for the measurement of instant utility. New insights will be provided when we know more about correlations between reported subjective well-being and physiological measures of well-being. Correlations over time and across people would be interesting, whereby people with different frames of reference could be studied. Time-series for physiological measures would be particularly interesting in order to assess whether people have changed their reference standards in self-reported happiness over time. Given the possible shortcomings of happiness measures today, one should at the same time keep in mind that the required quality of happiness data depends on its intended use. Moreover, the quality of the happiness data should be compared to alternative concepts of measuring people's level of well-being.

While there will be further progress in many branches of research on happiness and economics, the success of our endeavor will be determined, however, by the extent to which our findings are integrated into established economics. We see two main opportunities as to how research on happiness and economics can contribute to the core of economics in the future. We describe these in the following two sections.

3.1. *Toward a Psychologically Sounder Concept of Utility in Economics*

Econometric and experimental research methods, together with proxy measures for people's well-being, can inform economics about a utility concept with more psychological content and one that is closer to people's well-being than revealed behavior. There have, of course, been a considerable number of contributions along these lines already. In particular, there is the work by Kahneman and co-researchers (1991, 1997, 2000), by the Leyden Group around van Praag (1971, 1993; van Praag and Frijters 1999) and by Easterlin (this volume) (for a review see Frey and Stutzer 1999). Research leading to a psychologically sounder notion of individual well-being challenges various basic assumptions of the economic approach that are incorporated in utility theory.

Future research could deal with several questions:

- *Do people consciously maximize their utility?* This positive question is usually not asked, because it is taken for granted or even seen as a moral obligation in Western societies, that the pursuit of happiness is the main source of human motivation. In particular, economics is based on conscious rational choice. However, such an approach has been criticized as being unscientific. When modern economics was under way, psychologists like William James (1890) argued that scientists should take all possible motives into account in their theories. Behavior might not always aim at maximizing utility, but could be impulsive, follow obligations, and not be goal-oriented (for an overview of this debate, see Lewin 1996). Whether people explicitly follow the goal of maximizing happiness is thus open to empirical research (see e.g. Kityama and Markus 2000).

- *Should people try to maximize their utility?* This question is asked because people's attempts at assessing their own level of utility may be self-defeating. Schooler *et al.* (2003) argue that hedonic introspection may undermine the utility that researchers try to measure, because it can reduce individuals' sensitivity to their own hedonic experience (p. 8). Consistent with this claim, there are several studies finding that happy people are less introspective (e.g. Lyubomirsky and Lepper 1999). The above question is justified because the explicit pursuit of maximum happiness can actually undermine the ability to achieve it. A neat illustration is offered by Schooler *et al.* (2003), who study "the costs of trying to have a good time" on New Year's Eve 1999. With an e-mail questionnaire sent out before the big event, they asked 475 people how large a celebration they were planning, how much they expected to enjoy the event, and how much money and time they were expecting to spend on the party. After the event, people were asked the same questions with regard to their actual experiences. They found that those people who expected a great party were more likely to be disappointed than those who only expected a small celebration or no celebration at all. The difference between experienced and expected enjoyment was negatively correlated with people's anticipation, as well as with the time they expected to spend on preparations. The active pursuit of happiness may also be self-defeating, because people have faulty theories about happiness. People who see the source of a good life to a greater extent in terms of financial success consistently report lower self-esteem, vitality and life satisfaction (see e.g. Kasser and Ryan 1993; Diener and Oishi 2000).

• *Can people successfully predict their future utility?* Economics evidently assumes that this is possible. At least, no systematic deviations are expected for individuals who learn. In contrast, Scitovsky (1976) has criticized this view as "unscientific" because "it seemed to rule out—as a logical impossibility—any conflict between what man chooses to get and what will best satisfy him" (p. 4). Moreover, psychologists have studied people's success in forecasting utility they are about to experience in many careful experiments and surveys (for a review, see Loewenstein and Schkade 1999). While they find that people accurately predict whether an emotional experience primarily elicits good or bad feelings, people often hold incorrect intuitive theories about the determinants of happiness and, for example, underestimate the speed of adaptation to new experiences. We think that individuals make systematic mistakes in decision-making due to these misguided predictions. When deciding (rather than consuming), extrinsic attributes of choice options are more salient than intrinsic attributes. People underestimate intrinsic attributes and therefore devote too little time to their family, friends, or hobbies. They overestimate extrinsic attributes and therefore put too much effort into acquiring income and gaining status, which makes them worse off overall (Frey and Stutzer 2003).

- *Do people have preferences for processes over and above outcomes?* In the assessment of institutions, it is important to understand whether processes themselves are a source of utility. Recommendations for institutional design may be quite different if people appreciate autonomy, participation, or self-determination beyond outcomes. Data on subjective well-being allow direct empirical investigations of these aspects as a source of people's well-being (for an introduction to procedural utility, see Frey *et al.* 2004).

In section 4.1, we discuss a further path towards a psychologically sounder concept of utility in economics. We discuss, and empirically show, how the idea of relative utility can be better studied using data on subjective well-being.

3.2. Testing Economic Theories and Predictions

With a proxy measure for utility at hand, we can distinguish between competing theories that make similar predictions about people's behavior, but differ in what they put forward as people's utility level. This kind of test may become a powerful tool to falsify theories that have proved resistant to a multitude of observed behavior. Some examples can serve to illustrate the potential of happiness research in this respect.

- Systematically different theories exist to explain labor supply and unemployment over the business cycle. In new classical macroeconomics, a perfect labor market is assumed, people heavily substitute their labor supply over time due to changes in wages and interest rates and, if they are unemployed, this is voluntary. According to this view, the loss of income due to unemployment is chosen and unemployed people suffer no lower utility level. In contrast, new Keynesian macroeconomics diagnoses involuntary unemployment due to price and wage rigidities. Unemployed people would be willing to accept a job at the current wage rate, but cannot find one. If people lose their job, they suffer reduced utility.

   Based on unemployed people's behavior, it is very difficult to assess the relative importance of these two models of the labor market. However, individual reports of subjective well-being provide information about the utility level of unemployed people. It is possible to study whether unemployed people are better or worse off than people with the same income, but less leisure time. It is one of the most robust findings in research on happiness in economics that unemployed people suffer large non-pecuniary costs from their lot that are at odds with voluntary unemployment (e.g. Clark and Oswald 1994; Winkelmann and Winkelmann 1998).

- In related research, Stutzer and Lalive (2004) study the effect of the social norm to work on unemployed people's behavior. They find that a stronger social work norm in a community significantly reduces the duration of unemployment of those residents who are looking for a job. From this result, it is not possible to assess whether a stronger social work norm is effective as a result of social sanctions, or whether, in a community with a stronger norm, unemployed people get social support and information which enables them to find a job more quickly. However, the two scenarios lead to different predictions about unemployed people's well-being. While they are expected to be relatively better off if they get social support, they probably suffer even more when a stronger social norm to work primarily means social sanctions. First results for the life satisfaction of unemployed people across Swiss communities are consistent with the latter view.

- Economic models can make systematically different predictions about the effect of excise taxes on people's utility, while they may all predict reduced consumption of the good that is taxed. People suffer a loss when a normal good is taxed and experience increased utility when the tax helps to overcome a bad habit. Depending on what characteristics are assumed for particular forms of consumption like smoking, drinking alcoholic beverages or eating chocolate, people might advocate sin taxes to encourage individuals to improve their lot or oppose them as being discriminatory against particular pleasures in life.

Research on happiness can contribute to this debate and directly study the effect of, say, tobacco taxes on people's subjective well-being. In two longitudinal analyses across the US and Canadian states, Gruber and Mullainathan (2002) perform such a test with data from the General Social Survey. They analyze the effect of changes in state tobacco taxes on the reported happiness of people who are likely to be smokers. They arrive at the astonishing result that a real cigarette tax of 50 cents[2] significantly reduces the likelihood of being unhappy among predicted smokers. In fact, predicted smokers would, with

50 cent taxes, be just as likely to report being unhappy as those not predicted to be smokers (i.e. the proportion of smokers in the lowest happiness category would fall by 7.5 percentage points). This result favors models of time-inconsistent smoking behavior, in which people have problems with self-control.

- Many theories in regional, urban and public economics assume that arbitrage across markets and across space equate people's utility level, *ceteris paribus*. For example, people only accept more time spent commuting if they are either compensated with a higher salary or if they benefit from cheaper housing. Thus, there is a strong notion of equilibrium underlying economic models of location and federal competition. With data on subjective well-being, the prediction of equalized levels of utility can be tested directly. Stutzer and Frey (2003) estimate the effect of commuting time on people's satisfaction with life based on seven cohorts of the German Socio-Economic Panel. In contrast to the equilibrium prediction, a negative partial correlation between commuting time and life satisfaction is found that is robust to a number of alternative explanations. For economics, this result constitutes a commuting paradox.

The new strategy to test economic theories is exemplified in more detail in Section 4.2. Based on data on subjective well-being, we study crucial assumptions that underlie models of the marriage market and lead to completely different mating patterns in equilibrium.

4. Two Applications

4.1. *Relative Utility: The Role of Income Aspirations*

The concept of utility in economics is based on a very simple psychological notion. Economics assumes that people always know what is best for them and that they make decisions accordingly. Moreover, it is assumed that people's satisfaction depends on what they have in absolute terms. It is taken as self-evident that higher income and consumption levels provide higher utility.[3]

However, a psychologically sounder concept of utility should take into consideration that human beings are unable and unwilling to make absolute judgments. Rather, they are constantly drawing comparisons from their environment, from the past, or from their expectations of the future. Thus, people notice and react to deviations from *aspiration levels*.[4]

Most economists would not deny that utility is inherently relative in nature. Even founders of traditional economics, like Paul Samuelson, emphasized that utility functions are not constant: "Because man is a social animal, what he regards as 'necessary comforts of life' depends on what he sees others consuming" (1973: 218, cit. in Holländer 2001). Nevertheless, most economic models of human behavior assume invariant utility functions. Presumably, for reasons of the testability of the basic model, changing tastes have been widely neglected.[5]

We argue that income aspirations ought to be introduced in people's utility function in order to better understand their well-being. An individual's income aspiration can capture his or her concerns for relative income, as well as his or her adaptation to a previous income level. It is hypothesized that higher income aspirations reduce the utility people gain from a given income or consumption level. In a new and direct way, the effect of income aspirations on people's utility is empirically tested. We study panel data for Germany that includes individual data on reported satisfaction with life as a proxy measure for utility, as well as an income evaluation measure as a proxy for people's aspiration levels.[6]

(A) WHAT MAKES FOR THE RELATIVITY IN PEOPLE'S UTILITY?

There are two main processes forming individuals' aspirations, and producing the relativity in people's utility evaluation.

First, people make *social comparisons,* which drive their positional concerns for income. It is not the absolute level of income that matters most, but rather one's position relative to other individuals. This idea of *relative income* is one part of the more general aspiration level theory. Positional concerns are not a new aspect of human nature, but they are probably more pronounced today because of more extended possibilities for social comparison. Many economists in the past have noted that individuals compare themselves to significant others with respect to income, consumption, status, or utility. Marx (1849) expressed his view about the social aspect of utility most explicitly: "Our wants and pleasures have their origin in society; we therefore measure them in relation to society; we do not measure them in relation to the objects which serve for their gratification. Since they are of a social nature, they are of a relative nature." Veblen (1899) coined the notion of "conspicuous consumption", serving to impress other persons. The "relative income hypothesis" has been formulated and econometrically tested by Duesenberry (1949), who posits an asymmetric structure of externalities. People look upward when making comparisons. Aspirations thus tend to be above the level already reached. Wealthier people impose a negative external effect on poorer people, but not vice versa. As a result, savings rates depend on the percentile position in the income distribution, and not solely on the income level, as in a traditional savings function.

Second, people adapt to their new income or consumption level. Additional material goods and services initially provide extra pleasure, but this is usually only transitory. Higher utility from material goods wears off. Satisfaction depends on change and disappears with continued consumption. This process, or mechanism, which reduces the hedonic effects of a constant or repeated stimulus, is called *adaptation*.

Processes of hedonic adaptation supplement the socially comparative, or even competitive, processes in consumption. Together, they make people strive for ever higher aspirations.[7] It is but a short step from aspirations to individual welfare. According to aspiration level theory, individual well-being is determined by the gap between aspiration and achievement (Andrews and Withey 1976; Campbell *et al.* 1976; and Michalos 1985).

(B) HOW TO TEST THE EFFECT OF INCOME ASPIRATIONS ON INDIVIDUAL UTILITY?

Here we apply a new approach to studying the role of income aspirations in individual well-being. We take advantage of reported subjective well-being as a proxy measure for utility and combine it with a theoretically and empirically well-grounded concept for people's aspirations: the individual welfare functions (e.g. van Praag 1971; for a recent survey, see van Praag and Frijters 1999). In research on individual welfare functions, a cardinal relationship between income and expected welfare is established by asking individuals to add income ranges to a number of qualitatively characterized income levels.[8] Answering this "income evaluation question", they should take into account their own situation with respect to family and job. People's answers provide information about the income that is sufficient to meet their aspiration level, that is, the income that is required to reach mean expected welfare.

Based on proxy variables for people's income aspirations and their utility level, we can test the following proposition: Individuals' judgments of well-being are affected by their aspiration level Y^*, over and above the effect of income Y and other individual characteristics X. That means that income aspirations Y^* are a characteristic of individual i's "utility function".[9] According to aspiration level theory, higher income aspirations lead to lower subjective well-being, *ceteris paribus*.

$$U_{i,t} = f(Y_{i,t}, Y_{i,t}^*, X_{i,t}) \quad and \quad \delta U_i/\delta Y_t^* < 0$$

(C) EMPIRICAL TEST OF THE ROLE OF INCOME ASPIRATIONS

The proposition is empirically studied, using survey data for Germany from the German Socio-Economic Panel Study (GSOEP).[10] The GSOEP is one of the most valuable data sets for studying individual well-being over time. It was started in 1984 as a longitudinal survey of private households and persons in the Federal Republic of Germany and was extended to residents in the former German Democratic Republic in 1990. From this survey, we use the two cohorts of 1992 and 1997 that contain information about individuals' aspiration levels. Observations for the two waves are from all the samples available in the scientific use file (samples A to F). People in the survey are asked a wide range of questions with regard to their socio-economic status and their demographic characteristics. Moreover, they report their subjective well-being and their income aspirations. Reported subjective well-being is based on the question "How satisfied are you with your life, all things considered?" Responses range on a scale from 0 "completely dissatisfied" to 10 "completely satisfied". Income aspirations are captured by the question "Whether you feel an income is good or not so good depends on your personal life circumstances and expectations. In your case—the net household income ___ DM is just sufficient income".[11] For the proxy of people's aspiration levels, on average, an amount of DM 3,800 per month (at prices and purchasing power parities for 1999, approx. Euro 1,950) is reported. Average household income in the sample is DM 4,800 per month (at prices and purchasing power parities for 1999, approx. Euro 2,450).

The empirical analysis starts with a standard microeconometric happiness function. In order to make the interpretation of the results easier, least squares estimations are presented.[12] Individuals' reported satisfaction is regressed on income, a number of socio-demographic and socio-economic characteristics, as well as on the size of the household. Household income is positively correlated with reported satisfaction with life, *ceteris paribus*. The coefficient implies that doubling household income increases life satisfaction by 0.334 points on the ten-point scale.[13] The results for household size incorporate the fact that household income has to be shared among household members. However, household size also captures the fact that people live with others in what are probably close and supportive relationships. The results in panel A of Table 4.1 indicate that the two effects of household size on satisfaction with life have a negative net effect. Women are slightly more satisfied with life than men. People with a partner report, on average, higher satisfaction scores than those without. The partial correlation between age and life satisfaction is u-shaped with a minimum around age 50. People with more years of education report higher satisfaction scores than those with fewer years of education. Lower satisfaction scores are reported by self-employed people, non-working people, unemployed people, people living in Eastern Germany, and non-EU foreigners (compared to employees, people living in Western Germany, and nationals).

In panels B and C, the happiness function is extended to include the proxy measure for individuals' aspiration levels. It is thus tested whether, according to our proposition, individuals' judgment of well-being is relative to their income aspirations. The results in panel B show that a negative effect on subjective well-being is estimated for the measure of individuals' income aspirations. This means that people experience lower well-being when they have higher income aspirations, given their income level. A doubling of the aspiration level—measured by the income that is evaluated as "just sufficient"—reduces reported life satisfaction, on average, by 0.191 points. This result supports the basic underlying hypothesis that people's subjective well-being is negatively affected by their income aspiration level, controlling for the effect of income and other individual characteristics.

For the demographic control variables, coefficients similar in size to panel A are estimated. In contrast, the effect of household income on life satisfaction is larger (0.534) than in panel A. This indicates that, for a given aspiration level, higher income has a greater effect on well-being. The change in the size of the coefficient for household income provides indirect evidence that people adjust their aspiration levels according to their income level (see also the discussion in the next subsection).

An alternative interpretation of the results in estimation B suggests that the inference is clouded by unobserved personality traits that influence individuals' aspirations, as well as how they respond to subjective well-being questions. For instance, competitive people who have high aims in life may report higher aspirations and may also report lower satisfaction with life because they want to leave room for improvement. As a result, the observed correlation would be biased. However, idiosyncratic effects that are time-invariant can be controlled for if the same individuals are

Table 4.1. The effect of income aspirations on satisfaction with life, Germany 1992 and 1997 (dependent variable: satisfaction with life)

	A		B		C	
	pooled estimation		pooled estimation		individual fixed effects estimation	
	Coef.	t–value	Coef.	t–value	Coef.	t–value
Household income, ln	0.454	15.39	0.534	16.54	0.327	5.81
Income aspirations, ln			−0.259	−6.06	−0.323	−4.99
No. of household members, square root	−0.363	−5.83	−0.303	−4.81	−0.321	−2.50
Male			Reference group			
Female	0.055	2.08	0.059	2.23		
Age	−0.049	−7.57	−0.046	−7.06		
Age squared	0.48e−3	6.93	0.45e−3	6.45	0.09e−3	0.53
Years of education, ln	0.155	2.22	0.213	3.03	−1.963	−2.26
No children			Reference group			
Children	0.072	1.73	0.062	1.49	0.047	0.70
Single, no partner			Reference group			
Single, with partner	0.137	1.82	0.165	2.18	0.499	3.07
Married	0.196	3.06	0.227	3.53	0.753	4.25
Separated, with partner	−0.296	−1.25	−0.279	−1.18	0.458	1.17
Separated, no partner	−0.640	−5.08	−0.620	−4.93	0.041	0.18
Divorced, with partner	0.107	1.05	0.145	1.41	0.604	2.74
Divorced, no partner	−0.337	−4.05	−0.331	−3.99	0.340	1.66
Widowed, with partner	0.068	0.43	0.100	0.64	1.505	3.72
Widowed, no partner	−0.065	−0.80	−0.051	−0.63	0.511	2.37
Spouse abroad	−0.277	−1.12	−0.243	−0.99	0.616	1.27
Employed			Reference group			
Self-employed	−0.230	−3.44	−0.242	−3.62	−0.164	−1.36
Some work	−0.019	−0.23	−0.039	−0.49	−0.210	−1.83
Non-working	−0.135	−3.30	−0.151	−3.68	−0.188	−2.67
Unemployed	−0.857	−16.89	−0.871	−17.16	−0.734	−10.23
Maternity leave	0.165	1.79	0.152	1.65	0.023	0.17
Military service	0.684	1.34	0.658	1.29	−0.196	−0.24
In education	0.086	0.68	0.056	0.44	−0.309	−1.63
Retired	−0.052	−0.72	−0.069	−0.95	−0.139	−1.24
Western Germany			Reference group			
Eastern Germany	−0.837	−29.29	−0.819	−28.51	−1.009	−4.53
Nationals			Reference group			
EU foreigners	0.056	1.02	0.059	1.07		
Non-EU foreigners	−0.238	−5.02	−0.237	−5.01		
Year dummy 1997	−0.134	−5.46	−0.141	−5.74	−0.299	−3.55
Constant	7.101	103.98	8.071	46.40	7.857	25.02
Number of observations	19130		19130		19130	
Adjusted R^2	0.102		0.103			
Overall R^2					0.040	

Source: GSOEP.

re-surveyed over time. This is the case for our longitudinal data set, in which it is possible to consider a specific baseline well-being for each individual. The statistical relationship between income aspirations and reported subjective well-being is then identified by the change in aspirations between 1992 and 1997 for the same person.

Estimation C in Table 4.1 reports the result for an estimation with individual fixed effects that excludes spurious correlation due to time-invariant unobserved characteristics of people. Partial correlations again show a sizeable negative effect of income aspirations on life satisfaction. A doubling of the aspiration level reduces reported life satisfaction, on average by 0.237 points. Thus the results of the pooled estimation are confirmed.

(D) INTERPRETATION

The evidence presented indicates that people's well-being is better understood when their income aspirations are taken into consideration. Income aspirations are thus one aspect of a psychologically sounder concept of utility. With this extension, various empirical observations can be explained. For example, if average aspirations in society increase at the same rate as income per capita, it can be better understood why people in industrialized societies have not become happier over the last few decades, despite substantial growth in their economic wealth. This is consistent with citizens' voting behavior. It is found that citizens support the incumbent parties when economic conditions are good. However, citizens take into consideration the unemployment rate and the inflation rate much more than the rate of income growth (e.g. Nannestad and Paldam 1994). Another observation that can be better understood is the low correlation between income and reported subjective well-being. If people evaluate their economic well-being relative to their aspirations, rather than in an absolute way, a fraction of people in an objectively bad economic situation may still be highly satisfied, and another fraction of people living in objectively good economic conditions may still report being highly dissatisfied.

The extension of the utility concept with a proxy measure for aspirations leads immediately to the following questions: What factors determine people's income aspirations? Is there empirical evidence for the two processes that have been put forward as theoretical explanations of the formation of individual aspirations?

First, research on hedonic adaptation studies processes that reduce the effects of repeated sensory and cognitive stimuli (e.g. Frederick and

Loewenstein 1999). With regard to income, there is the notion that we get "used to" a higher income level. After a period of enjoyment, the hedonic effects of higher consumption adapt to a base level and cognitive changes in interests, values, and goals set in. In this process, people increase their aspiration level. The relation between individual income and income aspirations was empirically studied based on the concept of individual welfare functions by the Leyden Group (see e.g. van Herwaarden *et al.* 1977, van Praag and van der Sar 1988). As a robust result, it was found that aspirations increase with people's income level. Moreover, the results indicate that a higher income is not fully translated into higher income aspirations. Van Praag and his co-researchers find that the preference shift through higher individual income "destroys" about 60 percent of the expected welfare effect of an increase in income.

Second, there are social comparisons with relevant others. It is not the absolute level of income that matters most, but rather one's position relative to other individuals. Socially comparative, or even competitive, processes in consumption complement processes of hedonic adaptation. The empirical analysis of social comparisons is, however, difficult because one has to identify *who* the other people are that constitute the relevant reference group. For Veblen (1899), rich families like the Vanderbilts are setting the reference standards. For Duesenberry (1949), keeping up with the neighboring Joneses drives consumption aspirations. However, reference groups are only partly exogenously given, and to some extent may be actively chosen (Falk and Knell 2000). Even TV families in people's favorite soap operas may become the relevant others (Schor 1998).[14] Using the same proxy measure for income aspirations as applied here, the effect of social comparisons has been studied across Swiss communities (Stutzer 2004). It turns out that individuals' aspirations are systematically affected by the average income in the community where people live. The richer one's fellow residents are, the higher is an individual's aspiration level. This effect cannot be explained by a higher cost of living alone. It is shown that the aspiration levels of community members who interact within the community react much more to changes in average income than those of members who do not interact.

4.2. *Theories of Marriage: Which Couples Benefit?*

The second application relates to the possibility of new tests of economic theories and predictions using data on subjective well-being. This data provides an alternative way (i) of discriminating between theoretical models that explain similar patterns in behavior but lead to different predictions of individuals' levels of utility and (ii) of assessing auxiliary assumptions that often play a crucial role in the predicted behavior and equilibrium outcome of economic models.

One field in which different auxiliary assumptions lead to completely different predictions is family economics (Pollak 2002). Becker's seminal work on the economics of marriage (1973, 1974a) is based on the gains married people derive from household production and labor division.[15] Other theories focus on spouses' joint consumption of household public goods, or on reciprocity and social equality in homogamous[16] relationships. In the latter case, it is argued that the tendency for "like to marry like" facilitates compatibility of spouses' basic values and beliefs. While, based on Becker's model, mating is predicted to be negatively related to (shadow) wages, it is predicted to be positively related to education in the case of homogamous relationships. In order to study the validity of the assumptions underlying these two sets of models, data on subjective well-being can be studied to provide systematic evidence as to who benefits more and who benefits less from marriage.

In this section, we draw on our research, which is more fully described in Stutzer and Frey (2003a). Our empirical analysis studies whether couples with different potentials for specialization of labor and more or less difference in education systematically differ in their benefits from marriage.

(A) THE EFFECTS OF MARRIAGE ON SPOUSES' WELL-BEING

With marriage, people engage in a long-term relationship with a strong commitment to a mutually rewarding exchange. The spouse expects some benefits from the partner's expressed love, gratitude, and recognition, as well as from security and material rewards. This is summarized in the protection perspective of marriage. Of the protective effects, economists have, in particular, studied the financial benefits of marriage. Marriage provides basic insurance against adverse life events and allows gains from economies of scale and specialization within the family (Becker 1981). With specialization, one of the spouses has advantageous conditions for human capital accumulation in tasks demanded on the labor market. This is reflected in married people earning higher incomes than single people, *ceteris paribus* (e.g. Chun and Lee 2001).

There are a wide range of benefits from marriage that go beyond increased earnings. These benefits have been studied in psychology, sociology, and epidemiology. Researchers in these fields have documented that, compared to single people, married people have better physical and psychological health (e.g. less substance abuse and less depression) and that they live longer. The evidence for the effects on health has been reviewed, e.g. in Burman and Margolin (1992) and Ross *et al.* (1990). Waite and Gallagher (2000) additionally survey evidence on income, mortality, children's achievements, and sexual satisfaction. A survey that is focused on longitudinal evidence is by Wilson and Oswald (2002).

Recently, there has been an increasing interest in the effect of marriage on people's happiness. It has been found that marriage goes hand in hand with higher happiness levels in a large number of studies covering different countries and time periods (e.g. Diener *et al.* 2000; Stack and Eshleman 1998; see also Coombs 1991 and Myers 1999 for surveys). Married persons report greater subjective well-being than persons who have never been married or have been divorced, separated, or widowed.[17]

What characterizes couples who gain the most from marriage? This question sheds light on the channels providing the benefits from marriage. Here, related evidence is used to assess the crucial auxiliary assumptions in models of the marriage market. Economists have focused on the gains from specialization in household production, while sociologists and psychologists have emphasized increased emotional support and relational gratification. The latter is often related to homogamous couples, for instance with regard to social status measured in spouses' level of education.

(B) EMPIRICAL ANALYSIS OF THE DIFFERENCES IN HAPPINESS
   OF MARRIED PEOPLE

The two claims about the major sources of increased well-being in marriage are directly tested using data on reported satisfaction with life. As in the first application, we use panel data from the GSOEP. We restrict our analysis to people who got married during the 17 years of the sampling period and observe their well-being around marriage. Figure 4.1 shows average life satisfaction in the years before and after marriage, based on 21,809 observations for 1,991 people in Germany between 1984 and 2000. Average scores are calculated after taking respondents' sex, age, education level, parenthood, household income, household size, relation to the head of the household, labor market status, place of residence, and citizenship status into account.

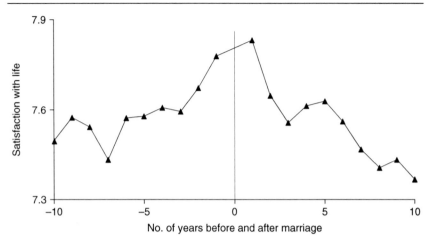

Figure 4.1. Life satisfaction around marriage

Note: The graph represents the pattern of well-being after taking respondents' sex, age, education level, parenthood, household income, household size, relation to the head of the household, labor market status, place of residence, and citizenship into account.

Source: GSOEP.

Figure 4.1 shows a noticeable pattern: As the year of marriage approaches, people report, on average, higher satisfaction scores. In contrast, after marriage, the average reported satisfaction with life decreases.

Several concepts may explain this pattern. Some psychologists put forward an event explanation that marital transitions cause short-term changes in subjective well-being (e.g. Johnson and Wu 2002). Others take it as evidence of adaptation (Lucas *et al.* 2003). Adaptation in the marriage context means that people get used to the pleasant (and unpleasant) stimuli they get from living with a partner in a close relationship, and after some time experience more or less their baseline level of subjective well-being. Whether this adaptation is truly hedonic, or whether married people start using a different scale for what they consider a satisfying life (satisfaction treadmill), is difficult to assess.[18]

In the current study, we are less interested in these patterns as such than in the large differences in life satisfaction for the newly married. In the first year after marriage, the standard deviation of reported satisfaction with life is 1.60 around a mean of 7.64. In the second year, the standard deviation is 1.59 and the mean 7.43 (on a scale between 0 for "completely dissatisfied" and 10 for "completely satisfied"). These numbers indicate that there are large differences in how spouses feel in their lives as newly wed couples. Here, we examine whether there are systematic differences for some sub-groups identified in theories of the marriage market.

First, the potential for specialization is studied. One of the main predictions of Becker's theory of marriage is that the gain from marriage is positively related to couples' relative difference in wage rates (1974*b*: S11). The reason is that a large relative difference in wage rates makes specialization between running the household and participation on the labor market more beneficial.

The hypothesis is studied graphically in Figure 4.2. The sample is divided into a group of couples who, on average, have above median relative difference in wage rates and one with below median difference.[19] The averages presented are estimated *ceteris paribus*. However, not all the control variables mentioned for Figure 4.1 are included. As specialization is expected

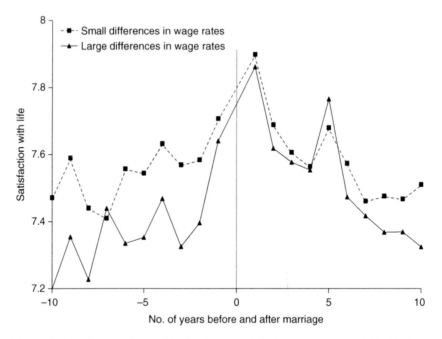

Figure 4.2. Differences in the (shadow) wage rate between spouses and its effect on life satisfaction around marriage

Note: The graph represents the pattern of well-being after taking respondents' sex, age, parenthood, household size, relation to the head of the household, labor market status, place of residence, and citizenship into account.

Source: GSOEP.

to provide benefits through increased household production, household income (as well as its close proxy education level) is not controlled for.

Figure 4.2 shows that there are no systematic differences in subjective well-being for the two groups in the years after marriage. However, *before* marriage, those individuals who go on to be in marriages with large differences in relative wage rates are less happy on average than those with small differences.[20] This indicates that couples with large differences in relative wage rates benefit more from marriage. This is a finding that supports one of the main predictions in Becker's model based on the gains from specialization.[21]

Second, possible benefits for homogamous couples are analyzed. Here, we look at couples' differences in the level of education, measured by the number of years of schooling. It is hypothesized that couples with small differences in the level of education gain more from marriage than those with large differences.

Figure 4.3 presents the result of a graphical analysis, applying the same test strategy as that previously used for specialization. Now the whole set

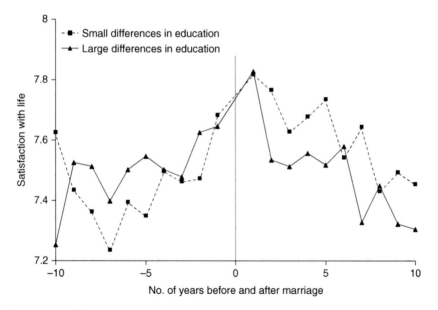

Figure 4.3. Differences in the level of education between spouses and its effect on life satisfaction around marriage

Note: The graph represents the pattern of well-being after taking respondents' sex, age, education level, parenthood, household income, household size, relation to the head of the household, labor market status, place of residence, and citizenship into account.

Source: GSOEP.

of control variables, as in Figure 4.1, is included. For the years before marriage, there are no systematic differences in the well-being of people who end up in marriages with small and large differences in education. However, after marriage, couples with differences in education below the median report, on average, higher satisfaction with life. For the first seven years, the joint statistical significance of the differences is higher than 99 percent. This finding supports the hypothesis that couples with similar educational background benefit more from marriage.

(C) INTERPRETATION

Basic assumptions about the gains from marriage or protection can be directly studied using data on subjective well-being. We find evidence that supports the specialization hypothesis emphasized in economics. Compared to their life satisfaction before marriage, couples with large relative wage differences, and thus a high potential gain from specialization, benefit more from getting married than those couples with small relative wage differences. However, the finding indicates that there are no systematic differences between the two groups after seven years of marriage. Our results also support theories emphasizing the importance of similarities between partners. Similar or homogamous partners are expected to share values and beliefs that facilitate a supportive relationship. We find that spouses with small differences in their level of education stand to gain, on average, more satisfaction from marriage than spouses with large differences. These tests of two auxiliary assumptions suggest that previous models of the marriage market—either focusing on specialization or on complementarities in consumption—each neglect an important aspect.

5. Concluding Remarks

Many people say that happiness is all they want or what they try to achieve in their life. It follows that economics is—or should be—about individual happiness. Only recently has economics started to address this claim directly and to study people's reported subjective well-being. In the meantime, research on happiness and economics has produced many interesting findings and insights about human well-being and its determinants.

We argue that future research on happiness in economics has huge potential, but that it needs to be guided more closely by theory. We propose two ways to test theories of happiness.

First, reported subjective well-being is a proxy measure for utility that is valid enough to contribute to a better understanding of utility itself. With a direct proxy for utility, it is again possible to have a utility concept with psychological content. Happiness research can address aspects like relativity in utility judgments, the prediction of experienced utility, or notions of procedural utility. This research is moving toward a concept of utility in economics that reflects more than the satiation of wants.

Second, happiness data offer a new way of distinguishing between different models of behavior. The abundance of theoretical models that can explain particular "stylized facts" in behavior stands in sharp contrast to empirical research, which lacks statistical tests to reject at least some models based on observed behavior. To the extent that these models make differentiated predictions about people's utility, they become testable and rejectable in turn.

We illustrate both ways of testing theories of happiness by presenting our own studies. Our first application extends the concept of utility to include people's income aspirations. We find that income contributes to people's well-being relative to their aspiration level. The estimated negative effect of income aspirations on reported satisfaction with life is sizeable and confirms the view that models of interdependent preferences and habit formation have much stronger implications for individual welfare than for the prediction of demand behavior (Holländer 2001).

Our second application tests two important assumptions underlying the marriage market in economics and sociology. While economic models focus on specialization and the division of labor, sociology emphasizes the advantages of homogamous relationships. We find evidence in support of both theories. Couples with a bigger potential for specialization, as well as those with smaller differences in the level of education, gain relatively more from marriage.

We forecast a prosperous future for research on happiness in economics. Testing theories of happiness has the potential to make significant contributions to the core of economics.

Notes

We are grateful to Reto Jegen, two anonymous referees and various participants at the conference on "The Paradoxes of Happiness" in Milan in 2003 for helpful comments. Data for the German Socio-economic Panel has been kindly provided by the German Institute for Economic Research (DIW) in Berlin.

137

1. This criticism also applies to our own efforts to study the effect of political institutions on reported subjective well-being (Frey and Stutzer 2000).
2. The average real cigarette tax in the United States (in 1999 US$) is 31.6 cents in the sample (Gruber and Mullainathan 2002: 14).
3. There are, of course, scientists who oppose this notion. Frank (1985a, 1999, this volume), Galbraith (1958), Hirsch (1976), Scitovsky (1976) and, more recently Schor (1998), studying consumer culture—in particular in the United States—emphasize the important role of socially formed aspirations and expectations for consumer satisfaction.
4. The importance of relative judgments for happiness is e.g. shown in laboratory experiments (Mellers 2000; Smith et al. 1989; and Tversky and Griffin 1991).
5. Among the few exceptions, the theories of preference change have concentrated on habit formation (e.g. Marshall 1890; Modigliani 1949; Pollak 1970; and more recently Carroll et al. 2000). Concepts of interdependent preferences due to comparisons with relevant others (see e.g. Frank 1985b; Pollak 1976; and Clark and Oswald 1998 for a survey) have remained rare. There is another class of interdependent utility models that focuses on fairness concerns rather than positional concerns (e.g. Becker 1974b; Fehr and Gächter 2000). Empirical studies that focus on individuals' distributive concerns, and which use data on reported subjective well-being, are e.g. Alesina et al. (2004), Hagerty (2000), Schwarze and Härpfer (2002), and Tomes (1986).
6. Related research has been conducted by Easterlin (1974, 1995, 2001, this volume), who uses the concept of aspirations as a frame of reference to resolve—as he calls it—the happiness paradox. The happiness paradox describes two striking observations in the relation between income and happiness: While people with higher income report, on average, higher satisfaction with life, raising everybody's income, on average, does not increase people's subjective well-being. It is argued, in the latter case, that individuals' aspirations grow hand in hand with income.
7. The concept of aspiration levels is well grounded in psychology and sociology (e.g. Irwin 1944; Lewin et al. 1944; and Stouffer et al. 1949), as is adaptation level theory in psychology (in particular Helson 1964; Brickman and Campbell 1971; Parducci 1995; and, for a modern discussion, Frederick and Loewenstein 1999).
8. For example, "Please try to indicate what you consider to be an appropriate amount for each of the following cases. Under my/our conditions, I would call a net household income per [month] of: about ___ very bad ... about ___ very good. Please enter an answer on each line ... " (van Praag 1993).
9. For convenience, an extended utility function is used rather than a state-dependent utility function $U_i = U_{i, Y^*}(Y_i, X_i)$ with the aspiration level Y^* defining the state.
10. For a detailed description of the GSOEP, see Burkhauser et al. (2001) and Haisken-DeNew and Frick (2001).

11. The proxy measure is focused on one category of the income evaluation question. In addition, people were asked what income they considered to be "very low", "low", "still insufficient", "good", and "very good".

12. Theoretically, ordered probit or logit estimations would be more appropriate to exploiting the ranking information contained in the originally scaled dependent variable "satisfaction with life". The respective results show that the estimation coefficients in the least squares estimations and the average marginal effects in ordered probit estimations are very similar. The respective estimates can be obtained from the author.

13. The coefficient in Table 4.1 refers roughly to a tripling of household income, because the logarithmic specification means that an increase in the transformed income variable by one is equivalent to an increase of household income by a factor e, i.e. approximately 2.718.

14. In a study of 5,000 British workers, Clark and Oswald (1996) formed a reference group, comprising persons with the same labor market characteristics. They conclude that the higher the income of the reference group, the less satisfied people are with their job. Social comparisons within the family are studied by Neumark and Postlewaite (1998) in order to test the role of relative income for utility. They find that the decision of a woman to undertake paid work depends on whether her sisters and sisters-in-law are employed, and how much they earn in their job. In a recent study for Germany, Ferrer-i-Carbonell (2002) combines individuals with a similar education level and age into an exogenous reference group. She finds a negative effect of this group's comparison income on reported satisfaction with life.

15. The progress in the theoretical analysis of marriage in economics is surveyed e.g. in Weiss (1997) and Brien and Sheran (2003).

16. Homogamy describes the tendency for "like to marry like". People of similar age, race, religion, nationality, education, attitudes, and numerous other traits tend to marry one another to a greater degree than would be found by chance (see e.g. Hughes *et al.* 1999).

17. The possibility of reversed causation is discussed and empirically studied e.g. in Mastekaasa (1992) and Stutzer and Frey (forthcoming).

18. There is also a selection explanation for the pattern. Many people might only marry if they expect to experience a rewarding relationship in the future. They predict their future well-being as spouses based on their current well-being. Therefore, the last year before marriage becomes the last year, because the couples experience a particularly happy time in their relationship.

19. Relative wage rates can be calculated because each person in the sample is matched with the socio-demographic characteristics of his or her spouse. Shadow wage rates for years during which the respondent or his or her spouse was not in the active labor force are estimated by using a simple procedure. Wages are approximated by the wage earned before or after the break—whatever was chronologically closer. It is assumed that where a person was to

start working again at the time of the interview, he or she would have to accept his or her last wage without general wage increases, or that he or she could get as high a wage as the one he or she gets in the future.

20. An *F*-test for the seven dummy variables that capture the differences in life satisfaction in the seven years before marriage is statistically significant at the 95 percent level.

21. Stutzer and Frey (forthcoming) also study the effect of actual specialization. It is found that actual division of labor seems to contribute to spouses' well-being, especially for women, and when there is a young family to raise.

References

Alesina, Alberto, Di Tella, Rafael, and MacCulloch, Robert (2004), "Inequality and Happiness: Are Europeans and Americans Different?" *Journal of Public Economics*, 88/9–10: 2009–42.

Andrews, Frank M., and Withey, Stephen B. (1976), *Social Indicators of Well-Being: Americans' Perceptions of Life Quality*, New York: Plenum Press.

Becker, Gary S. (1973), "A Theory of Marriage: Part I", *Journal of Political Economy*, 81/4: 813–46.

—— (1974*a*), "A Theory of Marriage: Part II", *Journal of Political Economy*, 82/2: S11–S26.

—— (1974*b*), "A Theory of Social Interactions", *Journal of Political Economy*, 82/6: 1063–93.

—— (1981), *A Treatise on the Family*. Cambridge, Mass: Harvard University Press.

Brickman, Philip, and Campbell, Donald T. (1971), "Hedonic Relativism and Planning the Good Society", in Mortimer H. Appley (ed.), *Adaptation Level Theory: A Symposium*, New York: Academic Press.

Brien, Michael, and Sheran, Michelle (2003), "The Economics of Marriage and Household Formation", in Shoshana Grossbard-Shechtman (ed.), *Marriage and the Economy: Theory and Evidence from Advanced Industrial Societies*, New York and Cambridge: Cambridge University Press.

Burkhauser, Richard V., Butrica, Barbara A., Daly, Mary C., and Lillard, Dean R. (2001), "The Cross-National Equivalent File: A Product of Cross-National Research", in Irene Becker, Notburga Ott, and Gabriele Rolf (eds.), *Soziale Sicherung in einer dynamischen Gesellschaft: Festschrift für Richard Hauser zum 65. Geburtstag*, Frankfurt and New York: Campus 354–76.

Burman, Bonnie, and Margolin, Gayla (1992), "Analysis of the Association between Marital Relationships and Health Problems: An Interactional Perspective", *Psychological Bulletin* 112/1: 39–63.

Campbell, Angus, Converse, Philip E., and Rodgers, Willard L. (1976), *The Quality of American Life: Perceptions, Evaluations, and Satisfactions*, New York: Russell Sage Foundation.

Carroll, Christopher D., Overland, Jody, and Weil, David N. (2000), "Saving and Growth with Habit Formation", *American Economic Review*, 90/3: 341–55.

Chun, Hyunbae, and Lee, Injae (2001), "Why Do Married Men Earn More: Productivity or Marriage Selection?" *Economic Inquiry*, 39/2: 307–19.

Clark, Andrew E. (1997), "Job Satisfaction and Gender: Why Are Women So Happy at Work?" *Labour Economics* 4/4: 341–72.

—— and Oswald, Andrew J. (1994), "Unhappiness and Unemployment", *Economic Journal*, 104/424: 648–59.

—— —— (1996), "Satisfaction and Comparison Income", *Journal of Public Economics*, 61/3: 359–81.

—— —— (1998), "Comparison-Concave Utility and Following Behaviour in Social and Economic Settings", *Journal of Public Economics*, 70/1: 133–55.

Coombs, Robert H. (1991), "Marital Status and Personal Well-Being: A Literature Review", *Family Relations*, 40/1: 97–102.

Csikszentmihalyi, Mihaly (1997), *Finding Flow: The Psychology of Engagement with Everyday Life*, New York: Basic Books.

Diener, Ed, Gohm, Carol L., Suh, Eunkook M., and Oishi, Shigehiro (2000), "Similarity of the Relations between Marital Status and Subjective Well-Being across Cultures", *Journal of Cross Cultural Psychology*, 31/4: 419–36.

—— and Oishi, Shigehiro (2000), "Money and Happiness: Income and Subjective Well-Being across Nations", in Ed Diener and Eunkook M. Suh (eds.), *Culture and Subjective Well-Being*, Cambridge, Mass.: MIT Press, 185–218.

Duesenberry, James S. (1949), *Income, Savings and the Theory of Consumer Behavior*, Cambridge, Mass.: Harvard University Press.

Easterlin, Richard A. (1974), "Does Economic Growth Improve the Human Lot? Some Empirical Evidence", in Paul A. David and Melvin W. Reder (eds.), *Nations and Households in Economic Growth: Essays in Honour of Moses Abramowitz*, New York and London: Academic Press, 89–125.

—— (1995), "Will Raising the Incomes of All Increase the Happiness of All?" *Journal of Economic Behaviour and Organization*, 27/1: 35–48.

—— (2001), "Income and Happiness: Towards a Unified Theory", *Economic Journal*, 111/473: 465–84.

—— (ed.) (2002), *Happiness in Economics*, Cheltenham: Edward Elgar.

Falk, Armin, and Knell, Markus (2000), "Choosing the Joneses: On the Endogeneity of Reference Groups", Working Paper No. 59, Institute for Empirical Research in Economics, University of Zurich.

Fehr, Ernst, and Gächter, Simon (2000), "Fairness and Retaliation: The Economics of Reciprocity", *Journal of Economic Perspectives*, 14/3: 159–81.

Ferrer-i-Carbonell, Ada (2002), "Income and Well-being: An Empirical Analysis of the Comparison Income Effect", Tinbergen Institute Discussion Paper No. 19/3, Amsterdam.

Frank, Robert H. (1985*a*), *Choosing the Right Pond*, New York: Oxford University Press.

Frank, Robert H. (1985b), "The Demand for Unobservable and Other Nonpositional Goods", *American Economic Review*, 75/1: 101–16.

—— (1999), *Luxury Fever: Why Money Fails to Satisfy in an Era of Excess*, New York: Free Press.

Frederick, Shane, and Loewenstein, George (1999), "Hedonic Adaptation", in Daniel Kahneman, Ed Diener, and Norbert Schwarz (eds.), *Well-Being: The Foundations of Hedonic Psychology*, New York: Russell Sage Foundation, 302–29.

Frey, Bruno S., Benz, Matthias, and Stutzer, Alois (2004), "Introducing Procedural Utility: Not Only What but also How Matters", *Journal of Institutional and Theoretical Economics*, 160/3: 377–401.

—— and Stutzer, Alois (1999), "Measuring Preferences by Subjective Well-Being", *Journal of Institutional and Theoretical Economics*, 155/4: 755–88.

—— —— (2000), "Happiness, Economy and Institutions", *Economic Journal*, 110/446: 918–38.

—— —— (2002a), *Happiness and Economics: How the Economy and Institutions Affect Human Well-Being*, Princeton: Princeton University Press.

—— —— (2002b), "What Can Economists Learn from Happiness Research?" *Journal of Economic Literature*, 40/2: 402–35.

—— —— (2003), "Economic Consequences of Mispredicting Utility", Mimeo, University of Zurich.

Galbraith, John Kenneth (1958), *The Affluent Society*, Harmondsworth: Penguin Books.

Gruber, Jonathan, and Mullainathan, Sendhil (2002), "Do Cigarette Taxes Make Smokers Happier?" NBER Working Paper No. 8872, Cambridge, Mass.: National Bureau of Economic Research.

Hagerty, Michael R. (2000), "Social Comparisons of Income in One's Community: Evidence from National Surveys of Income and Happiness", *Journal of Personality and Social Psychology*, 78/4: 764–71.

Haisken-DeNew, John P., and Joachim R. Frick (eds.) (2001), DTC—Desktop Companion to the German Socio-Economic Panel Study (GSOEP), Version 5.0. Berlin: DIW.

Helliwell, John F. (2003), "How's Life? Combining Individual and National Variables to Explain Subjective Well-Being", *Economic Modelling*, 20/2: 331–60.

Helson, Harry (1964), *Adaptation-Level Theory: An Experimental and Systematic Approach to Behavior*, New York: Harper and Row.

Hermalin, Benjamin E., and Isen, Alice M. (1999), "The Effect of Affect on Economic and Strategic Decision-Making", Mimeo, University of California, Berkeley.

Hirsch, Fred (1976), *The Social Limits to Growth*, Cambridge, Mass.: Harvard University Press.

Holländer, Heinz (2001), "On the Validity of Utility Statements: Standard Theory versus Duesenberry's", *Journal of Economic Behavior and Organization*, 45/3: 227–49.

Hughes, Michael D., Kroehler, Carolyn J., and Vander Zanden, James W. (1999), *Sociology: The Core*, New York: McGraw-Hill College.

Irwin, Francis W. (1944), "The Realism of Expectations", *Psychological Review*, 51: 120–6.

James, William (1890), *Principles of Psychology*, II, New York: Henry Holt.

Johnson, David R., and Wu, Jian (2002), "An Empirical Test of Crisis, Social Selection, and Role Explanations of the Relationship between Marital Disruption and Psychological Distress: A Pooled Time-Series Analysis of Four-Wave Panel Data", *Journal of Marriage and the Family*, 64/1: 211–24.

Kahneman, Daniel (2000), "Experienced Utility and Objective Happiness: A Moment-Based Approach", in Daniel Kahneman and Amos Tversky (eds.), *Choices, Values, and Frames*, New York: Cambridge University Press and Russell Sage Foundation.

—— and Varey, Carol (1991), "Notes on the Psychology of Utility", in Jon Elster and John E. Roemer (eds.), *Interpersonal Comparisons of Well-Being: Studies in Rationality and Social Change*, Cambridge: Cambridge University Press, 127–63.

—— Wakker, Peter P., and Sarin, Rakesh (1997), "Back to Bentham? Explorations of Experienced Utility", *Quarterly Journal of Economics*, 112/2: 375–405.

—— Krueger, Alan B., Schkade, David A., and Stone, Arthur A. (2004), "A Survey Method for Characterizing Daily Life Experience: The Day Reconstruction Method", *Science*, 306/5702: 1776–80.

Kasser, Tim, and Ryan, Richard M. (1993), "A Dark Side of the American Dream: Correlates of Financial Success as a Central Life Aspiration", *Journal of Personality and Social Psychology*, 65/2: 410–22.

Kitayama, Shinobu, and Markus, Hazel R. (2000), "The Pursuit of Happiness and the Realization of Sympathy: Cultural Patterns of Self, Social Relations, and Well-Being", in Ed Diener and Eunkook M. Suh (eds.), *Culture and Subjective Well-Being*, Cambridge, Mass.: MIT Press.

Lewin, Kurt, Dembo, Tamara, Festinger, Leon, and Sears, Pauline (1944), "Level of Aspiration", in J. McV. Hunt (ed.), *Personality and the Behavior Disorders*, i, New York: Ronald Press, 333–78.

Lewin, Shira B. (1996), "Economics and Psychology: Lessons for Our Own Day from the Early Twentieth Century", *Journal of Economic Literature*, 34/3: 1293–323.

Loewenstein, George, and Schkade, David (1999), "Wouldn't It Be Nice? Predicting Future Feelings", in Daniel Kahneman, Ed Diener, and Norbert Schwarz (eds.), *Well-Being: The Foundation of Hedonic Psychology*, New York: Russell Sage Foundation, 85–105.

Lucas, Richard E., Clark, Andrew E., Georgellis, Yannis, and Diener, Ed (2003), "Reexamining Adaptation and the Set Point Model of Happiness: Reactions to Changes in Marital Status", *Journal of Personality and Social Psychology*, 84/3: 527–39.

Lyubomirsky, Sonja, and Lepper, Heidi S. (1999), "A Measure of Subjective Happiness: Preliminary Reliability and Construct Validation", *Social Indicators Research*, 46/2: 137–55.

143

Marshall, Alfred (1890), *The Principles of Economics*, 8th edn. (1920), London: Macmillan.

Marx, Karl (1849), "Wage-Labour and Capital", http://eserver.org/marx/1849-wage.labor.capital/6-labor.and.capital.txt, May 2002.

Mastekaasa, Arne (1992), "Marriage and Psychological Well-Being: Some Evidence on Selection into Marriage", *Journal of Marriage and the Family*, 54/4: 901–11.

Mellers, Barbara A. (2000), "Choice and the Relative Pleasure of Consequences", *Psychological Bulletin*, 126/6: 910–24.

Michalos, A. C. (1985), "Multiple Discrepancies Theory (MDT)", *Social Indicators Research*, 16: 347–413.

—— and Zumbo, Bruno D. (2000), "Criminal Victimization and the Quality of Life", *Social Indicators Research*, 50/3: 245–95.

Modigliani, Franco (1949), "Fluctuations in the Saving-Income Ratio: A Problem in Economic Forecasting", *Studies in Income and Wealth*, 11: 371–443.

Myers, David G. (1999), "Close Relationship and Quality of Life", in Daniel Kahneman, Ed Diener, and Norbert Schwarz (eds.), *Well-Being: The Foundations of Hedonic Psychology*, New York: Russell Sage Foundation, 374–91.

Nannestad, Peter, and Paldam, Martin (1994), "The VP-function: A Survey of the Literature on Vote and Popularity Functions after 25 Years", *Public Choice*, 79/3–4: 213–45.

Neumark, David, and Postlewaite, Andrew (1998), "Relative Income Concerns and the Rise in Married Women's Employment", *Journal of Public Economics*, 70/1: 157–83.

Oswald, Andrew J. (1997), "Happiness and Economic Performance", *Economic Journal*, 107/445: 1815–31.

Parducci, Allen (1995), *Happiness, Pleasure, and Judgment: The Contextual Theory and its Applications*, Hillsdale, NJ: Erlbaum.

Pollak, Robert A. (1970), "Habit Formation and Dynamic Demand Functions", *Journal of Political Economy*, 78/4: 745–63.

—— (1976), "Interdependent Preferences", *American Economic Review*, 66/3: 309–20.

—— (2002), "Gary Becker's Contributions to Family and Household Economics", NBER Working Paper No. 9232, Cambridge, Mass.: National Bureau of Economic Research.

Ross, Catherine E., Mirowsky, John, and Goldsteen, Karen (1990), "The Impact of the Family on Health: The Decade in Review", *Journal of Marriage and the Family*, 52/4: 1059–78.

Samuelson, Paul A. (1973), *Economics*, 9th edn. New York: McGraw-Hill.

Schooler, Jonathan W., Ariely, Dan, and Loewenstein, George (2003), "The Pursuit and Assessment of Happiness can be Self-Defeating", in Isabelle Brocas and Juan D. Carrillo (eds.), *The Psychology of Economic Decisions, Volume 1: Rationality and Well-Being*, Oxford: Oxford University Press, 41–70.

Schor, Juliet B. (1998), *The Overspent American: Why We Want What We Don't Need*, New York: Basic Books.

Schwarze, Johannes, and Härpfer, Marco (2002), "Are People Inequality Averse, and Do They Prefer Redistribution by the State? Evidence From German Longitudinal Data on Life Satisfaction", IZA Discussion Papers No. 430, IZA Bonn.

Scitovsky, Tibor (1976), *The Joyless Economy: An Inquiry into Human Satisfaction and Dissatisfaction*, Oxford: Oxford University Press.

Smith, Richard H., Diener, Ed, and Wedell, Douglas H. (1989), "Intrapersonal and Social Comparison Determinants of Happiness: A Range-Frequency Analysis", *Journal of Personality and Social Psychology*, 56/3: 317–25.

Stack, Steven, and Eshleman, J. Ross (1998), "Marital Status and Happiness: A 17-Nation Study", *Journal of Marriage and the Family*, 60/2: 527–36.

Stouffer, Samuel A., Suchman, Edward A., DeVinney, Leland C., Star, Shirley A., and Williams, Jr., Robin M. (1949), *The American Soldier: Adjustment during Army Life*, Princeton: Princeton University Press.

Stutzer, Alois (2004), "The Role of Income Aspirations in Individual Happiness", *Journal of Economic Behavior and Organization*, 54/1: 89–109.

—— and Frey, Bruno S. (2003), "Stress that Doesn't Pay: The Commuting Paradox", IEW Working Paper No. 151, University of Zurich.

—— —— (Forthcoming), "Does Marriage Make People Happy, or do Happy People get Married", *Journal of Socio-Economics*.

—— and Lalive, Rafael (2004), "The Role of Social Work Norms in Job Searching and Subjective Well-Being", *Journal of the European Economic Association*, 2/4: 696–719.

Tomes, Nigel (1986), "Income Distribution, Happiness and Satisfaction: A Direct Test of the Interdependent Preferences Model", *Journal of Economic Psychology*, 7/4: 425–46.

Tversky, Amos, and Griffin, Dale (1991), "Endowment and Contrast in Judgments of Well-Being", in Richard J. Zeckhauser (ed.), *Strategy and Choice*, Cambridge, Mass. and London: MIT Press: 297–318.

van Herwaarden, Floor, Kapteyn, Arie, and van Praag, Bernard M. S. (1977), "Twelve Thousand Individual Welfare Functions: A Comparison of Six Samples in Belgium and The Netherlands", *European Economic Review*, 9/3: 283–300.

van Praag, Bernard M. S. (1971), "The Welfare Function of Income in Belgium: An Empirical Investigation", *European Economic Review*, 2: 337–69.

—— (1993), "The Relativity of the Welfare Concept", in Martha. Nussbaum and Amartya Sen (eds.), *The Quality of Life*, Oxford: Clarendon Press, 362–416.

—— and Frijters, Paul (1999), "The Measurement of Welfare and Well-Being: The Leyden Approach", in Daniel Kahneman, Ed Diener, and Norbert Schwarz (eds.), *Well-Being: The Foundations of Hedonic Psychology*, New York: Russell Sage Foundation, 413–33.

—— and van der Sar, Nico L. (1988), "Household Cost Functions and Equivalence Scales", *Journal of Human Resources*, 23/2: 193–210.

Veblen, Thorstein (1899), *The Theory of Leisure Class*, New York: Modern Library.

Waite, Linda J., and Gallagher, Maggie (2000), *The Case for Marriage: Why Married People are Happier, Healthier, and Better Off Financially*, New York: Doubleday.

Weiss, Yoram (1997), "The Formation and Dissolution of Families: Why Marry? Who Marries Whom? And What Happens Upon Marriage and Divorce", in Mark K. Rosenzweig and Oded Stark (eds.), *Handbook of Population Economics*, vols. 1A and 1B, Amsterdam, New York, and Oxford: Elsevier.

Wilson, Chris M., and Oswald, Andrew J. (2002), "How Does Marriage Affect Physical and Psychological Health? A Survey of the Longitudinal Evidence", Mimeo, Warwick University.

Winkelmann, Liliana, and Winkelmann, Rainer (1998), "Why are the Unemployed So Unhappy? Evidence from Panel Data", *Economica*, 65/257: 1–15.

Winkelmann, Rainer (2002), "Subjective Well-Being and the Family", Working Paper No. 0204, Socioeconomic Institute, University of Zurich.

5

Rethinking Public Economics: The Implications of Rivalry and Habit

Richard Layard

The aim of public policy should be to maximize people's happiness, suitably aggregated. This requires us to understand what actually produces happiness. In traditional economics, we simply assume that someone's current happiness depends on their current choice-set. The larger the choice-set, the happier the person. So if my choice-set increases and everyone else's remains the same, social welfare must increase.

But this conclusion completely ignores the impact of one person's pay rise on the welfare of his colleagues. Such interdependencies are a basic part of human experience, and a theory which ignores them is deeply misleading. In consequence some critics would have us discard the whole approach. But this is wrong. Instead we should expand our framework to take into account the full range of human experience, rather than rejecting it.

But how? Until recently we had to rely mainly on introspection or on observations of behavior—with no direct evidence about what produced happiness. But now we are accumulating more solid evidence on what actually affects happiness, and it confirms the powerful negative effect of other people's incomes. Whether we like it or not, human beings are rivalrous, and it is time for mainstream economics to incorporate this key fact of human nature.

There is a second key fact—habituation. Many forms of consumption give more pleasure at first than they do over the long haul. And people do not fully foresee this when they embark on a more expensive life-style.

Both these phenomena lead to serious market failures, which public policy needs to offset. Envy means that any income gain is a source of major negative externality—perhaps the biggest negative externality in modern society. Habituation involves major informational errors, which again lead to major inefficiency.

The purpose of this chapter is to see (in Section 2) what policy responses these phenomena require and more generally to see how they modify the standard propositions of public economics.[1] We shall find that rivalry and habit provide major new arguments for state activity. But first we need to establish the pervasive nature of the phenomena (in Part 1).

1. Evidence

There are two types of evidence.[2] The first, which is only circumstantial, points out that over time and across OECD countries rises in aggregate income are not associated with rises in aggregate happiness. The second type of evidence is microeconometric and tries to identify the actual mechanisms which are causing individual happiness.

In both cases we rely on people's responses to questions about happiness and job satisfaction. There is much evidence to support the objectivity and comparability of these answers. Individual self-reports of happiness are highly correlated with reports by others and with physical measurements of brain electro-encephelograms (EEGs) and smiling behavior (Diener and Suh 2000, chap. 1). Individual job satisfaction is highly correlated with quitting behaviour and with absenteeism (Freeman 1978). So let us look at what people say.

Aggregate Time Series and Cross-Sections

At the aggregate level, there has been no increase in reported happiness over the last 50 years in the US and Japan, nor in Europe since 1973 when the records began.[3] Nor has there been any particular change in the shape of the happiness distribution. These facts are remarkable, given the astonishing widening of the choice-set open to people in the Western world. The facts hold cohort by cohort—individual cohorts do not get happier over time despite the huge increase in their living standards.

The data here relate to questions like "Taken all together, how would you say things are these days—would you say you are very happy, pretty happy or not too happy?" Figure 5.1 shows the graph for the US.

Of course within countries the rich are always happier than the poor.[4] But over time, as absolute incomes rise, the happiness levels at each

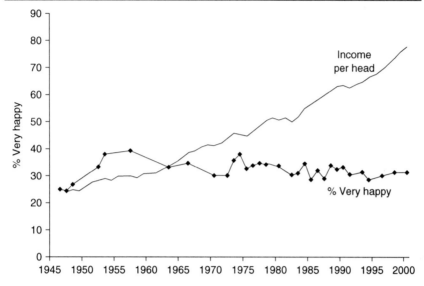

Figure 5.1. Income and happiness, US

Notes: The questions were:

AlPO: "In general, how happy would you say that you are—very happy, fairly happy or not happy?"; GSS: "Taking things all together, how would you say you are these days—would you say that you are very happy, pretty happy or not too happy?" The GSS get fewer replies in the top category than the AIPO for obvious reasons. (the difference between "pretty happy" and "fairly happy" and the reference to "these days" in the GSS). My approach is to accept the GSS replies and adjust all the AIPO ones to give the same AIPO reply in 1971 as the GSS reply in 1972.

Sources:

Income per head (adjusted for prices): Bureau of Economic Analysis, US Department of Commerce, NIPA Table 7.1, Real GDP per person per year.

Happiness: (1946–71:) American Institute of Public Opinion (AIPO) (Gallup), reported in T. W. Smith (1979) "Happiness: Time Trends, Seasonal Variations. Intersurvey Differences and Other Mysteries", *Social Psychology Quarterly* 42/1, (March), 18–30; 1972–2000: General Social Survey (GSS).

quartile fail to rise (see Table 5.1).[5] This suggests that the rich are benefiting from the level of their relative income, rather than from their absolute income.

Equally, if we compare countries, there is no evidence that richer countries are happier than poorer ones—so long as we confine ourselves to countries with incomes over $15,000 per head.[6] (For those who doubt whether happiness can be compared across countries I include Appendix 5.1, which should reassure them.)

At income levels below $15,000 per head things are different, since people are nearer to the absolute breadline. At these income levels richer countries *are* happier than poorer ones. And in countries like India,

Table 5.1. How happy are the rich and the poor? (US)

	Top quarter		Bottom quarter	
	1975	1998	1975	1998
Very happy	39	37	19	16
Pretty happy	53	57	51	53
Not too happy	8	6	30	31
Total	100	100	100	100

Mexico, and the Philippines, where we have time series data, happiness has grown as income levels have risen.[7] Moreover, within each poor country the happiness gap between rich and poor people is greater than it is in more prosperous parts of the world.[8] So economic growth is indeed more important for poor than for rich countries—as the diminishing marginal utility of income would lead us to expect.

The aggregate statistics raise the basic question of why in the West happiness has stagnated while incomes have exploded. But they cannot uncover the mechanisms at work. That requires microeconometric studies of happiness or of job satisfaction.[9]

Micro Evidence: Rivalry

The great majority of these studies show a strong negative effect of other people's incomes (rivalry) and of own lagged income (habit). On rivalry, in the US Blanchflower and Oswald (2000) found that a rise in the average income in the state where you live reduces your happiness by one-third as much as a rise in your own income increases it.[10] In Britain, Clark and Oswald (1996) found that a rise in the wages of comparable workers reduces your job satisfaction by as much as a rise in your own wage increases it.[11] Clark (1996) also showed that job satisfaction was adversely affected by the pay of your spouse. Comparisons also affect behaviour: if a woman's husband earns less than her sister's husband, the first woman is more likely to go out to work—in order to keep up with the living standards of her sister (Postlethwaite et al. 1998).

But perhaps the most telling indicator of the problem comes from a simple questionnaire administered to Harvard graduate students in public health. They were asked to choose between living in worlds A and B:[12]

A you earn $50k, and others earn $25k
B you earn $100k, and others earn $250k

Over half the students chose world *A*—so sensitive were they to the earnings of others. One can discuss ad nauseam why we make these comparisons. Some would call it envy but it is probably best thought of as a desire to exceed, or at least not fall below, the social norm.

Such sensitivity (though sad) would not distort choice if people were equally sensitive to all elements of other people's lives. For example, if people compared their leisure with others' as intensely as they compared their earnings, the private income–leisure choices of the individual would remain socially efficient. However, that is not how things are. People are much less sensitive to other people's leisure than they are to other people's earnings. The same students were asked to choose between worlds *A'* and *B'*:

A' You have two weeks' vacation and others have one week

B' You have four weeks' vacation and others have eight weeks

Only 20 percent of the students chose world *A'*. People compare their conspicuous consumption with others but are much less concerned with their comparative access to leisure, public goods, and inconspicuous consumption. That is why we should worry lest the latter get under-produced.

In reply to this, libertarians often argue that the rivalrous person has only himself to blame, and he should not be protected by public efforts to discourage conspicuous consumption. But this is to miss the mark. We are all rivalrous, to a greater or lesser degree. Which one of us would not suffer if all our colleagues except us got a raise? It is an intrinsic part of human nature, wired into the genes. When a monkey becomes top monkey, his serotonin count improves, and when he is displaced it falls.[13] This competitive instinct promoted survival in the wild. In our tamer world it is completely rational to limit those spheres of life where it survives in its more extreme forms, and to promote optimal levels of less rivalrous activity.

Micro Evidence: Habit

On the role of habituation, most studies find that lagged income has a negative effect on current happiness. In a panel study of individuals Clark (1999) found that job satisfaction in the UK is unaffected by the level of wages, and depends only on their rate of change—implying a strong negative effect of habituation coming from the lagged wage. At a more aggregate level, in a panel of countries Di Tella *et al.* (2002) found that lagged income reduced happiness by two-thirds as much as current income increased it. (Thus a steady rise in income did increase happiness somewhat, but in the historical record this effect was offset by the negative effects of other changes—higher divorce, crime, and so on.)

Another, less direct, approach to habituation is to ask people how much income they would need in order to lead a reasonable life. The Gallup Poll in the US has for many years asked, "What is the smallest amount of money a family of four needs to get along in this community?" Over time the answers rise in line with actual incomes. Many other studies have found similar results.[14]

A different approach is cross-sectional.[15] Each individual is asked, "What after-tax income would you consider for your family to be: very bad, bad, insufficient, sufficient, good, very good?" From these answers we can identify for each individual the income level which is mid-way between sufficient and insufficient. This "required income" varies strongly with the actual income of the individual—with a 10 percent rise in actual income predicting a roughly 5 percent rise in required income.[16]

The process at work here is the basic human process of adaptation, whereby people adjust to a change in circumstances, be it upwards or downwards. This is for example the mechanism that explains the famous endowment effect, whereby people suffer more from losing something than they would gain from obtaining it. One example of this is the mug experiment, where people are asked how much they would be willing to pay for a mug. They are then given the mug and asked how much they require to part with it. Their "selling" price is typically more than 50 percent higher than their "buying" price. This example illustrates, by extension, the importance which a standard of living acquires, once we have experienced it. It is what psychologists sometimes call the "hedonic treadmill".

But such processes of adaptation would cause no market failure if individuals foresaw them and took them into account. There is a lot of evidence that people do not correctly forecast how they will adapt.[17] For example, academics think that gaining tenure will make them happier for longer than it does—and so on. Even the participants in the mug experiment fail to forecast how much they will value the mug once they have it.[18] And, as for smoking, people's plans to smoke may indeed by affected by the future price of cigarettes as shown by Becker and Murphy (1988). But people still greatly under-predict their future cigarette consumption, given what they now consume. For example, among high school students who smoked a pack a day, only 32 percent expected to be doing it in five years time, compared with 70 percent who actually did it.[19] In fact almost all of us underestimate how much the level of living we adopt today will affect our utility function in the future.

But, again, it is crucial whether we adapt to some things more than others. For example, if we had 10 percent more leisure would we soon take it for granted in exactly the same way in which we might take for granted a 10 percent increase in our material standard of living? Frank (1999) makes a powerful case for the view that we would experience "gains that endure", if we had more social life, more time with our kids, less travel-time to work, more autonomy at work, more job security, and better health care. By contrast we rapidly adjust to a better car and a bigger house, with little continuing benefit. Remarkably, the time series reveal that, as people's income increase, their level of financial anxiety remains as high as ever.

To conclude, the evidence shows that, at the level of society as a whole, both rivalry and habit limit the effect of higher consumption upon social well-being. They also distort choice. To examine the extent of the distortion, we need to know how the negative effects of average consumption and own lagged consumption compare in magnitude with the positive effect of own current consumption. The evidence presented above shows that the negative effects are substantial, but not precisely defined. In what follows we shall assume that (i) the negative effect of average consumption upon utility is 0.3 times the positive effect of own current consumption and (ii) the negative effect of own lagged consumption is also 0.3 times the positive effect of own current consumption. Unless the effects are at least this large, it is extremely difficult to explain why happiness has been so stable in the OECD countries while real living standards have risen so much.

2. Policy

We can now ask how far the findings of Section 1 require us to rethink the standard propositions of public economics. To make a crude beginning, let me examine the following fairly standard propositions.

1. *Consumption–leisure choice*   The first-best solution would involve no marginal taxation of earnings. If taxes were needed to finance public goods, they should ideally be levied in lump-sum form (or be made as intra-marginal as possible).

2. *Cost–benefit analysis and public expenditure* Benefits should be valued by the amount that individuals would be willing to pay. Public expenditure should be undertaken when benefits exceed costs. Tax costs should allow for the excess burden of taxation.

3. *Choice between goods* Any consumption tax should be levied at the same rate on all goods and services unless there is strong evidence about differential complementarities with leisure.

4. *Redistribution* If lump-sum transfers could be made, these should equalize the marginal utility of income experienced by each individual. Since they cannot, we face an equity–efficiency trade-off.

How well do these propositions survive in the presence of the facts presented in Section 1? In answering, we shall assume all individuals to be identical, until we come to redistribution.

Consumption–Leisure Choice: The Effect of Rivalry

We can begin with the choice of hours of work. Since we are interested in how big an issue this is, we shall assume a specific utility function, the Cobb-Douglas,[20] with

$$u_i = (c_i - \beta c)^\alpha (1 - h_i)^{1-\alpha} = c_i^\alpha \left(1 - \beta \frac{c}{c_i}\right)^\alpha (1 - h_i)^{1-\alpha}$$

Here c_i is own consumption, c average consumption, and h_i is the fraction of time worked. As the right-hand expression shows, consumption is partly valued for its own sake, but partly also in relation to the consumption level in the rest of society. We shall assume that the wage is unity so that $c_i = h_i$.

We can now compare the optimum hours of work for society and for the individual. The social optimum maximizes utility taking c_i/c as fixed. Socially optimal hours are therefore $h = \alpha$. But the individual maximizes utility taking c as given. He therefore works for

$$h = \frac{\alpha}{\alpha + (1 - \alpha)(1 - \beta)}$$

He works longer than is optimal and the difference could be quite substantial. We shall assume that $\alpha = 0.4$ and (as we have said) that $\beta = 0.3$ Then optimal hours are 0.4 (say 40 actual hours out of a total of 100 "available"). But the individual, who ignores the negative externality which his work gives rise to, works nearly 20 percent more than is optimal.

He is working only partly for the intrinsic value of consumption but also partly to compete with the consumption of others.

This is an externality problem. When someone works an extra unit and increases his consumption by one unit, this affects the average level of consumption faced by the other members of society. To be precise, average consumption is raised by $1/n$, which reduces the utility of each of the other n people by $-\beta(1/n)\partial u/\partial c_i$. Since there are n others, the total negative externality measured in utils is $\beta \partial u/\partial c_i$. To prevent this loss of utility requires a tax of equal magnitude.[21] The optimal money tax is this externality measured in utils divided by the marginal utility of consumption. Thus the optimal tax rate is β.

If we imposed such a tax, we should force individuals to internalize the externality, choosing their hours solely on the basis of the absolute value of consumption—and ignoring its relative value altogether. We cannot stop people losing utility because they enviously compare themselves with others. But we can stop them losing further utility through self-defeating efforts to out-do each other.

Relative consumption, or indeed relative status or relative position of any kind, is in fixed supply. There is no point in people devoting energy to acquiring it. It is simply inefficient. So in this case a positive tax is efficient and a zero tax is inefficient.

Consumption–Leisure Choice: The Effect of Habit

A second mechanism which induces overwork is habit. If people adopt a higher living standard, they lose the option to return to their former living standard and experience the same utility as before from a given consumption. This negative effect of current consumption on future utility has been called by Frank a negative "internality". The distortion arises if the habituation effect is not foreseen. It operates precisely like the effect of an unforeseen addiction. In order to obtain a given amount of utility from this consumption an individual has to consume more and therefore to work harder.

Again, we are interested in the scale of the problem and the appropriate tax rate to offset it. Suppose that utility in period t is given as follows:[22]

$$u_t = f(c_t - \gamma c_{t-1}) \cdot v(1 - h_t)$$

We want the individual to maximize $\Sigma D^t u_t$, where D is the discount factor. This is subject to the intertemporal budget constraint, where for simplicity we shall assume that the real wage is constant and equal to one unit of consumption per unit of work. The budget constraint is therefore

$$\sum R^t(h_t - c_t) = 0$$

There are now two possible cases. In one the individual chooses h_t, c_t with foresight—taking note of the negative effect of lagged consumption reflected in the term $(-\gamma c_{t-i})$. In the other case the individual is myopic, behaving as if γ were zero. In both cases if $R = D$, the solution is a constant level of consumption and work, with zero saving.[23] But, when there is foresight, the level of work and consumption is less than when there is myopia.

To understand how hours are determined, we can write out the first two terms in the maximand Σu_t, beginning at period 0:

$$f(c_0 - \gamma c_{-1})v(1 - h_0) + Df(c_1 - \gamma c_0)v(1 - h_1) + \cdots$$

We now differentiate by h_0, allowing for the fact that the wage is unity. If habituation were foreseen (as would be optimal), hours would be given by

$$f_0'v_0 - \gamma Df_1'v_1 = f_0 v_0'$$

So in the steady state, where $f'v$ is constant, optimality requires

$$f'v(1 - \gamma D) = fv'$$

But, if habituation is not foreseen, hours are given by $f'v = fv'$.

How different are hours in the two cases? We shall again assume that u_t is Cobb-Douglas, with

$$u_t = (c_t - \gamma c_{t-1})^\alpha (1 - h_t)^{1-\alpha}$$

Then, with foresight, hours and consumption are

$$h = c = \frac{\alpha}{\alpha + (1 - \alpha)(1 - \gamma)/(1 - \gamma D)}$$

But, if habituation is not foreseen,

$$h = c = \frac{\alpha}{\alpha + (1 - \alpha)(1 - \gamma)}$$

which is substantially greater.[24] If we assume (as explained) that $\gamma = 0.3$ with $\alpha = 0.4$ and $D = 0.95$, then hours and consumption without foresight are 20 percent higher than with foresight. This is a serious error, and even if a half of the true habituation (γ) was foreseen, there would be roughly 11 percent more work and consumption than is optimal.[25]

Taxation is a natural way to remedy this. Assuming zero foresight, the optimal self-financing linear tax is given by

$$t = -D\frac{\partial u_1}{\partial c_0} \bigg/ \frac{\partial u_0}{\partial c_0} = \frac{\gamma Df'v}{f'v} = \gamma D$$

In this analysis the distorting effect of habit is not upon intertemporal choice but upon work effort. This is not obvious in a two-period analysis, but, once we take a long enough view, it is clear that the main problem concerns the *level* of the consumption profile, not its shape.

Finally, we can reintroduce rivalry and ask, What is the *overall* distortion in hours and what would the efficient tax be? The social maximand is

$$\sum f(c_{0i} - \beta c_0 - \gamma c_{-1i})v(1 - h_{0i})$$
$$+ D\sum f(c_{1i} - \beta c_1 - \gamma c_{0i})v(1 - h_{1i}) + \text{etc.}$$

Without foresight the individual will work 52 percent too hard.[26] This is a massive distortion. To find the optimal tax we note that the sum of the "externality" plus the "internal" distortion that are together caused by an extra unit of c_{0i} is $f'v(\beta + \gamma D)$.

The optimal tax rate is therefore

$$t = \beta + \gamma D$$

In our example this is 0.585.

The tax we have been discussing is efficient; it is not distorting. So the tax proceeds have no excess burden. There is however the crucial issue of how they should be spent. If we ignore redistribution until later, the tax proceeds could either be used for public expenditure or they could be redistributed. They should be used for public expenditure only if this passes the cost–benefit test. But in this context how should cost–benefit analysis be conducted?

Cost–Benefit Analysis and Public Expenditure

In order to highlight the issue, I shall begin with the case where no efficient tax of the kind discussed above is already being levied. The question we want to ask is this: "Would the representative individual wish to see a given public expenditure happen if it were financed by him *and* by other citizens?"

Suppose the expenditure were on providing a bridge. The benefit of providing the bridge would then be

(i) the value attaching to the bridge, *and*
(ii) the benefit from reduced consumption by others.

The cost has to be compared with the sum of the two items—not as in the standard theory with the value of the bridge alone.

To be more precise, let us consider a bridge that costs (in flow terms) Q per citizen per period. Suppose $u_i = (c_i - \beta c)^\alpha + \phi D$ where D is a dummy taking the value 1 when there is a bridge. The bridge should be built if the benefits in utils exceed the cost in utils. In other words

$$\phi + \alpha(c_i - \beta c)^{\alpha-1} \beta Q > Q\alpha(c_i - \beta c)^{\alpha-1}$$

or

$$\frac{\phi}{\alpha(c_i - \beta c)^{\alpha-1}} > Q(1 - \beta)$$

The left-hand side is the individual's willingness to pay (WTP) and this need not exceed the cost (Q). It need only exceed the cost times $(1 - \beta)$.

However this assumes that when we undertake the extra expenditure we are changing taxes. Suppose instead that we already have the efficient tax. The issue is then whether to spend the money or hand it back in lump-sum form. In this case we should compare willingness to pay directly with the cost. But we should not, as in standard theory, augment the cost by the excess burden of the taxation which finances it.

The issue of excess burden would only arise if we needed more public expenditure than could be financed by the proceeds of the efficient tax. In this case excess burden would begin to be an issue. But of course the tax distortion would be measured not by the tax rate but by the excess of the tax rate over the efficient tax rate.

Thus, whichever perspective we take, public expenditure is more likely to be justified than appears from the traditional analysis.

Inconspicuous Consumption

Let us now consider a different dimension of individual choice, between different forms of consumption. Some forms of consumption are much more visible than others. For example, people compare their cars and houses with other people's. But they do not compete in this way over job security, safety at work, adequate insurance, crime-free streets, or health-care services. Frank (1985) calls such items "inconspicuous consumption".[27] Others might call them "merit goods". These goods (g_i) cannot be provided without extra work or reduced conspicuous consumption (c_i). If we leave matters to the market, they will be underprovided precisely because "conspicuous consumption", which is partly self-defeating, will be overprovided.

For example, suppose an employer is willing to offer increased job security at a price equal to its cost to the employer. The individual, when deciding how much security to choose, will take into account the loss of relative consumption involved, as well as the loss of absolute consumption. He will thus demand less job security than he would demand if all his colleagues demanded it as well.

Algebraically, we shall now think in terms of a utility function

$$u_i = (c_i - \beta c)^\alpha \, g_i^\delta (1 - h_i)^{1-\alpha-\delta}$$

We can readily see what difference a collective decision on the inconspicuous good might make. If the decision were collective, everyone would work for $(\alpha + \delta)$ units and spend δ units of income on merit goods and α on consumption proper. But the isolated individual's choice would be different. In a tax-free world, he would work

$$h = \frac{\alpha + \delta(1 - \beta)}{1 - \beta(1 - \alpha)} > \alpha + \delta$$

And he would spend his money on consumption and merit goods according to

$$c = \frac{\alpha}{1 - \beta(1 - \alpha)} > \alpha$$

and

$$g = \frac{\delta(1 - \beta)}{1 - \beta(1 - \alpha)} < \delta$$

So he will overwork, overconsume, and underspend on merit goods. The underspending on merit goods could be substantial.

It is interesting to explore magnitudes. In our exposition so far we have ignored habit. But it happens that, broadly speaking, those goods which are bought for effect are also those which lose their luster most rapidly. So for simplicity we shall make β reflect both rivalry and habit, and we shall therefore assume $\beta = 0.585$ We shall also assume $\alpha = 0.3$ and $\delta = 0.15$.

So socially optimal hours are 0.45, with consumption being 0.30 and expenditure on merit goods 0.15. But left to his own, the individual works for 0.62 hours, consumes 0.51 and spends only 0.11 on merit goods.

How in practice could such an outcome be secured? Would it require regulation as Frank (1982) suggested? The answer is, not necessarily. We could simply forget about merit goods and tax conspicuous consumption correctly. If we did so, individual choice would reproduce the collective choice we have just described. The optimum tax rate on conspicuous consumption would now, as before, be β. The individual would then freely choose to work for $\alpha + \delta$ units and freely choose to buy δ units of the merit good. Provided the merit good is not itself taxed, its quantity will be correctly chosen. For example, suppose a firm could provide an extra unit of safety at work at a cost θ and a worker valued it more than $\theta(1 - \beta)$. He would then be willing to accept the wage cut of θ for the sake of the extra safety, since his consumption would only be reduced by $\theta(1 - t) = \theta(1 - \beta)$.

The design of tax systems to protect inconspicuous consumption from taxation is therefore extremely important.

Redistribution

Finally, redistribution. We need a tax-benefit schedule which finances redistribution and other public expenditure, in a way that maximizes the sum of utilities.[28] In the normal analysis there is an excess burden from any positive level of taxation. But our analysis shows that there may be no excess burden until quite high levels of taxation are reached. So the first obvious question is whether the tax levied in the name of efficiency could be high enough to achieve as much redistribution as was justified.

The answer is No. For at the efficient rate of tax there is no net excess burden of taxation. But unless the rate of tax is unity there will still be differences in net income, generating differences in the marginal utility of income. There will thus be a case for further redistribution, up to the point where the cost of further redistribution is as great as the gain from greater equality.

Consider the following example. Suppose first that everyone were the same and

$$u_i = (c_i - \beta c)^{\alpha}(1 - h_i)^{\beta}$$

With no tax, people would work

$$\alpha/(\alpha + (1-\alpha)(1-\beta))$$

rather than the efficient α. The efficient tax would be

$$-\frac{\partial u_i/\partial c}{\partial u_i/\partial c_i} = \beta$$

leading everyone to work for α units.

Suppose now that people differ in productivity. There are two groups of equal size with wage rates w_1 and w_2. Suppose we introduce a self-financing tax with a tax rate β and a total tax per person given by[29]

$$T_i = \beta w_i h_i - \tfrac{1}{2}\beta(w_1 h_1 + w_2 h_2)$$

With this tax each group will in fact work for α units.[30] Meantime the tax will have substantially reduced the income gap between the two groups. For example, if $w_1/w_2 = 3$ and $\beta = 0.585$, then the new ratio $c_1/c_2 = 1.5$. This difference means however that the marginal utility of consumption is still significantly different between the two groups, justifying a tax rate higher than β.

How much higher should the tax rate be? At the social optimum the marginal utility of income of the poor person relative to the rich should equal 1 plus the efficiency cost of a unit net transfer from rich to poor. How should we compute this cost?

Suppose $W_1 = 1$ and $W_2 = \lambda < 1$, and for simplicity we renormalize hours at unity (they will be little affected by a small additional self-financing tax). Then the total "proceeds" of the linear tax are $t(1 + \lambda)$. But the net transfer is only $0.5t(1 - \lambda)$ since, although the rich man pays t in tax, he gets back $0.5t(1 + \lambda)$ in handout. So the marginal tax "proceeds" are $2(1 + \lambda)/(1 - \lambda)$ times the marginal net transfer. Now the marginal excess burden per unit of tax revenue is $\eta t/(1 - t - \eta t)$ where η is the compensated elasticity of supply.[31] It follows that the marginal excess burden per unit of net transfer is higher than this and is in fact

$$\frac{\eta t}{1 - t - \eta t} \frac{2(1 + \lambda)}{(1 - \lambda)}$$

As for the relative marginal utility of income of group 2, it is given by approximately

$$\left(\frac{c_2}{c_1}\right)^{\alpha-1} = \left(\frac{(1-t)\lambda + \tfrac{1}{2}t(1+\lambda)}{1 - t + \tfrac{1}{2}t(1+\lambda)}\right)^{\alpha-1}$$

So we now know how to find the optimum tax rate—subject to one qualification. The excess burden has to be measured for the tax rate only in *excess* of its efficient level t^*.

To find the optimum overall tax rate (t) we set the relative marginal utility of group 2 equal to 1 plus the marginal excess burden per unit of net transfer. So

$$\left(\frac{(1-t)\lambda + \frac{1}{2}t(1+\lambda)}{1 - t + \frac{1}{2}t(1+\lambda)}\right)^{\alpha - 1} = 1 + \frac{\eta(t - t^*)}{1 - (1+\eta)(t - t^*)} \cdot \frac{2(1+\lambda)}{1 - \lambda}$$

Thus as underlying equality (measured by λ) increases, so the appropriate tax rate t decreases.

But how much tax is needed? A crude approximation of the UK income distribution is $\lambda = 1/3$—it gives the same coefficient of variation (0.5) as the existing income distribution. We can take $t^* = 0.585$. We have hitherto assumed $\alpha = 0.4$ and will continue to do so, though most of the work on public economics uses functions where marginal utility declines more rapidly. Since the compensated elasticity of supply (η) is $(1 - \alpha)$, the implied tax rate is 0.67.[32] This is a typical figure for the marginal tax rate in Europe including all direct and indirect levies.[33] (The share of taxes in GDP is considerably less, just under a half, due to tax exemptions.)

A quite different approach (not my own) might start from the libertarian view that redistribution should only be undertaken to the extent that those who pay for it wish it. We would then postulate that the rich care about the incomes of the poor, which are in effect for them a public good. However the rich find it painful to part with their wealth. But they find it less painful if all the other rich people are doing the same. This is an old argument in favour of collective decisions in favour of charity. Going back to our original welfare function, suppose that there are n rich people. Each of them has the following utility function

$$u_i = (c_i - \beta c)^\alpha + \phi \sum_j d_j$$

where d_j is the amount given to the poor by the j^t person.

If the individual gives one unit on his own his benefit is only ϕ. If all individuals give at the same time, each gets an extra benefit, consisting of two parts:

  (i) a bigger increase in receipts by the poor, and
  (ii) a gain from reduced consumption by others.

So the gain from a unit gift by each is now

$$\phi n + \alpha(c_i - \beta c)^{\alpha-1}\,\beta$$

This greatly exceeds ϕ, but the main reason is the first term rather than the second.

3. Conclusions

This chapter is intended as a challenge to the profession—not to throw away our tools, but to use them in a more realistic way. There is now enough evidence to demonstrate beyond doubt that, in the absence of taxes, rivalry and habit would lead to excessive, self-defeating effort.

To offset these distortions requires a significant tax rate. Such taxes are not distorting but efficient. Thus, when public expenditure is evaluated, the tax cost should not be increased for "excess burden" on the scale currently allowed for. And inconspicuous consumption (consumption which is not compared with the consumption of others) should be taxed much less highly than conspicuous consumption.

Economists have long been puzzled that the public votes for high levels of "manifestly distorting" taxation. But could it be that the public uses a more realistic model of human nature than many economists do? Could this explain why they agree to collective restraint of private spending for the sake of more public goods and a less frenzied life-style?

Social science is only beginning to examine the true determinants of utility, and to acknowledge that revealed preference reveals the part and not the whole. The studies we have so far yield variable parameters, and in addition we have our own introspection. All this evidence show that the phenomena we are discussing are big and important, and they should now be included in mainstream public economics.

Appendix 5.1. Inter-country Comparisons

Of course one could question whether the word "happy" (or "satisfied") means the same thing in different languages. If it does not, we can learn nothing by comparing different countries. However countries can be rated separately on three different measures: how "happy" they are, how "satisfied" they are, and what score they give to life, using a scale running from "worst possible life" to the "best". The ranking of countries is almost identical on all three measures.[34] This suggests that words are not causing a problem.

Moreover there is direct evidence, for a number of languages, that the words do have a stable meaning in the different languages. For example, a group of Chinese students were asked to answer the happiness question, once in Chinese and once in English, with three weeks between the two questions.[35] A control group of similar students were asked to answer the questions in English only on both occasions. The consistency between the first group's replies in Chinese and in English was as good as between the control group's two replies in English. Since the English and Chinese languages are very far apart, this finding is highly reassuring. Similarly we can take the three groups of Swiss—who speak French, German, and Italian. They give similar replies. And each group of Swiss people is happier than those who speak the same language but live next door in France, Germany, or Italy. So the country and the life, rather than the language, is the overriding factor influencing the replies.

But, again, might not people in some countries feel more impelled to give high or low replies to the question, because of local cultural norms? There is no evidence of this—for example, no clear tendency for individualistic countries to vote high or collectivist cultures to vote low.[36] And the concepts seem equally familiar in all cultures—getting response rates of around 99 percent.

Appendix 5.2. The Effects of Habit

In this appendix we examine first the optimal allocation (when the effects of habit are foreseen) and then the individual choice when the effects are not foreseen. We shall begin with the fairly general formulation

$$u_t = f(c_t - \gamma c_{t-1}) \cdot v(1 - h_t)$$

We assume the wage equals unity, and $R = D$.

Optimum Choice

The problem is

$$\text{Max} f(c_1 - \gamma c_0)v(1 - h_1) + Df(c_2 - \gamma c_1)v(1 - h_2) + \text{etc.}$$
$$+ \lambda(h_1 - c_1 + D(h_2 - c_2) + \text{etc.})$$

The first-order conditions for c_1, c_2, c_3 etc. are

$$f_1'v_1 - D\gamma f_2'v_2 = \lambda \qquad \text{(A1)}$$
$$f_2'v_2 - D\gamma f_3'v_3 = \lambda \qquad \text{(A2)}$$
$$f_3'v_3 - D\gamma f_4'v_4 = \lambda \qquad \text{(A3)}$$

etc.

We can multiply equation A2 by $D\gamma$, equation A3 by $(D\gamma)^2$, etc. and then add equations A1, A2, A3 etc. This yields

$$f_1'v_1 = \lambda(1 + D\gamma + D^2\gamma^2 + \text{etc.}) = \frac{\lambda}{1 - D\gamma} \qquad \text{(B1)}$$

In addition, if we start one period later,

$$f_2'v_2 = \frac{\lambda}{1 - D\gamma}, \qquad \text{(B2)}$$

and so on.

The first-order conditions for h_1, h_2, h_3 etc. are

$$f_1v_1' = \lambda \qquad \text{(C1)}$$
$$f_2v_2' = \lambda \qquad \text{(C2)}$$
$$\text{etc.}$$

The conditions B1, B2 etc. and C1, C2 etc. are satisfied by $c_t = c$ (constant), $h_t = h$ (constant), $c = h$ and

$$f'v(1 - D\gamma) = fv' \qquad \text{(D)}$$

(This assumes that c_0 is the same as the solution for c_1, c_2 etc.)

Myopic Choice

With myopia the individual behaves as if $\gamma = 0$. Thus he chooses $c_t = c$, $h_t = h$, $c = h$ but with

$$f'v = fv' \qquad \text{(E)}$$

Comparison

We can compare h chosen optimally with h chosen myopically. If u is Cobb-Douglas

$$u = (c - \gamma c)^\alpha (1 - h)^{1-\alpha}$$

So optimal choice (given by equation D) becomes

$$\frac{\alpha u(1 - D\gamma)}{c(1 - \gamma)} = \frac{(1 - \alpha)u}{1 - h}$$

Since $c = h$, this gives optimal hours of

$$h = \frac{\alpha}{\alpha + (1 - \alpha)(1 - \gamma)/(1 - D\gamma)}$$

By contrast private choice (given by equation E) yields

$$\frac{\alpha u}{c(1 - \gamma)} = \frac{(1 - \alpha)u}{1 - h}$$

so that

$$h = \frac{\alpha}{\alpha + (1 - \alpha)(1 - \gamma)}$$

Notes

1. Many of these issues have been raised before by among others Easterlin (1973), Hirsch (1976), Scitovsky (1976), Layard (1980, 2005) and above all Frank (1985 and 1999). But their analyses have had remarkably little impact on mainstream public economics. For example, the latest edition of J. Stiglitz, *Economics of the Public Sector* contains no treatment of these issues.
2. For surveys see Diener and Biswas-Diener (2002) and Inglehart and Klingemann (2000).
3. See e.g. Frey and Stutzer (2002).
4. There is a causal relationship running from income to happiness—see e.g. Winkelmann and Winkelmann (1998) and Gardner and Oswald (2001), who use panel data to prove it.
5. US data. General Social Survey tapes.
6. Inglehart and Klingemann (2000).
7. Diener and Oishi (2000).
8. Inglehart and Klingemann (2000).
9. For some discussion see Layard (2005).
10. Table 8, col. 4—but the controls for prices and unemployment were poor. Diener *et al.* (1993) claimed no effect of average income, but their statistical analysis was less comprehensive than Blanchflower and Oswald's.
11. Comparison income was measured using a regression equation of wages on characteristics.
12. Solnick and Hemenway (1998), quoted in Frank (1999).
13. Brammer *et al.* (1994).
14. Frank (1999).
15. Van Praag and Frijters (1999).
16. Similar results are found in nine different countries. The "required income" also varies with family size in a way that produces sensible equivalent scales for family income requirements.

17. Loewenstein and Schkade (1999).
18. Loewenstein and Adler (1995).
19. Loewenstein and Schkade (1999).
20. This gives a vertical labor supply curve—which is about right for men and women taken together.
21. See Layard (1980) for a fuller discussion.
22. I am grateful to Stephen Nickell for the analysis which follows. It is more general than the two-period case considered by Loewenstein *et al.* (2000).
23. For proof see Appendix 5.2. We assume that the initial level of lagged consumption is the same as the optimal level of present and future consumption.
24. It is also possible to show that, with a completely general concave utility function, hours and consumption fall as foresight increases.
25. The individual chooses $h = \alpha/(\alpha + (1 - \alpha)(1 - \gamma)/(1 - 0.5\gamma D))$.
26. The social optimum is $\alpha/(\alpha + (1 - \alpha)(1 - \beta - \gamma)/(1 - \beta - \gamma D))$ and the private optimum is $\alpha/(\alpha + (1 - \alpha)(1 - \beta - \gamma))$.
27. See also Frank (1982) for a mathematical analysis of its implications.
28. See e.g. Mirrlees (1971).
29. The efficient tax is strictly $\beta \sum_j (\partial u_j/\partial c_j) \sum_k (\partial u_k/\partial c_k)^{-1}$.
30. Since the tax is self-balancing, $c = (1/2)(w_0 h_0 + w_1 h_1)$. Thus $c_i - \beta c = w_i h_i (1 - \beta) + (1/2)\beta(w_0 h_0 + w_1 h_1) - \beta(1/2)(w_0 h_0 + w_1 h_1) = w_i h_i (1 - \beta)$.
31. See Layard (1980).
32. The solution to $1 = ((1 + t)/(3 - t))^{-0.6} + (2.4t - 1.404)/(1.6t - 1.936)$. For simplicity η is evaluated at zero lump-sum income.
33. Even in Britain it is at least 55%.
34. Veenhoven (2000: 10).
35. Shao (1993).
36. Veenhoven (2000: 10–11).

References

Becker, G., and Murphy, K. (1988), "A Theory of Rational Addiction", *Journal of Political Economy*, 96/4: 675–700.

—— Grossman, M., and Murphy, K. (1994), "An Empirical Analysis of Cigarette Addiction", *The American Economic Review*, 84/3: 396–418.

Blanchflower, D., and Oswald, A. (2000), "Well-Being over Time in Britain and the USA", NBER Working Papers, No. 7487.

Brammer, G., Raleigh, M., and McGuire, M. (1994), "Neurotransmitters and Social Status", in L. Ellis (ed.), *Social Stratification and Socioeconomic Inequality*, ii, Westport, Conn.: Greenwood.

Clark, A. (1996), "L'utilité est-elle relative? Analyse à l'aide de données sur les ménages", *Economie et Precision*, 121: 151–64.

—— (1999), "Are Wages Habit-Forming? Evidence from Micro Data", *Journal of Economic Behaviour and Organisation*, 39 (June): 179–200.

Clark, A. (2001), "What Really Matters in a Job? Hedonic Measurement using Quit Data", *Labour Economics*, 8 (May): 223–42.

—— and Oswald, A. (1996), "Satisfaction and Comparison Income", *Journal of Public Economics*, 61: 359–81.

Di Tella, R., Layard, R., and MacCulloch, R. (2002), "Accounting for Happiness", mimeo, London School of Economics.

Diener, E., and Biswas-Diener, R. (2002), "Will Money Increase Subjective Well-Being?", *Social Indicators Research*, 57: 119–69.

—— and Oishi, S. (2000), "Money and Happiness: Income and Subjective Well-Being across Nations", in Diener and Suh (2000).

—— Sandvik, E., and Seidlitz, L., (1993), "The Relationship between Income and Subjective Well-Being: Relative or Absolute?", *Social Indicators Research*, 28: 195–223.

—— and Suh, E. (eds.) (2000), *Subjective Well-being across Cultures*, Cambridge, Mass.: MIT Press.

Easterlin, R. (1973), "Does Economic Growth Improve the Human Lot? Some Empirical Evidence", in P. David and M. Reder (eds.), *Nations and Households in Economic Growth: Essays in Honor of Moses Abramovitz*, Palo Alto, Calif.: Stanford University Press.

—— (2001), 'Income and Happiness: Towards a Unified Theory', *Economic Journal*, 111: 465–84.

Frank, R. H. (1982), "Envy and the Optimal Purchase of Unobservable Commodities: The Case of Safety", in M. W. Jones-Lee (ed.), *The Value of Life and Safety*, Amsterdam: North-Holland.

—— (1985), *Choosing the Right Pond*, Oxford: Oxford University Press.

—— (1999), *Luxury Fever: Money and Happiness in an Era of Excess*. Princeton and Oxford: Princeton University Press.

Freeman, R. (1978) "Job Satisfaction as an Economic Variable", *American Economic Review*, 74: 549–71.

Frey, B., and Stutzer, A. (2002), *Happiness and Economics*, New Jersey: Princeton University Press.

Gardner, J., and Oswald, A. (2001), "Does Money buy Happiness? A Longitudinal Study using Data on Windfalls", Mimeo, University of Warwick.

Hirsch, F. (1976), *The Social Limits to Growth*, Cambridge, Mass.: Harvard University Press.

Inglehart, R., and Klingemann, H.-D. (2000), "Genes, Culture, Democracy and Happiness", in Diener and Suh (2000).

Kahneman, D., Diener, E., and Schwartz, N. (1999), *Well-Being: The Foundations of Hedonic Psychology*, New York: Russell Sage Foundation.

Layard, R. (1980), "Human Satisfactions and Public Policy", *The Economic Journal*, 90: 737–50.

—— (2005), *Happiness: Lessons from a New Science*, New York and London: Penguin Books.

Loewenstein, G., and Adler, D. (1995), "A Bias in the Prediction of Tastes", *Economic Journal*, 105/431: 929–37.

—— and Schkade, D. (1999), "Wouldn't it be Nice? Predicting Future Feelings", in Kahneman *et al.* (1999).

—— O'Donoghue, T., and Rabin, M. (2000), "Projection Bias in Predicting Future Utility", BDR Working Papers Series, 258.

Mirrlees, J. A. (1971), "An Exploration in the Theory of Optimum Income Taxation", *Review of Economic Studies*, 38 (April): 175–208.

Postlethwaite, A., Cole, H. L., and Mailath, G. J. (1998), "Class Systems and the Enforcement of Social Norms", *Journal of Public Economics*, 70/1: 5–35.

Shao, L. (1993), "Multilanguage Comparability of Life Satisfaction and Happiness Measures in Mainland Chinese and American Students", Mimeo, University of Illinois.

Scitovsky, T. (1976), *The Joyless Economy*, New York: Oxford University Press.

Solnick, S. J., and Hemenway, D. (1998), "Is More Always Better? A Survey on Positional Concerns", *Journal of Economic Behaviour and Organisation*, 37: 373–83.

van Praag, B., and Frijters, P. (1999), "The Measurement of Welfare and Well-Being: The Leyden Approach", in Kahneman *et al.* (1999).

Veenhoven, R. (2000), "Freedom and happiness: A Comparative Study in 44 Nations in the early 1990s", in Diener and Suh (2000).

Winkelmann, L., and Winkelmann, R. (1998), "Why Are the Unemployed So Unhappy? Evidence from Panel Data", *Economica*, 65: 1–15.

6

Mill between Aristotle and Bentham

Martha C. Nussbaum

Who is the happy Warrior? Who is he
That every man in arms should wish to be?

Wordsworth,
"Character of the Happy Warrior"

Man does not strive after happiness; only the Englishman does that.

Nietzsche, *"Maxims and Arrows"*

I

Powerful philosophical conceptions conceal, even while they reveal. By shining a powerful light on some genuinely important aspects of human life, British Utilitarianism concealed others. Its concern with counting each and every person obscured, for a time, the fact that some issues of justice cannot be well handled through mere aggregation of the interests of all. Its radical and admirable concern with suffering, with bringing all sentient beings from pain to a state of well-being and satisfaction, obscured, for a time, the fact that satisfaction might not be all there was to the human good, or even all there was to happiness. Other things might also be involved, such as activity, loving, fullness of commitment.

Indeed, so powerful was the obscuring power of Bentham's insight that a question that Wordsworth takes to be altogether askable, and which, indeed, he spends 85 lines answering—the question what happiness really is—soon looks to philosophers under Bentham's influence like a question whose answer is so obvious that it cannot be asked in earnest. Thus Henry Prichard, albeit a foe of Utilitarianism, was so influenced in his thinking about happiness by Bentham's conception that he simply assumed that any philosopher who talks about happiness must be identifying it with pleasure or satisfaction. When Aristotle asks what happiness is, Prichard argued, he cannot really be asking the question he appears to be asking, since the answer to that question is obvious: happiness is contentment or satisfaction. Instead of asking what happiness consists in, then, he must really be asking about the instrumental means to the production of happiness.[1] Nietzsche, similarly, understands happiness to be (uncontroversially) a state of pleasure and contentment, and expresses his scorn for Englishmen who pursue that goal, rather than richer goals involving suffering for a noble end, continued striving, activities that put contentment at risk, and so forth. Unaware of the richer English tradition about happiness represented in Wordsworth's poem, he simply took English "happiness" to be what Bentham said it was. So, much later, did Finnish sociologist Erik Allardt, when he wrote an attack on the idea that happiness was the end of social planning, entitling his book *Having, Loving, Being*—active things that he took to be more important than satisfaction, which Finns, heirs of Nordic romanticism, typically think quite unimportant.[2] Like Nietzsche, he understood the "happiness" of the social scientists to be a state of pleasure or satisfaction. (He is correct about the social scientists, if not about "happiness".)

There is, however, an older and longer tradition of thinking about happiness, the tradition represented in Wordsworth's poem. It derives from ancient Greek thought about *eudaimonia* and its parts, and is inherited via the standard English translation of *eudaimonia* as "happiness". According to this tradition, represented most fully in Aristotle's *Nicomachean Ethics*, what we all can agree about is that happiness is something like flourishing human living, a kind of living that is active, inclusive of all that has intrinsic value, and complete, meaning lacking in nothing that would make it richer or better. Everything else about happiness is disputed, says Aristotle, but he then goes on to argue for a conception of happiness that identifies it with a specific plurality of valuable activities, including activity in accordance with excellences[3] (valuable traits) of many sorts, including ethical, intellectual, and political excellences, and activities involved in love and friendship. Pleasure is not identical with happiness, but it usually (*not* always) accompanies the unimpeded performance of the activities that constitute happiness.

Something like this is the idea that Wordsworth is relying on, when he asks, in each of the many areas of life, what the character and demeanor of the "happy Warrior" would be, and answers that question. As J. L. Austin memorably wrote in a devastating critique of Prichard on Aristotle, "I do not think Wordsworth meant . . . : 'This is the warrior who feels *pleased.*' Indeed, he is 'Doomed to go in company with Pain | And fear and bloodshed, miserable train.' "

As Austin saw, the important thing about the happy Warrior is that he has traits that make him capable of performing all of life's many activities in an exemplary way, and he acts in accordance with those traits. He is moderate, kind, courageous, loving, a good friend, concerned for the community, honest,[4] not excessively attached to honor or worldly ambition, a lover of reason, an equal lover of home and family. His life is happy because it is full and rich, even though it sometimes may involve pain and loss.

John Stuart Mill knew both of these conceptions of happiness and was torn between them. Philosophically he declared himself a Utilitarian; despite his many criticisms of Bentham, he never stopped representing himself as a defender of Bentham's general line. He was also, however, a lover of the Greeks and a lover of Wordsworth, the poet whom he credits with curing his depression. The Aristotelian/Wordsworthian conception of happiness makes numerous appearances in his thought. Mill seems never to have fully realized the extent of the tension between the two conceptions; thus he never describes the conflict between them or argues for the importance of the pieces he appropriates from each one. The unkind way of characterizing the result is that Mill is deeply confused and has no coherent conception of happiness. The kinder and, I believe, more accurate way is that, despite Mill's unfortunate lack of clarity about how he is combining the two conceptions, he really does have a more or less coherent idea of how to combine them, giving richness of life and complexity of activity a place they do not have in Bentham, but giving pleasure and the absence of pain and depression a role that Aristotle never sufficiently maps out—in part because depression is a category that Aristotle never recognizes, as Mill, by dint of unfortunate experience, does. The result is the basis, at least, for a conception of happiness that is richer than either of its two sources, more capable of doing justice to all the elements that thoughtful people have associated with that elusive idea.

II

Bentham had a way of making life simpler than it is. He asserts that the only thing good in itself is pleasure, and the only thing bad in itself is pain.

From the claim that these two "masters" have a very powerful influence on human conduct, he passes without argument to the normative claim that they are the proper goals of conduct. And he also equates pleasure with happiness (sometimes with enjoyment of happiness), pain with unhappiness. The principle of utility is "that principle which approves or disapproves of every action whatsoever, according to the tendency which it appears to have to augment or diminish the happiness of the party whose interest is in question: or, what is the same thing in other words, to promote or to oppose that happiness". Utility, in turn, is defined in a manner that shows Bentham's characteristic disregard of distinctions that have mattered greatly to philosophers, both before and since:

> By utility is meant that property in any object, whereby it tends to produce benefit, advantage, pleasure, good, or happiness, (all this in the present case comes to the same thing) or (what comes again to the same thing) to prevent the happening of mischief, pain, evil, or unhappiness to the party whose interest is considered.

Ignoring or flouting the long Western philosophical tradition that had debated whether happiness could be identified with pleasure—a tradition in which the negative answer greatly predominated, the positive answer being given only by Epicureans—Bentham simply declares what he takes to be the case, and goes on from there. Nothing else is good but pleasure; pleasure and good are the same thing.

As for pleasure, an equally long philosophical tradition before Bentham had debated how we should understand its nature. Is it a single unitary thing, or many things? Is it a feeling, or is it a way of being active, or, perhaps, activity itself? We speak of pleasure as a type of experience, but we also refer to activities as "my pleasures", saying things like, "My greatest pleasures are listening to Mahler and eating steak". Such ways of talking raise two questions: is pleasure a sensation at all, if such very different experiences count as pleasures? And is it single? Could there be any one thing that both listening to Mahler's Tenth and eating a steak have in common?

These questions were subtly discussed by Plato, Aristotle, and a whole line of subsequent philosophers. Bentham simply ignores them. As Mill writes in his great essay "On Bentham", "Bentham failed in deriving light from other minds". For him, pleasure is a single homogeneous sensation, containing no qualitative differences. The only variations in pleasure are quantitative. They can vary in intensity, duration, certainty or uncertainty, propinquity or remoteness, and, finally, in causal properties (tendency to produce more pleasure, etc.). The apparent fact that pleasures differ in quality, that the pleasure of steak-eating is quite different from the pleasure of listening to Mahler's Tenth, bothered Bentham not at all; he does not discuss such examples. Perhaps the reason for this problem is that Bentham's deepest concern is with pain and suffering, and it is somewhat more plausible to think of pain as a unitary sensation varying only in intensity and duration. As Mill says, this is "the empiricism of one who has had little experience"—either external, he adds, or internal, through the imagination.

Nor was Bentham worried about interpersonal comparisons, a problem on which economists in the Utilitarian tradition have spent great labor. For Bentham there was no such problem: when we move from one person to many people, we just add a new dimension of quantity. Right action is ultimately defined as that which produces the greatest pleasure for the greatest number. Moreover, Bentham sees no problem in extending the comparison class to the entire world of sentient animals. One of the most attractive aspects of his thought is its great compassion for the suffering of animals, which he took to be unproblematically comparable to human suffering.[5]

Another problem that has troubled economists in the Benthamite tradition is that of evil pleasures. If people get pleasure from inflicting harm on others, as so often they do, should that count as a pleasure that makes society better? Most economists who follow Bentham have tried to do some line-drawing here, in order to leave the most sadistic and malicious pleasures out of the social choice function. In so doing, they complicate the system in a way that Bentham would not have approved, introducing an ethical value that is not itself reducible to pleasure or pain.

Activity plays no special role in Bentham's system. The goal of right action is to maximize pleasure, understood as a sensation. That is the only good thing there is in the world. So, in effect, people and animals are understood as large containers of sensations of pleasure or satisfaction. Their capacity for agency is of interest only in the sense that it makes them capable of choosing actions that produce utility. But in terms of the end result, agency really does not matter. A person who gets pleasure by being hooked up to an experience machine (a famous example of the late Robert Nozick) is just as well off as the person who gets pleasure by loving and eating and listening. Even when we are thinking about nonhuman animals, this is a very reduced picture of what is valuable in life; where human beings are concerned, it evidently leaves out more or less everything.

What is attractive about Bentham's program is its focus on urgent needs of sentient beings for relief from suffering and its determination to take all suffering of all sentient beings into account. But Bentham cannot be said to have developed anything like a convincing account of pleasure and pain, of happiness, or of social utility. Because of his attachment to a strident simplicity, the view remains a sketch crying out for adequate philosophical development.

III

Unlike Bentham, Aristotle sees that the question about happiness is a very difficult question. He is aware of many different answers people have given to that question. Some identify happiness with pleasure, some with honor, some with the life of virtue, some with the life of reflection or thought. But progress can be made, he suggests, if we pin down some key areas of agreement. In book I of the *Nicomachean Ethics*, he sets about that task. He argues that there is general agreement about several formal characteristics of happiness. It must be *most final*, that is, inclusive of all that has intrinsic value. It must be *self-sufficient*, by which he means that there is nothing that can be added to it that would increase its value. (He immediately makes clear that self-sufficiency does not imply solitariness: the sort of self-sufficiency he is after is one that includes relationships with family, friends, and fellow citizens.) It must be *active*, since we all agree that happiness is equivalent to "living well and doing well". Moreover, we think that a person who is inactive all through life ("asleep" he says, but we could think of a coma) is not in the least happy, but indeed quite miserable, even if he feels no pain and is in a very good ethical state. It must be *generally available*, to anyone who makes the right sort of effort, since we don't want to define happiness as something only a few can enjoy. And it must be relatively *stable*, not something that can be removed by any chance misfortune.

Aristotle concludes this (allegedly uncontroversial) part of his argument by arguing that there is a further deep agreement: happiness is made up of activity in accordance with excellence, either one excellence, or, if there are more than one, then the greatest and most complete. Scholars argue a lot about the precise understanding of this passage, but let me simply assert. At this point in his argument, Aristotle cannot be importing any precise or controversial content into the conception, and he explicitly says that he is not doing so. So he must mean, whatever the excellent activities of a human life are, happiness involves all of these in some suitable combination. He also makes it clear that the overall product is more than the mere aggregation of its parts: the way all the activities fit together to make up a whole life is itself an element in the value of the life.

In the remainder of the work, Aristotle moves through the areas of human life in which we characteristically act and make choices, trying to identify the excellent way of acting in each of these areas. He seems to think that there is relatively little controversy about the fact that courage, moderation, justice, etc. are worth pursuing: where the controversy occurs is in the more precise specification of what each of these is. Presumably the reason for this is that he conceives of these spheres of life as spheres in which we all have to make some choice or another: we have to have some way of facing the risk of death, some way of coping with our bodily appetites, etc. So there is no question of omitting that element altogether; one either does it well or does it badly, and the question is, what is it to do it well? Only with friendship and love does he face an imaginary opponent who urges the utter omission of these relationships as intrinsically valuable areas of human activity. But he brusquely dismisses that position by saying that nobody would want to live without friendship, even if he had all the other goods.

Where in all of this is pleasure? Early in the work, Aristotle dismisses the claim that pleasure is identical with happiness, saying that living for pleasure only would be "to choose the life of dumb grazing animals". Later he advances some further arguments against the identification. First of all, there is an issue about pleasure: it is by no means easy to say what it is. Aristotle himself offers two very different conceptions of pleasure, one in book VII and one in book X. The first identifies pleasure with unimpeded activity (not so odd if we remember that we speak of "my pleasures" and "enjoyments"). The second, and probably better, account holds that pleasure is something that comes along with, supervenes on, activity, "like the bloom on the cheek of youth". In other words, it is so closely linked to the relevant activities that it cannot be pursued on its own, any more than bloom can be cultivated by cosmetics. One gets it by doing the relevant activity in a certain way, apparently a way that is not impeded, or is complete. It is a kind of awareness of one's own activity. In any case, pleasure is not a single thing, varying only in intensity and duration (a position that Plato already knew and criticized). It contains qualitative differences, related to the differences of the activities to which it attaches.

But whatever one says about pleasure, one should still not say that it is identical with happiness. First of all, even if pleasure were single and homogeneous, happiness clearly is not: it is constituted by activities of many different sorts, which cannot be rendered commensurable on any quantitative scale.

Second, pleasure is just not the right thing to pitch on as a normative account of the good life for a human being. Some pleasures are bad, namely those that are closely associated with bad activities. Evil people have pleasure in their evil behavior. But happiness is a normative notion, meaning "the human good life", or "a flourishing life for a human being", so we cannot include evil pleasures in it.

Another problem, and a revealing one for Mill, is that some valuable activities are not accompanied by pleasure. Aristotle's example is Words-worthian (perhaps the source for Wordsworth's poem): the courageous warrior who faces death in battle for the sake of a noble end. It is absurd to say that this person is pleased at the prospect of death, says Aristotle. Indeed, the better his life is, the more he thinks he has to lose, and the more pain he is likely to feel at the prospect of death. Nonetheless, he is acting in accordance with excellence, and is aware of that; and so he is still happy. This just goes to show, says Aristotle, that pleasure does not always go along with the activities that comprise happiness, only most of the time.

The courageous warrior is still happy because he is living the sort of life he chooses, and it is a good one. There are other people whose circum-stances deprive them of happiness, according to Aristotle. But they do so by blocking activity. For example, if one is imprisoned and tortured, one is no longer happy—because all one's activities are terribly "impeded". If one encounters "the luck of Priam", here too, one can be "dislodged from happiness"—because friends, children, political activity, and indeed the entire sphere in which he lived and acted are suddenly snatched away by defeat and capture. So Aristotle does allow that certain sorts of misery are incompatible with happiness: but his question is not, "How does the person feel?" It is, instead, "What is the person able to do?" And he judges that in a wide variety of circumstances a good person will be able to use life's materials resourcefully and well, so as to continue being happy in a wide range of (somewhat reduced) circumstances.

IV

Mill's *Utilitarianism* is organized as an extended defense of Bentham's program against the most common objections that had been raised against it. Mill defends both the idea that pleasure is identical with hap-piness and the idea that right action consists in producing the greatest happiness for the greatest number. Along the way, however, without open defection from the Benthamite camp, he introduces a number of crucial modifications. First of all, he admits that Bentham's theory has given no clear answer to the question of what pleasure is: "To give a clear view of the moral standard set up by the theory, much more requires to be said; in particular, what things it includes in the ideas of pain and pleasure; and to what extent this is left an open question."

One thing that Mill does shortly make very clear, however, is that, for him, "Neither pains nor pleasures are homogenous". There are differences "*in kind*, apart from the question of intensity", that are evident to any competent judge. We cannot avoid recognizing qualitative differences, particularly between "higher" and "lower" pleasures. How, then, to judge between them? Like Plato in *Republic* book IX, Mill refers the choice to a competent judge who has experienced both alternatives.

This famous passage shows Mill thinking of pleasures as very like activities, or, with Aristotle, as experiences so closely linked to activities that they cannot be pursued apart from them. In a later text, he counts music, virtue, and health as major pleasures. Elsewhere he shows that he has not left sensation utterly out of account: he refers to "which of two modes of existence is the most grateful to the feelings". Clearly, however, the unity of the Benthamite calculus has been thrown out, to be replaced by an idea of competent judgment as to what "manner of existence" is most "worth having". And this talk of a "manner of existence which employs their higher faculties" suggests that, with Aristotle, he is thinking of this judge as planning for a whole life.

When Mill describes the way in which his judge makes choices, things get still more complicated. The reason an experienced judge will not choose the lower pleasures is "a sense of dignity, which all human beings possess in one form or other,... and which is so essential a part of the happiness of those in whom it is strong, that nothing which conflicts with it could be, otherwise than momentarily, an object of desire to them". So a sense of dignity is a *part* of what happiness is for many people: it acts as a gatekeeper, preventing the choice of a life devoted to mere sensation. Nozick's experience machine will clearly be rejected by this judge. Moreover, Mill continues, if anyone supposes that this sense of dignity will cause people to sacrifice some of their happiness, they are just confused: they "confoun[d] two very different ideas, of happiness, and content". One more of Bentham's equivalences has now been denied.

Summarizing his discussion, referring to the ancient philosophers he has been following, Mill writes, "The happiness which they meant was not a life of rapture; but moments of such, in an existence made up of few and transitory pains, many and varied pleasures, with a decided predominance of the active over the passive". At this point, Mill would appear to have jettisoned the identification of happiness with pleasure: for happiness is now "made up of" pleasures, and some pains, and activity; its "parts" include virtue and the all-important sense of dignity. Even though pleasure itself is complex and heterogeneous, standing in a close relation to activity, happiness is more complex still, including some pain, and extending to embrace the complexities of an extended "mode of existence". Happiness is, then, a full and active life, in Aristotle's manner.

And yet the emphasis on pleasure persists throughout the work; Mill cannot utterly leave it aside. And in one crucial passage, he shows us that his attitude toward pained virtue is subtly different from that of Aristotle, and of Wordsworth. Imagining a virtuous man in the present "imperfect state of the world's arrangements", he concludes that this man must sacrifice his own happiness, if he wishes to promote the happiness of others. Mill does not tell us enough about this man. If his sacrifice is very great, so that his life is deprived of activity, Mill's position may still be Aristotelian: for Aristotle, we recall, judges that Priam is "dislodged from happiness" by his many and great misfortunes. But if this man is more like the happy Warrior, enduring pain for the sake of a noble cause, then Mill is not Aristotle. Even though this man is living well and acting well according to his plan, the very fact of the adversity he faces (apparently political adversity, anxiety, and various types of pain) deprives him of happiness, according to Mill, although Aristotle and Wordsworth judge that such a person is happy.

V

Mill, then, appears to stop short of Aristotle and Wordsworth. People's emotional states and states of pleasurable and non-painful awareness remain crucial elements in happiness, even though pleasure is seen to be elusive and complex, and even though happiness itself consists at least partly in valuable activities. We might put this point by saying that Mill sets the bar of fortune higher than Aristotle does. Aristotle thinks that fortune dislodges a person from happiness only when it impedes activity so severely that a person cannot execute his chosen plan of life at all. The pained warrior is still happy because he can still live in his own chosen way, and that is a good way. For Mill, the presence of a great deal of pain seems significant beyond its potential for inhibiting activity. A life full of ethical and intellectual excellences and activity according to those excellences does not suffice for happiness, if pleasure (however we think about pleasure) is insufficiently present and if too much pain is present.

Why did Mill think this? Well, as he tells us, he had experienced such a life—not in a moment of courageous risk-taking, but during a long period of depression. This life was the result of an upbringing that emphasized excellent activity to the exclusion of emotional satisfactions, including feelings of contentment, pleasure, and comfort.

Mill, as he famously records, and as much other evidence demonstrates, was brought up by his father to be hyper-competent, and to share his father's shame at powerful emotions. Nor did he receive elsewhere any successful or stable care for the emotional parts of his personality. Mill's mother was evidently a woman of no marked intellectual interests or accomplishments, and she soon became very exhausted by bearing so many children. Her son experienced this as a lack of warmth. In a passage from an early draft of the *Autobiography* (deleted prior to publication at the urging of his wife Harriet), Mill speaks of her with remarkable harshness:

That rarity in England, a really warm-hearted mother, would in the first place have made my father a totally different being, and in the second would have made his children grow up loving and being loved. But my mother, with the very best of intentions, only knew how to pass her life in drudging for them. Whatever she could do for them she did, and they liked her, because she was kind to them, but to make herself loved, looked up to, or even obeyed, required qualities which she unfortunately did not possess. I thus grew up in the absence of love and in the presence of fear; and many and indelible are the effects of this bringing up in the stunting of my moral growth.

In his early twenties, Mill encountered a crisis of depression. He remained active and carried out his plans; but he was aware of a deep inner void. He tried to relieve his melancholy through dedication to the general social welfare, but the blackness did not abate. The crucial turning point is a very mysterious incident that has been much discussed:

I was reading, accidentally, Marmontel's *Memoirs*, and came to the passage which relates his father's death, the distressed position of the family, and the sudden inspiration by which he, then a mere boy, felt and made them feel that he would be everything to them—would supply the place of all that they had lost. A vivid conception of the scene and its feelings came over me, and I was moved to tears. From this moment my burthen grew lighter. The oppression of the thought that all feeling was dead within me, was gone. I was no longer hopeless: I was not a stock or a stone . . .

The crisis gradually lifts, and Mill finds great sustenance in Words-worth's poetry. He returns to society. Several years later, after several unproductive infatuations with women of artistic and poetic tastes, he meets Harriet Taylor at a dinner party.

The Marmontel episode has typically been analyzed in terms of an alleged death wish by Mill toward his father. The assumption of such interpreters is that Mill is identifying himself with Marmontel, and expressing the desire to care for his family, displacing the father he feared. No doubt this is not altogether misguided, for hostility toward his father is a palpable emotion in the narrative, if counterbalanced by a great deal of love and admiration. The problem with this account, however, is that Mill does not seem particularly keen on caring for others, either before or after this episode. Indeed, he tells us that he tried to lift his depression by active concern with the well-being of others, but that this effort did no good. Instead, the focus of his search is all on finding care for himself, and in particular for the emotions and subjective feelings that his father's edu-cation had treated as shameful. It seems to me much more likely that Mill above all identified with the orphaned family who were now going to receive the care that they needed. He imagines someone saying to him, your needs, your feelings of pain, deadness, and loneliness, will be recognized and fulfilled, you will have the care that you need. Your dis-tress will be seen with love, and you will find someone who will be everything to you.

If we now examine the original Marmontel passage, as interpreters of the *Autobiography* usually do not bother to do, it strongly confirms this reading. Marmontel makes it clear that his consolation of his family was accomplished through the aid of a difficult control over his own emotions, as he delivered the speech "without a single tear". But at his words of comfort, streams of tears are suddenly released *in his mother and younger siblings*: tears no longer of bitter mourning, he says, but of relief at receiving comfort.[6] So Mill is clearly in the emotional position not of the self-contained son, but of the weeping mother and children, as they are relieved to find a comfort that assuages sorrow.

In part, as the *Autobiography* makes clear, Mill's wish for care is fulfilled by a new relation to himself: he becomes able to accept, care for, nourish, and value the previously hidden aspects of himself. In part, too, he shortly discovers in Harriet Taylor—as her letters show, an extremely emotional person and very skilled at circumnavigating John's intellectual defenses—the person who would care for him as his mother (he felt) did not. And his strong statements of preference for French over British culture also show

how much he prized freedom of emotional expression, which seemed to release his own imprisoned emotions. (Perhaps another aspect of the Marmontel episode is the language in which the releasing text was written.)

To relate the *Autobiography* to the complexities of Mill's relation to Bentham and Aristotle is conjectural. But it is the sort of conjecture that makes sense, and, moreover, the sort that Mill invites. For Mill, then, we may suppose, the Aristotelian conception of happiness is too cold. It places too much weight on correct activity, not enough on the receptive and childlike parts of the personality. One might act correctly, and yet feel like "a stock or a stone". Here the childlike nature of Bentham's approach to life, which Mill often stresses, proves valuable: for Bentham understood how powerful pain and pleasure are for children and the child in us. Bentham did not value the emotional elements of the personality in the right way. He simplified them too, lacking all understanding of poetry (as Mill insists) and of love (as we might add). But perhaps it was the very childlike character of Bentham, the man who loved the pleasures of small creatures, who allowed the mice in his study to sit on his lap, that made him able to see something Aristotle did not see, the need that we all have to be held and comforted, the need to escape a terrible loneliness and deadness.

Mill's *Utilitarianism* is not a fully developed work. It frustrates philosophers who look for a tidy resolution to the many tensions it introduces into the Utilitarian system. But it has proven compelling over the ages because it contains a subtle awareness of human complexity that few philosophical works can rival. Here as in his surprising writings on women, Mill stands out, an adult among the children, an empiricist *with* experience, a man who painfully attained the kind of self-knowledge that his great teacher lacked, and who turned that into philosophy.

Notes

1. (1935), 27–39, famously discussed and criticized in Austin (1979), 1–31. My account of Prichard follows Austin's, including his (fair) account of Prichard's implicit premises.
2. Erik Allardt (1975), A brief summary of some of the argument in English can be found in Allardt (1993). (The original language of Allardt (1975) is Swedish because Allardt is a Swedish-speaking Finn.)
3. I thus render Greek *aretê*, usually translated "virtue". *Aretê* need not be ethical; indeed it need not even be a trait of a person. It is a trait of anything, whatever

that thing is, that makes it good at doing what that sort of thing characteristically does. Thus Plato can speak of the *aretê* of a pruning knife.

4. Here we see the one major departure from Aristotle that apparently seemed to Wordsworth required by British morality. Aristotle does not make much of honesty. In other respects, Wordsworth is remarkably close to Aristotle, whether he knew it or not.

5. He denied that animals suffered at the very thought of death, and thus he argued that the painless killing of an animal is sometimes permitted.

6. Marmontel (1999: 63): " 'Ma mère, mes frères, mes soeurs, nous éprouvons, leur dis-je, la plus grande des afflictions; ne nous y laissons point abattre. Mes enfants, vous perdez un père; vous en retrouvez un; je vous en servirai; je le suis, je veux l'être; j'en embrasse tous les devoirs; et vous n'êtes plus orphelins,' À ces mots, des ruisseaux de larmes, mais de larmes bien moins amères, coulèrent de leurs yeux. 'Ah!' s'écria ma mère, en me pressant contre son coeur, 'mon fils! mon cher enfant! que je t'ai bien connu!' "

References

Allardt, Erik (1975), *Att ha, alska, att vara: Om valfard i Norden (Having, Loving, Being: On Welfare in the Nordic Countries)*, Borgholm: Argos.

——(1993), "Having, Loving, Being: An Alternative to the Swedish Model of Welfare Research", in M. Nussbaum and A. Sen (eds.), *The Quality of Life*, Oxford: Clarendon Press, 1993, 88–94.

Aristotle, Ethica Nicomachea, ed. I. Bywatel, Oxford: Clarendon Press, 1894.

Austin, J. L. (1979), "*Agathon* and *Eudaimonia* in the *Ethics* of Aristotle", in Austin, *Philosophical Papers*, ed. J. O. Urmson and G. J. Warnock, Oxford and New York: Oxford University Press, 1–31.

Bentham, J. (1789), An Introduction to the Principles of Morals and Legislation, J. H. Burns and H. L. A. Hart edrs., Athlone P., London.

Marmontel, Jean François, *Mémoires*, Paris: Mercule de France, 1999.

Mill, J. S. (1981) [1874], Autobiography and Literary Essays, Collected works. Vol I. John M. Robson and Jack Stillinger. ed. By, Toronto and London: University of Toronto Press. Routledge & Kegan.

Mill, J. S. (1998) [1863], Utilitarianism, in "Collected Works". Vol X. John M. Robson and Jack Stillinger. ed. By, Toronto and London, University of Toronto Press, Routledge & Kegan.

Nozick, *Anarchy State and Utopia*, New York: Basic Books, 1974.

Plato, *Republic*.

Prichard, H. A. (1935), "The Meaning of *Agathon* in the *Ethics* of Aristotle", *Philosophy*, 10: 27–39.

7

Happiness and Political Philosophy: The Case of Nancy Mitford versus Evelyn Waugh

Matt Matravers

Happiness, or something like it, plays a significant role in many accounts of the foundations of justice and of our motivation to be just. Its role is more easily identified in the case of motivation. Thus, John Rawls argues that one reason we have to endorse our sense of justice is that life in a well-ordered society is better and more satisfying for all than life in an unjust society. Peter Singer argues that the good life is more satisfying and more fulfilling than a life of self-interest. In both cases, they appeal to the happy prospect of living "from the point of view of the universe" (*sub specie aeternitatis*) to explain why we might be motivated to behave justly. The role of happiness in the case of grounding justice is less clear, but I argue below that appeals to subjective welfare are essential in the constructions of justice offered by theorists as otherwise different as Tim Scanlon and David Gauthier. However, the evidence is that what makes us happy, and what makes us feel fulfilled, is what is local; our families, friends, and communities. Thus, if happiness is to play a role in liberal political philosophy—in theories that attempt to generate universal principles of justice—then liberals have to explain how this is possible given the local focus of the objects that make us happy. In this chapter, I address this puzzle. My goal is to uncover the role played by the appeal to happiness in contemporary political philosophy; to show why it is problematic; and to show that the problem may reveal a significant constraint on the scope of morality.

I want, then, to consider a tension in contemporary (Anglo-American) analytic political philosophy that arises when an appeal is made to the idea that acting morally has a pay-off in terms of the subjective well-being of the agent. The tension is caused by morality encompassing a wider range of relationships than the range that normally contributes to people's happiness. I begin by saying a little about happiness—a term that I will use fairly loosely—in political philosophy. I then consider the role of happiness in accounts of moral motivation and in accounts of the grounding of morality. Finally, I turn to the tension noted above. The aim is to show that the idea that acting morally has a pay-off in terms of subjective well-being appears not just in the utilitarian and mutual advantage traditions (the traditions of Bentham and Hobbes), where it might be expected, but also in contemporary neo-Kantian theories (which is much more surprising). If the tension exists, then, it is problematic for theories in all of the main schools of ethical thought.[1]

1. Happiness in Political Philosophy

Happiness, or subjective feelings of well-being, can play a role in at least two ways in political philosophy: they may be part of the theory of what might motivate us to behave justly or morally, and/or part of the theory of what it is to behave justly or morally toward others. That is, appeals to happiness can be uncovered in accounts of *moral motivation* and/or in accounts of the *grounding* of morality itself.

The role of happiness has been significant in both the utilitarian and virtue ethical traditions. Virtue ethicists, who often prefer to invoke the ancient idea of *eudaimonia*, characteristically connect acting virtuously and achieving *eudaimonia*, although the precise nature of that connection varies between different theorists. Where happiness has had the most explicit role is in classical utilitarianism. For Bentham, happiness both constitutes the good for human beings and, in the form of pleasure and pain, explains what motivates them. It is in the Kantian tradition of moral and political philosophy that happiness has played its least significant role. For Kant, morality demands that one does one's duty (for the sake of duty) whatever the consequences for the happiness of the agent or of others. I argue below that recent neo-Kantian liberal theories give more emphasis to happiness and, in so doing, call on resources more commonly associated with the utilitarian tradition. To see that, we need first to examine briefly the role of happiness in a recent utilitarian argument.

2. Happiness and Moral Motivation

For a (reasonably) straightforward consequentialist theorist like Peter Singer, what makes something right or wrong is its consequences (for Singer "consequences" are measured in terms of the occurrence of pain and suffering in sentient beings). What it is for an action to be morally right is for it to be the action that leads to greatest net utility when compared with the outcomes of all alternative actions, including doing nothing where that is an alternative. Singer's theory is very demanding and he is not slow to point out that someone who spends money developing her taste for fine wines rather than campaigning for the elimination of poverty or giving the money to Oxfam is in some sense morally pathological (Singer 1972). Singer recognizes that this creates a problem because acting from the narrow perspective of self-interest is not irrational. Self-interest and generalized benevolence "clash" (Singer 1997: 268–77). In short, and as Bentham and all utilitarians have known, the role of happiness in constituting the good (as the promotion of *general* well-being or happiness) can conflict with its role in motivating particular agents (where the concern is with the particular well-being or happiness *of the agent*).

Singer does not attempt to solve this problem. He knows what morality demands, but he agrees that rationality does not command that we should give priority to its demands over those of individual self-interest. However, he thinks that there are things that can be said to commend the moral life to us. His approach is on two fronts and is neatly summed up in an anecdote he tells about taking up a visiting appointment at New York University in 1973. Singer claims that he had never known anyone in therapy before he moved to New York. In New York, he found many of his colleagues were in daily therapy ("handing over a quarter of their annual salary to their analysts!"). When he enquired of his colleagues why they were doing this, "they said that they felt repressed, or had unresolved psychological tensions, or found life meaningless". Singer's response is instructive. He records,

I wanted to pick them up and shake them. These people were intelligent, talented, wealthy, and living in one of the world's most exciting cities . . . The *New York Times* was informing them every day of the state of the real world. They knew, for example, that in several developing countries, there were families that did not know where the next day's food was coming from, and children who were growing up physically and mentally stunted by malnutrition. They knew, too, that the planet could produce enough food for every human being to be adequately fed, but that it was so unequally distributed as to make laughable any talk of justice between nations.

His (perhaps somewhat unsympathetic) conclusion was that,

if these able, affluent New Yorkers had only got off their analysts' couches, stopped thinking about their own problems, and gone out to do something about the real problems faced by less fortunate people in Bangladesh or Ethiopia—or even in Manhattan, a few subway stops north—they would have forgotten their own problems and maybe made the world a better place as well. (Singer 1997: 245)

The anecdote contains both parts of Singer's argument: first, that contemporary commercial life, even when successfully pursued, does not make us happy. We have, he thinks, become self-obsessed; concerned only with satisfying our own wants and those of people we happen to like or love. Even when we succeed—perhaps especially when we succeed—we are left feeling empty and our lives seem meaningless. Moreover, in psychotherapists we see solutions instead of evidence of the very cause of the problem. Second, we can find meaning in our lives and thus the solution to our problems in orienting ourselves to projects that transcend our narrow self-interest: in particular, in taking up projects that attend to the condition of the world and the sentient beings within it. Taking up a project of this kind will, Singer thinks, give us meaning and happiness.

Singer is, of course, not the first to argue this. He does however make explicit an appeal that is implicit in many other theories. Put as boldly as possible, the appeal is this: you should do what is morally required of you, and this will not conflict with your self-interest, because doing what is required of you will make you happy. Thus, the conflict between self-interest and morality can be largely dissolved because what is in your self-interest properly understood is, it turns out, to be moral (at least, more often than not).

As noted above, we should not be surprised to find this kind of appeal in Singer who is, after all, a consequentialist. Consequentialists are predisposed to thinking about happiness and the problem of reconciling the motivation to pursue one's own interest and the motivation to pursue the general interest is well established in consequentialist thought. What would be more surprising is to find such an appeal in a neo-Kantian theory. Yet, the appeal is there. To demonstrate this, consider the recent work of two explicitly neo-Kantian theorists, John Rawls and Tim Scanlon.

Discussion of the concept of happiness does not appear all that much in Rawls's work. It is mentioned briefly in *A Theory of Justice*, but only as part of a discussion of the pursuit of a rational plan of life and what Rawls calls "the problem of hedonism" (Rawls 1971: §83), but not at all in *Political Liberalism* (Rawls 1993). Nevertheless, understanding Rawls's project as a whole is impossible without understanding the way in which it is underpinned by the ideal of a well-ordered society and the way in which that ideal is taken by Rawls to be a reason for people to regulate their pursuit of their conceptions of the good in accordance with the demands of justice. A well-ordered society is one in which all citizens can all look one another in the eye, both in the sense that all are of equal status and in the sense that none is ashamed. This second sense is important. According to Rawls's moral vision—a vision that survives (indeed, in part, explains) his turn to the political—those who benefit from an unjust distribution of the benefits and burdens of social cooperation ought to want the system to be changed. They ought to want this for there is a great good, a good that belongs in a well-ordered society to each citizen, "in free and equal citizens recognizing the duty of civility to one another and supporting the institutions of a constitutional regime" (Rawls 1998: 621; cf. Nagel 1995: 121).

Of course, Rawls's account of how we are best to realize the good of a well-ordered society changed between *A Theory of Justice* and *Political Liberalism*. What did not change was his conviction that a well-ordered society was a goal worth pursuing and that it could be shown to be so. Of course, some people might not be convinced, and such people could not be charged with irrationality, but they would thereby deny themselves access to a constituent element of living well when living with others. Thus, and often only implicitly, Rawls appeals to an argument not unlike Singer's, although one that is narrower in scope. Asked what might motivate a religious believer to give priority to the demands of civility, or what might motivate the talented (or lucky) to recognize the demands of the difference principle as legitimate, Rawls has an answer: they have reason to want to live together with others on just terms and they have this reason in part because there is a pay-off in terms of subjective well-being—in terms of happiness—that arises from living in such a society.

A similar argument appears more explicitly in Scanlon's work. Scanlon's original account of moral motivation relied on a desire to act in ways that could not be reasonably rejected by others. This desire, Scanlon thought, was triggered in us when we correctly understood our relations with one another (Scanlon 1982). In his recent book, *What We Owe to Each Other* (1998), Scanlon replaces desire with reason and claims that reason motivates us. So, we have reason to behave morally toward one another and that reason is normally sufficient to motivate us to do so. Scanlon's account of reasons and their motivational power is complex, but the core of it is that we have reason to want our lives to go a certain way and, given that, we are motivated to perform actions that will achieve this. With respect to morality we have reason to behave in a certain way because we have reason to wish to live in "unity" with our fellows (Scanlon 1998: 154). Scanlon's account of moral motivation thus has much in common with that of John Stuart Mill from whom he borrows the phrase: "the social feelings of mankind; the desire to be in unity with our fellow creatures" (Mill 1987: 303).

Much of Scanlon's book is an attempt to explicate the notion of "living in unity" with fellow human beings, and much of the argument depends on the phenomenological accuracy that Scanlon claims for his account. The core of the argument is that we have reason to live in this way because it is better for us to do so. That is, standing in this relationship with others is appealing in itself, "worth seeking for its own sake" as Scanlon puts it (1998: 162). It is also a positive value for the individual; living in unity with others is a critical ingredient of living well. There is, as I put it above, a pay-off in terms of subjective well-being.

The idea of living in unity with our fellows plays a role not only in Scanlon's account of moral motivation, but also in grounding his con-tractualism. As noted above, Scanlon's defense of his contractualism is partly that it is phenomenologically accurate. In our relations with one another we are governed by a concern to act reasonably; to act in ways that cannot be reasonably rejected by others. Thus, this concern is built into the very structure of Scanlon's contractualism. What is clear, then, is that there is in the neo-Kantianism of both Rawls and Scanlon, just as in Singer's consequentialism, an appeal to the subjective well-being that is achieved when acting morally.

3. Happiness in the Grounding of Morality

Theorists—at least non-utilitarian theorists—who appeal to subjective well-being to ground morality are more unusual than those who slip some thoughts about well-being into their accounts of moral motivation. This is hardly surprising since to justify morality by appealing to its happiness-creating properties seems both implausible and, even if plausible, too contingent. So, we are skeptical when Socrates alleges that the unjust man who is caught and punished ought to be happier than the unjust man who gets away with it (Plato 1960). And morality, it is thought, binds us whether it makes us happy or not.

That said, theorists in what is called the "mutual advantage" tradition have always appealed to the pay-off that accompanies moral rules. In this tradition, the *locus classicus* of which is Hobbes's *Leviathan*, we have reason to coordinate our activities through binding rules because such rules are mutually advantageous. David Gauthier (1986), a contemporary neo-Hobbesian, thus argues that what he calls "constrained maximizers" (those who are disposed to adhere to agreed rules) will do better for themselves in normal conditions than "straightforward maximizers" (those whose disposition allows them to consider free-riding on the compliance of others). "Better", for Gauthier, is defined in terms of a variant of preference satisfaction and that, of course, is not the same thing as happiness. Nonetheless, the appeal to subjective well-being in the grounding of morality is there. If the agent could not do better in cooperation, and by complying with his agreements, than he could as an independent, then morality would not be relevant for him. His relations with others would not be moral or immoral, but amoral.

It is generally agreed that Gauthier cannot show the rationality of constrained maximization (Matravers 2000, chap. 6). In other words, he cannot show that it is rational to become the kind of person who constrains the pursuit of her self-interest in accordance with her agreements (even where it would be better, in the individual instance, to defect). Rational self-interest, then, cannot ground morality. However, it is possible to defend a version of the mutual advantage approach. If we understand the fundamental challenge *not* as one of justifying morality to a rational non-tuist, but as defeating the idea that the moral person is making a mistake in being moral (in allowing moral norms to regulate the pursuit of his self-interest), then there is hope. That is, it may be possible to show that it does not follow from the failure of Gauthier's project that the moral person would be better off if he could shed his commitment to morality. To do this, an appeal has to be made to subjective well-being. To summarize an argument made at length elsewhere (Matravers 2000): we typically achieve subjective well-being by living a life in which our choices are congruent with our settled beliefs, emotions, and values and, crucially, our beliefs, emotions, and values are socially constituted. In short, living what we think of as worthwhile lives matters to us—makes us happy—and measures of "worthwhileness" are a product of our relations with others. If this is right, we have reason to go beyond what is *commanded* by rationality. We have reason to make an "existential commitment" to the rules of cooperation which allow us to flourish together with others. Subjective well-being, then, plays a critical part in the account. It explains why we have reason not to shed our commitments to morality as if they were mere fetishes, and it shows why, in normal conditions, we have reasons (all be it not decisive reasons) to endorse the priority we give to morality as a constraint on our pursuit of narrow self-interest.

To put the point simply: it is often thought that mutual advantage cannot succeed in closing the gap between *self-interest* and *morality*, because an agent motivated by self-interest will always be better off retaining the option of defecting from the agreement and free-riding. The free-rider, as the name suggests, when successful gets everything the moral person gets, but without paying the costs. My argument is that this is not necessarily true. The free-rider fails to get certain goods, goods that are only available to those who have made the commitment to morality. And these goods contribute to the agent's subjective well-being (Matravers 2000, chaps. 7–8).

It might be helpful to sum up the argument to this point. For Singer, Rawls, and Scanlon, a person can be motivated to behave morally because, they argue, thinking of oneself as living together with others and committing oneself to doing so in accordance with the demands of morality has a pay-off in terms of subjective well-being. Moreover, in the mutual advantage tradition and (arguably) in Scanlon's account, there is a more foundational role for subjective well-being. The fact that living in unity with others has a pay-off is important in the justification of morality, not just in the account of moral motivation.

4. Nancy Mitford and Evelyn Waugh

In both contemporary utilitarianism and neo-Kantian theories, then, it is important that living a moral life contributes to happiness, at least under normal conditions. That it does so is plausible only if living together with others in certain ways contributes to our subjective well-being. I am going to assume that these claims are established. What I want to consider is who the "others" are in these arguments. In particular, it seems to me that there is a tension here: moral rules are generally thought to hold universally or, in the mutual advantage tradition, to hold between those who can cooperate for mutual advantage. Yet, on the face of it, the evidence is that human beings normally find happiness in local communities, in their families, amongst friends, and so on. The tension arises because the psychological evidence suggests that it is living in unity with *some* people that matters to us, not living in unity with *all* people or with all those with whom we might enjoy mutually advantageous cooperation.

Consider the following interchange between Nancy Mitford and Evelyn Waugh. Toward the end of 1948, Mitford, who had moved to Paris, wrote to Waugh to say that she was deliriously happy and regretted only the end of "heavenly 1948". Waugh, an idiosyncratic Roman Catholic and equally idiosyncratic conservative, was never deliriously happy and at the time was living in England under a socialist government he abhorred. He immediately admonished Mitford for her frivolity, commenting that even the most appalling of people would, as he put it, "not say: 'Heavenly 1948' of, I suppose, the blackest year in the world's history since 1793" (Mosley 1996: 118).

Nancy Mitford thought Waugh had simply missed the point. She replied,

Don't be angry with me for being happy, you must know as well as I do that happiness doesn't depend on exterior or political events & that the findings of [the] U[nited] N[ations] O[rganization] or fresh demands for peace in Nanking are not enough to damp one's spirits for more than the 5 minutes it takes to read them of a morning. I live among good & happy people & my days are unclouded from morning to night. (ibid. 119)

Waugh remained unconvinced, beginning his next letter, "of course I am cross with you for being happy. It is entirely indecent." Yet, Nancy Mitford had a point, one that we now know to be backed up by the psychological evidence: happiness does not depend on exterior events, but on successful intimate relationships. Moreover, her claims are potentially damaging even for someone who appeals, as the mutual advantage argument summarized above does, not so much to the first-order facts about what makes us happy, but to second-order considerations of how social interaction structures the way in which our choices can make us happy. The stark truth might be that some, perhaps most, people will find happiness in, or will understand their choices in relation to norms that belong to, small social groups. In addition, these groups and the norms that are expressed in their social interaction might be such that others find them morally repugnant.

In short, the tension is this: neo-Kantian moral theory has inherited from Kant, and through him from the Judaeo-Christian tradition, the idea that morality has universal application to human beings conceived of as free and equal. However, shorn of the metaphysical underpinnings provided by Kant, a gap appears between what Nagel calls the "personal" and "impersonal" standpoints (Nagel 1991). That is, the danger is that the demands of morality seem to be alien imperatives that frustrate the individual's pursuit of his self-interest. Some neo-Kantians, including Rawls and Scanlon, have tried to fill this gap in part by appealing to the subjective well-being that normally accompanies living on moral terms with others. Yet, if our subjective well-being is tied to relationships that are close to home then it would seem that this strategy is mistaken.[2]

Given that the gap between the individual and the demands of morality is a recognized problem in neo-Kantian moral theory, perhaps it is enough simply to conclude that the appeal to happiness will not do the trick in closing this gap and that, therefore, neo-Kantians had better keep working. What about those in the mutual advantage tradition who think that this gap cannot be closed by those who assume equality between human beings and, therefore, that a commitment to morality must be grounded in the subjective well-being of persons? For them, there may be no way to avoid the tension. Justice, in the mutual advantage tradition, holds between those engaged in mutually advantageous cooperation (on some accounts, between those for whom such cooperation is available) and there are reasons to think that the scope of mutually advantageous cooperation extends beyond the scope of those relationships that contribute to those feelings of subjective well-being that are available to the moral agent and not to the free-rider. And if living in unity with others— in my sense of living in a way in which one's choices are congruent with one's socially constituted settled beliefs, emotions, and values—is defined relative to a small group then we have reason to renounce our commitment to morality in our relations with those with whom we cooperate, but who are not part of this group.

That said, perhaps this pessimistic conclusion can be tempered for two reasons. First, there has been an explosion of work recently on the idea of "relational goods", and on questions of how affective states can be incorporated into our understandings of rationality (this volume is in part testament to this).[3] Second, if "fellow feeling" is an important component of living well then it can be used to advance the argument that Rawls unsuccessfully attempts: that injustice can be bad even for those who apparently do best under it. And that is an argument of immense political significance, even if its scope is less wide than we would intuitively wish it to be.

Notes

1. I shall not deal with the tradition of virtue ethics. This might be thought surprising given that happiness—or *eudaimonia*—plays a central role in this tradition. However, the argument is based around trying to uncover the role of happiness and then show that if what makes us happy is "local", then there is a tension with the aspiration to universality normally associated with morality. Virtue ethics thus does not fit: there is nothing to uncover—since *eudaimonia* is usually a central concept within any virtue ethical theory—and many virtue ethicists will not "feel" the tension identified, since they locate moral actions and the virtues in small communities.

2. In a passage that I must admit I find hard to interpret, Scanlon seems to concede that there might be problem in appealing to our living in unity with our fellows. Having argued that "standing in [a just] relation to others is appealing in itself" (Scanlon 1998: 162), he goes on to consider a society in which this is not thought to be the case. "If everyone in my society sees the world as divided between 'them', the outsiders to whom nothing is owed, and 'us', who are bound by relations of blood, affection, and patronage, then", he writes, "I really am faced with a choice between actual ties with my fellow citizens—strong and warm, perhaps, if also fierce—and the requirements of morality, grounded in an ideal of relations with others that must remain purely ideal". He goes on to note that he has "tried to argue that we are not in fact faced with this choice, but it must be conceded that others could be" (Scanlon 1998: 166).

3. Sugden's recent work seems to me to be of the first importance for any plausible future account of social norms (see his contribution to this volume).

References

Gauthier, David (1986), *Morals by Agreement*, Oxford: Clarendon Press.

Matravers, M. (2000), *Justice and Punishment: The Rationale of Coercion*, Oxford: Oxford University Press.

Mill, J. S. (1987), *Utilitarianism and Other Essays*, ed. Alan Ryan, Harmondsworth, Middlesex: Penguin Books.

Mosley, C. (1996), *The Letters of Nancy Mitford and Evelyn Waugh*, London: Hodder & Stoughton.

Nagel, T. (1991), *Equality and Partiality*, New York: Oxford University Press.

——(1995), *Other Minds: Critical Essays 1969–1994*, Oxford: Oxford University Press.

Plato (1960), *Gorgias*, trans. W. Hamilton, Harmondsworth, Middlesex: Penguin Books.

Rawls, J. (1971), *A Theory of Justice*, Cambridge, Mass.: Harvard University Press.

——(1993), *Political Liberalism*, New York: Columbia University Press.

—— (1998), *"Commonweal* Interview with John Rawls", in S. Freeman (ed.), *John Rawls: Collected Papers*, Cambridge, Mass.: Harvard University Press.

Scanlon, T. (1982), "Contractualism and Utilitarianism", in A. Sen and B. Williams (eds.), *Utilitarianism and Beyond*, Cambridge: Cambridge University Press.

—— (1998), *What We Owe to Each Other*, Cambridge, Mass.: Harvard University Press.

Singer, P. (1972), "Famine, Affluence and Morality", *Philosophy and Public Affairs*, 1/3: 229–43.

—— (1997), *How are We to Live?*, Oxford: Oxford University Press.

8

The Connection between Old and New Approaches to Financial Satisfaction

Bernard M. S. van Praag

1. Introduction

"Happiness", the subject of this timely book, is one of the most pressing issues for the behavioral sciences in general and for economics in particular. As I am an economist by upbringing, I will restrict myself mostly to the economic viewpoint, although there will inevitably be points of tangency with the other behavioral sciences, especially with psychology.

Economists agree that individuals strive for the greatest happiness. Let us assume two situations x_1 and x_2 and let us assume that the two situations generate happiness values W_1 and W_2, where $W_2 > W_1$. Then the individual will choose x_2, if that situation is in his choice set. It follows that the function $W(x)$ describes a very basic aspect of human behaviour. Choice between scarce things is the core subject of economics.

It is therefore natural that economists have developed a choice model, where human choice behaviour is described as maximizing a function W on a relevant choice set. One of the first economists to proposed this was Edgeworth in his book *Mathematical Psychics* (1881). He thought of W as a *cardinal* concept. If $W(x_1) = 1$ and $W(x_2) = 2$, then the individual derives twice as much utility[1] (or happiness) from x_2 as from x_1.

Pareto (1909) was the first to raise doubts about the practical possibility of observing and estimating the function W. Moreover, he showed that in the case of static consumer behaviour we do not need to know the function itself but only its contour lines, the so-called indifference curves which are described by the equations:

$$W(x) = C \tag{1}$$

where C stands for a constant. The same set of indifference curves is described by

$$\varphi(W(x)) = \varphi(C) \tag{2}$$

where $\varphi(.)$ stands for an arbitrary monotonously increasing function.

The set of indifference curves defines an equivalence class of functions, $\varphi(W(x))$, that have the same contour lines.

In the meantime there arose a growing aversion among economists toward "psychologizing". The term "happiness" was abandoned for "ophelimity" and later on for "well-being", "welfare", or for the still less emotionally loaded term "utility" or "satisfaction".

The practical difficulty in estimating the function W was annoying for economists and it led to the gradual emergence of the axiom that utility was immeasurable. Notice that an axiom is not proven but proposed and accepted. The high priest of this dogma was Lionel Robbins (1932) and it was supported by Hicks (1939), Samuelson (1947), and Houthakker (1950). We may say that after 1950 an economist was not taken seriously unless he professed his belief in this dogma.

As a consequence, in consumer theory the use of a cardinal utility function was either completely abandoned or it was used just as a handy instrument to describe indifference curves. The latter function was called the ordinal utility function. To one net of indifference curves corresponds a whole equivalence class of ordinal utility functions, satisfying equation (2).

However, there were some problems left. The first point arose with decisions under uncertainty. If we accept the von Neumann–Morgenstern model, where we have a lottery L with outcomes x_1 and x_2 and corresponding probabilities p and $(1 - p)$, the individual is assumed to decide on expected utility

$$E(W) = pW(x_1) + (1 - p)W(x_2) \tag{3}$$

Now it is clear that if we replace W by a non-linear monotonously increasing transformation $\varphi(W)$ and we have two lotteries L_1 and L_2, then it may be that L_1 is preferred to L_2 when we use W and that L_2 is preferred to L_1 when we use $\varphi(W)$. It is obvious that given uncertainty W is required to be a cardinal utility concept. That is, $\varphi(W)$ is defined up to a positive affine transformation, that is, $\varphi(W) = \alpha W + \beta$ with $\beta > 0$. Actually, by observing lottery behavior for various values of p we can estimate the values of W up to a positive linear transformation. We notice however that in the limiting situation where $p \to 1$ we are back to the situation of choice under certainty. Hence, if we assume that the certainty situation is a special case of the more general uncertainty situation we see that we cannot simultaneously maintain the validity of the unmeasurability axiom and Von Neumann–Morgenstern (VNM) theory.

Ragnar Frisch stated in 1959: "To me the idea that cardinal utility should be avoided in economics is completely sterile. It is derived from a very special and indeed narrow part of theory, viz., that of static equilibrium".

In van Praag (1968) I added to this quote (p. 158): "This author agrees completely with Frisch's value judgment. The above-mentioned controversy seems to me the reason why there is found nowhere a really synthesizing analysis which brings under one denominator the theories of consumer behavior in a certain world and in an uncertain world. A similar story may be told with respect to decisions over time" (e.g. saving, investment).

It is indeed true that static consumer behaviour may be described by an ordinal utility concept. It follows that we cannot estimate and identify a cardinal utility function by observing static consumer behaviour when prices vary. But this fact does not entail that cardinal utility would be unmeasurable *per se* or that it is a ridiculous concept. The statement only indicates that we should look for another measurement method.

There remains a rather basic observation to be made. When we have two alternative situations x_1, x_2 and x_3, in most cases individuals will not only be able to say that they prefer x_2 to x_1 and x_3 to x_2, that is $W(x_1) < W(x_2) < W(x_3)$, but they are also able to say whether the improvement going from x_1 to x_2 is more or less than the improvement associated with going from x_2 to x_3. Individuals are able to compare utility differences. But this is just what is necessary and sufficient to have a cardinal utility function (see Suppes and Winet 1954).

One of the other methods by which we may investigate how individuals evaluate specific positions is not by observing their choice behavior, but much more simply by asking them how they evaluate those alternatives, either on a *verbal* scale ranging from "very bad" to "very good" or on a discrete (or ideally continuous) numerical finite scale, for instance from 0 to 10 or from 0 to 1.

In this framework we shall assume that satisfaction is always measured on a finite interval scale, preferably $[0, 10]$. That is, however the position is described, whether by a vector x, by a verbal description, or by an image, vignette, etc., also denoted by x, satisfaction will be described by a numerical function $S(x)$, where worst positions are evaluated by 0 and best positions by 1.

This is the method, developed in the 1990s, which employs so-called "satisfaction questions". Subjects investigated include job satisfaction (Clark and Oswald 1994), health satisfaction (Ferrer-i-Carbonell and Van Praag 2002), financial satisfaction, or satisfaction with "life as a whole" (van Praag *et al.* 2003).

In this chapter we shall focus on financial satisfaction (FS). Let us assume that financial satisfaction is a function $U(y; x)$ of household income y and other personal characteristics x. Our question is then whether we can derive this function from the FS question.

It turns out that there are four ways to derive a meaningful function $U(.)$ from the FS question. We will explain in Section 2 their connection, similarity, and differences.

As some readers may know, in the 1970s van Praag (1971) and van Praag and Kapteyn (1973) were considering the same problem. They formulated a different question module, the income evaluation question (IEQ) and attempted to estimate a cardinal utility function of income $U(y; x)$, which was called the individual welfare function of income (WFI).

In Section 3 we critically consider this second but earlier WFI approach in more detail and we will see that the IEQ yields two utility function estimates, where one may be identified as a *decision* utility function and the other as an *experienced* utility function in the sense of Kahneman *et al.* (1997). The functions derived from the FS approach may be identified as variants of the *experienced* utility function. It turns out that the *experienced* utility functions derived from either of the two methods are identical up to a positive linear transformation.

In Section 4 we present some empirical evidence.

In Section 5 we conclude that the IEQ stores more information than the FSQ at the expense of the fact that it requires more information from the respondent and is thus harder to answer. A second point is that it seems hard (but perhaps not impossible) to apply the IEQ approach to domains other than financial satisfaction. Moreover, we make some observations on the state of the art and the embedding of the happiness results in behavioral sciences in general and in economics in particular.

2. Four Methods of Analysis for the Satisfaction Question

The income satisfaction question we are using runs as follows:

How satisfied are you with your household income.............................
(Please answer by using the following scale, in which 0 means totally unhappy and 10 means totally happy)

This question is posed in the German Socio-Economic Panel (GSOEP). A similar question is posed in the British Household Panel Survey (BHPS). The only difference between the two modules is that the British survey questionnaire distinguishes between seven categories, while the German question has eleven response categories. The question is put in many other surveys as well. We notice that the response categories are explicitly described in terms of *numerical* grades, for example, from 0 to 10. In other modules the response categories are *verbal*, ranging from "very bad" to "very good". The verbal version is somewhat older and preferred by some as being more readily understood by respondents, although it is also thought that words may not carry the same sense for each respondent, diminishing the validity and the interpersonal comparability of the question.

The numerical version gives less room for ambiguity. As most individuals have been familiar with numerical evaluations since their school days, it may be surmised that the evaluations may be interpreted as cardinal evaluations. It is obvious that, although the satisfaction question requires a categorical answer, the underlying phenomenon is continuous.

Let us assume that individuals t in the population are ordered on the interval [0, 1] according to their satisfaction, such that there is a fraction t of the population in the interval [0, t]. It is obvious that we may define the satisfaction $S(t)$ of individual t as $S(t) = t$. In that case satisfaction is a purely relative phenomenon. For instance, if $t = 0.6$, it implies that 60 percent of the population is less satisfied than t and hence t's satisfaction is 0.6. However, as we do not know the function S, it is obvious that any other increasing function on [0, 1] may be just as credible. It is the objective of this chapter to achieve more clarity on that. The response categories correspond with the intervals of a partition of the unit interval. We assume a model of the type

$$S(t) = g[\alpha \ln (y) + \beta \ln(fs) + \gamma + \varepsilon] \tag{4}$$

where $g(\cdot)$ is an increasing function, where y stands for household income, *fs* stands for family size, and ε is a random disturbance term with

$E(\varepsilon) = 0$ which is uncorrelated with the structural part of the equation. In the sample y and fs are random variables as well. For convenience we define the variables $\ln(y)$ and $\ln(fs)$ as deviations from their means. This may evidently be rewritten as

$$Z = \alpha \ln(y) + \beta \ln(fs) + \gamma + \varepsilon \tag{5}$$

Where $Z = g^{-1}(S(t))$. As this chapter does not focus on empirical results we have only two explanatory variables here.

A. Ordinal Probit

Let us assume a random sample of size N, consisting of respondents n. The usual and first method to estimate this relation is by ordered probit (OP), where it is assumed that the error term ε is $N(0,1)$ distributed. Equation (5) implies that $Z \in (-\infty, \infty)$. The response categories for Z correspond with intervals $(\mu_{i-1}, \mu_i]$. In terms of the original t the response classes are $(t_{i-1}, t_i]$. For an individual who evaluates his financial satisfaction as i_n this implies that $\mu_{i_n-1} < Z_n \le \mu_{i_n}$. The log-likelihood of the sample is

$$L(\mu, \alpha, \beta) = \prod_{n=1}^{N} [N(\mu_{i_n} - \alpha \ln(y_n) - \beta \ln(fs_n) - \gamma)$$
$$- N(\mu_{i_n-1} - \alpha \ln(y_n) - \beta \ln(fs_n) - \gamma)], \tag{6}$$

where $N(\cdot)$ stands for the standard-normal distribution function. This is maximized with respect to μ, α, β. Generally, we are most interested in the parameters α, β, which determine the trade-off ratio between y and fs. The μ parameters are called the *nuisance* parameters; they are mostly overlooked. Here, we are especially interested in the μ parameters, because they give insight into the cardinalization which is implicitly applied by using the Probit model. It is easy to assess the μs by equalizing moments. More precisely, we have for the conditional probability that individual n's satisfaction will be found in the ith satisfaction interval

$$P(\mu_{i-1} < Z_n \le \mu_i \mid y_n, fs_n) = N(\mu_i - \alpha \ln(y_n) - \beta \ln(fs_n) - \gamma)$$
$$- N(\mu_{i-1} - \alpha \ln(y_n) - \beta \ln(fs_n) - \gamma) \tag{7}$$

The *marginal* probability for an *arbitrary* individual n to be found in the ith satisfaction interval is then (see Greene 1991) the average of those individual conditional probabilities averaged over the individuals in the sample. We find

$$P(\mu_{i-1} < Z \le \mu_i) = p\lim_{\to N} \frac{1}{N} \sum_{1}^{N} P(\mu_{i-1} < Z \le \mu_i \mid y_n, fs_n) \tag{8}$$

$$= p\lim_{\to N} \frac{1}{N} \sum_{1}^{N} \Big[N(\mu_i - \alpha\ln(y_n) - \beta\ln(fs_n) - \gamma)$$
$$- N(\mu_{i-1} - \alpha\ln(y_n) - \beta\ln(fs_n) - \gamma) \Big]$$
$$= [N(\mu_i - p\lim[\alpha\ln(y_n) + \beta\ln(fs_n)] - \gamma)$$
$$- N(\mu_{i-1} - p\lim[\alpha\ln(y_n) + \beta\ln(fs_n)] - \gamma)]$$
$$= [N(\mu_i - \gamma) - N(\mu_{i-1} - \gamma)]$$

Hence, the marginal distribution is asymptotically normal. However, the marginal probability is well-known. It is the fraction $P_i (= (t_i - t_{i-1}))$ of respondents whose responses have placed them in the *ith* satisfaction interval. It follows that we have the equations

$$N(\mu_1 - \gamma) = p_1$$
$$N(\mu_2 - \gamma) - N(\mu_1 - \gamma) = p_2$$

$$\tag{9}$$

$$1 - N(\mu_{10} - \gamma) = p_{11}$$

from which the values $(\mu_i - \gamma)$ $(i = 1, \ldots, 10)$ may be identified. Notice that μ and γ cannot be separately identified. Mostly it is assumed either that $\mu_1 = 0$ or that $\gamma = 0$. We assume that $\mu_1 = 0$. It follows that if the individual's response is i, it implies that his Z is in the interval $(\mu_{i-1}, \mu_i]$. We can even calculate its conditional expectation $\ddot{Z}_i$ according to a well-known formula for the normal distribution as

$$\ddot{Z}_i = E(Z \mid \mu_{i-1} < Z \le \mu_i) = \frac{n(\mu_{i-1}) - n(\mu_i)}{N(\mu_i) - N(\mu_{i-1})} \tag{10}$$

Let us now consider the limiting case where we have an infinitely fine categorization.

In that case system (8) may be described by the relation $N(Z) = t$ or inversely $Z = N^{-1}(t)$. In this case we have the satisfaction function $S(t) = t$.

B. *Probit OLS (POLS)*

Although ordered probit is now included in all relevant software packages, it is still less easy and significantly less flexible than good old ordinary least squares (OLS). Equation (10) suggests that OP might be substituted by an OLS procedure. We call that procedure Probit OLS (POLS).

Instead of taking a response category i_n as our observation to be explained, we take $\ddot{z}_{in}$ as the variable to be explained. We notice that $\ddot{z}_{in}$ can assume only k discrete values, where k is the number of response categories. We observe that this expression does not depend on the individual characteristics y, fs. This is analogous to the usual regression situation where the "left-hand" variable to be explained is directly observed without "correcting" for additional information about the respondent, as revealed by explanatory variables.

It follows that we look at the regression model

$$\ddot{Z}_{i_n} = \alpha \ln(y_n) + \beta \ln(fs_n) + \gamma + \varepsilon_n \tag{11}$$

We notice that the error term is a discrete random variable. However, if the number of observations is large, we may apply all large-sample results and deal with this OLS equation as usual.

More precisely, we may write the model as

$$Z = \ddot{Z} + \eta = \alpha \ln(y) + \beta \ln(fs) + \gamma + \varepsilon \tag{12}$$

The true latent observation is written as the sum of its conditional expectation *plus* a rounding-off error η, caused by the fact that we can only observe the *interval* in which the true Z is situated. We may rewrite this equation as

$$\ddot{Z}_i = \alpha \ln(y) + \beta \ln(fs) + \varepsilon + \eta_i \ (i = 1, \ldots, k) \tag{13}$$

This may raise the question whether we might also just as well take the untransformed response variable $i(i = 0, \ldots, 10)$ itself as our dependent variable to be explained. This would yield the regression equation

$$i = \alpha \ln(y) + \beta \ln(fs) + \varepsilon \tag{14}$$

This is a generalization of the linear probability model (see Greene 1991: 813). Indeed we might do this but the results are statistically and intuitively not very attractive, unless we have only two response categories. There are two reasons for its unattractiveness. First, the range of the variable to be explained is finite instead of the real axis, which the model specification would logically require. Second, contrary to the practice in POLS, the values of the variable to be explained are equi-distanced by definition. In contrast, in POLS they are defined by the overall sample distribution. This explains as well, why the linear probability model works for a phenomenon, which is two-valued, but not for multi-valued phenomena. In two-valued cases it is equivalent to POLS, except for an affine linear transformation.

C. Interval Regression (Cardinal Probit (CP))

If we drop our conventional prejudice toward cardinalism, we cannot deny that respondents who answer a satisfaction question by giving a numerical response are attempting to make a cardinal evaluation in terms of a finite interval scale. It stands to reason that responses are not very accurate, but the view that the respondent would have no intention of evaluating and, consequently, that his answers do not have any information value, may be safely discarded.

Now we look at a third method which also makes use of the *cardinal* information in the financial satisfaction question. It is this cardinal information which is neglected by ordered probit. If somebody is evaluating his satisfaction level by a 7, it does not imply that his satisfaction is *exactly* equal to 7. For instance, the exact evaluation might be 6.75 or 7.25, but due to the necessary discreteness of the responses we have to round it off at 7. However, it would be very unlikely when the exact evaluation was 7.75, for in that case we would round off to 8. More precisely, we assume that if somebody responds 7 his *true* evaluation will be in the interval [6.5, 7.5]. A similar reasoning holds for all other response values. For the extremes we use an obvious modification. The observed value 0 corresponds to the interval [0, 0.5] and the value 10 to [9.5, 10]. If we normalize the scale from [0, 10] to the [0, 1] interval, the intervals will be [0, 0.05], ... ,(0.95, 1].

Let us now assume that satisfaction S may be explained to a certain extent by a vector of explanatory variables x, including log income. More precisely, we assume

$$S = N(\beta'x + \beta_0; 0, \ 1) \tag{15}$$

where $N(\cdot)$ stands for the (standard) normal distribution function. We stress that (15) is a non-stochastic specification. For estimation purposes we add a random term and assume

$$S = N(\beta'x + \beta_0 + \varepsilon; 0, \ 1) \tag{16}$$

We see that satisfaction is determined by a structural part and a random disturbance ε. We assume the random disturbance ε to be normally distributed with expectation equal to zero. Its variance σ^2 has to be estimated. As usual, we assume that $cov(x, \varepsilon) = 0$. Notice that this model, and especially the specification of equations (15) and (16), is an assumption. If another model fitted the data better, we would have to replace it. However, let us assume it holds.

In that case the probability of response 7 is

$$P[0.65 < U \leq 0.75] = P[N^{-1}(0.65) < \beta'x + \beta_0 + \varepsilon \leq N^{-1}(0.75)]$$
$$= N(u_{0.75} - \beta'x - \beta_0) - N(u_{0.65} - \beta'x - \beta_0) \tag{17}$$

Comparison with equation (7) reveals that the likelihood is equal to the probit likelihood except that the unknown μ_is are replaced by known normal quantiles u_i. The βs are estimated by maximizing the log-likelihood.

It follows that it is possible to estimate a cardinal satisfaction function from the same data by using the additional cardinal information. It is an empirical matter which model is chosen.

This cardinal probit (CP) approach is a special case of what is sometimes called the group-wise or interval regression method in the literature, where information on the regressand is only available group-wise. This is frequently the case in public statistics, for example, with respect to household income which is only known per income bracket.

D. Cardinal OLS (COLS)

The reader will not be surprised that the trick of equation (10), which we used to define the POLS method, can be used in the cardinal setting as well. We define

$$\ddot{Z}_i = E(Z \,|\, u_{i-1} < Z \leq u_i) = \frac{n(u_{i-1}) - n(u_i)}{N(u_i) - N(u_{i-1})} \tag{18}$$

and we formulate the regression equation

$$\ddot{Z}_i = \alpha \ln(y) + \beta \ln(fs) + \varepsilon + \eta_i \quad (i = 1, \ldots, k) \tag{19}$$

In this section we have listed four possible methods of estimating an explanatory model for satisfaction. The difference between methods A and C is that A does not employ cardinal information in the satisfaction question, while C does employ that additional information. Methods B and D may be viewed as derivatives of A and C, respectively. The essential difference is between the acceptance or non-acceptance of the cardinal information. The two variations B and D are of much practical importance, as they make it possible to replace the non-linear Probit method by more easily applicable OLS.

The question now is how the different estimates are related. We leave this question until Section 4 and revisit a much older competitor.

3. The Income Evaluation Question

It is sometimes forgotten that the present wave of happiness research was preceded in the 1970s by another attempt which certainly had points in common with the present literature. This cluster of research is now frequently called the Leyden School after the Dutch university where this research started. Van Praag, Kapteyn, and Hagenaars were the main contributors. This line of research was started by van Praag (1968, 1971) and it may be seen as a forerunner to the present satisfaction question research.

In the spirit of the economic literature of that time it was assumed that satisfaction with income was synonymous with welfare or well-being. Although economists (including this author) also paid lip service to the idea that income was *only* a dimension of life, this feature of reality was ignored in practice in developing theory and applied research, where income was seen as the only determinant of welfare. Now we would say that the Leyden School was focusing on financial satisfaction. In this sense the subject of Leyden was narrower than that of present happiness research where various life domains like employment (Clark and Oswald 1994) and health (Ferrer-i-Carbonell and van Praag 2002) are studied as well. However, we should also realize that in those days so-called "subjective" satisfaction questions were not put in surveys to which economists had access. There were some "soft" surveys organized by sociologists or psychologists where such questions could be found, but those surveys did not contain reliable information about income and other "economic" variables. Sociologists and psychologists were not interested in those mundane regions of life and left it to the "dismal science" to bother about the effect of income.

The Leyden results are empirically based on the so-called income evaluation question (IEQ). The IEQ has been posed in various countries. Here we are especially interested in comparing the outcomes with the previous results, derived from the income satisfaction questions. Fortunately, the IEQ has been posed in the GSOEP data set in the 1992 and 1997 cohorts. This gives us the opportunity to make a direct comparison between the results based on the financial satisfaction question with those derived from the IEQ. We utilize the 1997 cohort.

Our first question here is whether the IEQ provides at least the same information as the financial satisfaction (FS) question. Our second question is whether the results derived from the IEQ are comparable or nearly the same as the results derived from the FS-question. Third, we are interested in whether the IEQ provides *more* information than the financial satisfaction question.

The IEQ runs as follows:

THE INCOME EVALUATION QUESTION (IEQ)
(MID-INTERVAL VERSION)

Whether you feel an income is good or not so good depends on your personal life circumstances and expectations.
In your case you would call your net household income:

  a very low income if it equaled DM ——
  a low income if it equaled DM ——
  a still insufficient income if it equaled DM ——
  a just sufficient income if it equaled DM ——
  a good income if it equaled DM ——
  a very good income if it equaled DM ——

There are several wordings of this question around. First, the number of levels has varied between five and nine. When it was first posed in a Belgian survey (van Praag 1971), nine verbally described levels were used. In Russian surveys (see Ferrer-i-Carbonell and van Praag 2001) five levels were used. Second, in the earliest versions (1971) the question was formulated as:

THE INCOME EVALUATION QUESTION (INTERVAL VERSION)

Given my present household circumstances, I would consider a monthly household income

An income below $???		as a very bad income
An income	between $???? and $???	as a bad income
An income	between $???? and $???	as an insufficient income
An income	between $???? and $???	as a sufficient income
An income	between $???? and $???	as a good income
An income	above $????	as a very good income

When introducing a question of this type, which requires more from a respondent than the usual financial satisfaction question, survey agencies predicted that the response ratio would be very bad and that, if there were any response, the respondents would not take the question seriously. It appeared in practice that such questions had a lower response than the usual questions but not dramatically so. It is possible also that the response is incomplete, but the question may still be used if at least *three* levels are filled in. Moreover, the amounts should be ordered in the sense that a good income requires a higher amount than a bad income. Finally, the response is considered to be unrealistic if a *very bad* income is much higher than the respondent's current income or a *very good* income is much less than current income. Such cases represent a small percentage of the response and they are usually excluded from further analysis.

The essential difference between the FS question and the IEQ is the inversion of stimulus and response. In the FS question, own current income, say y_c, is the stimulus and the individual's evaluation on a finite interval scale is the response. In the IEQ the stimuli are evaluations, expressed in terms of verbal labels like "bad" and "good". The responses are income levels y_{bad} and y_{good}. As different individuals have a different idea of what is a "good" or a "bad" income, it is obvious that we do not obtain *one* financial satisfaction function, but that each responding individual will have his own FS function. Therefore, van Praag (1971) used the term *individual welfare function of income* (WFI).

We now analyse the results of the IEQ. Let us denote the answers of individual n by $c_1, \ldots, c_6$. We can analyze these in one of two ways. The first method is an ordinal analysis where we consider the separate answers and look for regression equations

$$\ln(c_i) = \alpha_i \ln(y_c) + \beta_i \ln(fs) + \gamma_i + \varepsilon_i \quad (i = 1, \ldots, 6) \tag{20}$$

The question is then what these coefficients are and whether these coefficients are equal over the six equations. We leave the empirical results to the next section.

Now we look at the cardinal concept of the individual welfare function of income (WFI). In van Praag (1968) it was argued that individual welfare (read financial satisfaction in present-day terminology) was measurable as a cardinal concept between 0 and 1. In 1968 this was almost a heretical idea, not in favour with mainstream economics (see e.g. Seidl 1994 for a fierce but belated critique). The approximate relationship was argued to be a log-normal distribution function with parameters μ and σ. We notice that the specification (16) is also a log-normal specification if one of the dimensions of the vector x is $\ln(y_c)$. In later years van Praag (1971) and van Praag and Kapteyn (1973) estimated the μ and σ per individual on the basis of the response on the IEQ. They assumed for the "mid-interval" version of the IEQ that the answers $c_1, \ldots, c_6$ correspond with satisfaction levels $1/12$, $(2i-1)/12$ and $11/12$ respectively; this was called the equal quantile assumption (van Praag (1991, 1994) provided empirical evidence for this assumption). Moreover, it was assumed that satisfaction $U(c; \mu, \sigma) = \Lambda(c; \mu, \sigma)$ where $\Lambda(c; \mu, \sigma) = N(\ln(c); \mu, \sigma)$. The function $\Lambda(\cdot)$ stands for the log-normal distribution function. Estimation of μ and σ is possible for each individual. We have six or, more generally, k observations per individual and we assume that

$$N\left(\frac{\ln(c_i) - \mu}{\sigma}\right) = \frac{(2i-1)}{12} \tag{21}$$

We note that the c-value is comparable to $\ddot{z}$ in the cardinal probit situation of six observations per individual by COLS. The only difference is that the cs are equated to interval *medians* instead of interval *means*. We estimate the parameters μ and σ for each individual observation n by

$$\hat{\mu}_n = \frac{1}{6}\sum_{i=1}^{6} \ln(c_{in}) \quad \text{and} \quad \hat{\sigma}_n^2 = \frac{1}{5}\sum_{i=1}^{6} \ln(c_{in} - \hat{\mu}_n)^2 \tag{22}$$

Then the estimated $\hat{\mu}_n$ is explained over the sample of N observations by the equation

$$\hat{\mu}_n = \alpha \ln(y_{c,n}) + \beta \ln(fs_n) + \gamma \tag{23}$$

where $y_{c,n}$ stands for the *current* income of individual n. Later on we shall consider those regression results. Here we already note that both coefficients are always estimated as significantly positive. The income effect α equals roughly 0.6 and the family size coefficient β equals 0.10.

Up to now it has proved difficult to explain the σ parameter, which van Praag (1968, 1971) called the *welfare sensitivity* parameter, sufficiently by means of individual explanatory variables. It seems to vary over individuals in a random manner. Like many other studies, we too assume σ to be constant over individuals in the same population. We set it equal to the average over individuals. Hagenaars (1986) found from international comparisons that the parameter σ appears to be related to the log-standard deviation of the population's income distribution. Her result suggests that welfare sensitivity is higher in more unequal societies. In the present survey (GSOEP 1997) we found an average value of $\sigma = 0.453$.

We can now find the evaluation of any income y by someone with individual parameters $(\mu(y_c), \sigma)$. This equals

$$N(\ln(y); \mu(y_c), \sigma) = N\left(\frac{(\ln(y) - \mu(y_c))}{\sigma}\right)$$

$$= N\left(\frac{(\ln(y) - \alpha \ln(y_c) - \beta \ln(fs) - \gamma)}{\sigma}\right) \quad (24)$$

or using its ordinal equivalent on the $(-\infty, \infty)$ axis

$$\frac{(\ln(y) - \mu)}{\sigma} = \frac{(\ln(y) - \alpha \ln(y_c) - \beta \ln(fs) - \gamma)}{\sigma} \quad (25)$$

We notice that the IEQ effectively introduces *two* concepts of an individual welfare function. The first concept is generated by keeping μ constant. It gives a schedule of how individuals evaluate varying (fictitious) income levels from the perspective of their own income, which is kept unchanged at the present level. We call this the *virtual* or *short-term* welfare function. It can be estimated for a specific individual by posing the IEQ to that individual.

The second concept is the welfare function according to which individuals with *different* incomes evaluate their *own* income *in reality*. This is an inter-individual concept. We call it the *true* or *long-term* welfare function. This function must be derived by using a sample of different individuals. From (23) it follows that the true welfare function is

$$N\left(\frac{(\ln(y_c) - \mu(y_c))}{\sigma}\right) = N\left(\frac{(\ln(y_c) - \alpha \ln(y_c) - \beta \ln(fs) - \gamma)}{\sigma}\right)$$

$$= N\left(\ln(y_c); \frac{\beta \ln(fs) + \gamma}{1 - \alpha}, \frac{\sigma}{1 - \alpha}\right) \quad (26)$$

Hence, it is also log-normal with parameters

$$\left(\frac{\beta \ln fs + \gamma}{1 - \alpha}, \frac{\sigma}{1 - \alpha}\right)$$

In Figure 8.1a we sketch both functions. We see that the true welfare function has a much weaker slope than the virtual. This implies that income changes are *ex ante* perceived as more significant than when they are experienced in reality. Actually, the two concepts correspond to the

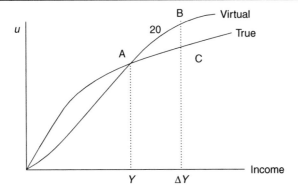

Figure 8.1a. The virtual and true welfare functions

two concepts of the *decision* and the *experienced* utility function, distinguished by Kahneman *et al.* (1997). The virtual welfare function describes the way in which a specific individual evaluates different income levels, irrespective of whether his real income or a (remote) prospect is being considered. It is the perceived *ex ante* relationship between income and welfare on which the individual bases his *decisions*. The true welfare function describes how individuals who *experience* those incomes themselves evaluate incomes in reality.

The welfare function maps incomes onto the evaluation range [0, 1]. A second (and easier) way to consider the welfare function is to map the range onto the real axis $(-\infty, +\infty)$ and to consider the function $u(y)$

$$u(y) = ((1 - \alpha) \cdot ln(y) - \beta \cdot ln(fs) - \gamma)/\sigma \qquad (27)$$

The two representations are ordinally equivalent. We call the latter the linear transformation. The linear transformations of the virtual and the true welfare functions are sketched in Figure 8.1b. The short-term version corresponds to $\alpha = 0$. It follows again that the short-term function is much steeper than the long-term function.

The difference between the short- and long-term concepts is best explained by the following simple thought experiment. Let us assume that somebody with an initial income y gets an income increase of Δy, yielding a new income $y + \Delta y$. Initially the increase will be evaluated by his short-term welfare function yielding an increase from point A to point B. After a while income norms will adapt to the new situation and this will be reflected in the parameter μ that will increase by $\alpha \cdot \Delta y$. Hence, after initial euphoria there will be some disappointment, as the evaluation falls from point B to point C.

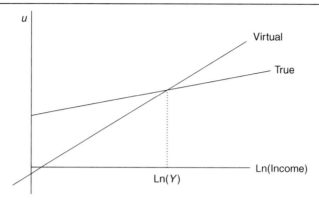

Figure 8.1b. The virtual and true welfare functions (linear transformation)

This is the so-called *preference drift* effect, which was introduced and estimated by van Praag (1971). It is absent only when $\alpha = 0$. If $\alpha = 1$, in the long term an income increase will not yield any increase in satisfaction.

We notice that the IEQ effectively introduces *two* concepts of an individual welfare function. The *virtual* welfare function describes the way in which a specific individual evaluates different income levels. It is the perceived *ex ante* relationship between income and welfare on which the individual bases his *decisions*. The *true* welfare function describes how individuals who *experience* those incomes themselves evaluate incomes in reality.

The most interesting point is that different individuals have a different idea of what presents a "good" income, a "sufficient" income, etc. This depends on their own net household income and their household circumstances, in this case characterized by their household size. It shows that evaluations are relative. Where $\alpha = 0$, the evaluations would be wholly absolute, that is, independent of current income. Where $\alpha = 1$ the evaluation is completely relative. We will see from the table that we are somewhere in between, as α turns out to be about 0.5 or 0.06. The phenomenon that evaluations drift along with rising income has been termed preference drift (see van Praag 1971). This is measured by α. This is similar to an effect independently discovered by the psychologists Brickman and Campbell (1971), which they called the *hedonic treadmill effect*. These authors and also Easterlin (1974, 1995, 2001) tend to the hypothesis that adaptation will be complete, that is, $\alpha = 1$. We were unable to establish this result empirically.

Obviously this is a puzzling effect. The evaluation of a specific income in combination with a specific household to support should, ideally and according to traditional economic models, be independent of the situation of the evaluator. However, we see that in practice it does depend on the income of the evaluator. It shows most clearly that the notion of "a good income" is partly relative and psychologically determined. This holds too for the situation of "poverty" (see Goedhart *et al.* 1977).

4. Empirical Evidence

Let us now proceed to an empirical analysis. We consider the GSOEP data set and more precisely the 1997 cohort,[2] where we restrict ourselves to the subset of West German workers. The data set is especially interesting because it contains the financial satisfaction question and the IEQ simultaneously. We shall now compare the empirical outcomes of the approaches described above.

In Table 8.1 we tabulate the response fractions for the eleven categories.

In Table 8.2 we present the ordered probit estimates of the unknown parameter values.

In Table 8.2 we present three estimates of the financial satisfaction equation to be estimated. The first version is the one described in equation (5). We have two explanatory variables, namely, household income and the number of children plus 1.[3] In the second version we distinguish between children under 17 living at home and other persons living in the household. The latter class will be called "adults". In the third specification we add a third variable, "family structure", which equals 0 if the respondent lives alone, 1 if the household has two working adults, and 2 if

Table 8.1. Response frequencies for income satisfaction for West German workers, 1997[4]

Satisfaction categories	Relative frequencies in %
0	0.00%
1	0.30%
2	1.05%
3	2.74%
4	5.34%
5	12.31%
6	13.60%
7	24.46%
8	25.62%
9	10.03%
10	4.55%
No. of observations	4964

Table 8.2. Estimates of three different income satisfaction equations by ordered probit, GSOEP 1997

Variable	Effects	t-ratio	Effects	t-ratio	Effects	t-ratio
Constant	−3.061	−10.224	−3.093	−10.232	−3.128	−10.319
Ln(household income)	0.734	20.251	0.738	20.113	0.738	20.093
Ln(family size)	−0.223	−6.800				
Ln(adults)			−0.223	−6.269	−0.246	−6.751
Ln(children + 1)			−0.128	−3.680	−0.164	−4.465
Family structure					0.070	2.844
Intercepts*						
μ_0	−∞		−∞		−∞	
μ_1	−∞		−∞		−∞	
μ_2	0		0		0	
μ_3	0.556		0.556		0.557	
μ_4	1.049		1.048		1.049	
μ_5	1.495		1.495		1.496	
μ_6	2.057		2.057		2.058	
μ_7	2.482		2.482		2.483	
μ_8	3.134		3.134		3.136	
μ_9	3.970		3.970		3.972	
μ_{10}	4.617		4.617		4.620	
μ_{11}	+∞		+∞		+∞	
N	4964		4964		4964	
Log−likelihood	−9310		−9310		−9306	
Pseudo R^2	0.020		0.020		0.021	

Note: $^*\mu_1 = \infty$, because the first response category is empty in this sample.

there are two adults in the household of which only one has paid work. This ordering reflects the idea that household chores are pretty fixed and that they are easier to bear by a family with one person working outside than by a family where the two adults are working in a paid job. The single person or the incomplete family bears the heaviest burden in this respect.

The estimation results, when we use POLS, are given in Table 8.3.

We see that the corresponding t-values are almost the same. The coefficients look like multiples of each other except for the constant.

The Estimates yielded by the cardinal CP or interval-regression approach are shown in Table 8.4 and once again we see that the ratios of coefficients are almost the same while the t-ratios hardly differ.

Finally we use the COLS approach with yields Table 8.5 and again we see that the ratios of coefficients and the t-ratios are almost the same.

The four methods used have the same objective, that is, the estimation of the equation

$$Z = \alpha \ln(y) + \beta \ln(fs) + \gamma + \epsilon \qquad (28)$$

Table 8.3. POLS results for the income satisfaction equations, GSOEP

Variable	Effects	t-ratio	Effects	t-ratio	Effects	t-ratio
Constant	−5.475	−19.849	−5.504	−19.663	−5.534	−19.770
Ln(household income)	0.678	19.829	0.681	19.581	0.681	19.584
Ln(family Size)	−0.206	−6.624				
Ln(adults)			−0.205	−6.122	−0.227	−6.597
Ln(children + 1)			−0.118	−3.645	−0.152	−4.407
Family structure					0.065	2.842
N	4964		4964		4964	
Adjusted R^2	0.073		0.073		0.075	

Table 8.4. The financial satisfaction question estimated by cardinal probit

Variable	Effects	t-ratio	Effects	t-ratio	Effects	t-ratio
Constant	−2.524	−18.236	−2.536	−18.055	−2.550	−18.159
Ln(household income)	0.342	19.923	0.343	19.652	0.343	19.657
Ln(family size)	−0.102	−6.568				
Ln(adults)			−0.101	−6.019	−0.112	−6.480
Ln(children + 1)			−0.060	−3.697	−0.076	−4.430
Family structure					0.032	2.765
σ	0.466	94.190	0.466	94.190	0.465	94.184
N	4964		4964		4964	
Log−likelihood	−9500		−9500		−9496	
Pseudo R^2	0.0198		0.0199		0.0202	

Table 8.5. The financial satisfaction question estimated by COLS

Variable	Effects	t-ratio	Effects	t-ratio	Effects	t-ratio
Constant	−2.464	−16.738	−2.477	−16.575	−2.492	−16.678
Ln(household income)	0.354	19.388	0.355	19.123	0.355	19.126
Ln(family size)	−0.108	−6.515				
Ln(adults)			−0.107	−5.966	−0.118	−6.427
Ln(children + 1)			−0.063	−3.669	−0.081	−4.403
Family structure					0.034	2.766
N	4964		4964		4964	
Adjusted R^2	0.070		0.070		0.072	

where Z stands for a satisfaction index. The equation may be used for the derivation of family equivalence scales.[5] If $\ln(fs)$ increases to $\ln(fs) + \Delta fs$, the question arises by how much the individual has to be compensated in his income $\ln(y)$. We find

$$\Delta \ln(y) = -\frac{\beta}{\alpha} \Delta \ln(fs) \qquad (29)$$

215

Table 8.6. Equivalence scale parameter calculated via different methods

Method	OP	POLS	CP	COLS	IEQ
β/α	0.32	0.30	0.30	0.30	0.26

It follows that the indifference curves between income and family size are described by

$$y = y_0 (fs/fs_0)^{\beta/\alpha} \tag{30}$$

where y_0 and fs_0 stand for the reference income and reference family size, respectively. Now it is interesting to see whether the ratio β/α is the same, irrespective of the four methods used. We give the different values in Table 8.6.

We see that the values of the ratio, estimated via four different methods, are virtually identical. Actually, this is less surprising than it looks if we realize that this equivalence scale describes an indifference curve which is defined by the financial satisfaction question. Everybody who evaluates his income by the same number is on the same indifference curve. The four methods yield different monotonic transformations of satisfaction, but their ordinal information is the same. The fifth column, derived from the IEQ, will be considered in a moment.

Let us now consider what the relationship is between POLS and COLS estimates. As before, we denote the ordinal variable belonging to a specific response category as $\ln(\ddot{z})$ and the corresponding cardinal value as $\ln(\dddot{z})$. We assume $\ln(\dddot{z}) = f(\ln(\ddot{z}))$. As the categories are ordered, we may assume that $f(\cdot)$ is a monotonically increasing function. Let us assume for a moment that both variables would be exactly measured on a continuous scale instead of on a discrete scale, then the marginal distributions of both variables would be normally distributed with parameters $(\ddot{\mu}, \ddot{\sigma})$ and $(\dddot{\mu}, \dddot{\sigma})$, respectively.

We may express a fraction of respondents to a specific category either with respect to $\ddot{z}$ or with respect to $\dddot{z}$. We have

$$N(\ln(\ddot{z}); \ddot{\mu}, \ddot{\sigma}) \equiv N(f(\ln(\ddot{z}); \dddot{\mu}, \dddot{\sigma})) \tag{31}$$

which implies

$$\frac{\ln(\ddot{z}) - \ddot{\mu}}{\ddot{\sigma}} = \frac{f(\ln(\ddot{z})) - \dddot{\mu}}{\dddot{\sigma}} \tag{32}$$

It follows that the function $f(\cdot)$ is a linear affine transformation. We have

$$\ln(\ddot{z}) = \frac{\dddot{\sigma}}{\ddot{\sigma}}\ln(\ddot{z}) + D \tag{33}$$

where D is a constant which can be easily calculated. Indeed if we apply this regression (on k observations) we find for the German data the regression result

$$\ln(\ddot{z}) = 0.5359\ln(\ddot{Z}) + 0.1965$$

with an R^2 of 0.99.

It follows that, if $\ln(\ddot{z})$ is a linear combination of variables x, then the same will hold for $\ln(\ddot{z})$, where the trade-off ratios will be the same.

It follows that OP, POLS, CP, and COLS are for practical purposes *equivalent* for the computation of trade-off ratios. The C versions employ the *cardinal* part of the information as well.

The implicit cardinalization on which probit and POLS are based will from now on be called the *frequentist* cardinalization because it is based on the frequency distribution of satisfaction levels. The cardinalization on which CP and COLS are based will be called the *satisfaction* cardinalization. We note that one is a linear transformation of the other.

It is evident that we may also derive family equivalence scales from the IEQ. The estimates of equation (23) are presented in Table 8.7.

It is obvious that we may derive individual welfare function household equivalence scales by requiring that households with different family sizes fs_0 and fs_1 enjoy an equal welfare level according to the true welfare function. This implies that the indifference curve is described by

$$y = y_0\left(\frac{fs}{fs_0}\right)^{0.121/0.473} \tag{34}$$

Table 8.7. The IEQ estimates for μ

Variable	Effects	t-ratio	Effects	t-ratio	Effects	t-ratio
Constant	3.611	54.308	3.572	52.302	3.574	52.309
Ln(household income)	0.527	61.964	0.533	60.667	0.533	60.644
Ln(family size)	0.121	14.819				
Ln(adults)			0.090	8.093	0.089	7.958
Ln(children + 1)			0.096	11.976	0.083	5.355
Family structure					0.011	0.963
σ	0.453		0.453		0.453	
N	3962		3962		3962	
Adjusted R^2	0.631		0.632		0.632	

where the ratio β/α is replaced by $\beta/(1-\alpha)$. We note that this power is 0.26. This value is evidently very well in line with the other values in Table 8.6. Hence our conclusion is that the ordinal information which can be extracted from the true welfare function is the same as that which is provided by the FS question.

Obviously, we may also try to explain the six separate responses to the IEQ, that is, the household cost levels $\ln(c_i)$. The resulting regression equations are given in Table 8.8.

The errors are strongly correlated as we see from Table 8.9.

For a more extensive ordinal analysis see van Praag and van der Sar (1988), where similar results for other data sets are to be found. Our conclusion is that the coefficients for the separate levels are not equal, but that they follow exactly the same pattern as in van Praag and van der Sar. At a low level of satisfaction the dependency on own income is considerable at 0.442, but it increases as the level of satisfaction increases, up to 0.593 at the highest level of satisfaction.

The family size effect β behaves in just the opposite way. It falls with rising levels of satisfaction (see also Van Praag and Flik 1992) for a comparison with other European data sets). We may characterize the effect of family size as reflecting *real needs*, while the dependency on own income stands for a *psychological* reference effect. Our findings may

Table 8.8. Ordinal Analysis of the Six Level Equations of the IEQ

	C_1		C_2		C_3		C_4		C_5		C_6	
	Effects	*t*-ratio	Effects	*t*-ratio	Effects	*t*-ratio	Effects	*t*-ratio	Effects	*t*-ratio	Effects	*t*-ratio
γ_i	3.499	33.653	3.422	42.488	3.447	46.647	3.558	51.176	3.788	51.033	3.961	41.326
α_i	0.468	35.134	0.507	49.193	0.527	55.774	0.539	60.572	0.550	57.904	0.571	46.534
β_i	0.165	12.870	0.149	14.996	0.141	15.490	0.130	15.144	0.089	9.706	0.056	4.715

Note: System Weighted R^2 0.2318.

Table 8.9. The Cross-Model Error Correlation Matrix

	C_1	C_2	C_3	C_4	C_5	C_6
C_1	1	0.906	0.836	0.744	0.611	0.467
C_2	0.906	1	0.963	0.887	0.784	0.630
C_3	0.836	0.963	1	0.951	0.856	0.706
C_4	0.744	0.887	0.951	1	0.917	0.772
C_5	0.611	0.784	0.856	0.917	1	0.899
C_6	0.467	0.630	0.706	0.772	0.899	1

then be summarized as: when individuals become richer, their real needs become less pressing and their norms become more determined by reference effects.

We may calculate for each verbal level i the income amount y_i, which is evaluated by i. For that level there holds

$$\ln(y_i) = \alpha_i \ln(y_i) + \beta_i \ln(fs) + \gamma_i \qquad (i = 1, \ldots, 6) \qquad (35)$$

which yields

$$\ln(y_i) = \frac{\beta_i \ln(fs) + \gamma_i}{1 - \alpha_i} \qquad (i = 1, \ldots, 6) \qquad (36)$$

We notice that the resulting family size elasticity is $\beta_i /(1 - \alpha_i)$. We notice that the elasticities and the corresponding household equivalence scales hardly vary between the satisfaction levels i.

Now we present the household equivalence scales for the six levels i and those derived from the μ equation side by side (see Table 8.10).

We see that the differences between all the subjective scales are rather small.

Van Praag and Flik (1992) derived equivalence scales for various European countries by the same IEQ method. They noticed that the scales in various countries are not the same, reflecting cultural differences and differences in social systems. See also Hagenaars (1986) and Goedhart et al. (1977).

Finally, it is interesting to compare the results derived from the IEQ responses with our results, based on financial satisfaction responses. The resulting trade-offs, derived from the true WFI, and the ratios found earlier are very similar. The additional result that we can derive from the IEQ, and which we cannot find from financial satisfaction questions because they only refer to current income, is the *virtual* WFI. As noted before, the true

Table 8.10. Household equivalence scales derived from the IEQ, GSOEP 1997

Household size	C_1	C_2	C_3	C_4	C_5	C_6	μ
1	81%	81%	81%	82%	87%	91%	84%
2	100%	100%	100%	100%	100%	100%	100%
3	113%	113%	113%	112%	108%	105%	111%
4	124%	123%	123%	122%	115%	109%	119%
5	133%	132%	131%	129%	120%	113%	127%
6	141%	139%	139%	136%	124%	115%	133%
7	147%	146%	145%	142%	128%	118%	138%
8	154%	152%	151%	148%	131%	120%	143%

WFI corresponds to the *experienced* utility function and the virtual WFI to the *decision* utility function.

5. Conclusion

Let us now summarize the conclusions of this chapter.

- We found that income satisfaction can be explained by objective factors. This yields trade-off coefficients between family size and income and trade-off coefficients between adults and children.

- We found that the ordered probit method is based on an implicit frequentist utility assumption, which may be interpreted as a cardinalist approach as well.

- We saw that we may replace the ordered probit method by the method of probit-adjusted ordinary least squares (POLS) and that the results do not vary except for a multiplication factor.

- We found that we can use the cardinal information in financial satisfaction questions, leading to a cardinal probit—and a cardinal OLS—approach.

- The frequentist and the cardinalist approach imply two different cardinalizations of satisfaction, which are related by an affine linear transformation.

- The empirical estimates according to these four estimation methods are strongly related and yield (almost) identical trade-off ratios.

- The POLS and COLS methods are computationally easier.

- An earlier method of studying income satisfaction in a quantitative way was developed by van Praag and Kapteyn (the Leyden School). In this chapter we compare the results they derived from the income evaluation question with results derived from the financial satisfaction question (FSQ). We found that both methods yield approximately the same trade-off coefficients.

- The FSQ yields an experienced utility function in the terms of Kahneman *et al.* The IEQ yields a virtual *and* a true individual welfare function, concepts which coincide with Kahneman *et al.*'s *decision* utility and *experienced* utility functions, respectively. The implication of this comparison is that most results derived by WFI analysis or in the spirit of the Leyden School could have been derived by analysis of the FSQ as well.

- The FSQ is easier for respondents to answer than the IEQ. Moreover, the IEQ format does not seem applicable when we ask about health satisfaction, housing satisfaction, and so on, while the FSQ can be used. However, the IEQ yields information on the decision utility function which the FSQ cannot provide.

Notes

This chapter is partly based on chapter 2 of (2004) van Praag and Ferrer-i-Carbonell (2004).

1. We shall not differentiate between the terms utility, well-being, and happiness.
2. We use here a preliminary unauthorized release of the 1997 cohort, which differs slightly from the final authorized version. In the final version there are a few observations in category 0 as well. See also Plug *et al.* (1997).
3. We add one so that we do not get a non-defined logarithm of zero if the number of children equals zero.
4. See n. 1.
5. See also van Praag (1971), van Praag and Kapteyn (1973).

References

Brickman, P., and Campbell, D.T. (1971), "Hedonic Relativism and Planning the Good Society", in M. H. Apley (ed.), *Adaptation-Level Theory: A Symposium*, New York: Academic Press, 287–302.

Clark, A. E., and Oswald, A. J. (1994), "Unhappiness and Unemployment", *Economic Journal*, 104: 648–59.

Edgeworth, F. Y. (1881/1961), *Mathematical Psychics*, New York: A. M. Kelley.

Easterlin, R. A. (1974), "Does Economic Growth Improve the Human Lot? Some Empirical Evidence", in P. A. David and M. W. Reder (eds.), *Nations and Households in Economic Growth: Essays in Honor of Moses Abramowitz*, New York: Academic Press, 89–125.

——(1995), "Will Raising the Incomes of All Increase the Happiness of All?" *Journal of Economic Behavior and Organization*, 27/1: 35–47.

——(2001), "Income and Happiness: Towards a Unified Theory", *Economic Journal*, 111: 465–84.

Ferrer-i-Carbonell, A., and van Praag, B. M. S. (2001), "Poverty in Russia", *Journal of Happiness Studies*, 2: 147–72.

————(2002), "The Subjective Costs of Health Losses due to Chronic Diseases: An Alternative Model for Monetary Appraisal", *Health Economics*, 11: 709–22.

Frisch, R. (1959), "Dynamic Utility", *Econometrica*, 32: 418–29.

Goedhart, T., Halberstadt, V., Kapteyn, A., and van Praag, B. M. S. (1977), "The Poverty Line: Concept and Measurement", *Journal of Human Resources*, 12: 503–20.

Greene, W. H. (1991), *Econometric Analysis*, New York: Macmillan.

Hagenaars, A. J. M. (1986), *The Perception of Poverty*, Amsterdam: North-Holland.

Hicks, J. R. (1939), "The Foundations of Welfare Economics", *Economic Journal*, 49: 696–712.

Houthakker, H. S. (1950), "Revealed Preference and the Utility Function", *Economica*, 17: 159–74.

Kahneman, D., Wakker, P. P., and Sarin R. (1997), "Back to Bentham? Explorations of Experienced Utility", *Quarterly Journal of Economics*, 2: 375–405.

Pareto, V. (1909), *Manuel d'économie politique*, Paris: Giard et Brière.

Plug, E. J. S., Krause, P., van Praag, B. M. S., and Wagner, G. G. "Measurement of Poverty: Exemplified by the German Case", in *Income Inequality and Poverty in Eastern and Western Europe*, Heidelberg: Physica-Verlag, 69–89.

Robbins, L. (1932), *An Essay on the Nature and Significance of Economic Science*. London: Macmillan.

Rowntree, B. S. (1941), *Poverty and Progress*, London: Longmans, Green and Co.

Samuelson, P. A. (1947), *Foundations of Economic Analysis*, Cambridge, Mass: Harvard University Press.

Seidl, C. (1994), "How Sensible is the Leyden Individual Welfare Function of Income?" *European Economic Review*, 38/8: 1633–59.

Suppes, P., and Winet, M. (1954), "An Axiomatization of Utility Based on the Notion of Utility Differences", *Management Science*, 1: 259–70.

van Praag, B. M. S. (1968), *Individual Welfare Functions and Consumer Behavior. A Theory of Rational Irrationality*, Ph.D. thesis, Amsterdam: North Holland.

——(1971), "The Welfare Function of Income in Belgium: An Empirical Investigation", *European Economic Review*, 2: 337–69.

——(1991), "Ordinal and Cardinal Utility: An Integration of the Two Dimensions of the Welfare Concept", *Journal of Econometrics*, 50: 69–89.

——(1994), "Ordinal and Cardinal Utility: An Integration of the Two Dimensions of the Welfare Concept", Revision of (1991) in R. F. Blundell, I. Preston, and I. Walker (eds.), *The Measurement of Household Welfare*, Cambridge: Cambridge University Press.

——and Ferrer-i-Carbonell, A. (2004), *Happiness Quantified, A Satisfaction Calculus Approach*, Oxford: Oxford University Press.

——and Flik, R. J. (1992), "Poverty Lines and Equivalence Scales: A Theoretical and Empirical Investigation", in *Poverty Measurement for Economies in Transition in Eastern Europe*, International Scientific Conference, Warsaw, 7–9 October, Polish Statistical Association, Central Statistical Office.

——Frijters, P., and Ferrer-i-Carbonell, A. (2003), "The Anatomy of Subjective Well-Being", *Journal of Economic Behavior and Organization*, 51/1: 29–49.

——and Kapteyn, A. (1973), "Further Evidence on the Individual Welfare Function of Income: An Empirical Investigation in the Netherlands", *European Economic Review*, 4: 33–62.

——and van der Sar, N. L. (1988), "Household Cost Functions and Equivalence Scales", *Journal of Human Resources*, 23: 193–210.

9

Towards a Theory of Self-Segregation as a Response to Relative Deprivation: Steady-State Outcomes and Social Welfare

Oded Stark and You Qiang Wang

1. Introduction

People who transact individually in markets also belong to groups. Both the outcome of the market exchange and the satisfaction arising from the group affiliation impinge on well-being. But how and why do groups form and dissolve? The pleasure or dismay that arises from group membership can be captured in a number of ways and relative position is an appealing measure. A plausible response to transacting in a market that confers an undesirable outcome is to transact in another market (when the latter exists and participation in it is feasible). Labor migration is an obvious example. Similarly, one reaction to a low relative position in a given group could be a change in group affiliation. What happens then when people who care about their relative position in a group have the option to react by staying in the group or exiting from it?

We study this particular response in order to gain some insight into how groups form when individuals care about their relative position. To enable us to focus on essentials, we confine ourselves to an extremely stark environment. We hold the incomes of all the individuals fixed;[1] we restrict attention to a setting in which incomes are equally spaced; we start with all individuals belonging to a single group (exit is not an option) and then allow the formation of a second group (exit is feasible); and we allow costless movement between groups. We first use a payoff function that is the negative of the sum of the income differences between one individual and others in his group who have higher incomes. Next we use a payoff function that is the proportion of those in the individual's group whose incomes are higher than the individual's times their mean excess income. We derive stark and unexpected results. In the first case we find that the process converges to a steady-state equilibrium of individuals across groups wherein clusters of income sub-groups exist in each group. There is no unique cut-off point above or below which individuals move. In addition, the steady-state distribution differs from the steady-state distribution that would have obtained had group affiliation been chosen so as to maximize rank. In the second case we find that the process converges to a steady-state equilibrium wherein the individual with the highest income is alone in one group while all other individuals belong to the second group. Once again, the steady-state distribution is inconsistent with rank maximization. We characterize and explore the social welfare repercussions of the process.

Suppose there are two groups, *A* and *B*, and that the deprivation of an individual whose income is *x* arises only from comparisons with other individuals in his group; nothing else matters. We abstract from the intrinsic value of *x*. However, this is of no consequence whatsoever since *x* is retained (the individual's income is held constant) across groups. We are thus able to study group-formation behavior that is purely due to deprivation. The individual prefers to be affiliated with the group in which his deprivation is lower. When equally deprived (a tie), the individual does not change groups. The individual cannot take into account the fact that other individuals behave in a similar fashion. However, the individual's payoff, or utility, depends on the actions of all other individuals whose incomes are higher than his. A key feature of this situation is that tomorrow's group-selection behavior of every individual is his best reply to today's selection actions of other individuals. What will be the steady-state allocation of individuals across the two groups? What will be the allocation that minimizes the societal relative deprivation?

We employ two measures of relative deprivation. We motivate our use of these measures in Sections 2 and 3 below. Measuring social welfare as the inverse of the population's total relative deprivation, we find that while in both cases the level of social welfare associated with the steady-state distribution is higher than the level of social welfare that obtains at the outset, the steady-state allocations do not confer the maximal level of social welfare. Most interestingly, we also find that the allocation of individuals across the two groups that a welfare-maximizing social planner will choose is *identical* in the two cases. Thus while we admit a variance in perception and measurement and in the ensuing steady-state out-comes, we also point to a uniformity in policy design. From the per-spective of a social planner this finding is of no trivial consequence. When a policymaker finds it difficult to unearth the precise manner in which individuals perceive relative deprivation, he could infer preferences from behavior: when there is a correspondence between observable steady states and hidden perceptions, policy analysts can await realization of the former to deduce the latter and then tailor their policy response to the inferred structure of preferences. Yet if the policy response to alternative structures of preferences happens to be invariant to these structures, awaiting realization of the steady states is not necessary and the policy intervention becomes more efficient.

Let there be a finite discrete set of individuals whose incomes are $x_1, x_2, \ldots, x_n$ where $x_1 \le x_2 \le \cdots \le x_n$. In Section 2, the relative deprivation of an individual whose income is x_j and whose reference group consists of the n individuals is defined as $D(x_j) = \sum_{x_i > x_j} (x_i - x_j)$ and $D(x_j) = 0$ if $x_j \ge x_i$ for $i = 1, 2, \ldots, n$. In Section 3, the relative deprivation of an individual whose income is x_j is defined as $RD(x_j) = \sum_{i=j}^{n-1} [1 - P(x_i)](x_{i+1} - x_i)$ for $j = 1, 2, \ldots, n-1$ where $P(x_i) = Prob(x \le x_i)$, and $RD(x_j) = 0$ if $x_j = x_n$. Note that both measures incorporate rank-related information beyond rank. In a population of two individuals, the rank of the individual whose income is 2 is the same regardless of whether the other individual's income is 3 or 30. However, both $D(\cdot)$ and $RD(\cdot)$ duly differentiate between these two situations. Both measures imply that regardless of their distribution, all units of income in excess of one's own are equally distressing. As will be shown in Section 3, $RD(\cdot)$ further implies that a given excess income is more distressing when received by a larger share of the individual's ref-erence group. ($RD(2)$ is higher in a population of two individuals whose incomes are 2 and 3 than in a population of three individuals whose incomes are 1, 2, and 3.)

2. The Steady-State Distribution when Relative Deprivation is Measured by $D(x_j)$

You board a boat in Guilin in order to travel on the Lijiang River. You can stand either on the port side (left deck) or on the starboard side (right deck) admiring the beautiful cliffs high above the banks of the river. Moving to the port side, you join other passengers, several of whom are taller than you. They block your view of the scenery. You notice that the starboard side is empty so you move there, only to find that other passengers who were disturbed by taller passengers have also moved to that side. You find your view blocked, which prompts you, as well as some other passengers, to return to the port side. And so on. Do these shifts come to a halt? If so, what will the steady-state distribution of passengers between the two decks look like? Will the steady-state distribution confer the best possible social viewing arrangement?

Incomes in the small region R where you live are fully used for visible consumption purposes. Any income (consumption) in your region that is higher than yours induces discomfort—it makes you feel relatively deprived. Another region, R', identical in all respects to your region except that initially it is unpopulated, opens up and offers the possibility that you, and for that matter anyone else, can costlessly move to R'. Who moves and who stays? Will all those who move to R' stay in R'? Will some return? And will some of those who return move once more? Will a steady-state distribution of the population across the two regions emerge? At the steady-state distribution, will the aggregate deprivation of the population be lower than the initial aggregate deprivation? Will it be minimal?

Consider a simple case in which there are ten individuals and individual i receives an income of i, $i = 1, \ldots, 10$. Suppose that initially all individuals $1, \ldots, 10$ are in group A. Group B just comes into existence. (For example, A can be a village, B—a city; A can be a region or a country, B—another region or country; and so on. In cases such as these we assume that the individual does not care at all about the regions themselves and that moving from one region to another is costless.) Measuring time discretely, we will observe the following series of migratory moves. In period 1, all individuals except 10 move from A to B because the deprivation of individual 10 is zero, while the deprivation of all other individuals is strictly positive. In period 2, individuals 1 through 6 return from B to A because every individual in region B except 9, 8, and 7 is more deprived in B than in A. When an individual cannot factor in the contemporaneous response of other individuals, his decision is made under the assumption of no group substitution by these individuals. In period 3, individual 1 prefers to move from A to B rather than be in A, and the process comes to a halt. Thus, after three periods, a steady state is reached such that the tenth and sixth through second individuals are in region A, while the ninth through seventh and first individuals are in group B. Figure 9.1 diagrammatically illustrates this example.[2]

What can be learned from this simple example? First, a well-defined rule is in place that enables us to predict group affiliation and steady-state

Period 0		Period 1		Period 2		Period 3	
Region A	Region B	Region A	Region B	Region A	Region B	Region A	Region B
10		10		10		10	
9			9		9		9
8			8		8		8
7			7		7		7
6			6	6		6	
5			5	5		5	
4			4	4		4	
3			3	3		3	
2			2	2		2	
1			1		1		1

Figure 9.1. The group-formation process and the steady-state distribution

distribution across groups. Second, until a steady state is reached, a change in group affiliation by any individual n is associated with a change in group affiliation by all individuals $i = 1, 2, \ldots, n-1$. Third, the number of individuals changing affiliation in a period is declining in the (rank) order of the period. Fourth, the number of inter-group moves by individuals never rises with their income; individuals with low incomes change affiliations at least as many times as individuals with higher incomes. Fifth, the deprivation motive leads to a stratification steady-state distribution where clusters of income groups exist in each region rather than having a unique cut-off point above or below which individuals move. Sixth, the steady-state distribution differs from the distribution that would have obtained had group affiliation been chosen so as to maximize (ordinal) rank: under pure rank maximization the individual whose income is 3 would have ended up in B rather than in A.

Suppose that when equally deprived in A and B, the individual prefers A to B (an infinitesimal home preference). The steady state reached in this case differs from the steady state reached under the original assumption that when equally deprived (a tie) the individual does not migrate. Looking again at our example we will have the sequence shown in Figure 9.2. Interestingly, in the case of $(x_1, \ldots, x_n) = (1, \ldots, n)$ and an infinitesimal home preference, the number of periods it takes to reach the steady state is equal to the number of complete pairs in n, and the number of individuals who end up locating in A is $n/2$ when $n = 2m$, $(n-1)/2$ when $n = 4m - 1$ or $(n+1)/2$ when $n = 4m - 3$, where m is a positive integer.

Changing the incomes of all individuals by the same factor will have no effect on the pattern of migration. This homogeneity of degree zero property can be expected; when the payoff functions are linear in income

Period 0			Period 1			Period 2			Period 3	
Region A	Region B		Region A	Region B		Region A	Region B		Region A	Region B
10			10			10			10	
9				9			9			9
8				8			8			8
7				7		7			7	
6				6		6			6	
5				5		5				5
4				4		4				4
3				3		3				3
2				2		2				2
1				1		1				1

Period 4			Period 5	
Region A	Region B		Region A	Region B
10			10	
	9			9
	8			8
7			7	
6			6	
	5			5
	4			4
3			3	
2			2	
1				1

Figure 9.2. The migration process and the steady-state distribution with an infinitesimal home preference

differences, populations with income distributions that are linear transformations of each other should display the same migration behavior. Thus the propensity prompted by aversion to deprivation to engage in migration by a rich population is equal to the propensity to engage in migration by a uniformly poorer population. Migration is independent of the general level of wealth of a population.

Interestingly, the result of a non-uniform equilibrium distribution has already been derived, at least twice, in the very context that constitutes our primary example, that is, migration. Stark (1993, chap. 12) studies migration under asymmetric information with signaling. Employers at destination do not know the skill levels of individual workers—they only know the skill distribution. Employers are assumed to pay all indistinguishable workers the same wage based on the average product of the group of workers. Employers at origin, however, know the skill levels of individual workers and pay them a wage based on their marginal product. When a signaling device that enables a worker's skill level to be completely identified exists, and when the cost of the device is moderate, the equilibrium distribution of the workers is such that the least skilled migrate without investing in the signaling device, the most skilled invest in the signaling device and migrate, and the medium skilled do not migrate. Banerjee and Newman (1998) derive a qualitatively similar result. They study a developing economy that consists of two sectors: a modern, high productivity sector in which people have poor information about each other, and a traditional, low productivity sector in which information is good. Since from time to time individuals in both sectors need consumption loans that they may have difficulty repaying, collateral is essential. The superior information available in the traditional sector enables lenders to better monitor borrowers there as opposed to those in the modern sector. The superior access to credit in the traditional sector conditional on the supply of collateral, and the higher productivity in the modern sector prompt migration from the traditional sector to the modern sector by the wealthiest and most productive workers, and by the poorest and least productive employees. The wealthy leave because they can finance consumption on their own and do not need loans; the most productive leave because they have much to gain; and the poorest and the least productive leave because they have nothing to lose—they cannot get a loan in either location.

A crucial assumption of both Stark's and Banerjee and Newman's models is that information is asymmetric. So far, no migration study has analytically generated an equilibrium distribution of three distinct groups under symmetric information, nor has a migration study analytically generated an equilibrium distribution of more than three groups. As the present example yields an equilibrium distribution of more than three groups, and it does so under symmetric information, our example contributes to the theory of migration.

3. The Steady-State Distribution when Relative Deprivation is Measured by $RD(x_j)$

In earlier studies on relative deprivation and migration (Stark 1984, Stark and Yitzhaki 1988, and Stark and Taylor 1989, 1991) we drew largely on the writings of social psychologists, especially Runciman (1966), to formulate a set of axioms and state and prove several propositions, and we conducted an empirical inquiry. The measure of relative deprivation of an individual whose income is y, yielded by our analytical work for the case of a continuous distribution of income, is $RD(y) = \int_y^\infty [1 - F(x)]dx$ where $F(x)$ is the cumulative distribution of income in y's reference group. We have further shown that $RD(y) = [1 - F(y)] \cdot E(x - y \mid x > y)$: the relative deprivation of an individual whose income is y is equal to the proportion of those in y's reference group who are richer than y times their mean excess income. Our empirical work indicates that a distaste for relative deprivation, when relative deprivation is measured by RD, matters; relative deprivation is a significant explanatory variable of migration behavior.

Suppose there are n individuals and that individual i receives income i. Thus the configuration of incomes is $(1, \ldots, n - 1, n)$. Suppose that initially all the individuals $1, \ldots, n - 1, n$ are in region A. Region B opens up. (For example, migration restrictions are eliminated, or B comes into existence.) We measure time discretely.

Claim 1: If the configuration of incomes is $(1, \ldots, n - 1, n)$, then the process of migration in response to relative deprivation reaches a steady state in just one period. Moreover, at the steady state, the individual with income n remains in region A while the rest of the population stays in region B.

Proof: It is trivial that in period 1 the individual with income n stays in region A while the rest of the population migrates to region B. Now consider the action of the individual with income i, where $i = 1, \ldots, n - 1$. If the individual remains in region B, the individual's relative deprivation will be $(n - i)(n - 1 - i)/[2(n - 1)]$.[3] If the individual returns to A, the individual's relative deprivation will be $(n - i)/2$. Note that $(n - i)(n - 1 - i)/[2(n - 1)] < (n - i)/2$ for $i = 1, \ldots, n - 1$. We thus have the result of the Claim. Q.E.D.

Corollary: Given the above setup and a real number $\alpha > 0$, the process of migration in response to relative deprivation will be identical in the two populations $P = \{1, \ldots, n - 1, n\}$ and $P_\alpha = \{\alpha, \ldots, \alpha(n - 1), \alpha n\}$.

Proof: The proof of the Corollary is a replication of the proof of Claim 1 since the two measures of relative deprivation in the proof of Claim 1 are multiplied by α, and therefore the inequality in the proof of Claim 1 carries through to the case of the Corollary. Q.E.D.

It follows that the propensity prompted by relative deprivation to engage in migration by a rich population is equal to the propensity prompted by relative deprivation to engage in migration by a uniformly poorer population. The pattern of migration is independent of the general level of wealth of the population.[4]

Note that the steady state is independent of whether individuals migrate simultaneously (as assumed) or in the order of their relative deprivation (with the most relatively deprived migrating first, the second most relatively deprived migrating second, and so on). In the latter case the steady state is reached after $n - 1$ periods rather than in just one period.

The steady-state distribution differs from the distribution that would have obtained had group affiliation been chosen so as to maximize (ordinal) rank: under pure rank maximization the individuals with incomes $n - 3, n - 4, n - 6, \ldots, n - (n - 2)$ if n is an even number, and the individuals with incomes $n - 3, n - 4, n - 6, \ldots, n - (n - 1)$ if n is an odd number, would have ended up in region A rather than in region B.

Each of the two groups that form in the steady state is smaller than the original single group. It might therefore be suspected that migration is caused partly or wholly by an aversion to crowding. It is easy to see, however, that this is not so. When 1,000 individuals, each with income y, are in region A there is crowding but no migration; when ten individuals, five with income $y > 1$ each and five with income $y - 1$ each are in region A there is little crowding but much migration.

4. Societal Relative Deprivation and Social Welfare

Suppose we measure social welfare by the inverse of the population's total deprivation, where total deprivation is the sum of the deprivation of all the individuals constituting the population. It follows that social welfare is maximized when total deprivation is minimized. Consider first the case in which the payoff function is the negative of the sum of the income differences between one individual and others in his group who have higher incomes. While the social welfare associated with the steady-state distribution is higher than the social welfare associated with the initial period 0 allocation, individualistic group-formation behavior fails to produce maximum social welfare. The minimal total deprivation (*TD*) obtains when $(n, n - 1, \ldots, i)$ are in A and $(i - 1, i - 2, \ldots, 1)$ are in B where $i = (n/2) + 1$ if n is an even number and, as can be ascertained by direct calculation, where $i = (n + 1)/2$ or $i = (n + 3)/2$ when n is an odd number.[5]

Consider next the case in which the payoff function is the proportion of those in the individual's group whose incomes are higher than the individual's times their mean excess income. The steady-state allocation has n in region A and $(n-1, \ldots, 1)$ in region B. This allocation is Pareto efficient. However, the minimal total relative deprivation (TRD) obtains when $(n, n-1, \ldots, i)$ are in region A and $(i-1, i-2, \ldots, 1)$ are in region B where $i = (n/2) + 1$ if n is an even number, and where $i = (n+1)/2$ or $i = (n+3)/2$ when n is an odd number.[6]

In both cases then, the policy response to the steady-state distributions attained by individuals who, while pursuing their own betterment, do not achieve a collectively preferred division is to distribute the population across the two regions in precisely the same manner.

As long as the number of different incomes is larger than the number of (reference) groups, total relative deprivation will not be minimized at zero. If there are as many groups as there are different incomes, total relative deprivation will be zero.

Adopting the perspective that social welfare is maximized when total relative deprivation is minimized is not as ad hoc as it may appear to be. Consider the following social welfare function: $SW = \bar{y}(1 - G)$ where $\bar{y} = (\sum_{i=1}^{n} y_i)/n$ is income per capita in a society consisting of n individuals whose incomes are $y_1, y_2, \ldots, y_n$ and G is the Gini coefficient of income inequality. (It is easy to see that SW is higher upon an increase in any individual's income, and upon a transfer of any income from a high-income individual to a low-income individual.) It can be shown that $(\sum_{i=1}^{n} y_i)G = TRD$ where TRD stands for the total relative deprivation of the population.[7] Thus, SW can be rewritten as $SW = \bar{y} - (TRD/n)$: social welfare is the difference between income per capita and relative deprivation per capita. Since in the present setting incomes are kept intact, $\bar{y}$ is constant and SW is maximized when TRD is minimized.

We have implicitly assumed that region B is not subject to a capacity constraint: there is room in region B for the entire population but for one member. For the sake of concreteness, consider the case of an even n; of migration proceeding in the order of the intensity of relative deprivation; and of relative deprivation being measured by RD. We have seen that while individuals $1, 2, \ldots, n-1$ prefer to relocate to region B, it would be socially optimal to have only individuals $1, \ldots, n/2$ move there. Hence, if it so happens that region B can accommodate only up to one half of the population, migration will come to a halt precisely at a level that is socially optimal. We thus have an example in which a constraint on mobility is conducive to the attainment of maximal social welfare rather than constituting a hindrance to such an attainment.

5. Conclusions and Complementary Reflections

We have presented an analysis that contributes to the large and growing literature on the theory of non-market, social interactions pioneered by Schelling (1971, 1972) and recently added to, among many others, by Stark (1999), Glaeser and Scheinkman (2000) who provide a useful synthesis, and Becker and Murphy (2001).

We note that individuals belong to groups, clubs, neighborhoods, and various associations. When given a choice, individuals may want to revise their affiliation—form a new group, change their neighborhood, join another club, associate with others. Several considerations, both absolute and relative, impinge on these choices. In this chapter we have singled out for close scrutiny one such consideration—a distaste for relative deprivation. We have studied several repercussions when this measure is used as the exclusive determinant of affiliation.

We have assumed a given and uniform dislike of relative deprivation. Relative deprivation is a sensitive measure that encompasses rank-related information beyond mere rank. (It tells us that 1 compared to 3 is worse than 1 compared to 2, even though in both instances 1 ranks second.) An important question that is not addressed in this chapter is where the aversion to relative deprivation or, for that matter, the distaste for low rank, originates. Postlewaite (1998) argues that since over the millennia high rank conferred an evolutionary advantage in the competition for food and mating opportunities, the concern for rank is likely to be hard-wired (part of the genetic structure). More generally though, any setting in which rank impinges positively—directly or indirectly—on consumption ought to imply a concern for rank.[8] The study of why an aversion to relative deprivation exists and why individuals exhibit distaste for low rank invites more attention.

It is plausible to stipulate that the distaste for low rank will not be uniform across societies. Consequently, the extent of self-segregation across societies will vary. Since segregation is visible, whereas preferences are not, an inference may be drawn from the observed segregation to the motivating distaste, with more segregation suggesting stronger distaste.

We have shown that when individuals who initially belong to one group (costlessly) act upon their distaste for relative deprivation and self-select into any one of two groups, they end up splitting into two groups in a manner that is sensitive to the way in which relative deprivation is sensed and measured. However, when the social planner's response to a split is not sensitive to the way in which relative deprivation is conceptualized nor, for that matter, to the particular configuration of the split, there is no need to exert effort to unearth the specific configuration of the underlying motive or to await a particular manifestation of the behavior that the motive prompts.

We have described an endogenous process of voluntary segmentation into distinct groups; the division of the population into groups is not the outcome of an exogenous imposition of segregation. Assuming no comparisons between members of one group and another, we have shown that, as a consequence, aggregate relative deprivation is lowered. In broader contexts, the group partitioning could also be associated with improved social welfare as a result of reduced social tensions, fewer conflicts, less crime, and a mediated quest for status (as the inequality between those who compete with each other for status is reduced).

The opening of another region, B, facilitates shedding one's relative deprivation by allowing a group to split into two. Consider a reverse process, wherein regions A and B merge into a single composite region that constitutes everyone's reference group. In all cases (except the degenerate case in which all individuals have exactly the same income) the population's relative deprivation is bound to rise. Groups who are less well off in terms of absolute income will be better off in terms of well-being if they are allowed to secede, without any change in absolute income. Conversely, a group that is less well off in terms of absolute income that is forced to merge with a group that is better off in terms of absolute income becomes worse off. The pressure to form a separate state, for example, can be partially attributed to this aversion to relative deprivation; when such an aversion exists, the sole individual with less than 1 in B may prefer that option to having 1 in A, where 2 is present.

These considerations relate to federalism. The process of adding new members to a federation of nations usually draws on the expectation that in the wake of the integration, the incomes of the citizens of the new member nations will rise. The European Union, however, has taken great pains to ensure that the incomes of the citizens of the would-be member nations rise substantially *prior* to integration. Our approach suggests a rationale. To the extent that integration entails the formation of a new reference group, relative deprivation when 1 joins 2 would be reduced if $1\frac{1}{2}$ were to join 2, and would be eliminated altogether if 2 were to join 2.

The idea that externalities impinge asymmetrically on individuals' well-being and behavior has been with us for many years. Early proponents of this idea were of the opinion that the well-being of individuals rose in what they had and declined in what more prosperous people had. References of pioneering works that come readily to mind are Duesenberry (1949) who argued that individuals look up but not down when making comparisons, Stouffer *et al.* (1949) who, in spite of studying quite different behavior, independently argued likewise, and Davis (1966) who observed that in choosing higher performance career fields, which generally require graduate training, students in colleges and universities in the US were heavily influenced by their subjectively assessed relative standing in their college or university rather than by the subjective quality of the institution, *and* that they adjusted their career choices in a manner corresponding to their subjective (relative) standing in their college or university, tilting toward the low performance fields as their *relative* standing declined.[9] (As social psychologists, Stouffer *et al.* and Davis have carefully searched for the relevant set of individuals with whom comparisons are made—the reference group.) A recent manifestation of the asymmetric externalities idea takes the diametrically opposite view that while the utility of an individual rises in his own consumption, it declines in the consumption of any of his neighbors if that consumption falls below some minimal level; individuals are adversely affected by the material well-being of others in their reference group when this well-being is sufficiently lower than theirs (Andolfatto 2002). Our impression though is that in the course of the intervening five decades, the bulk of the theoretical work has held the view that individuals look up and not down, and that the evidence has overwhelmingly supported the "upward comparison" view.[10] (Helpful references are provided and reviewed in Frey and Stutzer (2002) and in Walker and Smith (2002).) The analysis in the preceding sections is in line with, and draws on this perspective. Nonetheless, it could be of interest to reflect on the manner in which our results will be affected if comparisons were to assume a symmetrical or quasi-symmetrical nature. It is easy to see why such a revised structure of preferences will not even yield a steady-state distribution to begin with. An example will suffice. Consider the first case and rewrite the payoff function of an individual whose income is x_j as follows: $D(x_j) = \sum_{x_i > x_j}(x_i - x_j) + \sum_{x_k < x_j} \alpha(x_k - x_j)$. Throughout this chapter we have assumed that $\alpha = 0$. Let us now have $\alpha > 0$, however small, retain the assumption of two regions, and consider the simplest case of $n = 2$. In this setting a steady state will never be reached: while 1 will want to separate from 2, 2 will want to stay with 1. There will be repeated and endless cycles. Let $\alpha = 1$ and consider the case of $n = 3$. Again, a steady state will not be reached and cycles will ensue: in period zero, 3, 2, and 1 are in A. In period one, 3 and 2 stay in A while 1 moves to B. (3 has the minimal sum of gaps (-3) which, if he were to move, would rise to (0); 2 has a sum of (0) and thus stands to gain nothing by moving; 1 has the sum of (3) which, upon a move, will be reduced to (0).) In period two, 3 and 2 move to B since each contemplates the move to result in a lowering of his period-one relative deprivation (from (-1) to (-2) and from (1) to (-1), respectively). But now 3, 2, and 1 are in B, which is the same configuration as that of period zero, prompting 1 to move to A, and so on. Alternatively, if we let $\alpha = -1$, implying that individuals seek to minimize the sum of absolute income gaps (in either direction), we will find once again, as can easily be verified, that a steady state will not be reached. The results obtained in this chapter constitute, therefore, a contribution to the study of group formation when affiliation choices are guided by an aversion to falling behind others, and when this aversion is modeled through particular measures that go beyond the crude measure of rank. The results are appealing both intuitively and analytically, and are consistent with a large body of theoretical and empirical literature.

Appendices

To differentiate between the cases that correspond to payoff functions $D(x_j)$ and $RD(x_j)$, we refer to total relative deprivation in the first case as TD, and to total relative deprivation in the second case as TRD.

Appendix 9.1

I

To find the division of a population of n individuals across groups A and B that confers the minimal total deprivation (TD) we proceed in two steps. First, given the size of the two groups, we show that the minimal TD is reached when high income individuals are in one of the groups and low income individuals are in the other group. (That is, the income of *any* individual who is in one group is higher than the income of *any* individual who is in the other group.) Second, given this distribution, we show that the minimal TD is reached when *half* of the individuals are in one group and the other half are in the other group.

Lemma: Let n be a fixed positive integer. Consider $\{a_1, a_2, \ldots, a_n\}$ where $a_1 < a_2 < \cdots < a_n$ and the a_i's are positive integers. Let $S(a_1, a_2, \ldots, a_n) = \sum_{1 \le i,j \le n} |a_i - a_j|$. Then $S(a_1, a_2, \ldots, a_n)$ reaches its minimum if and only if $a_{i+1} = a_i + 1$ for $i = 1, 2, \ldots, n-1$.

Proof: For any $i < j$, we have $|a_i - a_j| = |a_j - a_{j-1}| + |a_{j-1} - a_{j-2}| + \cdots + |a_{i+1} - a_i|$.

Therefore, $|a_i - a_j| \ge j - i$ and $\left(\underset{\text{for all } i,j}{|a_i - a_j| = j - i}\right)$ if and only if $\left(\underset{\text{for } i=1, 2, \ldots, n-1}{a_{i+1} = a_i + 1}\right)$. It follows that $S(a_1, a_2, \ldots, a_n)$ reaches its minimum if and only if $a_{i+1} = a_i + 1$ for $i = 1, 2, \ldots, n-1$. (This minimum is $n(n^2 - 1)/3$.) Q.E.D.

Corollary: Consider the configuration of incomes $(1, \ldots, n-1, n)$. Let there be two groups, A and B, with $(i_1, i_2, \ldots, i_{n_A})$ in A, and $(j_1, j_2, \ldots, j_{n_B})$ in B, $n = n_A + n_B$. Let $TD = TD_A + TD_B$. Then, if n, n_A, n_B are fixed, TD reaches its minimum if and only if $(j_1, j_2, \ldots, j_{n_B}) = (1, 2, \ldots, n_B)$ or $(i_1, i_2, \ldots, i_{n_A}) = (1, 2, \ldots, n_A)$; that is,

either

Region A	Region B
n	
$\vdots$	
$n_B + 1$	
	n_B
	$\vdots$
	1

or

Region A	Region B
n	
$\vdots$	
$n_A + 1$	
	n_A
	$\vdots$
	1

Proof: Note that $TD_A = (1/2) S(i_1, i_2, \ldots, i_{n_A})$, $TD_B = (1/2) S(j_1, j_2, \ldots, j_{n_B})$. Thus, for fixed n_A, n_B, $\min TD_A \Leftrightarrow \min S(i_1, i_2, \ldots, i_{n_A})$, $\min TD_B \Leftrightarrow \min S(j_1, j_2, \ldots, j_{n_B})$. Assume that TD reaches its minimum at $(i_1^*, i_2^*, \ldots, i_{n_A}^*)$, $(j_1^*, j_2^*, \ldots, j_{n_B}^*)$. Without loss of generality, assume that $n \in (i_1^*, i_2^*, \ldots, i_{n_A}^*)$. Then, if $(i_1^*, i_2^*, \ldots, i_{n_A}^*) \ne (n_B + 1, \ldots, n)$, then $(j_1^*, j_2^*, \ldots, j_{n_B}^*) \ne (1, \ldots, n_B)$. By the Lemma, we have that $TD_A(i_1^*, i_2^*, \ldots, i_{n_A}^*) > TD_A(n_B + 1, \ldots, n)$, and $TD_B(j_1^*, j_2^*, \ldots, j_{n_B}^*) > TD_B(1, \ldots, n_B)$. Thus, $TD((i_1^*, i_2^*, \ldots, i_{n_A}^*), (j_1^*, j_2^*, \ldots, j_{n_B}^*)) > TD((n_B + 1, \ldots, n), (1, \ldots, n_B))$, which contradicts the assumption that TD reaches its minimum at $(i_1^*, i_2^*, \ldots, i_{n_A}^*), (j_1^*, j_2^*, \ldots, j_{n_B}^*)$. Hence, $(i_1^*, i_2^*, \ldots, i_{n_A}^*) = (n_B + 1, \ldots, n)$, and $(j_1^*, j_2^*, \ldots, j_{n_B}^*) = (1, \ldots, n_B)$. Conversely, by the Lemma, we have that $TD_A(i_1, i_2, \ldots, i_{n_A}) \ge TD_A(n_B + 1, \ldots, n)(or(1, \ldots, n_A))$, and $TD_B(j_1, j_2, \ldots, j_{n_B}) \ge TD_B(1, 2, \ldots, n_B)(or(n_A + 1, \ldots, n))$. Therefore, TD reaches its minimum at either of the two configurations. We have thus proved the Corollary. Q.E.D.

II

From the Lemma we know that the minimum of $S(a_1, a_2, \ldots, a_n)$ is $n(n^2 - 1)/3$. The total deprivation TD of $(n, n-1, \ldots, 1)$ is $1/2$ of this minimum, that is, $TD = n(n^2 - 1)/6$. Let $n = n_A + n_B$, $n \geq 2$, $n_A \geq 1$. Then, by the Corollary, $TD_A = n_A(n_A^2 - 1)/6$, $TD_B = n_B(n_B^2 - 1)/6$. Therefore, $TD = (n_A(n_A^2 - 1)/6) + ((n - n_A)[(n - n_A)^2 - 1]/6) = (n^3 - 3n^2 n_A + 3n n_A^2 - n)/6$.

We seek to solve $\min_{1 \leq n_A \leq n} TD$. Since $(dTD/dn_A) = (1/6)(-3n^2 + 6n n_A)$ and $d^2 TD/(dn_A)^2 = n > 0$, we have that the minimal TD obtains when $dTD/dn_A = 0$, that is, $n_A = n/2$. Therefore, if n is an even number, half of the n individuals will be in each of the two groups. With $TD_A = TD_B = n(n^2 - 4)/48$, $TD = TD_A + TD_B = n(n^2 - 4)/24$.

Appendix 9.2

I

Section I of Appendix 9.2 is identical to Section I of Appendix 9.1 except that TD in Appendix 9.1 is replaced by TRD in Appendix 9.2.

II

We next determine the size of the sub-groups that brings TRD to a minimum.

Let $(n, \ldots, i)$ be in region A, and let $(i-1, \ldots, 1)$ be in region B. Total relative deprivation in A is:[11]

$$TRD_A = \frac{1}{n-i+1} \cdot 1 + \frac{2}{n-i+1} \frac{1+2}{2} + \cdots + \frac{n-i}{n-i+1} \frac{1+2+\cdots+n-i}{n-i}$$

$$= \frac{1 + (1+2) + \cdots + (1+2+\cdots+n-i)}{n-i+1} = \frac{(n-i)(n-i+2)}{6}.$$

Total relative deprivation in B is:

$$TRD_B = \frac{1}{i-1} + \frac{2}{i-1} \frac{1+2}{2} + \cdots + \frac{i-1-1}{i-1} \frac{1+2+\cdots+i-1-1}{i-1-1}$$

$$= \frac{1 + (1+2) + \cdots + (1+2+\cdots+i-2)}{i-1} = \frac{i(i-2)}{6}.$$

Hence, $TRD = TRD_A + TRD_B = (1/6)[(n-i)(n-i+2) + i(i-2)]$. We seek to solve $\min_{1 \leq i \leq n} TRD$. Since $dTRD/di = (1/3)(-n + 2i - 2)$ and $d(TRD)^2/di^2 = 2/3 > 0$, we have that the minimal TRD obtains when $dTRD/di = 0 \Rightarrow -n + 2i - 2 = 0 \Rightarrow i = (n/2) + 1$. If n is an even number then the i that brings TRD to a minimum is $i^* = (n/2) + 1$, and, by direct calculation, $TRD = (1/12)(n^2 - 4)$. If n is an odd number, direct calculation yields that when $i = (n+1)/2$, $TRD = (1/12)(n^2 - 3)$, and that when

$i = (n+3)/2$, $TRD = (1/12)(n^2 - 3)$. Therefore, if n is an odd number, the i that brings TRD to a minimum is $i^* = (n+1)/2$ or $i^* = (n+3)/2$.

The result pertaining to the optimal split of the n individuals between the two regions can also be obtained by noting that for $(1, 2, \ldots, n)$, $TRD = (n^2 - 1)/6$. (This equation can be inferred, for example, from the expression above of $TRD_B = i(i - 2)/6$ by setting $i - 1 = n$.) Let $n = n_A + n_B$, $n \geq 2$, $n_A \geq 1$. Then $TRD_A = (n_A^2 - 1)/6$ and $TRD_B = ((n - n_A)^2 - 1)/6$. Therefore, $TRD = (2n_A^2 + n^2 - 2n \cdot n_A - 2)/6$. We seek to solve $\min_{1 \leq n_A \leq n} TRD$. Since $dTRD/dn_A = (4n_A - 2n)/6$ and $d(TRD)^2/(d^2 n_A) = 4/6 > 0$, we have that the minimal TRD obtains when $dTRD/dn_A = 0 \Rightarrow 4n_A - 2n = 0 \Rightarrow n_A = n/2$. Therefore, if n is an even number, half of the n individuals will be in each of the two regions. With $TRD_A = ((n/2)^2 - 1)/6$ and $TRD_B = ((n/2)^2 - 1)/6$, $TRD = TRD_A + TRD_B = 2((n/2)^2 - 1)/6 = (1/12)(n^2 - 4)$.

Notes

1. When utility is derived both from absolute income and from relative income, and the utility function is additively separable, the difference in utilities across groups is reduced to the difference that arises from levels of relative income. Holding absolute incomes constant should not then be taken to imply that the individual does not care about his absolute income, and it enables us to study behavior that is purely due to considerations of relative income.

2. Since the myopic adjustment dynamics is deterministic, that is, the distribution in period t completely determines the distribution in period $t + 1$, it follows that starting with everyone in A, the process will converge (if at all) to a unique steady state. To see this most easily, note that the richest individual will never move. Given the richest individual's immutable location, the second-richest individual has an optimal location and will need at most one period to get there. Given the stable location of the first two individuals, the third richest individual will have his own optimal location, which will be reached at most one period after the second individual has "settled down", and so on. No individual will have to move more times than his descending-order income rank. This reasoning assures us of convergence. As to uniqueness, allowing individuals to choose locations in a descending order of incomes well defines a path, and one path cannot lead to two destinations; the resultant "profile" is the only possible steady-state distribution.

3. In the case of $(x_1, \ldots, x_n) = (1, \ldots, n)$, $RD(x_j) = \sum_{i=j}^{n-1} (1 - i/n)$ (recall the last paragraph of Section 1). Since in this arithmetic series $a_1 = 1 - j/n$, $a_{n-j} = 1 - (n-1)/n$, and the number of terms is $n - j$, it follows that

$$RD(x_j) = \sum_{i=j}^{n-1} \left(1 - \frac{i}{n}\right) = \frac{\left(1 - \frac{j}{n} + 1 - \frac{n-1}{n}\right)(n - j)}{2} = \frac{n-j}{2n}(n - j + 1).$$

The relative deprivation of the individual with income i in region B can also be calculated by using this formula:

$$RD(i)|_{i \in B} = \frac{(n-1)-i}{2(n-1)}\left[(n-1)-i+1\right] = \frac{n-i}{2} \cdot \frac{n-1-i}{n-1}.$$

4. Note that the results of this section apply even if the population is multiplied by a natural number k. To see this, consider the configuration of incomes $\left(\underbrace{1,\ldots,1}_{k},\ldots,\underbrace{n,\ldots,n}_{k}\right)$. In period 1 the k individuals with income n stay in region A while the rest of the population migrates to region B. Now consider the action of an individual with income i, where $i = 1, \ldots, n-1$. If the individual remains in region B, the individual's relative deprivation will be $(n-i)(n-1-i)/[2(n-1)]$ (as when $k=1$). If an individual with income i were to return to A, the individual's relative deprivation would be $(k/(k+1))(n-i)$. Since for any natural number k, $(k/(k+1))(n-i) > (n-i)(n-1-i)/2(n-1)$, the result of Claim 1 holds also for the case in which the population is multiplied by k.

5. The proof is in Appendix 9.1.

6. The proof is in Appendix 9.2.

7. The proof is Appendix 2 of Stark and Wang (2004).

8. In poor societies with meager assets, rank can serve as a proxy for collateral, making it easier for individuals to obtain credit.

9. Notably, students judged themselves by their "local standing" in their own college or university (that is, standing within their reference group) rather than across colleges or universities (that is, across reference groups). This self-assessment and the resulting response implied that being a "big frog in a small pond" or a "small frog in a big pond" mattered even when the absolute size of the "frog" did not change. Davis concluded that when parents who aspire for their son to opt for a higher-performance career field send their son to a "fine" college or university, "a big pond", they face a risk of him ending up assessing himself as a "small frog" thereby ending up not choosing a desirable career path.

10. For example, it has been argued that given the set of individuals with whom comparisons are made, an unfavorable comparison could induce harder work. This idea is captured and developed in the literature on performance incentives in career games and other contests. (Early studies include Lazear and Rosen (1981), Rosen (1986), and Stark (1990).) Loewenstein et al. (1989) provide evidence that individuals strongly dislike being in an income distribution in which "comparison persons" earn more. Clark and Oswald (1996) present evidence that "comparison incomes" have a significant negative impact on overall job satisfaction.

11. $\sum_{k=1}^{n}(1+2+\cdots+k) = \sum_{k=1}^{n}\frac{(1+k)k}{2} = \frac{1}{2}\sum_{k=1}^{n}k + \frac{1}{2}\sum_{k=1}^{n}k^2 = \frac{1}{2}\frac{(1+n)n}{2} + \frac{1}{2}\frac{n(n+1)(2n+1)}{6} = \frac{n(n+1)(n+2)}{6}$. Substituting $n-i$ for n yields the last expression of TRD_A.

References

Andolfatto, David (2002), "A Theory of Inalienable Property Rights", *Journal of Political Economy*, 110: 382–93.

Banerjee, Abhijit V., and Newman, Andrew F. (1998), "Information, the Dual Economy, and Development", *Review of Economic Studies*, 65: 631–53.

Becker, Gary S., and Murphy, Kevin (2001), *Social Markets: Market Behavior in a Social Environment*, Cambridge, Mass.: Harvard University Press.

Clark, Andrew E., and Oswald, Andrew J. (1996), "Satisfaction and Comparison Income", *Journal of Public Economics*, 61: 359–81.

Davis, James A. (1966), "The Campus as a Frog Pond: An Application of the Theory of Relative Deprivation to Career Decisions of College Men", *American Journal of Sociology*, 72: 17–31.

Duesenberry, James S. (1949), *Income, Savings and the Theory of Consumer Behavior*, Cambridge, Mass.: Harvard University Press.

Frey, Bruno S., and Stutzer, Alois (2002), *Happiness and Economics: How the Economy and Institutions Affect Human Well-Being*, Princeton: Princeton University Press.

Glaeser, Edward, and Scheinkman, Jose A. (2000), "Non-Market Interactions", Cambridge, Mass.: National Bureau of Economic Research, Working Paper 8053.

Lazear, Edward P., and Rosen, Sherwin (1981), "Rank-Order Tournaments as Optimum Labor Contracts", *Journal of Political Economy*, 89: 841–64.

Loewenstein, George F., Thompson, Leigh, and Bazerman, Max H. (1989), "Social Utility and Decision Making in Interpersonal Contexts", *Journal of Personality and Social Psychology*, 57: 426–41.

Postlewaite, Andrew (1998), "The Social Basis of Interdependent Preferences", *European Economic Review*, 42: 779–800.

Rosen, Sherwin (1986), "Prizes and Incentives in Elimination Tournaments", *American Economic Review*, 76: 701–15.

Runciman, Walter G. (1966), *Relative Deprivation and Social Justice: A Study of Attitudes to Social Inequality in Twentieth-Century England*, Berkeley: University of California Press.

Schelling, Thomas (1971), "Dynamic Models of Segregation", *Journal of Mathematical Sociology*, 1: 143–86.

——(1972), "A Process of Residential Segregation: Neighborhood Tipping", in Anthony H. Pascal (ed.), *Racial Discrimination in Economic Life*, Lexington, Mass.: Lexington Books.

Stark, Oded (1984), "Rural-to-Urban Migration in LDCs: A Relative Deprivation Approach", *Economic Development and Cultural Change*, 32: 475–86.

——(1990), "A Relative Deprivation Approach to Performance Incentives in Career Games and other Contests", *Kyklos*, 43: 211–27.

——(1993), *The Migration of Labor*, Oxford and Cambridge, Mass.: Blackwell.

Stark, Oded (1999), *Altruism and Beyond: An Economic Analysis of Transfers and Exchanges within Families and Groups*, Cambridge: Cambridge University Press.

—— and Taylor, J. Edward (1989), "Relative Deprivation and International Migration", *Demography*, 26: 1–14.

—— (1991), "Migration Incentives, Migration Types: The Role of Relative Deprivation", *The Economic Journal*, 101: 1163–78.

—— and Wang, You Qiang (2004), "On the Quest for Status as an Intervening Variable between the Distribution of Wealth and Growth", Manuscript, University of Bonn, Bonn.

—— and Yitzhaki, Shlomo (1988), "Labour Migration as a Response to Relative Deprivation", *Journal of Population Economics*, 1: 57–70.

Stouffer, S. A., Suchman, E. A., Devinney, L. C., Star, S. A., and Williams, Jr., R. M. (1949), *The American Soldier: Adjustment during Army Life*. Princeton: Princeton University Press.

Walker, Iain, and Smith, Heather J. (2002), *Relative Deprivation: Specification, Development, and Integration*, Cambridge: Cambridge University Press.

10

Happiness in Hardship

Ruut Veenhoven

Many philosophers have associated happiness with trouble-free living. Some 2,300 years ago, the Greek philosopher Epicure defined happiness as the absence of pain and advised his followers to avoid the social rat race and retreat into contemplative communes (Poot 2005). Likewise, the nineteenth-century German philosopher Schopenhauer saw happiness as "not suffering too much" and also advised one should live a tranquil solitary life (Schalkxs 2005).

This view on happiness is also found in utopian fantasy, where the ideal society is typically depicted as ordered and without problems. In these earthly paradises there is no social conflict, no competition, and no jealousy. In Skinner's *Walden Two*, for instance, all such nasty troubles have been eradicated by psychological condition techniques (Skinner 1948).

The idea of happiness as trouble-free living is also common in religious thinking, in particular in beliefs that renounce the world. Happiness is seen to have existed in paradise and is expected in heaven, both sanctuaries from hardship. It is not seen as something that can be realized in an earthly existence. At best one can reduce suffering a bit by withdrawing from worldly life as much as possible.

This theory is in fact one of the reasons why many philosophers see little value in happiness. A common objection against the utilitarian "greatest happiness principle" is that happiness is mere sullen contentment and that this peace of mind requires a sheltered society, such as the technocratic paradise of *Brave New World*. "Self-actualization" is typically mentioned as an alternative end-value that promises more pith.

In line with this philosophy, several empirical investigations have tried to demonstrate that happiness is antithetical to problems, in particular to social problems. Most of this research was instigated by welfare institutions, eager to legitimize their existence. Much to the regret of investigators and their commissioners, some of the findings do not fit this theory too well. It appears that people can be quite happy, in spite of considerable problems in society and in their private lives. These unexpected results have given rise to disenchantment with the concept of happiness. They have fueled doubts about biased measurement and false consciousness and given support to theories that denounce happiness as mere mental illusion.

I will describe this research in more detail below and then entertain the question: Does this mean that happiness is truly illusionary? I start with a quick overview of the field.

Study of Happiness

Empirical research on happiness started in the 1960s in several branches of the social sciences. In sociology, the study of happiness developed from "social indicators research". In this field, "subjective" indicators were used to supplement traditional "objective" indicators and "happiness" became a main subjective indicator of social system performance (Andrews and Withey 1976; Campbell 1981). In psychology, the concept was used in the study of mental health. Jahoda (1958) saw happiness as a criterion for "positive mental health" and items on happiness figured in the pioneering epidemiological surveys on mental health by Gurin *et al.* (1960) and Bradburn (1969). At that time happiness also figured in the ground-breaking cross-national study of "human concerns" by Cantril (1965) and came to be used as an indicator of "successful aging" in gerontology (Neugarten *et al.* 1961). Twenty years later, the concept appeared in medical outcome research. Happiness is a common item in questionnaires on "health related quality-of-life" such as the much-used SF-36 (Ware 1996). Lately, economists, such as Oswald (1997), Frank (1999), and Frey and Stutzer (2002) have also picked up the issue.

The study of happiness has been rapidly institutionalized over the past few years, most investigators have joined forces and formed the International Society for Quality of Life Studies (ISQOLS).[1] There is a specialized academic journal, the *Journal of Happiness Studies*,[2] and research findings are easily obtainable in the World Database of Happiness.[3]

Concept

Happiness is defined as the degree to which people evaluate their overall quality of present life as a whole positively. In other words, how much they like the life they live.

When we appraise how much we appreciate the life we live, we seem to use two sources of information: affectively, we estimate how well we feel generally, and at the cognitive level we compare "life as it is" with perceived standards of "how life should be". The former, affective source of information seems to be more important than the latter cognitive one (Veenhoven 1996: 33–5).

I refer to these "subtotals" in the evaluation of life as respectively "*hedonic level of affect*" and "*contentment*". I use the terms "*happiness*" or "*life satisfaction*" for the comprehensive judgment. These definitions have been delineated in detail in earlier publications (Veenhoven 1984, chap. 2; 2000).

Measurement

Measurement has long been understood to be "objective" and "external" assessment, analogous to the measurement of blood pressure by a doctor. By now, we know that happiness cannot be measured this way. Steady physiological correlates have not been discovered, and probably never will be. Nor have any overt behaviors been found that can be linked consistently to inner enjoyment of life.

Like most attitudinal phenomena, happiness is only partially reflected in behavior. Though some social behaviors tend to be more frequent among the happy, such as being active, outgoing, friendly, such conduct is also observed among some unhappy persons. Likewise, non-verbal behaviors such as frequent smiling or enthusiastic movements appear to be only moderately related to self-reports of happiness. Consequently, estimates of people's happiness by their peers are often wrong. Suicidal behavior is probably more indicative of unhappiness. Almost all people who attempt to or commit suicide are quite unhappy. However, not all the unhappy resort to suicide. In fact, only a fraction does.

Inference from overt behavior being impossible, when determining degrees of happiness or unhappiness, we must make do with questioning. That is, simply asking people how much they enjoy their life as a whole. Such questions can be posed in various contexts: clinical interviews, life-review questionnaires, and common survey interviews. The questions can be posed in different ways: directly or indirectly, using single or multiple items.[4] A common survey question is:

Taking all things together, how happy would you say you are: very happy, quite happy, not very happy, not at all happy?

245

Such questions are commonly used in survey research. The validity and reliability of such simple self-reports however are to be doubted. In earlier publications I have considered the objections and inspected the empirical evidence for claims of bias. I concluded that responses to these questions do adequately reflect how much people enjoy their life, though not very precisely. For more detail and references, see Veenhoven (1984, chap. 3 and 1998).

Investigations

Measurement of happiness is used in an increasing number of investigations. Happiness is now a common item in large-scale population surveys, such as the Eurobarometer and the World Value Studies. Measurement of happiness also figures in many studies of specific groups, such as single mothers, students, or lottery-winners. The bulk of these studies revolve around a single questionnaire, but there are a number that contain follow-up studies and there have even been some experimental investigations.

To date, happiness has been assessed in some 3,000 empirical investigations and the volume of research on happiness is increasing exponentially. The findings of all this research are stored in the above-mentioned World Database of Happiness (WDH 2003), which contains data on assessments of how happy people are (distributional findings) and differences in conditions of more and less happy people (correlational findings). These findings are easily accessible on the web (www.worlddatabaseofhappiness.eur.ul).

Paradoxical Findings

Many of the findings are in line with the theory of happiness as living a trouble-free life. Average happiness is much lower in nations that are afflicted by poverty, war, and injustice than in nations that are not. Likewise, individual happiness is lower after personal calamities such as widowhood or job loss. Still there are also findings that contradict this theory and suggest that there are also some troubles we can live with.

Happiness in an Imperfect Society

Social ills are often mentioned as a source of unhappiness, both chronic social problems and sudden crises in society. Yet not all tribulation we read about in the newspapers really affects the happiness of citizens.

Chronic Social Problems

On the political right, criminality is often mentioned as a major threat to happiness, while the left stresses persistent inequality. All parties seem to agree that the increasing pace of life reduces happiness in modern society. Opinions are strong on this matter, but the empirical evidence is surprisingly weak.

Criminality

There is much concern about crime, in particular about violence. The media have reported more on matters related to violence and bloodshed in the last decade and murder rates have actually risen in several countries. There is widespread public support for safety policies: But does this evil really reduce average happiness in the country?

One check is to compare happiness in nations that differ in the degree of prevalence of criminality. A plot of happiness against homicide rates is given in Figure 10.1. Though there is a tendency for there to be

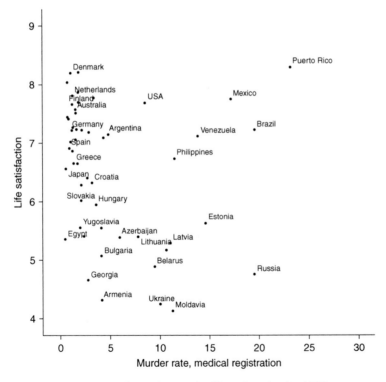

Figure 10.1. Happiness and murder rate in 55 nations in the 1990s

lower happiness in the most homicidal nations, the tendency is modest, $r = -0.36$, and it is not clearly visible.

This unexpected result could be caused by the Latin American nations, where people are fairly happy in spite of high homicide rates. Possibly Latin culture involves some compensators and thus distorts the big picture. I checked this possibility by considering three parts of the world separately, the rich Western nations, former communist countries, and Latin America. Yet I did not find much relation when considering these sets of nations separately (data not shown). Since happiness also depends on the economic development of the country I also controlled for income per head. This reduced the correlation even more: the partial correlation is only -0.20.

Another check is to compare over time and see whether rising homicide rates are followed by a decline in happiness. There is no evidence for such a trend; happiness rose somewhat over the last decade in most Western nations and also in nations reputed to have rising criminality, such as the USA. More sophisticated trend analysis may show otherwise, but it is unlikely to reveal a strong effect.

Inequality

There is also much concern about inequality in modern society, and in particular about the widening gap between rich and poor. This societal evil is denoted by terms like "social exclusion" and "new poverty" and ranks high on the political agenda. Yet again there is little evidence for detrimental effects on happiness.

A chart of happiness and income inequality in 45 nations in the 1990s is presented in Figure 10.2. In this plot we again see little relation between inequality and happiness. Though happiness is indeed high in egalitarian countries such as Denmark, it is also high in unequal Latin American nations such as Brazil. In this picture the former communist countries combine equality with misery. Together this means that the correlation between happiness and income equality is zero.

Again, various intervening variables may distort this picture. Yet statistical control for income per head does not produce the expected negative relationship. Instead, a positive correlation emerges: the partial correlation is $+0.42$! Within country comparisons across regions yielded somewhat different results (Alesina *et al.* 2001; Oswald and Blanchflower 2003), but these effects are small in size.

Comparison over time is difficult in this case, since income inequality has not changed much over the last decade in affluent nations. In spite of much talk about a growing split in society, income inequality appears to

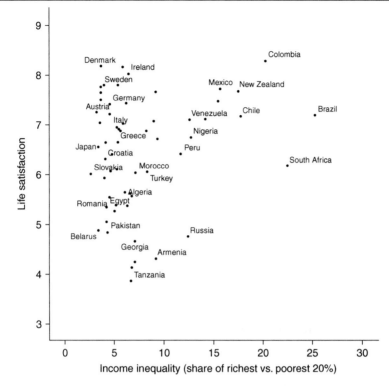

Figure 10.2. Happiness and income inequality in 52 nations in the 1990s

have increased only in Britain and the USA (Ritakallio 2001). Yet happiness did not decrease in either of these countries (Veenhoven 2003).

Time Pressure

There is good evidence of a growing pace of life in modern society. We spend more hours at work and on other scheduled activities and have less free time. This development is usually described as harmful. Garhammer (2002) calls it "time stress" and Schorr's (1991) bestseller on this subject is entitled *The Overworked American*. A lot of people believe that it is the curse of the era. However, the available data do not suggest that this is detrimental to happiness, at least not for average happiness in affluent nations.

A comparison of European nations in the 1990s is given in Figure 10.3. Happiness is again plotted vertically and an indicator of time pressure horizontally. Instead of the predicted negative relationship, we see a

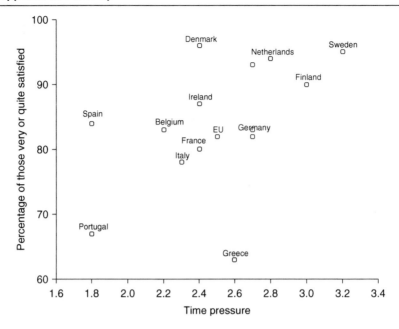

Figure 10.3. Happiness and time pressure in EU nations in the 1990s
Note: High work speed/tight deadlines: 0 = never; 6 = all the time.

positive one, happiness being lowest in relaxed Portugal and highest in speedy Sweden. Obviously, this result could be due to intervening factors, such as economic affluence and political democracy. Statistical control for such variables does abate the positive correlation, but does not reveal the expected negative relationship.

Comparison over time does not reveal any harm to happiness either. Though time pressure has risen over the last decade, average happiness did not decline; in Figure 10.4 we can see that happiness has risen somewhat in Western Europe since the 1970s. Not only has happiness risen, life expectancy is also still on the increase. We get older than ever and also live longer without disability (WHR 2002). All this suggests that growing time pressure does not really hurt.

Sudden Crisis

Possibly we are more vulnerable to unexpected trouble, since we cannot accommodate to this so easily and because it undermines the predictability of our existence. Data on this are scarce as yet, but the available findings suggest again that we can live with some turmoil in society.

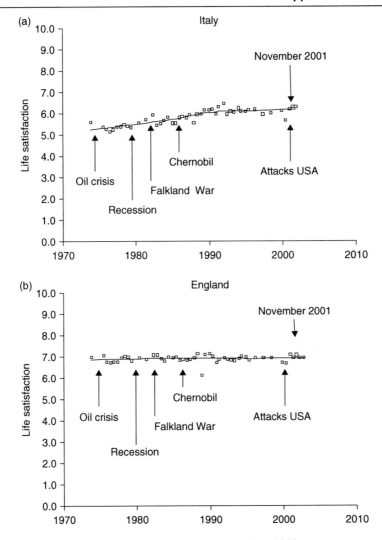

Figure 10.4. Trends in happiness in two nations, 1974–2002

Economic Recession

There is much concern about the effects of economic recession on the individual citizen and these miseries are described vividly in the media. It is easy to imagine that recession hurts: it involves bankruptcies, job insecurity, and cutting down on consumption, all of which shatter aspirations and expectations. Yet again, the impact on overall well-being appears to be small in present-day affluent societies.

Together with the late Aldi Hagenaars, I took stock of the effects of the 1980–82 economic recession on the well-being of Europeans (Veenhoven 1989). We found that the decline of the economy provoked concern about finances and job, but did not affect general well-being. In some countries there was a short-lived dip in life satisfaction, but not in all. We did not find any rise in stress. Reports of depression and anxiety in surveys did not peak and sales of antidepressants and sedatives did not rise. General practitioners registered fewer stress-related complaints in the Netherlands and the number of suicides did not rise.

Possibly recessions have hurt more at other times and in other places, in particular in less affluent societies. Still this suffices to demonstrate that setbacks do not always harm happiness.

September 11

The unexpected attack on the Twin Towers in New York is another case. Several commentators saw this as the end of happiness in the Western world, since the event glaringly showed the vulnerability of modern society to forces such as terrorism and the unpredictability of history. In response, trend analysts searched for evidence of sinking morale, but found very little.

The trend in happiness in the UK and in Italy since the early 1970s is depicted in Figure 10.4. These pictures show no dip in happiness after September 2001. Similar trend graphs for other western nations can be found in Veenhoven (2003) nor did an analysis of Gallup polls in the USA reveal any dip either (Gallup 2002).

Figure 10.4 also depicts some other crises in these countries in the late twentieth century. As one can see, there is no consistent pattern of reaction. In the UK, happiness dipped after the 1986 Chernobyl accident, but not after the 1973 oil crisis, while it also dipped after the successful Falkland War. The case of Italy shows no dips after disturbing events at all, but rather a continuous rise in happiness.

Happiness in Spite of Personal Misfortune

At the individual level there are also examples of things hurting less than expected. I present some illustrative cases below.

Physical Handicaps

The most illustrative case is the happiness of severely handicapped people; in particular paralysed accident victims. Being confined to a hospital bed forever would seem the worst that can happen to a person. These people are indeed desperate in the beginning, yet most of them adjust after a time. Average happiness in this group remains lower than average, but not as low as one would expect. The results of two investigations are summarized in Table 10.1.

Old Age

A related case is old age. This is typically not seen as the best phase of life, because of the inevitable losses involved in growing old. Young adulthood is commonly seen as the happiest time of life (Harris 1997). Yet empirical studies have found surprising little relationship between happiness and age. Figure 10.5 shows average life satisfaction by age group in Western Europe. At first sight there seems to be no difference at all, but on closer inspection one can see a slight U pattern. Life-satisfaction is high among adolescents and drops somewhat in adulthood, in particular in the thirties. There is a rise around retirement age, which extends into old age. People over 80 are most satisfied with life.

Table 10.1. Happiness and handicap

		Average happiness
1.	Accident victims, in rehabilitation	5.9
	Controls	7.6
2.	Disabled for 20 years	5.0
	General population	5.4

Sources: (1) Brickman *et al.* (1978); (2) Schulz and Decker (1985).

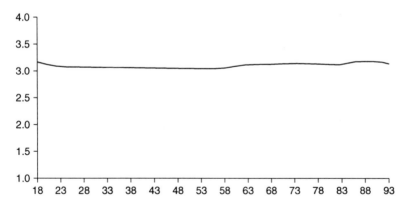

Figure 10.5. Happiness and age in eight EU nations, 1980s
Source: Veenhoven and Okma (1999).

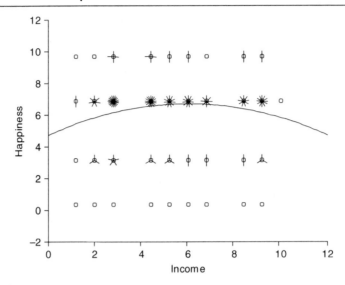

Figure 10.6. Happiness and income in Italy, 1995

Poverty

Surprisingly, for economists in particular, the poorest people are not much less happy than the richest in affluent societies. This phenomenon is illustrated in the flower chart shown in Figure 10.6, which presents the relationship between happiness and income position in Italy in 1995. The icons in the flower chart denote the number of respondents; the more flowery the sign, the more people in that category. As one can see, happiness is highest in the medium income brackets and hardly differs between the highest and the lowest incomes.

The differences are greater when intervening variables, such as age and family situation, are taken into account, but even the most sophisticated studies show modest sized effects at best (Oswald and Blanchflower 2003; Saris 2001). Follow-up studies have shown that changes in income, in particular income loss, affect happiness. Yet the effects appear to be short-lived, even in a poor nation like Russia (Schyns 2000).

Explanations for Happiness in Hardship

These paradoxical findings are dealt with in two ways: one is to denounce them as misapprehension; the other is to seek causal mechanisms.

There is No Paradox

If the paradox is illusory, the illusion can be both in the perception of happiness and in the perception of hardship. There are arguments for both explanations.

Less Happy than Surveys Suggests

Since the beginning of empirical research on happiness, there have been doubts about the high levels reported in general population surveys. Social critics are unwilling to believe that so many people really do enjoy life in this unjust society and attribute the findings to false measurement and false consciousness.

False Measurement

Several methodological objections have been raised against the unexpectedly high levels of happiness found in Western nations. One of the misgivings is that most people have no opinion about their satisfaction with life. When questioned, they may be more aware of how happy they are expected to be, and report this instead. Though this may happen incidentally, it appears not to be the rule. Most people know quite well whether or not they enjoy life. Eight out of ten Americans think about it every week. Responses to questions about happiness tend to be prompt. Non-response to these items tends to be low, both absolutely ($\pm 1\%$) and relatively to other attitudinal questions. "Don't know" responses are also infrequent.

A related assertion is that respondents mix up how satisfied they actually are, with how satisfied other people might think they are, given their life situation. If this were so, people considered as being well off would typically report high life satisfaction, and people regarded as disadvantaged should follow suit with low-satisfaction reports. This pattern does occur, but it is not general. For instance, in the Netherlands a good education is seen as being required for a good life, but the highly educated appear slightly less satisfied with life in comparison to their less educated counterparts.

Another objection concerns the presence of systematic bias in responses. It is assumed that questions on happiness are interpreted correctly, but that the responses are often biased by social desirability. There is indeed evidence of some social desirability bias; it has been shown that the same people report more happiness in a face-to-face interview than on a written questionnaire. The difference is modest however: less than 10 percent of the scale range. If we take this into account, average life satisfaction in Western Europe would be 6.7 instead of 7.4, which is still above the midpoint of this ten-step scale.

False Consciousness

Another qualm is that people are reluctant to acknowledge their unhappiness and therefore make themselves believe that they are happier than they actually feel.

Some clinical studies have tried to demonstrate such ego-defensive distortion by comparing responses to single direct questions with ratings based on in-depth interviews and projective tests. The results are generally not much different.

Another test is to compare self-estimates of general happiness with less obtrusive measures of mood level. One such measure is the Affect Balance Scale, which involves questions about specific affects during the past few weeks. Scores on this scale appear to be highly correlated with self-reports of happiness; at the nation level the correlation is $+0.69$.[5] Another method is to measure average mood using experience sampling. A study among students found a strong correlation ($r = +0.61$) between average mood as assessed by diary records and an overall estimate of happiness (Wessman and Ricks 1966).

The above objections imply that research using these measures to determine happiness will fail to find any meaningful correlations; if self-reports of happiness tap mere "hot air", there will be little correspondence with "hard" indicators of well-being. Yet this is clearly not the case. At the nation level, there are high correlations with economic affluence, political freedom, and institutional quality. The explained variance amounts to some 75 percent (Veenhoven 1997). At the individual level, happiness appears to predict longevity. A long-term follow-up study showed that nuns who were happy in their twenties lived about seven years longer than their sisters who had been unhappy at that time in their life (Danner *et al.* 2001). In this context it is also worth realizing that the high levels of happiness in present-day society go together with an unprecedented length of life.

Life Less Bad Than We Think it is

There may also be a paradox in the perception of hardship. The adversities considered may be less dire than we think they are. This could be due to over-reporting of bad news in the media and the over-emphasizing of hardships by politicians and social scientists.

The case of criminality is a good example. Newspaper coverage of homicides tripled in the USA during the last decade, while the homicide rate actually fell.[6] Likewise, there has been much political hubbub about the "new poverty" since the 1980s, whilst income differences remained largely the same in Western Europe and actually decreased somewhat in France and Italy (Ritakallio 2001).

There seems to be system in this perceptual distortion. Biologically, we are probably quite alert to hazards, since this adds to survival chances. This may be one of the reasons why bad news sells. Next there are also institutional incentives for the overstatement of peril; both politicians and social scientists earn their living by exploiting problems. This can be seen to lead to a pattern of "worried happiness"; because we are alert to potential hazards we cope adequately and therefore enjoy life, but we remain aware.

Paradox has Logic

This brings us to substantive explanations for the observed paradoxes of happiness. One explanation holds that subjective happiness is insensitive to objective harm. Another is that we can live with some troubles and even need the challenge.

Happiness is Not Sensitive

The most common explanation for cases of happiness in hardship is that happiness does not really depend on external conditions, but is rather produced by internal psychological states. One explanation of this kind holds that happiness is "relative", the other is that happiness is a "trait".

Happiness is Relative

A common theory of happiness assumes that we compare life as it is to conceptions of how life should be. Standards of how life should be are seen to draw on perceptions of what is feasible and what other people have. These standards of comparison are thought to adjust. The more money we earn and the more our neighbors have, the higher the amount of money we will deem necessary for a decent living.

At the individual level, this theory predicts that happiness is a short-lived phenomenon. We will be happy when life approaches an ideal, but in coming closer to that ideal we will set higher demands and end up equally unhappy as before. Likewise, social comparison will impede lasting happiness. When we have overtaken the Jones, our reference drifts upward to the Smiths, and we feel unhappy again. This theory has many variations.

At the societal level, the theory implies that average happiness will fluctuate around a neutral level. Because individual citizens oscillate between happiness and unhappiness, the average will be in between. Social comparison is also likely to result in a neutral average; the happiness of the citizens who do better is balanced by the unhappiness of the ones who do worse. Consequently, average happiness should be approximately the same in all countries.

Empirical evidence Some often-cited investigations claim support for this theory. Easterlin (1974) saw the theory proved by his observation that happiness is as high in poor countries as it is in rich countries. Brickman *et al.* (1978) assert that happiness is relative because they found that lottery winners are no happier than paralyzed accident victims are.

I have exposed these sensational claims elsewhere (Veenhoven 1991). Average happiness is *not* the same in all nations and does *not* tend to a neutral level. I have also checked some other implications of the theory that happiness is relative. One such implication is that changes in living conditions, to the good or the bad, do not permanently affect the appreciation of life. However, there is good evidence that we do not adjust to everything; for instance, we do not adjust to the misfortune of having a handicapped child or the loss of a spouse. Another implication I checked is that earlier hardship favors later happiness. However, survivors of the Holocaust were found to be less happy than Israelis of the same age who were not affected by it. All in all, there is no empirical support for the theory that happiness is relative.

Theoretical flaws Proponents of this theory see happiness as a purely cognitive matter and do not acknowledge affective experience. They focus on conscious wants and neglect unconscious needs. In contrast to "wants", "needs" are not relative. Needs are absolute demands for human functioning, which do not adjust to any and all conditions; in fact, they mark the limits of human adaptability. Below I will argue that an evaluation of life draws on need gratification in the first place and is therefore not relative.[7]

Happiness is a Trait

Another explanation of examples of happiness in hardship holds that happiness is a fixed disposition. This theory operates at the individual level and at the societal.

Personal character trait The individual-level variant sees happiness as a psychological trait: a general tendency to like or dislike things. This tendency is seen to stem from inborn temperament or early experience. This trait is believed to shape the perception of life experiences and the overall evaluation of life. On this view, hardship will not affect happiness too much; discontented people will always be disgruntled and the habitually satisfied will always see the sunny side of things.

I have taken stock of the empirical evidence for this theory elsewhere (Veenhoven 1994, 1995; Ehrhardt *et al.* 2000). I inspected whether happiness is (1) temporally stable, (2) cross-situationally consistent, and (3) innerly caused. None of these appeared to be the case. With respect to the first question, it appeared that happiness does not remain the same over time, particularly not over the length of a lifetime. Individuals revise their evaluation of life periodically. Consequently happiness changes quite often, both absolutely and relatively toward others. Second, happiness appears to be sensitive to changes in living conditions. Improvement or deterioration is typically followed by a rise or decline in the appreciation of life. This appears for instance in the sequel of widowhood and divorce. Lastly I established that happiness is not entirely an internal matter. Though evaluations of life are influenced by personal characteristics, these inner alignments modify the impact of environmental effects rather than determining them.

National character trait The societal variant of this theory (folklore theory) assumes that happiness is part of the national character. Some cultures tend to have a gloomy outlook on life, whereas others are optimistic. Russia is often mentioned as an example of the former kind, and the USA as an example of the latter. On this view, Russia-like cultures remain unhappy in spite of prosperity, whilst US-like cultures remain happy in spite of hardship.

I have also examined the empirical evidence for this theory (Veenhoven 1994, 1995, 2001). I first inspected whether the differences in average happiness in nations are indeed unrelated to variation in the objective quality of living conditions in these nations. This appeared not to be the case. As noted earlier, societal qualities such as economic development and political freedom explain about 75 percent of the variation in average happiness. I next inspected whether happiness is lower than expected on the basis of these qualities in nations with a reputation for misanthropy, such as France and Russia. This appeared not to be the case. Lastly, I considered the happiness of migrants. I compared their appreciation of life with average happiness in the country of settlement and with happiness in their country of origin. If happiness reflects the quality of the conditions one lives in, the happiness of migrants in a country must be close to the level of autochthons. If, however, happiness is a matter of socialized outlook, the happiness of migrants must be closer to the level in their motherland. I considered the happiness of first-generation migrants in Australia and West Germany. The trait theory failed this test also.

Happiness Needs No Paradise

The other explanation holds that subjective happiness depends on objective well-being, but that we can cope with some hardship and even flourish when confronted with challenge. This explanation draws on the "liveability" theory of happiness (Veenhoven 1995), which is also referred to as "need theory" (Lucas and Diener 2000). This explanation can be summarized as follows.

Hedonic Affect Serves as an Adaptation Compass

Humans can feel good or bad and this capacity is likely to exist in all mobile organisms. The prime biological function of this capacity is to inform the organism whether it is in a liveable biotope or not. Flora can do without this ability, since it cannot move.

Mood level most informative Humans can also differentiate between momentous emotion and general background mood. The latter is most informative for deciding whether one is in a good place. Other higher animals, such as cats, also seem to be able to react to how well they generally feel in an environment. Unlike cats, humans can reflect on mood and can probably estimate mood level over longer periods.

Primacy of Affect In evolution, this affective orientation capacity preceded the development of cognition. The human ability to reason about one's situation was added to an existing capacity for intuitive affective appraisal and did not replace it. Cognition serves a secondary role in appraisals. This can be seen in the fact that affective reactions precede cognitive evaluation (Zajonc 1980) and that evaluation is not really possible when one's capacity to appraise "how it feels" is impaired.

Happiness Draws on Hedonic Level of Affect

The focus on general mood and primacy of affect also applies to the overall evaluation of life. As noted earlier, happiness judgments draw primarily on affective information, in particular on hedonic level of affect. Happiness is not "calculated" by comparing life as it is to standards of how life should be, but rather "inferred" from how well one feels generally. The basic heuristic is "I feel good, hence I am happy" (Schwartz and Strack 1991).

Happiness Linked to Needs

Hedonic level of affect reflects the gratification of basic needs. "Needs" are requirements for functioning that are so vital that evolution has safeguarded their fulfillment by means of hedonic signals. There are different need-affect circuits in the human body, for instance, separate signal systems for monitoring food intake and companionship. The total of these signals is displayed in hedonic mood. Like the green or red lights on some machines, good and bad moods indicate whether the organism is thriving. Unlike emotions, mood does not signal specific problems.

"Needs" should not be mixed up with "wants". Not everything wanted is really needed and the pursuit of wants can even be detrimental to need gratification. Needs are given by nature and limited in principle. Wants are products of our thinking and as such endless.[8] Needs are absolute, wants are relative (Veenhoven 1991).

Needs for "Functioning" Require some Challenge

A main class of needs is "functioning needs". Maslow (1970) referred to this kind as "growth needs" or "self-actualization needs". All organisms have a drive to use and develop their potentials. The survival value is rather obvious; trained organisms have a better chance than untrained ones. Again there seem to be different reward circuits, linked to different capabilities. In thinking animals, the need for intellectual stimulation is quite pronounced. The pleasure that accompanies fully functioning has been described as "flow" (Csikszentmihalyi 1997).

In children, the needs for functioning are manifested most clearly in play. Children play for fun, not for any external reward. In adults, functioning needs seek competition at work and challenging leisure activities, such as mountain climbing. Wants often serve as a means to keep going and this is one of the reasons why wants have no limit.

These Needs Developed in Harsh Conditions

The human species did not develop in paradise, but in the conditions of a hunter-gatherer life in the African Rift Valley. Life was hard in that

There is no paradox

- Less happy than surveys suggest
    - False measurement   *false*
    - False consciousness   *false*
- Life less bad than we think it is   *true*

Paradox has logic

- Happiness not sensitive to any hardship
    - happiness is relative   *false*
    - happiness is a trait   *false*
- Happiness needs no paradise   *probable*

Figure 10.7. Explanations for paradoxical findings

situation and not very secure. Hence it is likely that evolution gave rise to an ability to face such adversities. Though reason tells us that it might be better to avoid trouble, we nevertheless thrive when putting these abilities in to practice.

In several earlier publications I have argued that need theory is the best explanation for the observed pattern of happiness (Veenhoven 1991, 1994, 1995, 2000). This theory also provides a plausible explanation for the cases of happiness in hardship presented in this chapter.

In Sum

The various explanations for the paradox of happiness in hardship reviewed in this chapter are summarized in Figure 10.7. It also recapitulates my view of their reality value, which reduces to the conclusion that there is no paradox. The illusion of a paradox is based on over-estimation of hardship and in false theories of happiness.

Conclusion

Though happiness calls for liveable conditions, we can deal with hardship and even thrive when challenged to cope with it. Paradise is not a prerequisite for happiness.

Notes

1. International Society for Quality of Life Studies: www.cob.vt.edu/market/isqols. In addition to this social science association, there is a health-science-oriented association, named International Society for Quality of Life Research: www. isoqol.org
2. *Journal of Happiness Studies*: http://springerlink.metapress.com
3. World Database of Happiness: www.worlddatabaseofhappiness.eur.ul
4. An overview of acceptable measures of happiness can be found in the World Database of Happiness, Item bank.
5. This correlation appears in an analysis of 40 nations in the 1990s, using the dataset "states of nations" (www.eur.nl/fsw/research/happiness/statesofnations).
6. Between 1990 and 1996 the homocide rate dropped from 9.8 to 7.3 in the USA (UN-DY 1993/1998, table 21).
7. The theory applies better to some domain satisfactions. For instance, income satisfaction appears to be largely a matter of comparison, and standards of reference on this matter have been shown to drift (van Praag 1993). There are also indications of comparison processes in satisfaction with health and satisfaction with job.
8. In economics it is commonly stated that "needs are endless". This assertion is based on observed buying behavior and in fact concerns "wants" rather than "needs".

References

Alesina, A., DiTella, R., and MacCulloch, R. J. (2001), *Inequality and Happiness: Are Europeans and Americans Different?* Working Paper 8198, Cambridge, Mass.: National Bureau of Economic Research.

Andrews, F. M., and Withey, S. (1976), *Social Indicators of Well-Being: American Perceptions of Life-Quality*, New York: Plenum Press.

Bradburn, N. M. (1969), *The Structure of Psychological Well-Being*, Chicago: Aldine Publishing.

Brickman, P., Coates, D., and Janoff-Bulman, R. (1978), "Lottery Winners and Accident Victims. Is Happiness Relative?", *Journal of Personality and Social Psychology*, 36: 917–27.

Campbell, A. (1981), *The Sense of Well-Being in America*, New York: McGraw Hill.

Cantril, H. (1965), *The Pattern of Human Concern*, New Brunswick, NJ: Rutgers University Press.

Csikszentmihalyi, M. (1997), *Finding Flow: The Psychology of Engagement with Everyday Life*, New York: Basic Books.

Danner, D. D., Friessen, W. V., and Snowdon, D. A. (2001), "Positive Emotions in Early Life and Longevity: Findings from the Nun Study", *Journal of Personality and Social Psychology*, 80: 804–13.

Easterlin, R. A. (1974), "Does Economic Growth Improve the Human Lot? Some Empirical Evidence", in P. A. David and W. R. Melvin (eds.), *Nations and Households in economic growth*, New York: Academic Press, 89–125.

Ehrhardt, J. J., Saris, W. E., and Veenhoven, R. (2000), "Life-Satisfaction over Time: Analysis of Change in Ranks in a National Population", *Journal of Happiness Studies*, 1: 177–205.

Frank, R. H. (1999), *Luxury Fever: Why Money Fails to Satisfy in an Era of Excess.* New York: The Free Press.

Frey, B. S., and Stutzer, A. (2002), "What can Economists Learn from Happiness Research?", *Journal of Economic Literature*, 40: 402–35.

Gallup (2002), "American's Mood: Has September 11th Made a Difference?", www.gallup.com/poll/releases/pr011217.asp

Garhammer, M. (2002), "Pace of Life and Enjoyment of Life", *Journal of Happiness Studies*, 3: 217–56.

Gurin, G., Veroff, J., and Feld, S. (1960), *Americans View their Mental Health: A Nation Wide Interview Survey*, New York: Basic Books.

Harris, L. (1997), *The Myth and Reality of Aging in America*, Washington: National Council on the Aging.

Inglehart, R. (1990), *Culture Shift in Advanced Industrial Society*. Princeton: Princeton University Press.

Jahoda, M. (1958), *Current Concepts of Positive Mental*, New York: Basic Books.

Lucas, R. E., and Diener, E. (2000), "Explaining Differences in Societal Levels of Happiness: Relative Standards, Need Fulfillment, Culture and Evaluation Theory", *Journal of Happiness Studies*, 1: 41–78.

Maslow, A. H. (1970), *Motivation and Personality*, New York: Harper & Row.

Neugarten, B. L., Havighurst, R. J., and Tobin, S. S. (1961), "The Measurement of Life Satisfaction", *Journal of Gerontology*, 16: 134–43.

Oswald, A. J. (1997), "Happiness and Economic Performance", *The Economic Journal*, 1815–31.

—— and Blanchflower, D. (2004), "Well-Being over Time in Britain and the USA", *Journal of Public Economics*, 88: 1359–86.

Poot, G. (2005), "Happiness in the Garden of Epicure", paper under review.

Ritakallio, V.-M. (2001), *Trends of Poverty and Income Inequality in Cross National Comparison*, Luxembourg Income Study Working Paper 272, Differdange, Luxembourg: INSTEAD.

Saris, W. E. (2001), "The Relationship between Income and Satisfaction: The Effect of Measurement Error and Suppressor Variables", *Social Indicators Research*, 53: 117–36.

Schalkxs, R. (2005), "Arthur's Advice", paper under review.

Schimmack, U., and Diener, E. (eds.) (2003), "Experience Sampling Methodology in Happiness Research", *Journal of Happiness Studies*, special issue, 4–1.

Schorr, J. (1991), *The Overworked American*, New York: Basic Books.

Schulz, R., and Decker, S. (1985), "Long-Term Adjustment to Physical Disability", *Journal of Personality and Social Psychology*, 48: 1162–72.

Schwarz, N., and Strack, N. (1991), "*Evaluating One's Life: A Judgment Model of Subjective Well-Being*", in F. Strack, M. Argyle, and N. Schwarz (eds.), *Subjective Well-Being: An Inter-Disciplinary Perspective*, Oxford: Pergamon Press, 27–48.

Schyns, P. (2000), "The Relationship between Income, Changes in Income and Life-Satisfaction in West Germany and the Russian Federation. Relative, Absolute or a Combination of Both?" in E. Diener, and D. R. Rathz (eds.), *Advances in Quality of Life Theory and Research*, Dordrecht: Kluwer, 83–110.

Skinner, B. F. (1948), *Walden Two*, New York: Macmillan.

(UN-DY), *United Nations Demographic Yearbook*, New York: United Nations.

van Praag, B. M. (1993), "*The Relativity of Welfare*", in M. Nussbaum and A. Sen (eds.), *The Quality of Life*, Oxford: Clarendon Press. 362–85.

Veenhoven, R. (1984), *Conditions of Happiness*, Dordrecht: Kluwer Academic.

—— (ed.) (1989), *Did the Crisis Really Hurt? Effects of the 1980–82 Economic Recession on Satisfaction, Mental Health and Mortality*, Rotterdam: Universitaire Pers.

—— (1991), "Is Happiness Relative?", *Social Indicators Research*, 24: 1–34.

—— (1994), "Is Happiness a Trait? Tests of the Theory that a Better Society Does Not Make People any Happier", *Social Indicators Research*, 32: 101–60.

—— (1995), "The Cross-National Pattern of Happiness", *Social Indicators Research*, 43: 33–86.

—— (1996), "Happy Life-Expectancy. A New Comprehensive Measure of Quality-of-Life in Nations", *Social Indicators Research*, 69: 1–57.

—— (1997), "Progrés dans la compréhension du bonheur" (Progress in the Understanding of Happiness), *Revue Québécoise de psychologie*, 18: 29–74.

—— (1998), "Vergelijken van geluk in landen" (Comparing Happiness across Nations), *Sociale Wetenschappen*, 42: 58–84.

—— (2000), "The Four Qualities of Life: Ordering Concepts and Measures of the Good Life", *Journal of Happiness Studies*, 1: 1–39.

—— (2001), "Are the Russians as Unhappy as They Say They Are? Comparability of Self-reports across Nations", *Journal of Happiness Studies*, 2: 111–36

—— (2003), "*Average Happiness in Nations: Trend 1946–2001*". World Database of Happiness, Distributional Findings in Nations, Trend Report 2002/1, www.worlddatabaseofhappiness.eur.ul

—— and Okma, P. (1999), "Is langer leven nog wel leuk? Levensvoldoening van hoogbejaarden in 8 EU landen", *Sociale wetenschappen*, 42: 38–62.

Ware, Jr., J. E. (1996), "The SF-36 Health Survey", in B. Spilker (ed.), *Quality of Life and Pharmaco-economics in Clinical Trials*, Philadelphia: Leppincott-Raven Publishers, 337–45.

WDH (2003), "World Database of Happiness: Continuous Register of Research on Subjective Appreciation of Life", Erasmus University Rotterdam, The Netherlands, www.eur.nl/fsw/research/happiness

Wessman, A. E., and Ricks, D. F. (1966), *Mood and Personality*, New York: Holt, Rhinehart & Winston.

World Health Report (WHR) (2003), Geneva: World Health Organization.

Zajonc, R. B. (1980), "Feeling and Thinking: Preference Needs no Inference", *American Psychologist*, 35: 151–75.

11

The Evolution of Caring

Charlotte D. Phelps

1. Introduction

Forces observed in motion in the latter half of the twentieth century in the United States have gathered momentum. This chapter focuses on the contribution of interactions between economic change and psychological factors to changes in Americans' reports of overall happiness. I will show evidence that is consistent with an evolutionary explanation of the paradoxes of happiness in economics. My thesis is that caring[1] behavior and love have survived the competition for scarce resources because caring parents nurture caring offspring. The argument hinges on the interdependence between the development of a secure attachment and exploratory behavior. My hypothesis builds on Hazan and Shaver's (1990, 1994) model of attachment processes. Their model builds on Bowlby's (1969, 1973, 1980, 1988) attachment theory.

Attachment theory examines the causes and consequences of human parent–infant interactions. Trained in the psychoanalytic tradition, Bowlby (1969, 1973, 1980) was troubled by its focus on fantasy and by inconsistencies between psychoanalytic theory and his own observations of children's behavior. He searched the ethological literature for answers to his questions and found similarities between human and animal behavior that placed human development in an evolutionary continuum. An excerpt from Hazan and Shaver (1994) describes attachment theory:

As a result of selection pressures, infants evolve behaviors that function to maintain proximity to a protector/caregiver. Adult care giving is regulated by a complementary behavior system. Babies smile, and parents find the smiles rewarding. Babies cry, and parents are motivated to soothe them. Parents move away, and babies follow visually or physically. These two systems conspire to create the kind of relationship that fosters the infant's survival. ... In evolutionary terms, it has been adaptive for human young to feel safe enough to engage in play and exploration only as long as a familiar protector is available to respond if needed. (pp. 2–3)

Hazan and Shaver hypothesized that attachment behaviors are gradually redirected from parents to peers. They constructed a model of attachment processes that distinguishes four developmental phases: infancy, early childhood, late childhood/early adolescence, and adulthood. They argued that adult work is functionally similar to Bowlby's concept of exploration:

To learn about and become competent at interacting with the physical and social environment, one must explore. But exploration can be tiring and even dangerous, so it is desirable to have a protector nearby, a haven of safety to which one can retreat. ... The exploration system can function optimally only when the attachment system is relatively quiescent ... In other words, attachment needs are primary; they must be met before exploration can proceed normally. (Hazan and Shaver 1990)

To test their model, they gathered data from two surveys: a love and work questionnaire in the Sunday magazine supplement of one of Colorado's largest circulation newspapers and one that was distributed by mail. The newspaper survey included a question about overall happiness. Respondents were asked to evaluate which is more important "my relationship" or "my work". Those who were securely attached reported significantly higher levels of overall happiness than those who were anxiously attached or avoidant. Those who were securely attached also rated love relationships more important than work. There were no significant differences between the types of attachment in ratings of happiness or unhappiness with income.

My research model is similar to theirs in that it uses psychoanalytic theory to investigate social interaction and frames the investigation in developmental processes.[2] I used ratings of the affective quality of the voices of survey respondents' mothers to categorize the subjects by attachment type. I tested the hypothesis that securely attached adults have higher levels of work satisfaction than insecurely attached adults. I also tested hypotheses about marriage and parenting satisfaction. I argue that having children and enjoying parenting are symptomatic of valuing love more than valuing work, so securely attached adults should report higher levels of both parenting and work satisfaction than insecurely attached adults.

268

The model I constructed to test these hypotheses is a life-cycle model of personality and well-being. It assumes that events such as marriage and births of children are endogenous. It explains why people "tend to display repeating patterns of events... promotions, unemployment, marriage, birth of children" (Headey and Wearing 1989).[3]

It incorporates Erikson's (1950/1963) theory of personality development. Erikson distinguished eight stages of man. Infant sexuality—oral, anal, and genital are typically grouped together. Latency, puberty, and adolescence comprise the middle stage. Young adulthood, adulthood, and maturity comprise the last stage.

I tested the hypotheses with data from the *Patterns of Childrearing* archive. The data are especially well suited to testing hypotheses about personality development because they include observations from the first and third broad stages of development. They also include TAT fantasy-based measures that enable a test of Freud's hypothesis that unconscious motives influence behavior. The first TAT observation was from young adulthood (age 31) and the second observation from adulthood (age 41).[4]

TAT is an abbreviation for a Thematic Apperception Test, a method of personality assessment based on imaginative stories composed in response to picture cues.[5] Concepts from attachment theory are easily mapped onto the TAT motives. The affiliation motive measures the need for love, and the achievement motive measures the adult need to explore. The stories of the *Patterns* subjects reveal gender differences in the long-run effects of childhood interactions with both parents.

There were six picture cues in the tests that the *Patterns* subjects took. The stories indicated how they perceived different social situations. The network of theme-coded images in the picture stories enabled the developmental process to be traced from infancy to adulthood. Stories about the picture of a couple sitting on a bench and the picture of an engineer sitting at his desk aroused thoughts about the decision to commit and intimacy (Sternberg's (1988) concept of companionate love).[6] The picture of a couple in a nightclub differentiated between romantic love, infatuated love, and non-love (Sternberg, ibid.). The picture of a ship's captain and the picture of two women scientists in a laboratory aroused thoughts that were sensitive to vestiges of parent–child power relationships. The picture of a man and woman performing on trapezes aroused thoughts about risks associated with exploratory behavior.

The life-cycle model incorporates goal processes and socialization processes. Although there is broad agreement that five traits explain behavior, Diener and Lucas (1999) noted disagreement on the processes that relate behaviors to wellbeing. They distinguished five different models of processes: temperament, congruence, cognition, goals, and socialization.

TAT motives distinguish between goal processes. The goal of the achievement motive is the satisfaction from competing with standards of excellence. The goal of the affiliation motive is satisfaction from being warmly received or loved. The goal of the power motive is satisfaction from having impact.

Differences in the affective tones of the mothers' voices contribute to tracking socialization processes across situations. The tones show consistencies across situations that are characteristic of personality traits.[7] The different tones are clues to differences in the environments in which the subjects bonded with their parents.

I will present the evidence and develop the argument in eight sections. In Section 2, I will describe how attachment types have been measured in child development research and summarize those experimental results. In Section 3, I will give an overview of the *Patterns of Childrearing* data. Three nested samples are used in the chapter. Descriptive statistics, a test for sample selection bias, and the method used to analyze the mothers' voices are set out in Appendix 11.1. In Section 4, I will state hypotheses about attachment processes and present tests of the hypotheses. The first tests are framed in terms of insecure attachments. A second set of tests is framed in terms of secure attachments. In Section 5, I will present profiles of the personality development of two subjects in the core sample. The first profile illustrates ambivalent attachment processes. The second illustrates avoidant processes. In Section 6, I will present evidence of the robustness of inferences from the *Patterns* data with data from the 1957 and 1976 nationwide surveys of American mental health (Gurin *et al.* 1975; Veroff *et al.* 1982). In Section 7, I will suggest social policies that I believe would improve the well-being of Americans. In Section 8, I will briefly describe the model and summarize the results.

2. Measures of Attachment Types from Child Development Research

Ainsworth *et al.* (1978) designed the experiment that is used to measure attachment types. It is called "The Strange Situation". They related observations of caregiver–infant interactions in their child-development laboratory to home observations of interactions between caregivers and infants. They classified their observations in three categories: secure, avoidant, and anxious/ambivalent. Other investigators have replicated the experiment. Campos *et al.* (1983) reported that distributions in American samples average: 60 percent secure, 25 percent avoidant, and 15 percent ambivalent.

The following paragraphs, based on Hazan and Shaver (1994), describe typical behaviors in the three major patterns:

Secure In the laboratory, a typical securely attached infant was distressed when the mother left the room, was comforted by her return, and engaged in active exploration with toys as long as she was present. During home observations made before the laboratory visits, caregivers were judged to be consistently available and responsive.

Anxious/Ambivalent In the laboratory, these infants appeared both anxious and angry and were preoccupied with their caregivers to such a degree that it precluded exploration. In the home, caregivers typically exhibited inconsistent responsiveness to the infant's signals, being sometimes unavailable or unresponsive and at other times intrusive.

Anxious/Avoidant In the laboratory, these infants appeared not to be distressed by separations, avoided contact with their caregivers, and kept their attention directed toward the toys (although with less apparent interest and enthusiasm than the securely attached infants). In the home, caregivers consistently rebuffed or deflected their infants' bid for comfort, especially for close bodily contact.

3. An Overview of the Patterns Data

The subjects were born in 1946–7 and reared in suburban Boston. When they were aged 5, Sears *et al.* (1957) interviewed their mothers about childrearing practices and recorded the interviews. McClelland (1977–8) and McClelland and Franz (1987–8) measured their motives with Thematic Apperception Tests in follow-ups at ages 31 and 41.[8]

The data link three generations: grandparents, parents, and children. The mothers that the Sears researchers interviewed are the grandparents. Some of the subjects had never married by age 41; some had no children. The average family size was two children. One subject had her sixth child between ages 31 and 41. At age 41, the parents rated their satisfaction from parenting on a scale from 0 to 100. The lowest reported value in the sample was 40 and the highest 100.

The data comprise three nested samples. The largest has 43 subjects, all of whom took the TAT at ages 31 and 41.

The middle-sized sample has 20 subjects. The measures of voice affect are for subjects in this sample. Independent judges rated "thin slices" from the recordings with respect to 11 adjectives. These measures are the data for testing the hypotheses that attachment is based on emotion socialization. They are relevant to the nature versus nurture debate. I think that some attributes of voice quality are inherited and that some are learned in early childhood.

The adjective ratings were based on "thin slices" taken from the recorded answers that mothers gave to three interview questions. The letter (a) in the statistical tables denotes that the measure was derived from an analysis of the answer to a question about mother–infant warmth. The question was especially suitable for a test of the economic hypothesis (Barro and Becker 1989) that altruistic parents invest more in their children than selfish parents. The question asked the mother whether she had time to spend with the baby besides the time that was necessary for feeding, changing, and regular care and what she did in that time: whether she cuddled, sang to the baby, and that sort of thing. The letters (bc) in the tables indicate that the measure is an average of thin slices from answers to questions about interaction between the mother and child and between the father and child.

The core sample (the smallest sample in the nest) consists of ten subjects who took both TATs and for whom there are voice data. That sample enables us to show that motives mediate the effect of the adjective ratings on the subjects' behaviors and satisfactions. It also enables us to show that changes in motivation are consistent with adult personality development.

4. Hypotheses, Tests, and Results

First I will give the logic that links attachment theory to motivation theory to adult love and work behavior; the logic of what may seem a leap from infancy to adulthood. The logic resides in four steps of a behavioral sequence: (1) Warmth in mother's aural cues contributes to her child's secure attachment, and anxiety in aural cues contributes to an insecure attachment. (2) In young adulthood (age 31), memories of mother's (and father's) voice in infancy and early childhood influence perceptions of current social interactions in the subject's life. Positive affect from early childhood affiliation experiences is an antecedent of the perception of affiliation behaviors and affiliation possibilities in adult social interactions. Negative affect is an antecedent of the absence of the perception of affiliation. Positive affect from early childhood exploratory experiences is an antecedent of the perception of achievement behavior and achievement possibilities in the family and in the workplace. Negative affect is an antecedent of the absence of perception of achievement. (3) Perceptions are antecedents of instrumental actions. (4) If an instrumental action results in goal attainment (affiliation and/or achievement), the subject experiences positive affect. If an instrumental action fails, the subject experiences negative affect.

Here are two examples from infancy to illustrate how a secure attachment is formed. The first example illustrates the development of the affiliation motive and a secure attachment. It draws on an illustration that both McClelland (1985: 137) and Hazan and Shaver used. The examples use terms in the same context as the preceding paragraph. McClelland used the terms to describe a behavioral sequence. A motive develops with countless repetitions of similar behavioral sequences.

Example 1: A mother coos to her baby. (Cooing is an aural cue.) In response, the baby looks at mother. (Looking is an instrumental action.) Then mother cuddles and kisses her baby. (Cuddling and kissing are rewards.) The consummatory response consists of the baby feeling pleasure (positive affect) from being cuddled and kissed.

The second example illustrates the development of the achievement motive through exploratory behavior. It is adapted from an account of an experiment on the development of language in a text on child development (Newcombe 1996: 216). Learning to talk is an example of an exploratory behavior and that evolves into goal-seeking behavior, the goal being satisfaction from mastery. In the experiment, a mother nurses her baby while a loudspeaker emits a particular syllable, such as ba. (At 1 month infants can discriminate among phonemes—sounds like ba, bu, or da). The infant's rate of sucking begins to slow because she is becoming bored by the sound ba.

Example 2: The syllable emitted from the loudspeaker is changed to da (aural cue). The baby sucks faster (Instrumental Action.) Boredom is relieved and the rate of intake of milk increases. (Variety and food are rewards.) The consummatory response is the positive affect the baby feels from experiencing variety and from satisfying the hunger motive.

McClelland listed the consummatory experience of mild variety as a reward that contributes to the development of the achievement motive.

Next it is necessary to give more information about my choice of TAT measures for the regressions. Previous research based on TAT motives showed that affiliation behavior is situation specific, but that achievement behavior is generalized across situations (Terhune 1969). Therefore I used picture-specific measures for the affiliation and intimacy motives, and I summed the scores for the achievement motive across all six pictures in each TAT. Although picture-specific measures were used in both nation-wide surveys of mental health (Gurin *et al.* 1975: Veroff *et al.* 1982), other researchers usually do not use them.[9]

The picture I chose to measure affiliation and intimacy thoughts is especially apt for capturing thoughts about choices that require allocating time between the family and market work. It portrays a man working at his desk. A photograph of his family is on the desk. McClelland and Franz (1992) referred to the man as "an engineer" in their description of the picture.

Table 11.1 shows the results of regressions of the affiliation and intimacy motives on adjective ratings of the mothers' voices. Table 11.2 shows the result of a regression of the achievement motive on the adjective ratings. Table 11.3 shows the results of regressions of work satisfaction on Anxious (bc), the achievement motive, and the affiliation motive. The regressions are controlled for socio-economic status in the family of origin, gender, and ethnicity.

Here are the results.

Hypothesis 1 There are gender, ethnic, and socio-economic differences in the strength of affiliation and intimacy motivation.

The results in Table 11.1 are consistent with the hypothesis. All the control variables are significant (p-value < 0.01): subjects reared in a white-collar family wrote stories with less affiliation and intimacy imagery about the engineer than subjects reared in a blue-collar family; women wrote stories with more affiliation and intimacy imagery than men; subjects reared in a Jewish family wrote stories with more affiliation and intimacy imagery than subjects of other ethnic origin.

Hypothesis 2 Fear of rejection is an antecedent of the affiliation and intimacy motives.

One of the unresolved questions in the history of research on affiliation motivation concerns fear of rejection. McClelland (1985: 356) observed: "Throughout the history of the n Affiliation score, investigators have suspected that it represents primarily a fear of rejection...".[10] My conjecture is that depressed mothers were often unresponsive in responding to their children's demands for attention.

Table 11.1. TAT picture of an engineer: affiliation and intimacy scores in stories subjects wrote at age 31, regressed on adjective ratings of their mothers' voices at age 5

	(1) Affiliation	(2) Intimacy	(3) Intimacy
Constant	−16.613**	−0.327	−8.799*
	(−6.027)	(−0.330)	(−2.489)
Sesfo	−6.291**	−1.745**	
	(−9.418)	(10.382)	
Gender	4.813**	1.481**	
	(6.726)	(9.082)	
Anxious (bc)			2.562*
			(2.692)
Depressed (bc)	4.531**	−0.674**	
	(6.830)	(−4.358)	
Emotional (a)		0.769*	
		(4.901)	
Jewish	11.166**	2.337**	
	(10.372)	(9.470)	
Adjusted R-squared	0.957	0.989	0.410
F-ratio	39.953**	131.651**	7.249*
N	8	8	10

Notes: t-statistics in parentheses; *p*-value significant at the 5% level; **p-value significant at the 1% level. N = 10 in the core sample. There are missing values for reported ethnicity. Coded values for socio-economic status family of origin are white collar = 1, otherwise zero; for gender females = 1, otherwise zero. The ethnicity variable differentiates between Irish, Italian, and Jewish. Irish and Italian are classified in the "all other" category in this table. Four subjects were reared in blue-collar families. Three are men. Two are Jewish, three are Irish, and one is Italian ethnicity.

Table 11.2 Sum of achievement scores in stories subjects wrote at age 31 about six pictures, regressed on adjective ratings of their mothers' voices at age 5

Constant	49.456**
	(6.131)
Gender	−1.712
	(−1.796)
Anxious (bc)	−3.817
	(−2.423)
Dominant (a)	−7.215*
	(−5.095)
Italian	−6.961*
	(−3.811)
Adjusted R-squared	0.826
F-ratio	9.282*
N	8

Notes: (*t*-statistics in parentheses; *p*-value significant at the 5% level; **p-value significant at the 1% level. N = 10 in the core sample. There is a missing value for the achievement motive at age 31.

Table 11.3 Work satisfaction at age 41, regressed on affiliation scores in stories about the picture of an engineer at age 31 and the sum of achievement scores in six pictures at age 31 and adjective ratings of mothers' voices at age 5

	(1)	(2)	(3)	(4)
Constant	364.647*	354.378*	386.292**	399.123**
	(14.090)	(34.197)	(24.909)	(35.698)
Sesfo	−6.115			
	(−2.042)			
Gender	−30.095*	−28.332*	−35.353**	−35.361*
	(13.168)	(−28.445)	(−19.733)	(−32.614)
Anxious (bc)	−63.220	−64.281*	−69.658**	−73.924*
	(10.720)	(−22.329)	(−18.499)	(−24.275)
Achievement	−16.649*	−14.567**		
	(13.867)	(−41.803)		
Ach* Income			−2.769**	−2.750*
			(−25.096)	(−40.795)
Affiliation		2.852		1.342
		(4.628)		(2.112)
Adjusted R-squared	0.990	0.998	0.993	0.997
F-ratio	120.000	521.300*	241.911*	496.454*
N	6	6	6	6

Notes: t-statistics in parentheses; *p*-value significant at the 5% level; **p*-value significant at the 1% level. $N = 10$ in the core sample. Eight subjects worked; two women were full-time housewives. A man who was employed did not report work satisfaction.

The results in columns (1) and (2) of Table 11.1 are consistent with the hypothesis of fear of rejection. The coefficient of the adjective Depressed (bc) is a significant positive antecedent of affiliation (p-value < 0.01) and a significant negative antecedent of intimacy (p- value < 0.01). I think that children who had a very depressed mother learned to use more instrumental actions to evoke a warm response from their mothers than other children and that they had fewer experiences of intimacy with their mothers than other children. As a result, they had a larger repertory of affiliative instrumental actions in adulthood than those who had a secure attachment. They also had lower levels of aspiration for intimacy than other young adults. They were not aware of what they had missed in infancy and early childhood.

Other interesting findings pertinent to intimacy were: subjects who had a very emotional mother (high Emotional (a)) wrote stories with more intimacy imagery, and subjects who had a very anxious mother (high Anxious (bc)) wrote stories with more intimacy imagery. The latter finding suggests that children who have a very anxious mother listen attentively for cues about her feelings.

Hypothesis 3 Mother-anxiety and mother-intrusiveness deter exploratory behavior and are antecedents of a low achievement motive.

The results in Table 11.2 are consistent with the hypotheses. The coefficient of the measure of mother-anxiety has the expected sign, but is not statistically significant. The coefficient of Dominant (a), the measure of intrusiveness, is significant (p-value < 0.05) and has the expected sign.

Hypothesis 4 (Work satisfaction) Subjects who are insecurely attached—ambivalent or avoidant—have lower levels of work satisfaction than subjects who are securely attached.

The results in Table 11.3 are consistent with the hypothesis. The regression in column (1) omits the affiliation motive from the independent variables in order to focus on the hypothesis that exploratory behavior is an antecedent of the achievement motive, but the model does not explain the results. The model in column (2) is successful. The coefficient of Anxious (bc) is significant and negative ($p = 0.025$), confirming the alternative hypothesis that people who are securely attached experience higher levels of work satisfaction. The coefficient of the affiliation motive is positive, as hypothesized, although it is not statistically significant. The sign is consistent with the hypothesis that aspirations for warmth and affection in the family add to work satisfaction. The finding that women averaged lower levels of work satisfaction than men ($p = 0.022$) is consistent with the hypothesis that they experienced significant negative effect from doing more than half the childcare and more than half the household chores. (See Section 6 for corroborating evidence.) The coefficient of the achievement motive is significant and negative ($p = 0.006$), consistent with the hypothesis that the achievement motive measures aspirations for career success. At age 41, the subjects have unfulfilled career aspirations.

The models in columns (3) and (4) shows the effect of monetary incentives. Each subject's achievement motive is weighted by an index of his or her earnings. The results show that the incentive value of money increases with the strength of a person's achievement motive. This finding is consistent with McClelland's inference that "…money is not an incentive for subjects high in *n* Achievement, [but] they do use it as information on how successful their performance has been" (McClelland 1985: 248). Notice that the control for earnings exacerbates the negative effect of an insecure attachment. The small size of the sample hampers inferences. To preserve degrees of freedom, I excluded the affiliation motive from the model in column (3). The model in column (4) includes affiliation, and the signs of all the variables remain consistent with the hypothesis.

Hypothesis 5 (Parenting satisfaction) Subjects who are securely attached have higher levels of parenting satisfaction than subjects who are insecurely attached.

1. Tests with Data from the Core Sample

Tests of the hypotheses with data from the core sample are limited by the sample size. Nevertheless, the signs and relative magnitudes of the coefficients are consistent with results from the sample of 43. The model in Table 11.4 column (1) provides a negative frame for the test, and the sign of the coefficient of Anxious (bc) is negative, just as it was in the work satisfaction model. The model in column (2) provides a positive frame, and the coefficient of Confident (a) is positive. In both models, the coefficient of the affiliation motive is positive and larger than in the model of work satisfaction. When the achievement motive is added to the positive frame, the model explains the data perfectly. This result is consistent with the hypothesis that parenting is instrumental to the satisfaction of the

Table 11.4 Parenting satisfaction at age 41, regressed on affiliation scores in stories about the picture of an engineer at age 31 and the sum of achievement scores in stories about six pictures at age 31 and adjective ratings of mothers' voices at age 5

	(1)	(2)	(3)
Constant	245.588*	−133.422	−198.259
	(4.391)	(−2.074)	
Sesfo		34.694	44.717
		(2.992)	(1.662)
Gender	−15.266	36.720	41.461
	(−1.605)	(2.864)	(1.541)
Anxious (bc)	−40.870		
	(−2.933)		
Confident (a)		32.935	41.695
		(3.347)	(1.259)
Achievement			2.651
			(.564)
Affiliation	6.627	14.282	19.177
	(3.035)	(3.347)	(2.797)
Adjusted R-squared	0.615	0.671	1.000
F-ratio	4.199	4.062	
N	7	7	6

Notes: t-statistics in parentheses; *p*-value significant at the 10% level; *p-value significant at the 5% level; **p-value significant at the 1% level. N = 10 in the core sample. Three were not parents. In column (3), standardized coefficients are in parentheses.

achievement motive, a result that is also consistent with my earlier analysis of children as a source of wives' happiness (Phelps 1995: 62–3).

2. Tests with Data from the Sample of 43

In Section 3, I drew attention to the fact that Sears' interviewers coded a variable that rated mother–infant warmth on both the quality and the quantity of time the mother reported spending with her infant. If the mother said that she spent time with her infant besides the time that was necessary for regular care, they asked her if she cuddled and sang to the baby. The results of the model in Table 11.5 are consistent with the critical importance of warmth of maternal affection in infancy. The coefficient of mother–infant warmth is positive and significant (p-value < 0.05). In column (2), the affiliation motive controls the negative effect of very depressed mothers.

Notice that the ratings of Confident (a) are based on the answers to the question about cuddling and singing. That the two measures lead to the same inference is evidence of robustness.

Table 11.6 uses an analysis of variance to compare the average level of parenting satisfaction and work satisfaction attained by the subjects who had the benefits of maternal cuddling and singing. They rated parenting

Table 11.5 Parenting satisfaction at age 41, regressed on affiliation scores in stories about the picture of an engineer at age 31 and Sears ratings of mother–infant warmth (MIW) at age 5 (Ever-married subjects)

	(1)	(2)
Constant	75.201**	50.582**
	(11.303)	(3.742)
Sesfo	8.188	11.021
	(1.460)	(1.952)
Gender	2.152	3.368
	(0.361)	(0.567)
Affiliation Motive	3.889	4.551*
	(2.013)	(2.392)
MIW		3.377*
		(2.026)
Adjusted R-squared	0.105	0.196
F-ratio	2.171	2.762*
N	31	31

Notes: t-statistics in parentheses;* p-values significant at the 5% level; ** p-value significant at the 1% level. These data are from the largest of the *Patterns* nested samples. Thirty-one of the 43 reported parenting satisfaction.

279

Table 11.6 Mean differences in the level of parenting and work satisfaction at age 41 in stories about the picture of the engineer at age 31: presence versus absence of affiliation imagery: (results of analysis of variance)

	Presence of affiliation	Absence of affiliation	F
Parental satisfaction			
	93.546	77.778	7.947**
	5.298	25.509	
N	22	9	31
Work satisfaction			
	80.846	64.500	4.945*
	14.690	29.576	
N	26	10	36

Notes: Standard deviations in parentheses,* p-value significant at the 5% level; ** p-value significant at the 1% level. These data are from the largest of the *Patterns* nested samples. Thirty-one of the 43 reported parenting satisfaction. Thirty-six of the 43 subjects reported work satisfaction.

satisfaction 93, 15 points higher than work satisfaction. Insecure attachments constrained the satisfaction of the other subjects significantly in both domains: parenting (p-value < 0.01) and work (p-value < 0.05).

5. Profiles of the Pursuit of Happiness

In the introduction, I asserted that the model could explain why people tend to display repeating patterns of events in their lives. In this section, I present corroboratory evidence. I use the adjective ratings of voice affect to explain consistency in subjects' behavior, TAT motives to predict domain-specific outcomes, and changes in TAT scores to illustrate the adaptation of aspirations to events in the lives of two of the subjects.[11]

The three regressions equations in Table 11.7 are my analytical tools. In order to explain how to use the tools, I take a sequential approach to explaining outcomes. For the first subject, I begin by explaining choices in the domain of work, and then I explain the choices in the domain of the family. I hope the method I have adopted to explain my model will facilitate discussion of the cases. I believe that discussions of differences in inferences will advance our understanding of the origins of economic outcomes and psychological well-being. In the best of all possible worlds, readers will test the model with different data.

The first profile is of a man who wrote a story about the engineer with an affiliation score of 3. The second profile is of a woman who wrote a story

Table 11.7 Perspectives on developmental paths of adjustment between ages 31 and 41: increase in subjects' TAT scores from age 31 to age 41 regressed on adjective ratings of their mothers' voices at age 5 (score at age 41-score at age 31)

A. Increase in affiliation scores in stories about the picture of an engineer

Model	Increase in affiliation
	Coefficient, t-ratio
Constant	−3.215 (−0.358)
Active (a)	5.046 (3.522)*
Depressed (a)	−6.168 (−3.451)*
Irish	1.767 (1.508)
Adjusted R-squared	0.771
F-ratio	8.842, $p = 0.031$
N	8

B. Increase in intimacy scores in stories about the picture of an engineer

Model	Increase in intimacy
	Coefficient, t-ratio
Constant	−0.375 (0.180)
Anxious (a)	−5.236 (−8.844)**
Emotional (a)	4.978 (9.237)**
Adjusted R-squared	0.917
F-ratio	50.959, $p = 0.000$
N	9

C. Increase in Achievement scores in stories about six pictures

Model	Increase in achievement
	Coefficient, t-ratio
Constant	−7.550 (−0.553)
Anxious (bc)	−7.910 (−2.511)*
Dominant (a)	8.686 (3.569)**
Adjusted R-squared	0.627
F-ratio	7.730, $p = 0.022$
N	9

Model	Increase in achievement
	Coefficient, t-ratio
Constant	−7.615 (−5.035)**
Sesfo	5.923 (4.230)**
Gender	5.821 (3.944)**
Adjusted R-squared	0.771
F-ratio	14.447, $p = 0.005$
N	9

Note: t-statistics in parentheses, *p-value significant at the 5% level; **p-value significant at the 1% level. N = 10 in the core sample.

about the engineer with an affiliation score of zero. Both had a mother whose voice was rated above the mean of the core sample on the adjective Anxious (bc), a symptom of insecure attachment.[12]

1. *A Profile of Anxious/Ambivalent Attachment Processes*

Hazan and Shaver predicted attributes of an anxious/ambivalent adult's love and work relationship. The predictions included: preference for working with others rather than alone, "inability to finish work projects, difficulty meeting deadlines, and poorer work performance". The work history of this subject is consistent with their predictions. His earnings were below what they should have been for his level of education; below the level predicted by a human capital model.[13] He was employed as a "minor professional" and held a greater number of different jobs than the other people in the core sample. He was unemployed once.

Do the data offer an explanation for his career path? I believe they do. The judges in the thin-slice experiment rated his mother's voice above average on the adjectives Anxious (bc), Dominant (a), and Emotional (a) and below average on Warm (bc). The above average rating on Dominant (a) is consistent with intrusiveness; the below average rating on Warmth (bc) is consistent with a caregiver being sometimes unavailable or unresponsive.

He grew up in a family with a high level of mother–father disagreement. The Sears interviewer rating on mother–father disagreement when he was 5 was the highest in the core sample. So was the rating on father coolness. I conjecture that the high rating on the Emotional (a) dimension of his mother's voice resonated with her voice when she argued with her husband. Being socialized in an argumentative family environment may have contributed to this subject's having a "short fuse" when superiors at work made demands.

Easterlin's (1987) explanation of how the baby boomer generation attained their material aspirations provides a more positive frame for analyzing his choices and outcomes. At age 41 he had a family income that was 60 percent higher than his parents.[14] Data in his file show that he took the instrumental actions of Easterlin's successful baby boomers. He graduated from college and completed two years of postgraduate education, deferred marriage until age 35, and deferred having a child until age 40. His wife also had two years of postgraduate education and worked. He reported that her earnings were about half as high as his. At age 41, he rated satisfaction with work, marriage, and parenting equally at 95.

I think that the TAT stories and regression equations explain his high level of life satisfaction. At age 31, the affiliation score in his story about the engineer was 3, high relative to the means of the core sample and the sample of 43. The engineer in his story was daydreaming about his family's vacation in Maine and the vacation house he designed and built. At age 41, the profiled subject's affiliation score was 5. "He would much rather be there with his family than at work." The regression in Table 11.1 suggests that a major source of his high aspirations for establishing and maintaining a positive affective relationship in the family was socialization in a Jewish family.

The regression in Table 11.7A shows that the change in affiliation scores in stories about the engineer depends on countervailing effects of the adjectives Active (a) and Depressed (a). The coefficient of Active (a) is significant and positive ($p=0.024$), and the coefficient of Depressed (a) is significant and negative ($p=0.026$). This subject's affiliation score at age 41 was 5, 2 points higher than it was at age 31. His increase in affiliation can be traced to the rating of his mother's voice on Active (a). She had the highest rating in the core sample.

At age 31 his intimacy score for the story about the engineer was 2. Recall that Jewish ethnicity accounts for higher intimacy scores as well as higher affiliation scores. The regression in Table 11.7B shows that the change in intimacy scores in stories about the engineer depends on countervailing effects of the adjectives Emotional (a) and Anxious (a). The coefficient of Emotional (a) is significant and positive ($p=0.000$), and the coefficient of Anxious (a) is significant and negative ($p=0.000$). There was no change in his intimacy score.

The regression in Table 11.7C shows that the change in the sum of achievement scores across the six pictures depends on countervailing effects of the adjectives Dominant (a) and Anxious (bc). The coefficient of Dominant (a) is significant and positive ($p=0.012$), and the coefficient of Anxious (bc) is significant and negative (bc) ($p=0.046$). A second regression estimated with the data shows that that subjects reared in a white-collar family increased their achievement scores more than subjects reared in blue-collar families ($p=0.005$) and that females increased their aspirations for achievement scores more than males ($p=0.008$).

The gender difference may be a result of the fact that the women had probably completed family formation by age 41 and so looked forward to increasing their commitment to the world of work. This interpretation is consistent with Stewart and Chester's (1982) analysis of gender differences in achievement, affiliation, and power motives:

Overall, the research conducted using the sex-role relevant experimental arousal paradigm has tended to proceed on the assumption that the female sex role constrains achievement fantasy, but that the male sex role does not. To the extent that we have data relevant to this assumption, it appears that the opposite may be true. Men may be relatively constricted in the range of situations that elicits achievement motivation, while women may respond to cues for standards of excellence in many domains. (pp. 183–4)

At age 31, the profiled subject had one of the lowest achievement scores in the core sample. The regression in Table 11.2 explains this result by his mother's dominant and intrusive behavior. The coefficient of Dominant (a) in regression in Table 11.7C suggests that he was able to overcome the negative effect of intrusiveness through life experience. However, he did not capture the standard reward of a white-collar childhood. His achievement score decreased. He lowered his aspirations for career advancement, an indication he learned from his employment experience.

He did accomplish a primary goal of young adulthood, the goal of establishing a family. He married and had a child. At the time of the second TAT, his affiliation score shows he was increasing his commitment to maintaining warmth and affection in his family.

Sternberg's triangular theory of love provides another perspective and adds to an understanding of his development. I think that the TAT picture of the couple on the bench is a cue for the decision to commit. His scores for that picture were: affiliation = 3, intimacy = zero, and power = 2. The story was about a married man with a child who was having an affair; it dramatized a conflict between a commitment (affiliation imagery) to his wife and infatuation (power imagery) with his lover. My inference is that he resolved the conflict in favor of his wife because ten years later the scores for his story about that picture were: affiliation = 5, intimacy = 3, power = 0.

2. A Profile of Anxious/Avoidant Attachment Processes

The judges in the thin-slice experiment rated the voice of this subject's mother above the average of the core sample on both indicators of depression: Depressed (a) and Depressed (bc). Earlier in the chapter (Hypothesis 3), I argued that fear of rejection could be related to parental depression. The facts in this case strengthen my argument.

The TAT stories she wrote at age 31 give evidence that she was dissatisfied with her marriage. Two of the stories were about married couples that "split up" and divorced. She rated her marriage satisfaction 75.

Her story about the engineer suggests that it was her husband's lack of career success that most disturbed her. The data file shows that he had completed one year of graduate education and worked in a medium-sized business at age 41. She wrote: "He's worked for the same company for... 10 years; with a few promotions within the department, but still the same old office and the same drafting board work.... Tomorrow morning... he's going to look for a new job—a new company." She had aspirations for improving their standard of living.

A reason why she didn't divorce him might have been that he was instrumental in fulfilling her material aspirations. At age 41, she reported that their family income was 50 percent higher than her parents' income. By a money measure of happiness, she was a successful baby boomer.

The dissatisfaction she expressed in her TAT story provides an explanation for the timing of the births of her children. She married at age 23, after graduating from college, but waited to have children until she was 37. Then she had two, closely spaced. The oldest was 4 at the time of the second follow-up.

Perhaps the strongest evidence I found to support an avoidant classification is that, for the first two months after she was born, her grandmother was her primary caregiver. I made a note of this fact in 1998 when I listened to the unfiltered recording of the Sears' interviewer with her mother. It was not until I read Hazan and Shaver's article that I realized its significance. It is possible that the grandmother deflected the infant's bids for comfort, especially for close bodily contact.

I also made a note of the fact that her mother told the interviewer "she was a very placid-easy child". This comment suggests an explanation based on the child's temperament. However, I think that avoidant attachment is the stronger hypothesis.

The equations in Table 11.7 provide strong support for an avoidant diagnosis. The rating for her mother's voice was above the mean for Depressed (a), a negative influence on increasing affiliation. The rating for Emotional (a) was below the mean, a negative influence on increasing intimacy. The affiliation and intimacy scores for the story she wrote about the engineer at age 41 were zero, the same as ten years earlier.

Her TAT scores suggest an unconscious conflict. The scores in her stories about the couple on a bench, the cue for the decision to commit, were the same in 1977 and 1987: affiliation $= 1$, intimacy $= 2$.

She had companionate feelings for her husband, but they didn't sustain feelings of warmth and affection for the children. She assigned parenting satisfaction 70 points, the lowest rating in the core sample. I think she was still struggling with her infant fears of being abandoned.

For her, giving birth was primarily instrumental to achievement. She expanded the range of exploratory behavior. Her achievement score increased between 1977 and 1987. She anxiously increased her aspirations to explore.

6. Evidence on the Evolution of Caring from the 1957 and 1976 Nationwide Surveys of American Mental Health

Attachment theory provides a new perspective for evaluating the assumptions and predictions of Becker's (1993) model of altruism in the family. Becker related the domains of love and work by the opportunity cost of time—the wage rate. Because historically men have been the primary wage earners, a focus on the wage rate assigns more importance to the male parent than to the female parent in the evolution of caring. Empirical studies that Becker reported as tests of the evolution of altruism in families consist of regressions of son's income or earnings on father's income or earnings (ibid., chap. 7, table 7S1) and regressions of son's wealth on father's and grandfather's wealth (ibid., table 7S2).

Given that the primary attachment is between the mother and child, tests of the evolution of altruism in families should be based on mother–child data. The 1976 nationwide survey of American mental health collected those data. They enable hypotheses about the relationship between mother-motivation, parenting practices in the family, and parenting satisfaction to be tested and they form a link with the *Patterns* subjects at age 31.

A subset of the nationwide respondents took a six-picture TAT that was scored for achievement, affiliation, intimacy, and power (N = 354 women and 215 men). Five of the pictures shown to women differed from the ones shown to men. The sixth picture in the sequence was the same. It portrayed a man and woman, facing the viewer; the man was smoking a cigar.

Many subjects wrote stories about picture 6 that cast the couple in roles of husband and wife. Imagery in the stories that married women wrote explained differences in marital happiness, fertility, and differences in their evaluation of children as a source of happiness (Phelps 1995).

Twenty-one percent of wives wrote stories about picture 6 with affiliation imagery and no power imagery, 34 percent wrote stories with only power imagery, 8 percent with both affiliation and power, and 37 percent with no affiliation or power. Analysis of these data yielded results consistent with an attachment-theoretic explanation of the evolution of caring:[15]

A logit regression showed that "regardless of personality, children were a significant source of marital happiness to wives who reported that the present or both the present and the past was the happiest time" (Phelps 1995: 62.) Interviewers asked a follow-up question of the present-oriented respondents: "What are some of the things you feel pretty happy about these days?" The responses were categorized by type of satisfaction: that is, achievement, affiliation, power, and other. Wives who wrote affiliation stories were likely to give examples such as "my children's achievement in school, at the job"; "when my child graduated with honors"; "seeing them grow and develop; see them happy" (ibid., p. 62 and table 7, p. 63). These examples are consistent with the hypothesis that mothers who nurture securely attached children encourage exploratory behavior.

The marital regression showed that reports of affiliation satisfactions such as "I love my children" diminished with the number of children (ibid.), a finding of significance for advocates of family planning. A regression that explained wives' overall happiness placed marital happiness in a wider context and showed that there was diminishing marginal utility from children, regardless of ranking in the income distribution (Phelps 2001, table 3, p. 298). The probability of being very happy or somewhat happy increased with family income as expected, but controlling for family income, there was diminishing marginal utility from children, regardless of motivation.

The theme of diminishing marginal utility from children was repeated with a variation in the overall happiness regression for husbands (Phelps 2001, table 1, p. 296). Only husbands who wrote affiliation stories about picture 6 showed diminishing marginal utility. They were among those who were most like to report that they shared childcare time equally with their wives (Phelps 1991, table 7, p. 107).

In 1976, two-thirds of husbands with working wives and children under 12 years of age reported that their wife allocated more time to childcare than they did. There was a significant personality effect on the sharing of childcare time. Husbands who wrote power stories were significantly less likely to report sharing time equally (ibid.).

There were differences between husbands and wives in the perception of sharing childcare time. In the families where the wife allocated more time to childcare than the husband, all of the wives who wrote affiliation stories reported that their husband helped often or sometimes. None of them reported that their husband hardly ever helped (Phelps 2001, table 2B, p. 297).

These findings help to explain why Kahneman *et al.* (2004) found a low mean net affect for childcare in their survey of employed women in Texas. Childcare ranked sixteenth, marginally below housework in the list of 19 activities rated (p. 432). My conjecture is that the women experienced more negative affect (frustrated, depressed, angry, hassled, criticized) than positive affect (enjoyment, warm, happy), because most of them did not have help with childcare. The time away from work that they had available for intimate relations, socializing, dinner, relaxing, etc. was not sufficient to be "somewhat happy".

There was also good news in the analysis of the 1976 survey. It was that love has contributed positively and significantly to individual happiness in America, regardless of an individual's rank in the income distribution. America is known as "the land of opportunity". We have developed a socio-economic system that enables children nurtured by caring parents to climb the socio-economic ladder. A downside of the American dream is that the path to fame and fortune is lined with time and institutional constraints that make it difficult to succeed economically and maintain warmth and affection at home. The measures of objective happiness from Texas dramatize the impediments to the evolution of caring.

Changes in TAT scores between the 1957 and 1976 nationwide surveys shed light on how caring survived in spite of those constraints. In both years, the TAT given to men included the picture of the engineer. In the 1976 nationwide survey, two-thirds of the husbands who wrote affiliation stories about the picture of the man and woman (the picture that was common to both the male and female TAT) also wrote affiliation stories about the picture of the engineer. The positive correlation between the imagery in the two pictures indicates a strong motive for love. Both pictures inform inferences about the evolution of caring.

Between 1957 and 1976, there were massive changes in the structure of labor markets in the United States: the shift from manufacturing to a service economy, the increased labor force participation of women, and the entrance of the baby boomer generation. The data show that caring husbands in professional and managerial occupations increased their achievement motivation, adapting to changes in a way that is consistent with a prediction of attachment theory.

Changes in their network of workplace motivation included a significant increase in the percentage of achievement themes in stories about the engineer and in stories about a picture of men in a boardroom (Phelps 1991, table 3, p. 98). Their wives cooperated in adapting to the changes by increasing participation in the labor force. They were likely to be employed in occupations of the same status as their husbands.

Other changes in the network of family motivation suggest that caring husbands in professional and managerial occupations tended to stop daydreaming about a family vacation when they were in the office and to focus more on their work. A significant number of them allocated more time to their children when they were at home. This inference is based on the fact that the percentage of affiliation imagery in stories about the picture of a father and children seated at a breakfast table doubled between the two survey years, while the percentage of affiliation stories about the picture of the engineer decreased somewhat.

In blue-collar occupations, changes in the network of family motivation also show that men increased achievement motivation, but not as much as men in management (ibid., table 3, p. 98). The evidence shows that blue-collar men daydreamed more about affiliation with the family when they were at work, but didn't increase aspirations for affiliation with their children at breakfast. That many blue-collar work schedules do not permit having breakfast with children before they go to school may account for those TAT results. Other evidence from my 1991 article (tables 6 through 10) suggests that in blue-collar families, the wife often became the effective altruist.[16]

7. Some Suggestions for Social Policy

The results in the last section are powerful evidence of the need to implement systems of social support for the delivery of childcare in the United States. Thirty years have passed since the 1976 survey, and the facilities for delivering quality childcare are still not in place. I think that those who are interested in improving the well-being of Americans should do everything possible to mobilize political support to develop institutional structures that nurture healthy parent–child attachments.

Suggestions about how to do it have been made. For example, Bergmann (1999) made a careful study of the French system of childcare and gave valuable suggestions for how some of the French institutions could be tailored to Americans. Folbre (2001) outlined a proposal for a family-friendly workplace that would include parental leave for men as well as women. Both the Bergmann and the Folbre books include recommendations about how to finance the changes.

In his contribution to this volume, Easterlin identified different domains of happiness—health, marriage, and material aspirations—and observed that research on happiness suggests people allocate too much time to positional goods and insufficient time to family life and health, domains where attaining goals have lasting effect. In looking to the future, he wrote: "It is time to recognize that serious policy attention is needs to be directed to education as a vehicle for shaping more informed preferences."

The 21st Century Community Learning Centers is a program that illustrates an avenue for educating preferences. It began as a pilot in 1998. The program includes parents in the education of their preschoolers. The TAT is an instrument that social workers and psychologists could use to evaluate social interactions in the family. TAT-informed counseling might increase the possibilities of fostering the development of secure attachments.[17]

8. Conclusion

I have shown that a life-cycle model of personality integrated in a microeconomic model of the family predicts life satisfactions in the *Patterns of Childrearing* data. TAT stories the subjects wrote at age 31, together with childhood antecedents, predicted their economic outcomes and their life satisfactions at age 41. I also presented inferences from the 1957 and 1976 nationwide surveys of American mental health that corroborated inferences from the longitudinal analysis.

The *Patterns* results are consistent with the hypothesis that people increase their material aspirations when they attain their achievement goals, and lower their material aspirations when they are unsuccessful. In young adulthood, a major achievement goal is to establish a career. In adulthood, people consolidate their achievements.

In young adulthood, the primary affiliation goal is to establish a family. In adulthood, those who have been successful direct their aspirations toward maintaining the environments they have created. Those environments are safe havens from which they explore the world of work and more distant social interactions. I illustrated two kinds of safe haven in the profiles of subjects in pursuit of happiness.

To conclude, I have related my model and empirical findings to the literature on personality development across the life course. Caspi and Roberts (2001) surveyed that literature for evidence on the relation between change and continuity in personality. Like Hazan and Shaver, they focused on processes. I think that progress on explaining the paradoxes of happiness in economics has been handicapped by a lack of attention to processes and by the widespread acceptance of the set-point model of personality.

Caspi and Robert's overarching conclusion was: " ... that with time and age people become more adept at interacting with their environment such that personality consistency increases with age and is more common than change in midlife and old age" (p. 49).

They called attention to three issues that I addressed: (1) that historical context impacts the complexity of continuity and change; (2) that people often filter experiences and evoke responses in unconscious ways; and (3) that "people often attempt to select environments deemed suitable to their personality and by doing so reinforce continuity" (p. 62).

The TAT evidence I assembled on unconscious ways that people filter experience is particularly valuable. Seventy years have passed since Morgan and Murray (1935) designed the first Thematic Apperception Test to investigate the unconscious. The results reported in this chapter build on the contributions of two generations of scholars who explored different picture cues, developed methods of testing and scoring the TAT, and developed applications of the TAT to the study of lives.

Some researchers are skeptical of personality research based on Thematic Apperception Tests (e.g. Lilienfeld *et al.* 2000), because there are gaps in the literature demonstrating its scientific validity. Evidence in this chapter fills several gaps that Lilienfeld *et al.* identified. I am especially pleased to report the regressions results in Table 11.7, because I think they are evidence of the previously elusive test–retest reliability of the TAT.

Other evidence that has been elusive pertains to the hypothesis of fear of rejection. My inferences, based on the adjectives Depressed and Active, suggest that the children of mothers who suffered from depression have a fear of rejection. I would like to see future research that explores the relation between fear of rejection and Caspi and Roberts's hypothesis that people select environments that reinforce continuity in personality. I think that fear of rejection explains why many of the *Patterns* subjects decided to remain near their parents in Boston.

The TAT is a valuable instrument for studying evolution, because it captures thoughts about biosocial transitions that people are reluctant to reveal in answer to direct questions (Coombs, 1947).[18]

Appendix 11.1

1. Description of the First Survey in the *Patterns of Childrearing* data (N = 379)

In 1951, Sears *et al.* (1957), researchers at the Harvard Graduate School of Education, interviewed mothers of 379 kindergarten-aged children, one child per mother, selected from two towns in the Boston area. In selecting the initial sample, they attempted to obtain a balance for gender, ordinal position of the child in the family, and socio-economic status. They asked the mothers questions about parenting practices for their 5-year-old child and coded the interviews for a variety of maternal and paternal behaviors. Details of the sample selection, the interview procedure, coding, and reliabilities may be found in Sears *et al.* (1957).

2. Description of the Largest Sample in this chapter (N = 43)

One hundred and thirty subjects[19] responded to the McClelland follow-up in 1977–8; 94 responded to the McClelland and Franz follow-up in 1987–8. The sub-sample studied at age 41 was drawn from the address list of the earlier wave. "Checks on the sampling indicated that the (1987–8) sample was representative of the original sample: t tests of only 1 out of 27 demographic and 5 out of 135 parenting variables were significant at $p < 0.05$. There were proportionately fewer men in the 41-year-old follow-up than in the original study, $t(377) = 2.177$; $p < 0.05$" (Franz *et al.* 1991: 588).

All the respondents to the McClelland and Franz follow-up took a six picture TAT. Forty-six of them also took a six picture TAT in the McClelland follow-up. The picture-specific scores were archived for the second TAT, but not for the first. So it was necessary to rescore the first set of protocols. Some stories for three subjects were lost from the archive, reducing the sample size to 43 (27 women and 16 men). Psychologists at Hay/McBer rescored the 1977–8 stories. They maintain coding reliabilities between 85 and 95 percent.

I selected five parenting variables to predict the subjects' motives and economic outcomes at age 41 from the set of variables used by Franz *et al.* (1991) to predict social accomplishment and from the set of variables used by McClelland and Franz (1992) to predict work accomplishment. The five are: warmth of bond between infant and mother (MIW, Variable 067); severity of toilet training (SEV, Variable 092); mother–child coolness (MCC, Variable 132); father–child coolness (FCC, Variable 170); and amount of mother–father disagreement (MFD, Variable 179).[20]

Table 11.A1. Descriptive statistics of variables used in this chapter

	N	Min	Max	Mean	Std. Dev.
Sesfo[1]	43	0	1	0.651	0.482
Gender[2]	43	0	1	0.628	0.489
Nkids41[3]	36	0	6	1.500	1.159
Parsat at age 41	31	25	100	88.970	15.688
Wrksat at age 41	36	0	100	76.31	20.836
Marsat at age 41	29	10	100	78.97	26.050
Family income at age 41[4]	32	$15,000	$87,500	58.906	25.080
Parents' family income reported at age 5[5]	37	$10,695	$85,560	33.906	21.615
Relative income at age 41[6]	29	0.28	5.84	2.119	1.370
MIW, reported at age 5[7]	42	3	9	6.071	1.598
FCC, reported at age 5[8]	43	1	7	3.162	1.573
Affiliation age 31, engineer	43	0	6	1.907	1.630
Power age 31, engineer	43	0	2	0.093	0.426
Achievement age 31, sum of scores in 6 stories	38	0	10	4.553	2.688

Computed by the author from SPSS files in the *Patterns* archive.
Notes:
[1] Sesfo (Socio-economic status family of origin): this is a dummy variable; 1 denotes reared in a white-collar family; otherwise blue collar.
[2] Gender: this is a dummy variable; 1 denotes male, otherwise female.
[3] Nkids41: (Number of children at age 41) = NKIDS87 + NGONE. If MARST87 was equal to 1 or 6, NKIDS87 was assumed to be the same as VAR521. If MARST87 was equal to 1, 4, 6, or 9, NGONE was assumed to be zero. The variable names in the formula are those used in the machine-readable data file supplied by the Murray Center.
[4] Family income at age 41 (FAMINC87): data include non-salary income and were reported for the following class intervals: $10,000–19,000; $20,000–34,000; $35,000–49,000; $50,000–75,000; $75,000 or more. For closed intervals, I assumed each subject's income to be at the mean. I assumed $87,000 was the value of the upper open interval.
[5] Income of parents in 1952 (Variable 036): data are reported for the following class intervals: less than $2,000; $2,000–2,999; $3,000–3,999; $4,000–4,999; $5,000–7,499; $7,500–9,999; $10,000–$14,999; $15,000 or more. For closed intervals, I assumed each subject's income was at the mean. $20,000 was assumed to be the value of the upper open interval. I multiplied the original data by 4.278 to inflate them to 1987 dollars. Source for inflator: Statistical Abstract of the US 1998, Table 771, Purchasing Power of the Dollar.
[6] Relative income at age 41: family income at age 41 divided by income of parents in 1952.
[7] MIW (mother–infant warmth): 1 = cold...9 = warm and affectionate (VAR067).
[8] FCC (Father–child coolness: 1 = lots of affection always...5 (moderate attachment)...7 (VAR170).

Of these variables, only MIW is necessary to explain affiliation in the TAT stories about the picture of the engineer.

Bias in the Sample of 43

Although Franz et al. noted some differences between the characteristics of the respondents to their follow-up and those in the original survey, they did not emphasize the differences in their discussion of their results. I think the differences are important evidence of a bias in favor of over-sampling subjects who have high affiliation motives and low power motives.

They stated (p. 588): "In this sub sample, no sex differences occurred in 8 out of 10 dimensions; on the other 2 dimensions, mothers were significantly more likely to restrict expressions of sexuality such as nudity or masturbation, $t (74) = 2.13$, $p < 0.05$, and to inhibit assertion in girls, $t (74) = 2.95$, $p < 0.005$". McClelland and Pilon (1983) found that those parenting practices were childhood antecedents of the power motive.

Like McClelland and Franz (1992), I predicted the work accomplishment of the subjects at age 41. In addition, I tested for a bias that they did not consider. I computed the log-odds of a person who responded in 1987–8 also responding in 1977. I found a significantly larger proportion of male respondents in 1977 had a cold father. A larger proportion of female respondents had a cold mother. This bias is important for the study of attachment processes because previous research has shown that coldness is an antecedent of avoidant attachments (Hazan and Shaver 1994).

The results of the logit test are shown in Table 11.A2. The model chi-squared for the male subjects was 8.851 (39), $p < 0.05$. In the sample of 16 men, subjects were more likely to have had a COLDPA than in the overlapping sample of 39 men ($p < 0.05$). Of the 16, those who did not complete college had a COLDPA.

Table 11.A2. Determinants of the log-odds of being in the sample of 43 subjects (Logit regression results: wald–statistics in parentheses)

	Male subjects	Female subjects
Constant	0.995	0.777
	(0.511)	(0.488)
SESFO	−1.155	0.120
	(1.961)	(0.037)
FCC		−0.373
		(3.497)
COLDMA	−0.981	1.664
	(0.648)	(3.334)
COLDPA	1.863*	
	(5.305)	
−2 Log-Likelihood	43.118	65.166*
Model chi-squared	8.851*	6.845
Predictive accuracy	69.23%	61.54%
N	39	52

Notes: * p-value significant at the 5% level.
The sample was split into two groups. Group 1 consists of subjects who completed the Thematic Apperception Tests in 1977 and 1987 and provided data on all economic outcomes. Group 2 consists of subjects who completed the 1987 TAT. The logit gives the log-odds of a subject being in the first group. VAR067 was coded from cold to warm values on a nine-point scale. If VAR067 was less than 5, COLDMA = 1; otherwise COLDMA = 0. VAR170 was coded from warm to cold on a nine-point scale. If VAR170 was greater than 3, COLDPA = 1. If VAR170 was less than or equal to 3, COLDPA = 0. The minimum value of MIW was 3 and the maximum value 9 in the male and female sample of Group 1. The minimum value of FCC was 3 and the maximum value was 9 for the males of Group 1; the minimum value of FCW was 1 and the maximum value was 5 for the females of Group 1. I thank Damaraju Raghavarao for advice on the design of this test.

The data in the *Patterns* archive comprise a natural experiment (Duncan *et al.* 1999) rich in hypotheses to be tested with other data from other larger samples. The COLDPA bias in the male sample suggests the need for future research relating attachment processes to higher educational attainment. Why didn't the sons complete college? Was it because their fathers discouraged their efforts or did not encourage them? Did some of the fathers deny their sons financial support?

3. Description of the Sample of Adjective Ratings of Mother-Voices (N = 20)

The Sears interviews were recorded on Grays Audographs, blue discs. Many of the discs were destroyed after the interviews were transcribed and coded. I used the Murray Center grant for transcribing 32 discs to audiotapes and for the thin slice analysis of the tapes. The quality of the original recordings was sufficient for thin slice analysis in 20 of the 32 cases.

All 20 subjects took the TAT at age 41; 10 of them also took the TAT at age 31. Frequency distributions for the 20 subjects with respect to gender (8 men, 12 women) and socio-economic status family of origin (15 white-collar, 5 blue-collar) enable comparisons with two of the 1951 sampling criteria.

Method of the Thin-Slice Analysis[21]

Procedure Ten-second clips were taken from the answers of the mothers to three sets of questions. Set (a) consisted of questions coded under MIW; set (b) consisted of questions coded under MCC; set (c) consisted of questions coded under FCC. When their answers were uninterrupted by the interviewer, the clips were taken from the middle of the answer; otherwise, when the researcher interrupted the mother, the clips were taken from the beginning or end of the answer. If it was impossible to find a ten-second uninterrupted clip, no clips were taken for that mother. The best quality clip was chosen from each category, leaving three clips per mother. These clips were content-filtered using a Macintosh-based computer program (Sound Edit). The content-filtering procedure removed the high frequencies and rendered the clips undecipherable.

The content-filtered clips were recorded on to an audiotape in a random order. Another condition with the same clips in reverse order was compiled in order to control for order effects.

Raters Thirty-two independent raters (16 males and 16 females, mostly undergraduates) were recruited through sign-up flyers posted on the Harvard University campus. They judged the content-filtered audio clips on the following dimensions: active, anxious, cheerful, confident, depressed, dominant, emotional, enthusiastic, happy, optimistic, and warm. Liggon *et al.* (1992) used a similar set of adjectives to describe mothers' voices and explain their children's behavior.

Table 11.A3. Inter-rater reliabilities of 31 judges

Adjective	Reliability
Active	0.890205205
Anxious	0.932918021
Cheerful	0.940825835
Confident	0.930895320
Depressed	0.938381150
Dominant	0.934306699
Emotional	0.933876428
Enthusiastic	0.938951741
Happy	0.940561339
Optimistic	0.938951741
Warm	0.935965028

Subjects were able to rate the clips at their own pace, as they were instructed to pause the tape after each clip, make a rating of the clip, and then listen to the next clip. On average, it took subjects between 45 minutes and one hour to complete the study. When they had finished, subjects were debriefed and paid for their participation at the rate of $8 per hour.

Effective reliability was computed for each dimension (Rosenthal and Rosnow 1991). Judges' ratings were highly reliable (see Table 11.A3). Therefore data were collapsed across judges by taking the average judges' rating for each mother, question, and variable.

Question Effects Since mothers talked about different relationships in the three sets of questions asked, the data were analyzed to explore if the question type had an effect on the rating of the mother. For each dimension, a correlation between the averaged ratings for the three questions was computed. The correlation between the second and third sets turned out to be high and significant for all dimensions except for warmth. In order to decide whether to collapse the data for the second and third sets, the data were collapsed across dimensions and a new correlation between the questions was run. This analysis yielded a high correlation between the second and third sets $r = 0.773$, $p < 0.0001$, so the data were averaged across those sets.

4. Description of the Core Sample (N = 10)

This sample consists of the subjects in the voices sample that took both TAT tests. The subjects in the sample of 43 took the first TAT, but not the second.

Five of the pictures in the first TAT were used in the second. The sequence of pictures shown to the subjects differed in the two tests. Here is a description of the pictures. The numbers denote the sequence investigators used.

TAT at age 31 (1) Engineer sitting at a desk. There is a photograph of the man's family on the desk. (2) Couple sitting on a bench by the river. (3) Two women scientists in a laboratory. (4) A man and woman who are performing on trapezes. (5) Ship's captain talking to another man. (6) A couple in a nightclub. A guitarist is serenading them.

   TAT at age 41 (1) Ship's captain. (2) Engineer. (3) Couple sitting on a bench. (4) Two women scientists. (5) Man and woman performing on trapezes. (6) A man and a woman climbing a hill, leading two horses.

5. TAT stories about the Engineer Sitting at his Desk Written by the Profiles' Subjects at age 31

Male, married, one child: Marsat, Parsat, and Worksat = 95

A draftsman is pausing clearing his work to reflect on the picture of his wife, daughter, and son. He is contemplating a vacation that they are about to take for 2 weeks in Maine. His family is very important to him which coupled with his insecurity is why he keeps a picture of them at his work area. The home in Maine is one he has his designed and built. He would much rather be there with his family than at work. This will be the second summer vacation at the Main house. It will be a good vacation.

Female, married, two children: Marsat = 75; Parsat = 70; Worksat = n.r.

John is sitting at his desk in Waltham, as he has done every morning for the past 10 years; he's worked for the same company for those 10 years, with a few promotions within the department, but still the same old office and the same drafting board work. Gazing at the picture of his family he's thinking that he, and they could stand a change—not out of New England, because they (he & his wife) have been to other area in the U.S. but like N.E. the best. Tomorrow morning, that's when he's going to look for a new job—new company.

Notes

This research was supported by grants from the Henry A. Murray Research Center, Harvard University, the Smith Richardson Foundation, and Temple University. The data are archived in the *Patterns of Childrearing* file in the Murray Center. Robert R. Sears, Eleanor E. Maccoby, and Harry Levin (1952); David C. McClelland (1978); and David C. McClelland and Carol E. Franz (1988) collected the data. Carol Franz conserved recordings of the Sears' interviews and gave them to the Murray Center. At my request, Nalini Ambady directed a thin slice analysis of tapes transcribed from the original recordings. She sent me an Excel File with the results in autumn 2000. I gratefully acknowledge her expertise and cooperation.

   I especially want to thank Edward Zigler for informative and challenging discussions during early stages of the research in 1998–99 when I was a Visiting Fellow at Yale University in the Bush Center in Child Development and Social Policy. I also want to thank Roslyn Gorin for sustained support in the use of statistical software at Temple University, Luigino Bruni and Pierluigi Porta for organizing the conference on happiness, and referees at Oxford University Press for comments on drafts of this chapter.

1. Although many economists have adopted Becker's use of the word altruism to describe cooperative behavior in the family, I prefer caring, because it is a frame for the positive affect from childrearing.
2. Hazan and Shaver (1990) cited Erikson (1950), Maslow (1954), and Rogers (1961).
3. Headey and Wearing (1987) used the set-point model to explain an Australian panel study and listed this among questions to be answered in future research.
4. I used Singer and Singer's (1990) dating of the stages of personality development to demarcate young adulthood and adulthood.
5. The stories are scored for four themes: achievement (McClelland *et al.* 1953), affiliation (Heyns *et al.* 1958), intimacy (McAdams 1980), and power (Veroff 1958; Winter 1973). Affiliation and intimacy (McAdams 1980) are related measures of the desire for warmth and companionship. Affiliation emphasizes what people *do* to attain, maintain, or restore a close relationship. Intimacy emphasizes *feelings* of communality. The manuals are collected in Smith (1992).
6. Sternberg's (1988) concept of companionate love combines both affiliation and intimacy themes.
7. Winter *et al.* (1998) argued that the primary distinction between personality traits and motives is that traits measure consistencies in behavior across situations, while motives are situation specific.
8. The follow-ups spanned the years in parentheses.
9. See e.g. Winter *et al.* (1998). Another difference in method is that I used the "raw" scores, unadjusted for number of words per story.
10. McClelland and Pilon (1983) searched unsuccessfully for the childhood antecedents of the affiliation and intimacy motives.
11. Samples of their TAT stories are in Appendix 11.1.
12. DeNeve and Cooper's (1998) meta-analysis of 137 personality traits and subjective well-being provides a framework for relating the Big Five personality traits to my profiles of the pursuit of happiness. They identified Affiliation as a component of Agreeableness. The subject with an ambivalent attachment could be classified in the Factor of Agreeableness by the criterion of Affiliation. They identified Anxiety as a component of the Factor of Neuroticism. The subject with an avoidant attachment could be classified as Neurotic. Neuroticism was the strongest predictor of negative affect.
13. I used a human capital model to explain the earnings of the subjects in the sample of 43.
14. I adjusted the measure of relative income for family size by the formula that Easterlin (1987: 175) used to show that the baby boomer generation attained their material aspirations. I assigned the first child an adult equivalent value

of 0.4 and each additional child a value of 0.3. I assigned the first adult a value of 1.0 and each additional adult a value of 0.8.

15. "The wives who were happiest in their marriage were those who wrote stories with power imagery and no affiliation imagery. It is possible that a contributing factor was their mothers' permissiveness in childhood sexual experimentation. It is interesting to observe that they did not use their assertiveness to persuade their husbands to help with childcare" (Phelps 1995, table 6, p. 62).

16. In the Becker model, a family with an effective altruist maximizes family income. Effective is defined as earning more than half of family income. The head effects cooperation in the family through the power of the purse, through transfers of time or money that maximize own utility. S(he) takes the welfare of all family members into consideration.

17. Two teams of scholars evaluated the 21st century program after the first year (Dynarski *et al.* 2003; Mahoney and Zigler 2003). Robblee *et al.* (2004) evaluated the reports of both teams and observed: "Frequent participants were more likely than infrequent participants to report better social skills, to say that they are better at working with others in a group, to have better problem solving skills, and to feel less lonely" (p. 12). They concluded that it would take time to see whether the social skill differences would persist.

18. Coombs (1947) found that the desires "to have sexual relations with", "to atone", "to be consoled", and "to have a child" were among those reported significantly more frequently in a TAT than in an autobiography.

19. The mature children are the subjects.

20. Variable numbers refer to the Murray Center SPSS data file. The variable numbers are given because there is more than one measure for each of the concepts modeled.

21. Nalini Ambady and Heather Gray wrote most of this section. Svetla Gueorguieva ran the subjects and assisted Ambady and Gray in the data analysis.

References

Ainsworth, M. D. S., Blehar, M. C., Waters, E., and Wall, S. (1978), *Patterns of Attachment: A Psychological Study of the Strange Situation*, Hillsdale, NJ: Erlbaum.

Ambady, N., and Rosenthal, R. (1992), "Thin Slices of Expressive Behavior as Predictors of Interpersonal Consequences: A Meta-analysis", *Psychological Bulletin*, 111: 256–74.

Atkinson, J. W. (1957), "Motivational Determinants of Risk-Taking Behavior", *Psychological Review*, 64: 359–72.

Barro, R. J., and Becker, G. S. (1989), "Fertility Choice in a Model of Economic Growth", *Econometrica*, 572: 481–501.

Becker, G. S. (1993), *A Treatise on the Family*, 1st paperback edn., Cambridge Mass.: Harvard University Press; 1st published 1988.

Bergmann, B. R. (1986), *The Economic Emergence of Women*, New York: Basic Books.
—— (1999), *Saving Our Children from Poverty: What the United States Can Learn from France*, New York: Russell Sage.
Bowlby, J. (1969, 1973, 1980), *Attachment and Loss: Vols. 1, 2, and 3*, New York: Basic Books. 2nd edn. Revised and enlarged 1963, New York: W. W. Norton.
Bowlby, J. (1988), *A Secure Base: Parent-Child Attachment and Healthy Human Development*, New York: Basic Books.
Campos, J. J., Barrett, K., Lamb, M. E., Goldsmith, H. H., and Stenberg, C. (1983), *Socio-emotional Development*, in M. M. H and J. J. Campose (eds.) *Handbook of Child Psychology: vol. 2. Infancy and Psychobiology*, New York: Wiley, 783–916.
Caspi, A., and Roberts, B. W. (2001), "Personality Development across the Life Course: The Argument for Change and Continuity", *Psychological Inquiry*, 122: 49–66.
Coombs, A. W. (1947), "A Comparative Study of Motivations as Revealed in Theenatic Apperception Stories and Autobiography", *Journal of Clinical Psychology*, 3: 65–75.
Costa, Jr., P. T., and McCrae, R. R. (1985), *The NEO Personality Inventory Manual*, Odessa, Fla.: Psychological Assessment Resources.
DeNeve, K. M., and Cooper, H. (1998), "The Happy Personality: A Meta-Analysis of 137 Personality Traits and Subjective Well-being", *Psychological Bulletin*, 1242: 197–229.
Diener, E., and Lucas, R. E. (1999), "Personality and Subjective Well-Being", in D. Kahneman, E. Diener, and N. Schwarz (eds.), *Well-Being: The Foundations of Hedonic Psychology*, New York: Russell Sage Foundation.
Dynarski, Mark *et al.* (2003), "When Schools Stay Open Late: The National Evaluation of the 21st Century Community Learning Centers", Mathematica Policy Research, Inc. and Decisions Information Resources, Inc., prepared for the US Department of Education.
Duncan, G. J., Magnuson, K. A., and Ludwig, J. (1999), "The Endogeneity Problem in Developmental Studies", Working paper, Joint Center for Poverty Research, Northwestern University, Evanston, Ill.
Easterlin, R. A. (1987), *Birth and Fortune: the Impact of Numbers on Personal Welfare*, Chicago and London: The University of Chicago Press; 1st published 1980.
Erikson, E. H. (1950), *Childhood and Society*, 2nd edn. Revised and enlarged 1963, New York: W.W. Norton.
Folbre, Nancy (2001), *The Invisible Heart: Economics and Family Values*, New York: The New Press.
Franz, C. E., McClelland, D. C., and Weinberger, J. (1991), "Childhood Antecedents of Conventional Social Accomplishment in Midlife Adults: A 36 Year Prospective Study", *Journal of Personality and Social Psychology*, 604: 586–95.
Gurin, G., Veroff, J., and Feld, S. (1975), *Americans View their Mental Health, 1957*, SSA Study no. 3503, Ann Arbor: Survey Research Center, Institute for Social Research.

Hazan, C., and Shaver, P. R. (1990), "Love and Work: An Attachment-Theoretical Perspective", *Journal of Personality and Social Psychology*, 592: 270–80.

—— (1994), "Attachment as an Organizational Framework for Research on Close Relationships", *Psychological Inquiry*, 51: 1–22.

Headey, B., and Wearing, A. (1989), "Personality, Life Events, and Subjective Well-Being: Toward a Dynamic Equilibrium Model", *Journal of Personality and Social Psychology*, 574: 731–9.

Heyns, R. W., Veroff, J., and Atkinson, J. W. (1958), "A Scoring Manual for the Affiliation Motive", in J. W. Atkinson (ed.), *Motives in Fantasy, Action and Society*, Princeton: Van Nostrand, 205–18.

Kahneman, D., Krueger, A. B., Schkade, D., Schwarz, N., and Stone, A. (2004), "Toward National Well-Being Accounts", *American Economic Review*, 942: 429–34.

Liggon, C., Weston, J., Ambady, N., Colloton, M., Rosenthal, R., and Reite, M. (1992), "Content-Free Voice Analysis of Mothers Talking about their Failure-to-Thrive Children", *Infant Behavior and Development*, 15: 507–11.

Lilienfeld, S. O., Wood, J. M., and Garb, H. N. (2000), "The Scientific Status of Projective Techniques", *Psychological Science in the Public Interest*, 11: 27–59.

McAdams, D. P. (1980), "A Thematic Coding System for the Intimacy Motive", *Journal of Research in Personality*, 14: 413–32.

McClelland, D. C. (1985), *Human Motivation*, Glenview, Ill.: Scott, Foresman.

—— Atkinson, J. W., Clark, R. A., and E. L. Lowell, (1953), *The Achievement Motive*, New York: Appleton-Century-Crofts.

—— and Franz, C. E. (1992), "Motivational and Other Sources of Work Accomplishments in Mid-Life: A Longitudinal Study", *Journal of Personality*, 604: 679–707.

—— and Pilon, D. A. (1983), "Sources of Adult Motives in Patterns of Parent Behavior in Early Childhood", *Journal of Personality and Social Psychology*, 443: 564–74.

Mahoney, J. L., and Zigler, E. F. (2003), "The National Evaluation of the 21st Century Community Learning Centers: A Critical Analysis of the First-Year Findings", Yale University.

Maslow, A. (1954), *Motivation and Personality*, New York: Harper & Row.

Morgan, C. D., and Murray, H. A. (1935), "A Method for Investigating Fantasies: The Thematic Apperception Test", *Archives of Neurological Psychiatry*, 34: 289–306.

Newcombe, N. (1996), *Child Development: Change over Time*, 8th edn., New York: HarperCollins College Publishers.

Phelps, C. D. (1991), "The Disappearance of Polarized Altruism", *Journal of Economic Behavior and Organization*, 15: 91–113.

—— (1995), "Wives' Motives and Fertility" *Journal of Economic Behavior and Organization*, 27: 49–67.

—— (2001), "A Clue to the Paradox of Happiness", *Journal of Economic Behavior and Organization*, 45: 293–300.

Robblee, S., Berkowitz, S., and Sawhill, I. (2004), "Education Proposal in the 2004 Presidential Campaign: A Preliminary Assessment", Brookings Working Paper, Washington: The Brookings Institution.

Rogers, C. R. (1961), *On Becoming a Person*, Boston: Houghton Mifflin.

Rosenthal, R., and Rosnow, R. L (1991), *Essentials of Behavioral Research: Methods and Data Analysis*, New York: McGraw Hill.

Sears, R. R., Maccoby, E. E., and Levin, H. (1957), *Patterns of Child Rearing*, Evanston, Ill: Row, Peterson.

Singer, D. G., and Singer, J. L. (1990), *The House of Make-Believe: Children's Play and the Developing Imagination*, Cambridge, Mass: Harvard University Press.

Smith, C. P. (ed.) (1992), *Motivation and Personality: Handbook of Thematic Content Analysis*, New York: Cambridge University Press.

Sternberg, R. J. (1988), *The Triangle of Love: Intimacy, Passion, and Commitment*, New York: Basic Books.

Stewart, A. J., and Chester, N. L. (1982), "Sex Differences in Human Social Motives: Achievement, Affiliation, and Power", in *Motivation and Society: A Volume in Honor of David C. McClelland*, San Francisco, Washington, London: Jossey-Bass, 72–218.

Terhune, K. W. (1969), "A Note on Thematic Apperception Scoring of Needs for Achievement, Affiliation, and Power", *Journal of Projective Techniques and Personality Assessment*, 334: 364–70.

Veroff, J. (1958), "A Scoring Manual for Power", in J. W. Atkinson (ed.), *Motives in Action, Fantasy, and Society*, Princeton: Van Nostrand.

——Douvan, E., and Kulka, R. (1982), *Americans View their Mental Health, 1976*, 1st ICPSR edn., ICPSR 7948, Ann Arbor: Inter-University Consortium for Political and Social Research.

Winter, D. G. (1973), *The Power Motive*, New York: the Free Press.

——John, O. P., Stewart, A. J., Klohnen, E. C., and Duncan, L. E. (1998), "Traits and Motives: Toward an Integration of Two Traditions in Personality Research", *Psychological Review*, 1052: 230–50.

12

Happiness and Individualism:
A Very Difficult Union

Stefano Zamagni

Introduction

The thesis I am going to defend here is that what ultimately lies at the bottom of the many forms of reductionism within the economic discourse is not so much the assumption of self-interested behavior on the part of economic agents, nor the predominant use, in theoretical work, of the instrumental rationality paradigm. Rather, the real limiting element is to be found in an excessively restrictive portrait of human nature and human motivation, namely in individualistic anthropology according to which behind economic action there is an individual who has no other determination than that of *homo oeconomicus*. More specifically, the ineptitude of conventional economic theory to adequately address the happiness issue is to be attributed to a philosophical stance for which individuals are isolated in an atomistic theoretical construct. As a result, models are generated where what is analysed is essentially an autistic behavior: the understanding of the mental states of the other is simply not considered at all, nor are sympathy and empathy given a proper role in the explanation of economic decisions in interactive contexts. It is rather difficult to make sense of happiness in economics as long as one sticks to an anthropology that says that human beings are asocial, that their "true" nature is something outside human relationality. Basically, the reason is that whereas utility is the property of the relation between a human being and a good (or service), happiness expresses the property of the relation between a person and (at least) another person. In this sense, while an economic agent can maximize utility in isolation—as the story of Robinson Crusoe reminds us—it takes (at least) two to be happy.

The proposal I advance in this chapter is to substitute the notion of person for that of individual. A person is an individual who is in essential relation with others. As Pareyson wrote: "Human being is a relation; it is not that s/he is in relation, not that s/he has relationships, but s/he is a relation...with the other" (1995: 15). This implies moving from the individualistic perspective to the relational one. It is my contention that by opening itself to the relational approach, economic theory can manage to avoid the risk of sliding back to more or less sweetened holistic positions. That would be an unproductive regression. As argued by Demeulamere (2000), holism is back in fashion today, and for good reasons. But it certainly does not have the right answers to the most serious problems of present-day societies. For this reason, I agree with Elias when he argues against those philosophical set-ups that give "the impression that every human being is by nature fitted for living alone as an isolated individual" (1991: 51). The fact that human beings also live in the realm of symbols leads inevitably to the notion of relationality.

Although the *homo oeconomicus* paradigm appears lacking in terms of the anthropological dimension, it should not be believed that it does not contain anthropological assumptions. Consider, for example, the recent contribution by Jensen and Meckling (2001) whose title is: "The Nature of Man". Having recognized that understanding human behavior is fundamental to understanding how organizations, whatever they are, function, the authors acknowledge that much policy disagreement derives from substantial differences in the way we think about human nature. To cope with this serious problem they suggest: "we want a set of characteristics that captures the essence of human nature" (p. 3). What are these characteristics? Those condensed in the "resourceful, evaluative, maximizing model (REEM)"—a model founded an four postulates: "every individual is an evaluator; each individual's wants are unlimited; each individual is a maximiser; the individual is resourceful" (p. 4). While Jensen and Meckling are to be praised for not shying away from explicit statements concerning human nature, it should be noted that the notion of individual is taken for granted by them and regarded as unproblematic. The authors do not even suspect that "the essence of human nature" might be that of a person and not that of an individual. In so doing, they create an intellectual set-up that allows them to conclude that the explanatory power of REEM dominates that of all the other models of human behavior. And from such a conclusion they obtain the following normative prescription: "The challenge for our society and for *all organizations* in it, is to establish rules of the game and *educational procedures* that tap and direct the creative energy of REEM in ways that increase the effective use of our scarce resources" (p. 17; emphasis added).

The ultimate aim of the chapter is, basically, to stimulate an open debate on the anthropological foundations of economic discourse and more specifically to explore ways of incorporating the relational dimension into economic models of behavior in order to expand their grasp on reality. Emma Rothschild reminds us that from the 1770s to the 1820s, "economic life was intertwined, in these turbulent times, with the life of politics and the life of the mind. Economic thought was interwined with political, philosophical and religious reflection. The life of cold and rational calculation was interwined with the life of sentiment and imagination" (2001: 3). In a sense, the present contribution can be seen as a modest return to that mode of doing economic theory by presenting contemporary interwinings in a time that is no less turbulent than it was then.

In what follows, I first show that the several attempts made by the economic theory of altruism over the last quarter of a century to modify the assumption of self-interested behavior have not produced the desired effect. My reason for this is that altruistic behavior has been embedded within an individualistic set-up. Actually, not much can be gained from the abandonment of the self-interest hypothesis—which is, after all, quite convenient from an analytical point of view—as long as we remain within the individualistic paradigm. I shall also show that the attempt to expand the realm of application of the rational choice model by utilizing the principle of reciprocity, as currently defined, does not mark a decisive step forward, in spite of the undoubtedly important results so far obtained by this line of inquiry. Second, I shall argue that in order to be able to satisfactorily accommodate the happiness category within the economic discourse, what we need is a theoretical approach capable of merging relationality and freedom. Indeed, the consideration of the relational dimension alone risks bringing us back to holistic positions, such as the communitarian position where the individual is visualized as part of a social whole. On the other hand, the freedom dimension alone would maintain the limitations of the *homo oeconomicus*. It is the unity of relationality and freedom which does the job, a unity that modern economic theory has ceased to pursue for a long time.

It is a fact that, by conceiving of the social order as stemming from individuals and their conflicts, modern economics has departed a great deal from Adam Smith's idea of society as a "mirror" for the person.

Without this mirror—says Smith in his *Theory of Moral Sentiments*—the person will never come to know herself. Developing the ideas of Ferguson and Hume, Smith went further in stressing the moral autonomy of the self as central to both virtue and happiness. The self desires not only praise, but praiseworthiness; not only the respect of others, but her own self-respect. This is tantamount to saying that the other is a condition of the self, since the self to appreciate its own value has structural need for "hospitality", that is, of being recognized. I need other human beings to judge that I am worth preserving and, in so doing, to pave the way for happiness.

2. Altruism, sociality, relationality

2.1. *Three approaches to altruistic behavior*

The economic theory of altruism is, undoubtedly, the most articulated attempt to expand the reach of economics in order to explain the pro-social motivations of the agent. It certainly deserves the most careful attention both for the really remarkable number of studies that have been devoted to it over the last few decades, and because it forms a *sui generis* case of heterogenesis of ends: the intention of overcoming the limitations associated with the assumption of self-interested behavior through the introduction of the category of altruism has produced an unintended consequence. Let us see how.

There are three main approaches through which altruism has entered into economic discourse. With aptly chosen terms, Khalil (2001) called them: egocentric, egoistic, and altercentric. The first approach is connected to the classic contribution of Becker (1974), according to which altruistic behavior is fully compatible with the assumption of the max-imization of utility, once we admit the possibility of interdependence of individual utilities; in particular once we admit that the utility of the donor is positively connected to the utility of the donee. As a matter of fact, the idea that individuals derive utility from the welfare of those they feel "near" to goes back to Edgeworth: if the subject i has the situation of j at heart, $U_i = f(x_i, U_j)$, with $\partial U_i / \partial U_j > 0$, or $U_i = U_i(u_i(x_i), u_j(x_j))$, with $\partial U_i / \partial u_j > 0$. By showing that altruists may sacrifice part of their consumption or income for the benefit of others without suffering the slightest diminution of their own utility, Becker allowed neoclassical theory to explore pro-social behaviours.

But at what price has such a result been achieved? Indeed, a higher one than turns out to be convenient. To reduce altruistic behavior to a question of tastes or preferences—which is the only way altruism can enter as an argument of the utility function—means betraying the meaning of the term itself, a term first introduced by Auguste Comte (in 1875) to denote a disinterested motivation to act in the interest of others. According to Becker's conceptualization of altruisms, the donee is visualized in merely instrumental terms. So much so that an individual will behave altruistically only to the extent that *his* marginal utility equals *his* marginal cost. The utility of the donee, from the point of view of the donor, is nothing more than a mere consumer good. In turn, the interdependence of utilities can generate paradoxical results. Let us assume that agent *i* derives little utility from the consumption of the basket of goods available to her, whereas she derives great benefit from the welfare of *j*, measured by the utility function of the latter. It may then happen that *i*, to improve her own welfare, requires *j* to be no longer interested in her. As much as to say that the extreme altruism of *i* postulates (or motivates) the egoism of *j*. So much so that if *j* were also an altruist, then *i* would not derive any benefit from what she decides to do or to give to *j*.

As Gui (2000) clarifies, in the relationship of friendship, joys and misfortunes are shared in ways that are quite different from those prevailing in the case of the interdependence of utilities. Furthermore, it should be noticed that Becker's altruism tends to produce results of inefficiency in all the cases in which the number of those that practice it does not reach a specific critical mass, as Lindbeck and Weibull (1988), and Bernheim and Stark (1988), have demonstrated. And above all the Beckerian approach is not able to explain the problem of free-riding. In fact, the egocentric model of altruism predicts that the potential donor (e.g. of the donation to a non-profit organization) finds herself facing the classical problem of public goods: her gift, while it significantly affects her own costs, only marginally increases the overall income of the donee and his utility. Hence, she will not make the donation. And yet, the empirical evidence shows *ad abundantiam* that the prediction of generalized free-riding behavior does not turn out to be confirmed in reality.

The egoistic approach—in Khalil's terminology—linked to Axelrod's pioneering study and to Andreoni's idea (1990) of the "warm glow", does not fare much better. This approach explains reciprocity as a strategic act to improve the future benefit of the agent in infinitely repeated games. Although not originally intended as an explanation of altruism—but rather to explain cooperative behavior in contexts of social interaction of the prisoner's dilemma type—Axelrod's study has ended up by being utilized to represent that variety of altruism known as "calculating altruism": agents donate to others strategically to construct a useful reputation for themselves, and hence to induce donors to reciprocate the favor or the gift received. However, such an argument is really rather weak. To behave altruistically can serve to create a positive reputation only if others do not realize the underlying egoistic motivation. For an agent to be able to pass himself off as an altruist without being one, it has to be true that genuine altruism exists and that other people fail to distinguish between authentic and opportunistic altruism. After which, true altruism is still unexplained.

In a context of voluntary contribution to a public good, Andreoni shows how it is fully compatible with the assumption of self-interest that there are agents who derive utility directly from pro-social behavior: by acting in this way they would experience a "warm glow", in fact. On reflection, the coherence of the proposition that rational agents would find the meaning of their own altruistic action in the prospect of feeling themselves "at peace with their conscience" is quite suspect. As Bardsley and Sugden (2002) argue, the "warm glow" presupposes the rationality of behavior that one intends to explain with it. Consider the case of the voluntary contribution to a public good. If, as Andreoni's approach requires, the "warm glow" associated with the contribution is a consequence of the fact that the individuals believe that the act of donating is a duty or is good in itself, this means that an a priori belief in this sense must already exist. If this is not the case, we should be asking ourselves why rational agents should feel at peace with their conscience when they do something for which there is no reason at all. This means that it cannot be the "warm glow" that is the foundation for the altruistic action, since it presupposes that the reasons why it is a good thing to contribute voluntarily are already known. The "warm glow" approach is not just incoherent, but tends to produce paradoxical outcomes, according to the usual canons of reasonableness. Let's consider its application to the context of the family, where the public good is here identified with the welfare of the children. It turns out that the parents, because they are concerned with the welfare of their children and voluntarily contribute to it, would be labeled by Andreoni as "impure altruists", whereas the children, who are the receivers, would be called "pure altruists", since they contribute directly to the "public good". This paradoxical terminology betrays the ambiguities of an approach that makes use of the utility maximization apparatus to represent and study altruistic behavior.

Finally, what can be said of the altercentric approach, as it emerges from the work of Etzioni (1986), Frank (1988), Simon (1990), and others? For these scholars, the altruistic action derives, ultimately, from a moral imperative that, as such, turns out to be binding on the agent. Ethical altruism involves the interiorization of moral ideals capable of producing donative behavior in those that adopt them. This is so much the case that the ethical altruist is not interested in others as such. He is only concerned in abiding by a particular ethical principle that operates in the same way as the Kantian categorical imperative. Margolis (1982) suggests a variation on this approach, by dichotomizing the economic subject. The latter would then have not one, but two utility functions: the first would represent his self-interested preferences; the second his altercentric preferences, in the sense specified above. It is not hard to see why such an approach has not produced the hoped-for effects. How can the results stemming from the two utility functions be put together? Lacking a metatheory capable of assigning a definite system of weights to the two utility functions, how can altercentric preferences and self-interested preferences be aggregated?

The question arises, what is wrong with this approach? First, it denies the voluntary, free character of altruistic action. My donative disposition may well be the consequence of a particular ethical code, but if the latter is either imposed on me by some macro entity assumed as a primitive—whether the community Etzioni writes about, or the social class or the group or whatever—or it is not chosen by me, my freedom to decide is, at least partly, taken away, and with it the possibility of giving a rational foundation to pro-social behavior. Such a problem is also evident in the socio-biological version of the "moral gene" put forward by Frank in opposition to the well-known theory of the "selfish gene" due to Wilson, according to which, human action, even in its most altruistic moments, is always entirely functional to the evolutionary requirements of the "selfish gene". Secondly, altercentric altruism is an altruism without "the other". An altruist of this kind "feels" and acts as if the welfare of others were an end in itself, something meritorious independently of the knowledge of the other (Gui 2002).

A concrete way of understanding what consequences a perspective of this kind may lead to is to consider the recent experience of so-called humanitarian interventions. Those who follow closely the way in which certain policies of humanitarian aid are carried out in favor of dis-advantaged sectors of the population know how altruistic actions based on rapid and highly professional interventions, but forgetful or neglectful of the identity of the victims, show a basically anti-human side. In order to be there for everyone, one becomes indifferent toward all. Ignoring the otherness of the people one is claiming to help, the link with them is lost, precisely because of the illusion that one can be there for everyone. In this way, the humanitarian intervention quite often ends up by encouraging that culture of dependence that denies the very chance of progress of a community because it encourages people to put on the mask of victim, in order to be noticed.

To sum up, the ethical altruist is not addressing the person as such, but a generic needy being, with whom no actual relationship is ever established. The risk of slipping into a sort of spiritual autism is therefore the greatest danger behind ethical altruism. To be sure, this is an unfortunate consequence of the adoption of Kant's approach to ethics. As is well–known, this approach posits a duality between happiness on the one hand, and moral obligation on the other. What is more, the pursuit of happiness guided by the principle of economic rationality is seen as an essentially private quest by agents who know what is best for themselves. In such a way, happiness, conceived as a merely private affair, has been taken to overlap with utility. Yet happiness, like identity, is an interpersonal relation. They both come into existence in the course of personal interaction.

2.2. *The anthropology of* homo oeconomicus

The three approaches to altruistic behavior outlined above share a common strategy: to show that in order to explain pro-social behavior of an altruistic kind there is no need to give up the individualistic framework. According to this strategy, all that is required is that economic theory restricts itself to taking into consideration mechanisms (social norms; incentive schemes; moral codes) capable of guiding the agent's behavior toward imitation of *homo ethicus*, without expecting the former to cultivate the same thoughts or the same sentiments as the latter. In other words, nothing would stop the individual of modern utility theory from being able to cultivate a genuine passion for the welfare of others, and nothing would stop *homo oeconomicus* from binding himself to ethical principles that would lead him to interest himself in others. Pareto (1906) had long ago arrived at this conclusion when he wrote: "Those who accuse the scholar of *homo oeconomicus* of forgetting or even of sneering at . . . *homo ethicus* . . . are making a big mistake" (p. 48). Thus, on condition that our conception of self-interest is sufficiently broad, and on condition that the domain of the utility function is expanded properly—as for example Robbins had promised to do: "As far as we are concerned, our economic subjects can be pure egoists, pure altruists, pure ascetics, pure sensualists or else a mixture of all these drives" (1935: 95)—there is no need to free economics from the anthropology of *homo oeconomicus* in order to find a place for altruism.

Wicksteed (1933) was the first to gain a clear understanding of the significance of this conclusion when he stated: "A specific characteristic of any economic relation is not the egoism behind it, but *non-tuism*" (p. 180). With this last expression, the English economist was describing the fact that, in an economic relation, the lack of interest in *A* in the aims pursued by *B*, and vice versa, does not in any way imply that *A* acts exclusively for self-interested reasons. Indeed: "The economic relation does not exclude everyone else except myself from my mind; it includes potentially everyone else except you" (p. 174). And a little further on: "It is only when *tuism* guides my behavior that it ceases to take on a fully economic form. It is therefore nonsense to think of selfishness as the characteristic feature of economic life" (p. 179). Whence the important conclusion: "The idea of excluding benevolent or altruistic motivations from economic studies is ... completely meaningless" (p. 180). As can be seen, it is *non-tuism*, that is, the rejection of relationality, that is the barrier impeding modern economic theory from going beyond the study of "Robinsonades". As H. Gossen (1983) candidly admitted, economics is interested in Robinson "up to the point where Crusoe finds Friday". *Non-tuism* is the true barrier that prevents the treatment of economic relations between agents that, on the one hand, know each other (so that the interactions are not anonymous), and, on the other hand, possess an identity (so that the interactions cannot be impersonal).[1]

As we know from the history of economic thought, Wicksteed's conceptualization of the nature of the economic problem did not come to be accepted as the core element of mainstream economics until Lionel Robbins popularized it in his celebrated *An Essay on the Nature and Significance of Economic Science* (1932). After insisting that what matters, as far as the science of economics goes, is the condition of *non-tuism*, he writes: "All that this means is that my relation to the dealers does not enter into my hierarchy of ends. For me—who may be acting for myself or my friends or some civic or charitable authority—they are regarded merely as means" (ibid. 97). This is a remarkable passage. I cannot find a better statement to exemplify the negation of the relational dimension within the economic discourse. And in his Introduction to the 1933 edition of Wicksteed's *Common Sense*, Robbins adds: "Before Wicksteed wrote, it was still possible for intelligent men to give countenance to the belief that the whole structure of economics depends on the assumption of the world of economic men, each accentuated by egocentric or hedonistic motives. For anyone who has read *Common Sense*, the expression of such a view is no longer consistent with intellectual honesty. Wicksteed shattered this misconception once and for all" (p. xxi). In other words, it is not self-interest *per se* that characterizes economics whose domain is capable of including any type of human choice provided the agent neglects the identity of the individual he is dealing with or exchanging with.[2]

The question arises: why, after all, should a theory of altruistic motivations which remains within the horizon of individualism be an unproductive complication of economic analysis? The answer is that it would fail to capture the true nature of altruism. Nagel (1970) writes: "Altruism depends on the recognition of the reality of other persons, and the corresponding capacity of persons to consider themselves as individuals among others.... Altruism should not be confused with a general affection for the human race. It is not a feeling" (p. 3). And further on: "The general thesis to spread around concerning altruism is that we have a direct reason to promote the interests of others; a reason that does not depend on intermediate factors such as one's own interest or one's own deepest feelings of sympathy and benevolence" (p. 16). A word of clarification is not out of place here. Though the employment of terms such as "sympathy and benevolence" might lead one to think that Nagel's position is the opposite of Adam Smith's, in actual fact this is not the case. Indeed, behind Nagel's notion of altruism lies the idea that, among persons, relations are established of a different nature from those established between persons and things. (To recall, utility is the property of the relation between an agent and an object.) It follows that when I treat attention to the other as an argument of my utility function, at that same moment I reduce the subject to whom I am referring to a thing, to an object. Which is precisely what is excluded by Smith's theory of sympathy.

As is well-known, in Smith the story begins with an agent who is already capable of true sympathy, that is, with agents capable of distancing themselves from their selves without however rejecting their self-interest. The peculiar nature of the principle of sympathy lies in that it postulates *continuity* between the pursuit of self-interest—Smith's "virtue of prudence"—and the pursuit of the interest of others—the "virtue of beneficence" (Khalil 2001). For Smith, the motivation that drives the agent to satisfy both self-interest and the interest of others derives from the capacity to sympathize, in the one case with oneself, in the other with whoever has been marked out for benefits. It is precisely in view of this that Smith openly criticizes, on the one hand, Bernard Mandeville, the author of the famous *The Fable of the Bees*, who brought to its extreme consequences Hobbes's position, and on the other hand David Hume, who thought of sympathy as a sort of useful mechanism to enable us to calculate social welfare. (For Hume the person who regulated his behaviour by the rules of sympathy and good manners would make himself most agreeable to others thus promoting his own esteem and reputation.) For the author of *Theory of Moral Sentiments*, instead, sympathy cannot be the result of calculation, even if the latter is targeted at social welfare. If this happened, fraternity, or "fellow-feeling" in the sense defined by Sugden (2002), could certainly not originate from sympathy. To sum up, whereas Smith's individual is capable of sharing with others the surplus deriving also from an *individual* transaction, the selfish altruist is not. Whereas the former is capable of exercising empathy because he is able to see the situation of the other from the inside, the egocentric altruist is not. Finally, whereas the *homo Smithianus* makes the donative act derive from sympathy in the sense specified above, the altercentric altruist "has to" donate, because he cannot not do so (Khalil 2001).

We can now understand why and in what precise sense it is individualism, that is, the denial of the relational nature of the person, that is the ultimate limitation of standard economic theory. What is the foundation of relationality? To quote the expression Sen uses to translate Aristotle's *eudaimonia*, it is the self-realization of the person, that is, his/her flourishing. It is important to realize what the recognition of the other implies: not just his/her *right* to exist but also the *necessity* he/she exists so that I can exist, in relation with him/her.

2.3. On the distinction between relationality and sociality

What does an economics of altruism that recognizes the key role played by personal relations look like? First, if sociality is not simply desire *for* the other—an attitude which is perfectly compatible with individualism—but also the other's desire for me, altruism becomes an instance of reciprocal recognition. In this specific sense, it can be said that altruism precedes self-interest, since it determines but is prior to action. Even before it appears as a means for attaining an individual end, interaction with others thus appears as an end in itself. Indeed, individual ends themselves can be understood only after interpersonal relationship has been established. Clearly, such a sociality, which moves beyond ourselves toward the other, is only possible within an economy of the gift in which mutuality and reciprocity figure. Only then can my desire for the other not be an appetite—that having the other would satisfy. It doesn't take much to realize that an approach to altruism of this kind is a long way from that of current literature which argues that the interests of agent B can motivate the action of A only if the former are connected in some way (e.g. via externalities) to the interests of A, or else they are the precipitate of some deontological code that A has chosen to make her own. In criticizing the way economics commonly, deals with altruism, Nagel (1970) writes: "It has to be noted the way egoism must appear pretty strange in practice: not only does it have to manifest itself in the lack of direct interest in others, but also in the inability to consider my own interest as a source of interest for anyone else, except for instrumental reasons or else as a consequence of the operation of some feeling" (p. 84).

A second consequence the adoption of a relational perspective would generate is a way out of the intricate question—a cause of lasting confusion among economists—about the connection between relationality and sociality of the individual. That man is a social animal and as such, possesses an inner disposition to take part in society, interacting systematically with others, has been known for a long time. Similarly, it is known, at least from the times of the *Wealth of Nations*, that this positive orientation toward others tends to produce, in specific conditions, mutually beneficial results. From here comes the hurried conclusion according to which a sustainable social order, humanly acceptable, would have no need at all of relationality. Instrumental rationality and non-tuism of agents is all that one would need. This assertion, in recent years, has been strengthened by the conclusions arrived at by a vast biological literature. This has shown how, in quite a number of animal species, examples of social behavior can be observed that are in fact relationships of mutual assistance, based on something that is the biological analogue of rational and non-tuistic behavior. However, as stressed above, the social dimension has little in common with the relational one. Two recent developments in the economic theory of human behavior—one centered on the notion of expressive rationality and one based on the idea of collective rationality—help us to detect the difference between sociality and relationality.

As is well-known, the distinction between expressive (or extended) rationality and instrumental rationality goes back to Max Weber. It is well illustrated by Benn (1978) when he writes: "An action may be rational for a person leaving aside the pay-off afterwards. This happens if that action expresses dispositions or principles that the person cannot but express, given the character that she is happy to recognize as her own. Which corresponds to what is usually called 'to be true to ourselves'" (p. 3). More recently, Hargreaves Heap (1989) has explained why expressive rationality—which applies to both ends and means—is incompatible with the maximization of utility: agents are interested not only in the consequences of their own actions, but also in the significance these acts embody with respect to the purpose of the fulfillment of their identity. In view of its anti-consequentialist nature, expressive rationality manages to distinguish between the end of an action, and its outcome, whereas the instrumental rationality approach conflates the end of an action and its outcome as if they were the same thing. Furthermore, consider the line of research Sugden began with his widely known 1984 study of the theory of reciprocity (an agent honors the underwritten obligation in a game of contribution, on condition others honor their obligations), later developed with the notion of team preferences. Team preferences are none other than the expression of individuals' conceptions concerning the end the team pursues. These preferences do not necessarily stem from the individual preferences of the members of the team, nor are they compatible with the postulate of the maximization of utility (Sugden 2000).

Both the expressive rationality approach, and that of the "*we-rationality*", as expanded by Sugden, illuminate the basic difference between sociality and relationality. The social principle, understood as a tendency of people to live together, is essentially a principle of self-organization. As such, it is not exclusively typical of human beings, since it is also common to animals. What is typical of the person is the relationality which postulates that the others become a *you* and not merely an alter ego. It is the presence of this last component that guarantees that social relations can be seen as human relations. To put it another way, it is relationality that removes the risk that the self is hypostatized as a self-referential core of needs and preferences, with respect to which the interpersonal dynamic is discredited as extrinsic superstructure. Relationality ultimately hinges on the conception of the self: oneself is constituted by the recognition the other bestows upon her. In standard economics, the other only has instrumental significance. In turn, this implies that relations among agents are treated as relations "at arm's length" and not as "face-to-face" interpersonal relations (Gui 2003). This excludes all processes of relationality from theoretical examination. In fact, there is no way to account for a dispositional variable like relationality in economic explanations as long as one adheres to the idea that the only explanatory variables are preferences and incentives (or constraints).

3. Reciprocity, Exchange of Equivalents, and Rationality

3.1. *Two notions of reciprocity*

Economics has known for quite some time that social interaction produces externalities and that the latter tend to delay, if not actually to impede, the movement toward socially advantageous equilibria. This is so since there is a basic difference between social decisions—those that influence the utility of others—and individual decisions—those whose effects remain limited to the personal sphere of the agent. To clarify the point: whereas the quality and the intensity of my relationships with friends are not in any way affected by my decision to consume bananas instead of apples, my decision to have children or not, to obtain a university degree or not, and so on have direct effects on others. In fact, decisions of this kind help to define my identity and thus influence my relationships with others. It may thus happen, as Akerlof (1997) and Akerlof and Kranton (2000) note, that the main determinant of my choice is the impact I imagine my decision will have on the network of my relations with others; whereas the evaluation of the direct effects of my choice on my level of utility—which is what the standard theory restricts itself to considering—could be of secondary importance. In recent years, a theory of social interaction is emerging that is at variance with Becker's famous approach, in which social decisions remain anchored to individual values.

The main impulse behind the construction of a theory of this kind has come, in the course of the last decade, from research on the principle of reciprocity, which has produced a huge literature. On the fact that reciprocity represents an important determinant of human behavior there is nowadays plenty of empirical evidence. From the work of Kahnemann and Tversky on economic psychology, to that of Bewley on labor economics, to that of Sugden on the voluntary contribution to public goods, to that of Fehr and others on the enforceability of contracts[3], from all this literature it clearly emerges that reciprocating behavior cannot be explained in terms of self-interested preferences and behavior oriented to outcomes only. It is by now accepted that reciprocity is something different from both the so-called reciprocating altruism and direct reciprocity, as exemplified by the tit-for-tat strategy Axelrod speaks of. The reciprocating altruist, in fact, is disposed to reciprocate only if a reward is expected in the future (or else to avoid or remove future punishments) as a result of one's action. We know that reciprocating altruistic behavior can emerge as an equilibrium strategy in games infinitely repeated or else in finite games with complete information. We also know that this kind of behavior is perfectly compatible with self-interested preferences, since the prospect of future gains or the credible threat of future punishments can induce selfish but patient agents to make momentary sacrifices in the context of repeated games.

Reciprocity, on the other hand, is a behavioral answer to "perceived courtesy"—as Falk and Fischbacher (2001) put it—where the term "courtesy" is taken to mean both the sense of distributive equity and the intention to behave fairly. The force behind reciprocity is not based, then, on any kind of prospect of future gain. A reciprocating individual is disposed to make material sacrifices in favor of those who are similarly disposed, and to punish those who are not. For example, to punish unfair behavior in an ultimatum game set-up is a form of reciprocity. Again, in games of coordination, most of the laboratory experiments show that the players, first, tend toward an inferior equilibrium and then, unexpectedly, change their strategy and converge to the dominant equilibrium. For this inversion to take place it is necessary that several individuals choose actions that are not best replies to the results of the moves that occurred immediately beforehand. In other words a certain number of players "make sacrifices" in the short run to teach the other players the way to coordinate on the dominant equilibrium (Stahl 2001).

Sally (1995) considers the conclusions of over a hundred essays of political science, economics, sociology, and social psychology, written in the last 35 years, where the replies to iterated laboratory experiments of the prisoner's dilemma type are analyzed. The experimental results are in marked contrast with those of traditional game theory. Not only is the presence of behavior that is not self-interested noted, to a significant extent, but also the possibility of communication between players, before they take their decisions, plays an important role in the results (Frank 1997). Also in the presence of cheap talks, that is, dialogues that are of no use because not binding, it was seen that on average communication increases the probability of cooperative behavior by 45 percent in one shot games, and by 40 percent in metagames. Frey and Bohnet (1995) carried out experiments on a sample of 340, students from the University of Zurich who were asked to play three familiar games (the prisoner's dilemma, the dictator game, and the ultimatum game) under different conditions as far as the assignment of property rights, the rules of the game, and above all the possibility of interaction between the participants were concerned. The result, in some respects surprising, was that whenever the nature of the game did not lead to the choice of the cooperative strategy, the latter was arrived at by allowing the participants to abandon their anonymous relationships through forms of communication, including non-verbal ones, that made the identity of the players explicit. (In the case of the prisoner's dilemma cooperative behavior rose from 12 percent to 78 percent and in the case of the dictator game the fairness indicator rose from 52 percent to 92 percent.) [4]

There are two notions of reciprocity to be found in the vast literature on the subject. One, which remains within the consequentialist domain, is founded on aversion to injustice: it is aversion to unfair distributions that stimulates the reciprocating response. The other notion, based on the principle of perceived courtesy, takes into account not only the consequences of the action but also the intentions behind it. (In the ultimatum game, for example, a certain offer of money is rejected by the other player much more often if the person making the offer is evidently not well-intentioned than if the same offer signals a good intention—let us say because the proponent finds himself in a particular situation of need.) No doubt the second notion is an interesting development within the theory of reciprocity, since it allows us to represent the utility of the agent as a function not only of the pay-offs of the original game, but also of the term expressing the response to the courtesy perceived—a term that Falk and Fischbacher (2001) rightly call "utility of reciprocity". However, on reflection, the explanatory power of even the expanded theory of reciprocity is a good deal lower than one might expect. The reason is, basically, that both versions of the theory of reciprocity postulate the same individualistic framework that is also at the bottom of the theory of altruism considered in the previous section. In both cases, in fact, individuals possess interdependent preferences; that is, they are interested in some way in others' pay-offs as well as their own. The ultimate difference between the theory of reciprocity and the theory of altruism lies in a different specification of the interdependence of individual preferences, but the conceptual structure behind it is the same: the attribution of weights to the pay-offs of others persists, weights that enter, in some way, one's own preference function. In other words, this conceptual structure visualizes reciprocity as part of a person's preference function, by considering human preferences to include something like a preference for being a moral person.

It should be recalled that recent studies (Guth and Yaari 1992; Sethi and Somanathan 2001; Ok and Vega Redondo 2001) have tried to explain, in evolutionary terms, the emergence (and stability) of preferences of reciprocity in agents belonging to specific social groups. The declared purpose of this literature is to demonstrate that even the preferences of reciprocity are compatible, despite appearances, with the individualist statute. The idea, in short, is that when information is incomplete—and therefore preferences cannot be observed—preferences that are not individualistic are not credible and hence end up by being dominated by individualistic preferences. This follows from the fact that agents, though knowing the relative frequency of the various types in the population, do not know the preferences of those with whom they find themselves interacting. The conclusion Ok and Vega Redondo (2001) arrive at is that within large groups and in the presence of incomplete information, evolution inevitably favors individualistic preferences in agents that operate in market-type social contexts. Coricelli *et al.* (2000) make a similar attempt to explain reciprocity as an example of self-interested behavior generated by a mechanism of delayed gratification allowing the individual to enjoy the gains deriving from intertemporal exchanges. The argument, basically, is that since most exchanges are intertemporal, the agent who moves first must in some way trust that the other will later reciprocate. So, in order to maximize the benefits deriving from exchange, agents learn to resist their propensity to immediate gratification, that is, they learn to practice reciprocity.

3.2. *The relational nature of reciprocity*

It is not difficult to detect the weakness inherent in such a line of argument. The point is that in the literature referred to above the meaning of the term reciprocity is being juggled with. In fact, whereas reciprocity postulates knowledge of the identity of the other, and above all readiness on the part of the agent to stay in a relationship with the other, the current literature reduces reciprocity—which is a relation—to an element in an extended preference function. It is therefore obvious that if the other does not know who I am, that is, she does not know my identity, she is led to behave individualistically toward me, since it is precisely this mode of behavior that emerges as the one evolutionarily stable among all those generated by any other kind of "mutant". The fact is that identity of the self is the ability to recognize and to be recognized. This means that identity, like trusting, is an interpersonal relation. They both come into existence in the course of interaction.

In view of the above I believe the formulation of reciprocity proposed by Kolm (1994) to be more adequate as far as the present argument is concerned. To him, reciprocity is a series of bi-directional transfers, independent of each other and at the same time interconnected. Independence implies that each transfer is voluntary in itself, that is, free; in other words, no transfer constitutes a prerequisite for putting the other into action, since there is no external obligation capable of acting on the mind of the agent. It is precisely this characteristic which differentiates reciprocity from relations based on the principle of the exchange of equivalents. The latter, too, are constituted by a set of bi-directional transfers, but the element of voluntariness is, so to speak, global in the sense that it is applied within a set of transfers, and not to each single transfer taken by itself. In other words, the transfers implied by the exchange of equivalents relationship are each the prerequisite of the other, so that a third party (e.g. a judge) can always intervene to render contractual obligations enforceable. Nothing like this happens with reciprocity, even if it remains true that exchange of equivalents and reciprocity, to the extent both postulate voluntariness, are opposed to command relations. At the same time, however, there is much more freedom in reciprocity than in the exchange of equivalents where the transfer in one direction becomes obligatory by the transfer in the opposite direction. The other characteristic of reciprocity—the bi-directionality of the transfers—is what differentiates the latter from philantropy or pure altruism, which expresses itself in one-directional transfers. A third property characterizes reciprocity: transitivity—the reciprocating behavior does not need to be directed towards the person who triggered the reciprocity relation. The recipient of the reciprocating action could be a third party. It is precisely the property of transitivity which confers on reciprocity an essentially triadic structure.

The relation of reciprocity requires some form of balancing between what one gives and what one *expects* to obtain, or *expects* to be given to some third party; a balancing, however, that is not expressed in a definite magnitude (i.e. in a relative price), since it may vary according to the intensity with which moral sentiments such as sympathy, benevolence, the feeling of solidarity are put into practice by the agents involved in the relation. At the same time, reciprocity does not exclude the strategic dimension always present in any interpersonal interaction: if those who receive my transfer do not give me some sign of reciprocation, I shall break off relations with them. Note carefully the difference. In the exchange of equivalents relation, the determination of the equilibrium price logically precedes the transfer of property rights—only after the buyer and seller have agreed on the price of the object of their transaction can the transfer of property rights take place. In the relation of reciprocity, on the other hand, the transfer precedes, both logically and temporally, the countertransfer, and the agent who moves first cannot claim any right; in fact he entertains a mere expectation. Second, the reciprocity nexus can modify the pay-offs of the economic game itself, whether because the practice of reciprocity tends to stabilize pro-social behavior in agents who find themselves interacting in contexts of the prisoner's dilemma type, or because the practice of reciprocity—itself tends to modify endogenously the preference structure of the agents. As the basic trust game teaches us, if I find that I have need of others in circumstances in which I cannot credibly bind myself to some commitment for the future, a rational agent (rational in the sense of the theory of rational choice), though capable of helping me, will certainly not do so if, knowing that I too am a self-interested agent, he conjectures that I will not have the slightest interest in reciprocating the favor received. This will not be the case if my potential helper somehow knows that I am a person who practices reciprocity.[5]

To conclude, one can understand why, unlike what happens with exchange of equivalents relations, reciprocity—as here defined—cannot be examined along individualistic lines. The fact is that in a game of reciprocity, the other person assumes a special value, since s/he gives us back the relational sense of ourselves. By comprising an essentially communicative aspect, reciprocity builds social relations and sense of identity. This is why traditional economic theory, hinging on the notion of instrumental action, is unable to properly categorize reciprocity. Reducing choices of reciprocity to the maximization of *given* preferences simply misses one of the most interesting aspects of such choices.

3.3. *The emergence of reciprocity*

"The touchstone of social capital"—writes Putnam (2000)—"is the principle of generalized reciprocity: I'll do this for you now, without expecting anything immediately in return and perhaps without even knowing you, confident that down the road you or someone else will return the favor" (p. 134). The question arises: how reciprocating behavior can emerge and evolve in a context of social interaction such as that of a market economy? From a cultural viewpoint reciprocity may be visualized as (the dispositional counterpart of) specific social norms. So, the question above can be rephrased as: which reasons may induce people to adopt a norm such as that of reciprocity? As indicated in the Introduction, a relational perspective on social norms is particularly suited to recognize not only their relevance as far as the individual social relevance is concerned, but also their evolution over time.

The basic idea[6] in the literature on social evolution is that cultural traits, such as preferences, values, norms, habits, and identities, are not completely innate characteristics of individuals, but are rather endogenous, in the sense of being acquired through, or influenced by, various processes of cultural transmission and of social selection, which, in turn, are influenced by the economic institutions present in a society (Bowles 1998).

To fix ideas, suppose that Ms B is following an altruistic norm that prescribes, say, unilateral donations in certain well-determined situations. In a cooperative context, her donations may be reciprocated, so that it is easy to imagine possible scenarios where the norm turns out to be both (subjectively) highly satisfactory and (objectively) materially rewarding. There is therefore a good chance that B keeps following the altruistic norm and that she is even "imitated" by other people, so that the norm spreads over. Notice that, in this cooperative context in which there is a straightforward incentive to behave nicely, whether people adopt the norm because of its apparent material convenience or because of the arousal of a deeper commitment to what they perceive to be the underlying disposition is relatively irrelevant insofar as both possibilities yield the same behavioral prescription. In an opportunistic context, though, the altruist B may be materially exploited by others, with the consequence that, due to the undesirable pay-off implications of norm compliance, other people are likely to choose not to embrace it. On the other hand, even if she is materially worse off, B may gain a high intrinsic satisfaction from donation because she truly adheres to the norm she abides by and is happy to see other people well off because of her, even if this does not deliver in material terms. Can then one conclude that, apart from our nice B, nobody else will embrace the norm? Not at all: despite the negative material pay-off, some people may still find it attractive to do the same as B, insofar as they either believe that by adopting the altruistic disposition their subjective, non-material reward will more than compensate the material loss, or, even more radically, insofar as they choose to abide by the norm whatever its material or psychological implications in terms of well-being.

This simple example calls for some basic distinctions. First, a norm may be either embraced because it corresponds to an intrinsic disposition, as in the case of a true altruist, or instrumentally, because adopting the corresponding behavior turns out to be rewarding even if the individual would behave differently if he had to follow his intrinsic disposition, as in the case of an egoist who—in a context where other people are altruist with seemingly altruist partners and egoist with seemingly egoist partners—finds it egoistically convenient to pretend to be an altruist, and therefore follows an altruistic norm instrumentally. But, as the example suggests, even in the case of an intrinsic commitment to the norm, one has to distinguish between a truly unconditional commitment, that is, the choice to embrace the norm irrespectively of its consequences, and a "rational" commitment, that is, the choice to embrace it in view of the favorable trade-off between the psychological benefit and the material loss. We can therefore speak, respectively, of strong and weak non-instrumentality.

Second, in picking up more rewarding traits, social selection may consequently operate at different levels, according to whether the relevant rewards for selection purposes are material or psychological or some combination of the two. As shown in our example, in a cooperative context the selection mechanism may have little or no discriminatory power, whereas in an opportunistic context there is much more scope for discrimination. Clearly, in this latter case, strongly non-instrumental variants of the norm are not affected by the selection process insofar as they are not sensitive to pay-off comparisons of any kind, thereby playing the role of a "drift" factor (which may however bring about important consequences for the selection outcomes as they alter the relative convenience of, say, instrumental versus weakly non-instrumental altruism versus egoism.

In their (2001) paper, Sacco and Zamagni concentrate on reciprocity in a hawk-dove game and consider both the possibility that it is undertaken for instrumental reasons and that it is embraced out of intrinsic motivations[7] A robust result in their model is that, whatever the initial distribution of player types in the population, the evolutionary dynamics leads to an equal split of players acting as "hawks" and as "doves" (which corresponds to a mixed-strategy Nash equilibrium of the static game), at least as long as either intrinsic or instrumental reciprocity is represented in the population. Allowing for psychological externalities shows that, while "relational" players may eventually dominate in equilibrium, with beneficial social effects, positional players cannot, precisely because they impose negative externalities on one another.[8]

4. Happiness and the Gift Principle

How can individuality and sociality be reconciled? How can the idea of an agent who chooses autonomously and rationally be reconciled with the idea that rationality has to do not only with the satisfaction of preferences, but also with values, affections, emotions, human relations? My answer is that such an objective can be achieved if we are prepared to open the economic discourse to the principle of gift as reciprocity. Why and in what sense would the acceptance of the gift principle expand the horizon and explanatory power of economics? In a rightly famous essay, Guardini writes: "The human person cannot understand himself as if closed within himself, because he exists in the form of a relation. Although the person is not born from an encounter, it is certain that he becomes real only in the encounter" (1964: 90). If human beings discover themselves in the interpersonal relationship, fulfilling themselves in relation to others, it follows that their fundamental need is a need of relationality. If my being in relation with another can be justified only by considerations of opportunity—to obtain consensus or to resolve conflicts, as the neo-contractualist school of thought would have it—I shall never be able to escape from the "unsociable sociability" Kant talked about. If we think about it, behind the demand for a better quality of life lies a demand that goes well beyond the simple demand for goods "made well". Rather, it is a demand for care, for participation—in other words, for relationality. The quality we hear about today with ever increasing insistence does not just involve consumer goods in the familier sense, but also (and perhaps above all) the quality of human relations. If it is true, as I believe, that the quality of life has to do with the possibility of self-realization, whereas the increase in per-capita income only tells us of a greater spending capacity in the agent, then it is equally true that interpersonal relationships are real goods, and as such cannot be excluded from the domain of economic discourse.

How can economics recover the relational dimension, avoiding the Scylla of holism and the Charybdis of individualism? My answer is to open up economic theory to the gift principle. It is well-known that, in general, the need for relationality can be satisfied within two different structures of relationship: one is characterized by the practice of the gift, the other by the exchange of equivalents, that is, the contract. The relationality born from the gift is such that the encounter with the other always determines, to some extent, a modification of the self that, in its return to its own interiority, finds itself "richer" thanks to the encounter having occurred. This is not the case in the relationality born from a contract, whose regulating principle is rather the perfect symmetry between what is given and what can be claimed in exchange—the exchange of equivalents, in fact. It is indeed because of this characteristic that the power of the law can always intervene to give enforceability to the obligations born through contracts. Nobody would deny the importance in our societies of the structure of relationships between agents founded on contracts. However, one has also to recognize that such a structure is insufficiently strong to take into account the relational dimension. As a matter of fact, the donative action rejects the linear means–end model. As Godbout (2000) puts it, the linear model is constructed on a pattern of reasoning of the following kind: the agent has received after having given, *therefore* he has given with the aim of receiving: the end was to receive, and what was given was the means to that end. This is certainly not the way the gift principle works. The movement of the self toward a *you*, of which the self has need, is what defines the *proprium* of the donative action. One does not give with the purpose of receiving, but so that the other may give.

This latter qualification enables me to point out that there are two, quite different, notions of gift. As the school of Mauss[9] has shown, there is an idea of the gift, typical of pre-modernity, that nevertheless survives, at least in part, today. According to this idea, the gift should always be traced to an underlying exchange structure. This is the idea of the gift as *munus*, as an instrument to commit others, even as far as being able to manipulate them. (Just think of the classic analyses, of the anthropologists Marcel Mauss and Claude Levi-Strauss concerning phenomena such as Potlach, and the Kula.) According to this idea, the gift actually becomes paradoxically an obligation to conserve the social link: life in society requires the practice of gift giving, which ends up by becoming a social norm of behavior, a norm sometimes more binding than legal norms themselves.

It is not hard to see why this concept of the gift does away with both the spontaneity and the gratuitousness of the donative action. The latter of course may cultivate an interest, but it always has to be an interest *for* others, never an interest *to* others. As a matter of fact, the term interest literally means "to be among"; which means that to pursue an interest it is necessary to interact with others, using each other reciprocally, for there to be fruits for both. And yet contemporary culture has wandered so far away from the original meaning of the term interest that it is almost always taken to have a negative meaning. In itself, the gift is by no means incompatible with the interest of the giver, *if* this is understood as interest in being in relation with others. The gift—unlike the philanthropic act—is not an act which is an end in itself, but is the beginning of a relation, of a chain of reciprocal acts. In other words, that the gift is given on purpose, in view of the establishment of a link. The specific sense of this second notion of gift is, therefore, that the gift generates reciprocity. Whereas the gift as *munus* almost always generates dependence in those who receive it, and sometimes even submission, the gift as reciprocity frees the addressee of the act of giving from the "shame" of which Seneca speaks in the Tenth Letter to Lucilius, when he writes: "Human madness has reached the point that to do a great favor to someone becomes dangerous in the extreme: because he feels it shameful not to repay in like measure, he would like to eliminate his creditor. There is no hatred worse than the one that is born of a feeling of shame for having betrayed a benefit." If those who have gratuitously received are not placed in a position to reciprocate in some way, they will feel humiliated, and will end up by hating—sooner or later—their benefactor.

The strength of the gift as reciprocity does not lie in the thing given or how much—as is the case with gift as munus—but in the special human quality that the gift represents for the fact of being a relation. So it is the existence of a specific interest to give rise to the relation between donor and donee that constitutes the essence of the gift as reciprocity. In this lies the *value of bond*, an actual third value category to be added to the two categories that economics has always taken into consideration: use value and exchange value. To expand the horizons of research so as to include the value of bond is a real intellectual challenge, given that the relation between persons is in itself a good, that, as such, generates value.

The final difference between the gift as *munus* and the gift as reciprocity lies in the fact that the former is perfectly compatible with the individualistic paradigm—as are altruism and philanthropy—while the latter postulates the relational paradigm. It is precisely the concern that the so-called free gift (i.e. the gift as *munus*) can generate power and prestige that makes Mary Douglas write in her Preface to Mauss's famous book: "No gift must be free. What is wrong with the so-called free gift is the donor's intention to be exempted from exchanged gifts coming from those who receive" (1990, p. vii). In the light of the above, it can thus be said that the gift as reciprocity is an expression of free choice, that is, an act whose result cannot be foreseen and guaranteed on the basis of a determined causal chain. It is thanks to its profoundly free character that this type of gift is able to intervene on agents' personality, allowing them to experience happiness.

The theory of network games is a promising instrument of research that can be used to model the notion of gift as reciprocity. A network game (Ellison 1993; Morris 1997; Macy 1996) is defined, in addition to the familiar pay-off matrix, by the matrix of the social network whose elements quantify the weight of the relation that involves two or more agents. Each player is influenced by the others, as well as by the game, through the specific set of relations as expressed by the matrix of the social network. The Consideration of the fact that the agents are interested not only in the results of their interaction with others, but also in the relations that are interwoven between them allows to achieve a dual objective.[10]

In the first place, it explains behavior that, on the basis of traditional models of rational choice, would remain without any kind of justification (e.g. why people go and vote in political elections; why so many people practice reciprocity systematically; why there are so many persons involved in voluntary activities, etc). A second important objective is to throw light on one of the most intriguing dimensions of social welfare, on the fact that our well-being depends to a large extent on the consumption of that special category of goods that are relational goods. It is precisely the interpersonal dimension—as I have said above—that is neglected by the model of rational choice, a model that postulates an agent so completely taken up with the rational pursuit of her utility that she does not realize that to reach that end she has to manipulate, systematically and explicitly, the behavior and the choices of other agents.[11] This point is well taken by Zinkin when he observes: "There has to be a notion of giving without losing whatever one has given or receiving without taking away" (2000: 112).

The reduction of happiness to the category of utility generates serious explanatory problems, for the simple reason that a large number of social interactions and the great majority of practical decisions acquire meaning only thanks to the absence of instrumentality. The meaning of a generous action toward a friend, a child, or a business colleague lies precisely in its being gratuitous. If we found out that that action had sprung from a manipulatory logic, it would acquire a completely different meaning, with the result that the modes of response by the addressee of the action would completely change. "Chicago man"—as McFadden (1999) calls him—is an isolate, a solitary individual, and hence unhappy, so much so the more he is concerned for others, since this solicitude is none other than an idiosyncrasy of his preferences. "Chicago man" is even a species on the way to extinction, even in those market contexts where it had long been believed he could survive indefinitely—as, with intellectual honesty, McFadden documents. On the whole, as long as we remain within the sphere of private goods, the results that can be obtained within the traditional framework are still valid and offer effective explanations. This is not the case, however, when we are dealing with relational goods. The reason is very easy to grasp. The typical trait of relational goods is that an agent's consumption of them increases not only with the amount of time the agent devotes to socializing, but also with the socializing effort expended by other agents. In these cases the elegant simplicity of the traditional economic models disappears in a moment, since happiness has to be shared if it is to be enjoyed.

5. A Final Note

The reductionist route taken by economics, from the second half of the nineteenth century onwards has ended up by disarming critical thinking, with the results I have partly outlined in this chapter. For this the profession must accept its own responsibilities. For too long, generations of pupils have been led to believe that scientific rigor postulated an ascetic stance; that in order to be scientific, research had to free itself from any reference to values. We now have the result: ontological individualism—that is itself a value judgment, and a very strong one, indeed—has acquired the status of a "natural" assumption, that as such does not require any justification. It sets itself up as a benchmark that every other hypothesis on human nature "has to" measure itself against. Indeed, only to individualism is granted the privilege of naturalness in traditional economics.

I don't think we can continue along this path for long. A choice has to be made: either we remain anchored to *non-tuism* and are prepared to pay the price of not being able to offer an answer to the naive, but fundamentally true, observation of Saint-Exupary: "Men ... buy things all ready made at the shops. But there is no shop anywhere where one can buy friendship; and so men have no friends any more" (*Little Prince*). Or we agree to give up *non-tuism* and then we might be able to articulate all the consequences of the (unnoticed) intuition of Gossen, (1983) when he wrote: "most pleasures become actual pleasures only if other persons, too, participate in the enjoyment".

Abell has written: "The theory of rational action is the *necessary* point of departure with which to compare other kinds of theory" (1992: 186). Statements of this kind are far from being neutral and innocent, as one might be led to believe. The fact is that it is precisely through this kind of statement, uncritically repeated an infinite number of times, that the theory of rational choice has ended up by acquiring an actual "paradigmatic privilege": every other explanation of the agent's behavior has to "reckon" with that point of departure. Thus, for example, while one is forced to *explain why* someone makes a gift, non-tuistic behavior is considered completely natural, not needing any explanation. Why should one feel exempted from providing valid reasons for not donating, whereas the opposite is not the case?

It is proper to remember that individualism, as this is interpreted by standard economic theory, leads to a paradoxical outcome: the negation, in actual fact, of the individual. Indeed, the word individual has a meaning in a social context that emphasizes individual differences; and differences can emerge only in a social context of interaction. Put another way, individualism, understood as self-differentiation from others, has a meaning only when there are others around with whom comparison is possible. After all, communitarianism, as a specific and particular form of collectivism, differs from individualism only at one point: the "self" is a collective self ("my group"; "my nation"; "both"). But in neither case can we escape the same horizon. What changes is that the subject analyzed is, in the one case, the single individual, and in the other, the group or the class. In this sense, the rational choice model is more an atomistic model, rather than an individualistic one—a model according to which human beings are seen not as interacting individuals, but as self-sufficient monads without the need to relate to others.

As we have seen, the notion of *homo oeconomicus* has to do with the idea of desert, that is, with the idea of a human being in its insurmountable solitude. *Homo oeconomicus* is an autistic being. Agents cross one another in the market-place to sign up contracts and to do business, but they never really meet in order to recognize one another. Solitude is a state of separation not only from the other, but also from the self. Thus, it should come as no surprise to discover that, as long as we remain within the realm of traditional economics, it is practically impossible to talk about happiness in a proper and meaningful way.

Notes

1. In opposition to Tullock (1978), who had written "As a result of empirical research...the average human being is for around 95% an egoist in the strict sense of the term" (p. 29) and in open criticism of Mueller (1986), who had argued that "the only essential assumption for a descriptive and predictive science of human behavior is egoism" (p. 14), Kirzner (1990) writes: "Self-interest is certainly a central element, but it must be understood through the use of a good deal of subtlety. Properly understood, self-interest does not exclude altruistic motivation; it tells of tension towards an end, but not that the end has

to be egoistic. The ends the agent pursues can be altruistic or of other kinds" (p. 39). For an extension, see Zamagni (2002).

2. I can note, in passing, that Sen's paradox of the impossibility of being a Paretian liberal is due to the fact that the condition of non-tuism is not satisfied. If the two agents of the story Sen relates to exemplify his paradox were perfect non-tuists, the impossibility would not occur.

3. For bibliographical references to this literature see Sally (1995) and Fehr *et al.* (1997). The basic premise of this literature is that without contracts there can be no market. On the other hand, without the enforceability of agreements, contracts would not be stipulated. On the basis of the assumption of rational and selfish agents the standard approach to endogenous enforcement of contracts yields incentive-compatibility contraints. By introducing reciprocity as a component of rational behavior, these authors obtain a significant increase in the number of contracts that can be made enforceable, which of course generates gains in efficiency.

4. The measurement of equity is constructed in the following way. Let 100 be the sum assigned to the dictator. If he divides the sum into equal parts, the index of equity will be 100%; if the dictator attributes to the other the sum of 25, the equity measurement will be 50% etc. In the experiments carried out by Frey and Bohnet (1995), the other player receives on average the sum of 26 when the game is played in conditions of anonymity and the sum of 48 when the players learn to recognize themselves.

5. We owe to Sen (1967) one of the first attempts to propose a relational approach to reciprocity. To what extent is reciprocity, as here defined, practiced and how significant is it in real life? Unlike what one might believe, it is a rather widespread phenomenon, especially in advanced societies. Not only it is practiced within families, in small informal groups, in associations of various kinds, but the transactions' network based on reciprocity as ruling principle is present in all those enterprises that fill the world of non-profit organizations and cooperative firms. See Ben-Ner and Putterman (1997).

6. What follows in this paragraph is taken with changes and adaptation from Sacco *et al.* (2003).

7. They consider a game in which a given surplus has to be distributed between two players, who can either claim it for themselves or accommodate. Since distributive conflict is costly, they find it optimal to accommodate if the opponent claims and to claim if the opponent accomodates. The authors then study the evolution of diferent player types. They consider both "naive" players, who always play either as hawks or as doves, and "sophisticated" players, who choose their action according to their opponent's type. Such sophisticated players may have different motivational orientations, namely neutral (traditional self-interested "Best Reply" players), relational ("Rawlsian" players, who maximize the least advantaged player's pay-off) and positional ("Positional" players, who maximize the difference between their own and their opponent's pay-off).

8. See Sacco *et al.* (2003) for a review of the literature on evolutionary games where social selection leads to the diffusion of those traits that provide superior reward.

9. This is the acronym of the Anti-Utilitarian Movement in Social Science a recent current of French thought that numbers among its best-known writers S. Latouche, A. Caillé, and J. Godbout. See Godbout *et al.* (1998).

10. The "new paradigm of social economics"—as it has been called by Durlauf and Young (2001)—does not seem to me to be able to deal with the challenge that the acceptance of the principle of the gift poses. The idea that authors who share this paradigm start from is that many economic actions are marked by social interaction. The latter implies that the net private benefits deriving from a particular transaction increase with the increase in the number of those who are involved in the same transaction. (To work hard in a certain activity is less painful if others find themselves sharing the same activity as well.) We therefore have to model the interaction between group behavior and individual behavior, starting from the consideration of the way individuals' beliefs are formed on the behavior of those with whom they are interacting. Although able to explain quite a few phenomena (e.g. a certain number of social pathologies such as crime; leaving school early; or smoking), the new social economics does not get beyond the individualistic horizon, with all the consequences this choice involves.

11. An area of research where the relational approach has produced results of great importance is that of studies on people's quality of life. I'm thinking especially of the *Reports on Human Development*, brought out every year by the Development Program of the UN. Sen's contribution to their design, centered on the capacity approach, has been decisive, as has above all the philosophical thinking of Martha Nussbaum (2002) about the passage from the notion of the individual to that of the person. Of special interest is Nussbaum's argument aiming to show how the individualistic perspective is incapable of thinking of the human being as an "animal with needs".

References

Abell, P. (1992), "Is Rational Choice a Rational Choice of Theory", in J. Coleman and T. Fararo (eds.), *Rational Choice Theory*, London: Sage.

Akerlof, G. (1997), "Social Distance and Social Decisions", *Econometrica*, 65: 1005–27.

——and Kranton, R. (2000), "Economics and Identity", *Quarterly Journal of Economics*, 65: 715–53.

Andreoni, J. (1990), "Impure Altruism and Donations to Public Goods: A Theory of Warm-Glow Giving", *Economic Journal*, 100: 464–77.

Bardsley, N., and Sudgen, R. (2002), "Human Nature and Socialty in Economics", University of East Anglia, January.

Becker, G. (1974), "A Theory of Social Interaction", *Journal of Political Economy*, 82: 1063–93.

——(1996), *Accounting for Tastes*, Cambridge Mass.: Harvard University Press.

Ben-Ner, A., and Putterman, L. (eds.), (1997), *Economics, Values and Organizations*, Cambridge: Cambridge University Press.

Benn, S. (1978), *Political Participation*, Canberra: Australian National University Press.

Bergstrom, T. C. (1999), "Systems of Benevolent Utility Functions", *Journal of Public Economic Theory*, 1: 71–100.

Bernheim, B. D., and Stark, O. (1988), "Altruism within the Family Reconsidered: Do Nice Guys Finish Last?" in Zamagni (1995).

Bowles, S. (1998), "Endogenous Preferences: The Cultural Consequences of Markets and other Economic Institutions", *Journal of Economic Literature*, 36: 75–111.

Coricelli, G., McCobe, K., and Smith, V. (2000), "Theory of Mind Mechanism in Personal Exchange", in G. Hotano, N. Okada, and H. Tanabe (eds.), *Affective Minds*, Amsterdam: Elsevier.

Deci, E., Koestner, R., and Ryan, R. (1999), "A Meta-analytic Review of Experiments examining the Effects of Extrinsic Rewards on Intrinsic Motivation", *Psychological Bulletin*, 125: 627–68.

Demeulamere, P. (2000), "Individualism and Holism: New Controversies in the Philosophy of Social Sciences", *Mind and Society*, 2: 3–16.

Douglas, M. (1990), "No Free Gifts" in M. Mauss, *The Gift*, New York: Norton.

Durlauf, S., and Young, H. P. (eds.) (2001), *Social Dynamics*, Cambridge, Mass.: MIT Press.

Edgeworth, F. Y. (1881), *Mathematical Psychics*, London: Kegan Paul.

Elias, N. (1991), *The Symbol Theory*, London: Sage.

Ellison, G. (1993), "Learning, Local Interaction and Coordination", *Econometrica*, 61: 1047–71.

Etzioni, A. (1986), "The case for a Multiple-Utility Conception", *Economics and Philosophy*, 2: 159–83.

Falk, A., and Fischbacher, U. (2001), "A Theory of Reciprocity", CEPR, 3014, October.

Fehr, E., and Gachter, S. (2001), "Do Incentive Contracts Crowd Out Voluntary Cooperation?" University of Southern California, Research Paper, C01.3.

——and Kirchsteiger, G. (1997), "Reciprocity as a Contract Enforcement Device: Experimental Evidence", *Econometrica*, 65: 833–60.

Frank, R. H. (1988), *Passions within reasons: The Strategic Role of Emotions*, New York: W. W. Norton.

——(1997), "Non-verbal Communication and the Emergence of Moral Sentiments", in U. Segerstrale and P. Molner (eds.), *Non-verbal Communication: Where Nature meets Culture*, Mahwah, NJ: Erlbaum Associates Pu.

Frey, B. (1997), *Not Just for the Money an Economic Theory of Personal Motivation*, Cheltenham: Edward Elgar.

——and Bohnet, I. (1995), "Institutions affect Fairness: Experimental Investigations", *Journal of Institutions and Theoretical Economics*, 151/2: 286–303.

Gachter, S., and Falk, A. (2002), "Reputation or Reciprocity? An Experimental Investigation", *Scandinavian Journal of Econometrics*, 24.

Godbout, J. (2000), "Homo Donator versus Homo Oeconomicus", in A. Vandevelde (ed.), *Gifts and Interests*, Leuven: Peeters.

——Latouche, S., and Caillé, A. (1998), *Il Terzo paradigma: Antropologia filosofica dèl dono*, Turin; Bollati Boringhieri.

Gossen, H. H. (1983), *The laws of Human Relations*, 1st Pub. in German, 1859; English edn. by N. Georgescu Roegen, Cambridge, Mass.: MIT Press, 1983.

Guardini, R. (1964), *Scritti filosofici*, vol. II, Milan: Vita e Pensiero.

Gui, B. (1994), "Interpersonal Relations: A Disregarded Theme in the Debate on Ethics and Economics", in A. Lewis and K. E. Warneryd (eds.), *Ethics and Economic Affairs*, London: Routledge.

——(2000), "Beyond Transactions: On the Interpersonal Dimension of Economic Reality", *Annals of Public and Cooperative Economics*, 71: 139–69.

——(2002), "Più che scambi, incontri. La teoria economica alle prese con i fenomeni interpersonali", in Sacco and Zamagni (2002).

——(2003) "Più che scambi, incontri. La teoria economica alle prese con i fenomeni interpersonali", in P. Sacco and S. Zamagni (eds.), *Complessità relazione e comportament. economico*, Bologna: Il Mulino.

Guth, W., and Yaari, M. (1992), "Explaining Reciprocal Behaviour in Simple Strategic Games: An Evolutionary Approach", in U. Witt (ed.), *Explaining Forces and Change*, Ann Arbor: University of Michigan Press.

Hargreaves Heap, S. (1989), *Rationality in Economics*, Oxford: Blackwell.

Khalil, E. L. (2001), "Adam Smith and Three Theories of Altruism", *Louvain Economic Review*, 67: 421–35.

Kirzner, I. (1990), "Self-Interest and the New Bashing of Economics: A Fresh Opportunity in the Perennial Debate", *Critical Review*, 4: 27–40.

Kolm, S. (1994), "The Theory of Reciprocity and the Choice of Economic Systems", *Investigaciones economicas*, 18: 67–95.

Jensen, M. C., and Meckling, W. H. (2001), "The Nature of Man", in D. H. Chew (ed.), *The New Corporate Finance: Where Theory meets Practice*, 3rd edn., Irwin, Calif.: McGraw Hill.

Lindbeck, A., and Weibull, J. W. (1988), "Altruism and Time Consistency: The Economics of Fait Accompli", in Zamagni (1995).

Lutz, M. (1999) *Economics for the Common Good*, London: Routledge.

McFadden, D. (1999), "Rationality for Economists", *Journal of Risk and Uncertainty*, 3.

Macy, M. (1996), "Natural Selection and Social Learning in Prisoner's Dilemma", in W. B. Liebrand and D. M. Messik (eds.), *Frontiers in Social Dilemmas Research*, Berlin: Springer Verlag.

Margolis, H. (1982), *Selfishness, Altruism and Rationality: A Theory of Social Choice*, Cambridge: Cambridge University Press.

Meeks, J. G. (ed.) (1991), *Thoughtful Economic Man: Essays on Rationality, Moral Rules and Benevolence*, Cambridge: Cambridge University Press.

Morris, S. (1997), "Interaction Games: A Unified Analysis of Incomplete Information, Local Interaction and Random Matching", University of Pennsylvania, CARESS, WP 2.

Mueller, D. (1986), "Rational Egoism vs. Adaptive Egoism", *Public Choice*, 51.

Nagel, T. (1970), *The Possibility of Altruism*, Princeton: Princeton University Press.

Nussbaum, M. (2002), *Diventare persona*, Bologna: Il Mulino.

Ok, E., and Vega Redondo, F. (2001), "On the Evolution of Individualistic Preferences", *Journal of Economic Theory*, 97: 273–97.

Pareto, V. (1906), *Manuale di economia politica*, Milan: Società Editrice Libraria.

Pareyson, L. (1995), *Ontologia della libertà*, Turin: Einaudi.

Prendergast, C. (1999), "The Provision of Incentives in Firms", *Journal of Economic Literature*, 37: 7–63.

Putnam, R. (2000), *Bowling Alone: The Collapse and Revival of American Community*, New York: Simon and Schuster.

Rabin, M. (2002), "A Perspective on Psychology and Economics", *European Economic Review*, 46: 257–85.

Robbins, L. (1932/1935), *An Essay on the Scope and Nature of Economic Science*, 2nd edn. London: Macmillan; 1935; 1st pub. 1932.

Rothschild, E. (2001), *Economic Sentiments: Adam Smith, Condorcet and the Enlightenment*, Cambridge, Mass.: Harvard University Press.

Sacco, P., and Zamagni, S. (1997), "An Evolutionary Dynamic Approach to Altruism", in F. Farina, F. Hahn, and S. Vannucci (eds.), *Ethics and Economics*, Oxford: Clarendon Press.

——— (2001), "Civil Economy, Cultural Evolution and Participatory Development", in G. Mwabu and C. Ugaz (eds.), *Social Provision in Low-Income Countries*, Oxford: Clarendon Press.

——— (eds.) (2002), *Complessità relazionale e comportamento economico*, Bologna: Il Mulino.

——— Vanin, P., and Zamagni, S. (2003), "The Economics of Human Relationships", Department of Economics, Bologna, November.

Sally, D. (1995), "Conversation and Cooperation in Social Dilemmas", *Rationality and Society*, 7: 58–92.

——— (2001), "On Sympathy and Games", *Journal of Economic Behaviour and Organization*, 44: 1–30.

Sen, A. (1967), "Isolation, Assurance and the Social Rate of Discount", *Quarterly Journal of Economics*, 80: 112–24.

——— (1993), "Internal Consistency of Choice", *Econometrica*, 61: 495–521.

Sethi, R., and Somanathan, E. (2001), "Preference Evolution and Reciprocity", *Journal of Economic Theory*, 97: 273–97.

Simon, H. A. (1990), "A Mechanism for social selection and successful Altruism", *Science*, 250: 1165–8.

Smith, A. (1759/1976), *Theory of Moral Sentiments*, ed. D. D. Raphael and A. L. Macfie, Oxford: Clarendon Press, 1976.

—— (1776/1904), *An Inquiry into the Nature and Causes of the Wealth of Nations*, 1st published 1776; London: Methuen, 1904.

Stahl, D. (2001), "A Survey of Rule Learning in Normal Form Games", University of Texas Working Paper May.

Stigler, G. and Becker, G. (1977), "De Gustibus Non Est Disputandum", *American Economic Review*, 67/1: 76–90.

Sugden, R. (2000), "Team Preferences", *Economics and Philosophy*, 16: 175–205.

—— (2002), "Beyond Sympathy and Empathy: Adam Smith's Concept of Fellow Feeling", *Economics and Philosophy*, 18: 63–88.

Tullock, G. (1978), "Altruism, Malice and Public Goods", *Journal of Social and Biological Structures*, 1: 3–9.

Wicksteed; P. H. (1933), *The Common Sense of Political Economy*, ed. L. Robbins, London: Macmillan; 1910.

Wilson, E. O. (1975), *Sociobiology: The New Synthesis*, Cambridge, Mass.: Harvard University Press.

Zamagni, S. (ed.) (1995), *The Economics of Altruism*, Aldershot: Edward Elgar.

—— (2000), "Economic Reductionism as a Hindrance to the Analysis of Structural Change", *Structural Change and Economic Dynamics*, 11: 197–208.

—— (2002), "L'economia delle relazioni uman: verso il superamento dell'individualismo assiologico", in Sacco, P. and Zamagni S. (eds.).

Zinkin, L. (2000), *The Psyche in the Social World*, London: Macmillan.

13

Paradoxes of Happiness in Economics

*Luigi Pasinetti**

1. Introduction

To have organized a series of contributions on *Economics and Happiness* is—it must be admitted—an act of courage and at the same time a sign of dissatisfaction with the current state of economics. It was precisely the discovery, by Professor Easterlin (1973, 1974), of the "income paradox" (also known as the "Easterlin paradox") that has stimulated the recent resumption of enquiries into the relationship between wealth and happiness.

Since the Industrial Revolution of the eighteenth century, the Western economies have experienced an unprecedented and persistent growth of national income. But all empirical surveys that have been carried out consistently reveal that people have not become happier at the same rate. The connections between national income and happiness have become weaker and weaker over time. Some people would even deny that they exist at all. Why is this so? A young collaborator of mine with whom I carried out discussions on the "Easterlin paradox" reacted with unusual vehemence: "Where is the problem? Human beings are not robots. A robot is an automaton. It behaves in a pre-programmed way. It may possess a (sort of) brain, but it has no heart. Human beings have brains. Actually, they have minds, but they also have hearts. Besides being rational, they are purposeful, and they have *feelings*. Happiness is just one of the most profound feelings of human life, and it is not on sale in the market-place."

On any analysis, the feeling of happiness emerges as being a very complex one, and intrinsic to human nature. We may learn a lot about this from Professor Kahneman, who is entertaining us on the results of his research on cognitive processes—a subject for which he was awarded the

336

2002 Nobel Memorial Prize in Economics. In the past, when enquiries about mankind were still carried out within a unified vision, the conception of happiness had always been at the centre of keen speculation and dispute. Aristotle (*Nicomachean Ethics*) thought that "Happiness is the end for which human beings are designed". Roman philosophers, in particular Seneca (*Epistulae Morales ad Lucilium*, XLVIII) and Boethius (*The Consolations of Philosophy*), argued that happiness can be achieved by virtue and self-restraint (*ataraxia*), and medieval writers considered happiness the outcome of a good and religious life: "Happiness consists of the contemplation of God . . . not in bodily pleasures, and riches" remarked St Thomas Aquinas (*Summa Theologica*). On all these occasions, happiness was not seen as a temporary emotion, but as an enduring and long-lasting attitude of human beings—an attitude linked to ethical behavior and human perfection.

The achievement of happiness was perceived as important not only for each individual's perspective, but also for society as a whole. During the modern era, and in particular during the Enlightment period in the whole of Europe, philosophers and moral writers debated widely and increasingly on public happiness: the eighteenth century witnessed a flourishing debate particularly in Italy. Discussions on public happiness appear extensively in the writings of Cesare Beccaria, Pietro Verri, Carlo Cattaneo in Milan, Antonio Genovesi and Giuseppe Palmieri in Naples, as well as many others. Even a cursory look at their arguments, at two and a half centuries' distance, may give a sense of re-discovery today. At an institutional level, it is significant to note that both the American *Declaration of Independence* (1776) and the French *Declaration of Rights of Man* (1789) refer explicitly in their texts to the pursuit of happiness as one of the basic goals of society.

2. The Birth of Political Economy

Be that as it may, the fact is that when the Classical economists, with their works, laid the foundations of Political Economy as an autonomous discipline, between the end of the eighteenth century and the beginning of the nineteenth century, the central subject on which they concentrated was not happiness, but material wealth. Adam Smith's masterpiece was *An Inquiry into the Causes and Nature of the Wealth of Nations* (1776). And Ricardo's *Principles of Political Economy and Taxation* (1817), by continuing Smith's approach, concentrated on the distribution of income, which he considered as "the principal problem of Political Economy". In both cases, the subject of happiness was left on the sidelines. How can this be explained? Did they go astray?

I should like to argue that the Classical economists—in spite of appearances—chose in fact the correct way to lay the basis for the new "science of Political Economy". Smith, Ricardo, Malthus, and the other Classical economists started engaging in what I have had occasion to call the *analytical* stage of economic science.[1] Analysis requires abstraction, and abstraction requires a coherent and unambiguously definable subject of investigation. Their choice fell on material wealth.[2]

Admittedly, the focus on wealth narrowed the scope of their analysis, but offered a more coherent and less elusive subject for their inquiries than would have been the case with happiness; hence easing the task of identifying and studying it. Their choice was in fact vital to subsequent developments in economic theory. Moreover it is worth noting that, while the focus on wealth narrowed the *subject* of inquiry, the *line* of inquiry around the subject remained open to a vast range of factors connected with wealth, including non-economic factors. It is not at all surprising to note that Adam Smith, in his masterpiece, still openly discusses happiness, not as a subject he could objectively investigate, but as a possible aspect of life (both private and public) connected with wealth.[3]

More essentially, to focus on material wealth and income distribution, as the Classical economists chose to do, can be justified on at least three grounds.

- To begin with, the world in which the Classical economists lived was at the dawn of the Industrial Revolution. It was a world still facing the harsh problems of subsistence in a scenario of fears over the growth of population. In that historical context, it seemed reasonable to concentrate on the sheer quantity of goods to be produced and exchanged on the market-place as the major factor determining the well-being of people.

- Second, Classical economists were facing the terrific task of building the *foundations* of a new discipline. The search for basic, permanent, sectoral, and macroeconomic features of the emerging industrial economic systems—without committing themselves to (and yet not excluding) particular types of individual and social behaviour— appeared as the most fruitful and logical way to shape the emerging new "science of Political Economy". This task could not have been carried out if they had not concentrated on an objectively definable subject of investigation.

- Third, while they restricted their enquiry to material wealth, they did not make the mistake of excluding the multiplicity of factors that could be connected with it. Even at a superficial level, one can clearly perceive their ability in grasping the importance of the dynamic aspect of the nascent industrial world, opening extensive (even if, at times, unduly pessimistic) discussions on the multiple factors that can affect the direction and pace of expansion of the production of material goods.

3. From Political Economy to (Neoclassical) Economics

The founders of Political economy initially enjoyed a reasonably long spell of success, but in the second half of the nineteenth century their theories were challenged. For reasons that are indeed fascinating but still too little investigated, the crucial change took place when the focus of economic analysis shifted from an approach that had concentrated on the objective concept of wealth to an approach that emphasized the psychological element of human enjoyment. The value of economic goods began to be assessed no longer by the effort to produce them, but by the "utility" the consumer would derive from them. In this context, the role of individuals' preferences, on the one hand, and the role of scarcity, on the other, were singled out as the factors conferring desirability on economic goods. This was the starting point of Marginal economics. Quite surprisingly—in spite of all intervening discussions (and realized failures)—this subjective approach still remains today at the very heart of what we know as Neoclassical economics. There is no doubt that the advent of marginal analysis represented a profound change of paradigm in economics. It affected not only the *subject* of economic inquiry, but also the *method* by which the analysis was carried out.

While the Classical economists focused their enquiries on macroeconomic phenomena (the wealth of nations, income distribution, international trade), Neoclassical economists abandoned this approach altogether in order to concentrate on microeconomic phenomena. In particular, they concentrated on the subjective aspects of the behavior of economic agents. We all know how this change of perspective compelled them to analytically construct a hypothetical world, with hypothetical economic "agents", characterized by a very specific behavior: perfectly rational, utility maximizing, strictly individualistic, fully capable of knowing the past, the present, and even the future, in a typically static framework.

As a result, all economic relations came to rely on the preliminary study of their *micro*foundations—as these have been called—which consist in hypothesizing the existence of an atomistic society in which each individual maximizes his or her own utility. The analysis that has emerged from these assumptions may have gained in elegance (who could deny the beauty of the General Economic Equilibrium model?), but alas it has lost in generality and in empirical relevance. By concentrating on a specific behavior, marginal analysis actually ended up by imposing on the economic "agent" (and as a consequence on the economic system as a whole) the straitjacket of a strict, formally defined, behavior, as if it were that of an automaton. The *homo oeconomicus*—as he has been called—turned out to be deprived of all the richness, beauty, and freedom of human action. Amartya Sen, in discussing the peculiarities of these artificially conceived economic agents, perceptively defined them "rational fools" (Sen, 1977).

It is important to notice, from the point of view of the present Conference, that it becomes impossible to fit any reasonable notion of happiness into this analytical strait-jacket. Or rather, the only way to conceive it would be by reducing its multidimensional meanings and aspects to a mathematical, formally well-defined, utility function to be maximized under constraints. This operation of reducing human freedom and variety to just one kind of behavior (typically selfish, individualistic, hedonistic) is—I think—at the very basis of the many "paradoxes of happiness" which have been revealed by so many empirical surveys. It may indeed be a re-discovery to realize today that the method of analysis envisaged by the Classical economists led to quite different conclusions and possibilities. By concentrating on the study of the material wealth at a *macro*economic level, their analysis left entirely open the possibility of investigating any sort of human behavior at a microeconomic level, including of course the multidimensional aspects embodied in the concept of human happiness.

All this leads me to the conviction that this revival of interest in the relation between economic theory and human happiness could trigger two unexpected effects. On the one hand, it might help to highlight the limitations—more specifically the reductionist character—of the present state of economic theory. On the other hand, it might contribute to a resurgence of the long-forgotten *Classical approach* to Political Economy: an approach which may continue to add a lot to our knowledge, and in any case an approach which seems to me now to emerge as much more suitable for dealing with the richness and freedom of human action.

4. An Economic Analysis Open to Investigations on Human Happiness

To strengthen the contentions which I have just made, I should like to add at least four specific remarks to illustrate why the Classical approach to economics can offer a wider theoretical framework for the investigation of many topics concerning human behavior, and thus also of happiness.

First, wealth may not buy happiness, but it is difficult to carry out any reasonable discussion on happiness without allowing for a minimum amount of wealth to start with. This seems a good incentive to maintain the focus of economic theory on the objective concept of wealth, at least as a starting point. We know all too well that economic growth is not a gift of nature, but a fruit of human activity, requiring time, effort, and adaptation to change. Understanding the mechanisms that lie behind these phenomena and the effects that they bring to society remains a *conditio sine qua non* for society to pursue a better sense of well-being.

Second, the proposal, inspired by the Classical School, to provide economic analysis with *macro*-foundations entails starting our analysis from those characteristics of economic systems that do not depend on human behavior. This allows us then to go on to investigate—at a second stage of analysis, no longer limited to economics, but enlarged to the contributions of other social sciences—many and diverse patterns of human behavior, sometimes even incompatible with one another, without the fear of destroying the economic foundations which were laid at the first stage of investigation.

Third, a Classically inspired framework is favorable to the adoption of theories which are conceived from the outset in a dynamic setting. These kinds of theories would consider novelty, creativity, and human learning not as a perturbation of a (statically conceived) equilibrium, but as the essence itself of the basic movements of modern economies for which human beings must face the task of continuous adaptation.

Fourth, we do not even need to adhere to the widespread Neoclassical view that economics is all about means, not ends. We should not fear to go straight—as indeed Keynes did (1936)—to discussing ends and *social goals:* not only as regards full employment (the centre of Keynes's work), but also as regards an equitable distribution of income and wealth, and social justice in the determination of wages, prices, rates of interest. Within this line of analysis, appropriate notions of "common good" and of "public happiness" emerge, in my view, as more easily compatible with Classical analysis than with any type of economic analysis suggested by the utility-dominated approach to economics.

Notes

* This chapter is based on my opening remarks at the conference on "The Paradoxes of Happiness" in Milan, 2003. I am grateful for research assistance to GianPaolo Mariutti and for financial support to Università Cattolica S.C. of Milan (research D.3.2, 2002).

1. On the distinction between the analytical stage of economics (whose beginning is attributed to Adam Smith) and its pre-analytical stage (which was typical of most of the other authors who were writing in the eighteenth century) I should like to refer to Pasinetti (1986), where I dealt with the emergence of the *theory* of value, following Galiani's *Della Moneta* (1751).
2. This did not exclude attempts to build bridges between Wealth and Happiness. See in particular Thompson (1824), and also the "Essay on Population" by Malthus. The full title of Malthus's second edition was: *An Essay on the Principle of Population; or, a View of its Past and Present Effects on Human Happiness; with an Inquiry into our Prospects respecting the Future Removal or Mitigation of Evils which it occasions*, 1803; see the variorum edition, edited by Patricia James, Cambridge: Cambridge University Press, 1989.
3. See in particular book 5, chap. 1 of the *Wealth of Nations*.

References

Easterlin, Richard A. (1973), "Does Money Buy Happiness?", *The Public Interest*, 30 (Winter): 3–10.

——(1974), "Does Economic Growth Improve the Human Lot? Some Empirical Evidence", in Paul A. David and Melvin W. Reder (eds.), *Nations and Households in Economic Growth: Essays in Honour of Moses Abramowitz*, New York and London: Academic Press, 89–125.

Galiani, Ferdinando (1751), *Della Moneta*, Napoli: Raimondi.

Keynes, John Maynard (1936), *The General Theory of Employment Interest and Money*, London: Macmillan.

Malthus, Thomas R. (1989/1803), "An Essay on the Principle of Population; or, a View of its Past and Present Effects on Human Happiness; with an Inquiry into our Prospects respecting the Future Removal or Mitigation of Evils which it occasions", 2nd edn. 1803, republished in the *variorum edition*, ed. Patricia James for the Royal Economic Society, Cambridge: Cambridge University Press, 1989.

Pasinetti, Luigi L. (1986), "Theory of Value: A Source of Alternative Paradigms in Economic Analysis", in Mauro Baranzini and Roberto Scazzieri (eds.), *Foundations of Economics—Structures of Inquiry and Economic Theory*, Oxford: Basil Blackwell, 409–31.

Ricardo, David (1951/1817), *Principles of Political Economy and Taxation*, in Piero Sraffa (ed.), *Works and correspondence of David Ricardo*, vol. 1, Cambridge: Cambridge University Press.

Sen, Amartya K. (1977), "Rational Fools", *Philosophy and Public Affairs*, 6: 317–44.

Smith, Adam (1904/1776), *An Inquiry into the Nature and Causes of the Wealth of Nations*, 2 vols., ed. by Edwin Cannan, London: Methuen.

Thompson, William (1824), *An Inquiry into the Principles of the Distribution of Wealth Most Conducive to Human Happiness, applied to the Newly Proposed System of Voluntary Equality of Wealth*, London: Longman.

Index

abandonment 286
Abell, P. 328
absenteeism 148
absolute breadline 5, 149
accident victims 32, 34
  paralyzed 252–3, 258
accidents:
  depression and disorientation in the
    wake of 69
  risk of death and injury from 75, 84
accountability 6
achievement 132, 273, 274, 287
  aspiration and 125
  giving birth instrumental to 286
achievement motives 269, 270, 273,
    274, 277
  caring husbands increased 288
  gender differences in 284
  parenting instrumental to satisfaction
    of 278–9
achievement scores 283, 284, 286
across-the-board changes 68, 70, 71, 80, 81
adaptability limits 258
adaptation 2, 30, 57, 68–71, 73, 152, 260
  adverse changes in health 31–2
  and aspiration 9–12, 45–52, 280
  complete 31, 32, 34, 36, 45, 46, 212
  continuous 341
  evidence of 133
  exercise 77
  less than complete 41, 45, 52
  see also hedonic adaptation
addiction 15
  rational 116
  unforeseen 155
adjectives 272, 274, 276, 280, 282
  countervailing effects of 283
adolescence 253, 269
adrenaline 74, 75
adults/adulthood 38, 213–14, 253, 269
adversity 179, 256
  ability to face 262

aerobic exercise 76
Affect Balance Scale 256
affection 277, 284, 286, 312, 324
  difficult to succeed economically and
    maintain 288
  maternal 279
affective states 8, 92, 94, 102, 106
  causal relationships between 103
  correspondence of 101
  directly induced 98
  hedonic 245, 260–1
  lively consciousness of 97–8
  negative 8, 93, 100, 273
  positive 96, 107, 111, 272–3, 283
  post-consumption 95
  similar, tendency to activate 98
  stronger fellow-feeling of other's 105
  states subject to mirroring 99
affiliation 269, 270, 272–3, 277, 278, 288
  aspirations for 289
  negative influence on increasing 285
  see also group affiliation
affiliation motives:
  gender differences in 284
  picture-specific measures for 274
affiliation scores 274, 282, 284, 285,
    286, 287
  higher 283
affluent nations 248, 250, 251, 254
"affluent society" 2
age, *see* adolescence; adults; children;
    developmental phases; old age; young
    adulthood
agriculture 110
Ainsworth, M. D. S. 270
Akerlof, G. 316
Allardt, Erik 171
altruism 96, 97, 99, 103, 104, 107, 272,
    305, 312, 326
  altercentric 306, 309, 313
  Becker's conceptualization of 307
  calculating 308

Index

Printed in the United Kingdom
by Lightning Source UK Ltd.
134946UK00001B/195/A